The Author (left) with paper NDA for Rheomacrodex in 1965.

The Author, Mickey C. Smith

Government, Big Pharma, and the People

Government, Big Pharma, and the People
A Century of Dis-Ease

Mickey C. Smith

with

E.M. (Mick) Kolassa and Walter Steven Pray

A PRODUCTIVITY PRESS BOOK

Cover Photo by Robert Jordan

First published 2021
by Routledge
600 Broken Sound Parkway #300, Boca Raton FL, 33487

and by Routledge
2 Park Square, Milton Park, Abingdon, Oxon, OX14 4RN

Routledge is an imprint of the Taylor & Francis Group, an informa business

© 2021 Taylor & Francis

The right of Author to be identified as author of this work has been asserted by him in accordance with sections 77 and 78 of the Copyright, Designs and Patents Act 1988.

All rights reserved. No part of this book may be reprinted or reproduced or utilised in any form or by any electronic, mechanical, or other means, now known or hereafter invented, including photocopying and recording, or in any information storage or retrieval system, without permission in writing from the publishers.

Trademark notice: Product or corporate names may be trademarks or registered trademarks, and are used only for identification and explanation without intent to infringe.

Library of Congress Cataloging-in-Publication Data
A catalog record for this title has been requested

ISBN: 978-0-367-43335-2 (hbk)
ISBN: 978-0-367-43244-7 (pbk)
ISBN: 978-1-003-00249-9 (ebk)

Typeset in Garamond
by codeMantra

To Mary

Thy indistinct expressions seem

Like language utter'd in a dream

Yet me they charm whate're the theme.

My Mary!

And still to love though press'd with ill,

In wintry age to feel no chill,

To me is to be lovely still.

My Mary!

(Wordsworth – "To Mary Unwin")

Contents

Preface xvii
Acknowledgments xxiii

1 Introduction 1
    Health 2
    Woman as a Biological and Social Entity 4
    A Different Paradigm 5
    Health Care and Rights 6
    Drugs and Their Role in Society 9
    Drug Policy 11
    Big Pharma 16
    Drug-Related Problems 18
    The People 20
    What's Ahead 21
    Conclusion 23

2 The "Four P's" 25
    Introduction 25
    Marketing as an Actualizing Process 26
    The Marketing Mix – The "Four P's" 27
        The Right Product 27
        The Right Price 28
        The Right Place 28
        Spreading the Word – Promotion 29
    The Pharmaceutical Marketing System 29
        Product 30
        Price 30
        Place 30
        Promotion 30
        Product 32

  From Medicine to Your Mouth (or Wherever)................................33
   Molecular Modification...34
   Generic Products..34
  Place..35
   Mail-Order Prescriptions 37
   The Wholesaler...37
  Price..38
   Price Listing in Direct to Consumer Advertising.....................41
   Retail Pricing..42
   Hospital Pricing 43
  Promotion..43
   Personal Selling – Detailing...45
   Print Media...46
   Other Forms of Promotion..47
   Meetings and Exhibits 48
   Samples..48
   Direct-to-Consumer Advertising (DTC) 48
   "Off-Label" Information...50
   Social Costs and Benefits of Promotion 51
   What to Do...53
 Government and the Four P's 55
  Product 56
  Price..56
  Place..56
  Promotion..57
 Conclusion...57

3 Investigators and Investigations...59
 Introduction..59
 The Hearings..61
  The Grand Inquisitor – Estes Kefauver..61
   On Patents 65
   On Competition..66
   On Promotion...66
   On Brand Names..67
   On Profits 68
   On Prices...68
   Minority Views 70
  FDA under the Microscope – A Resignation and a Whistle Blower...77
   Dr. Welch...77

  Dr. Barbara Moulton 78
   Conclusion/Kefauver 80
 Gaylord Nelson – Son of Torquemada 81
  Other Drugs and Issues 82
  Conclusion/Nelson 83
 The Fountain Hearings 84
 Senator Kennedy Joins the Fray 85
  Conclusion/Kennedy 88
 Small Business Problems in the Drug Industry – Dingell 89
 Drug Efficacy Problems – Fountain 91
 Moss on Drug Abuse 93
 Fountain Redux 94
 Congressman Rogers on Transition 96
 Senator Humphrey and the Literature 98
 A Newcomer – Congressman Lionel Van Deerlin 100
 Senator Fountain "One More Time" 101
 Senator Kennedy Returns 102
 FDA under the Microscope Again 106
 Kennedy – Not Too Tranquil 109
  Conclusion/Kennedy 112
 Gore on Pharmaceutical R&D 113
 Senator Fountain Again 117
 Claude Pepper for the Old Folks 119
 Zomax in the Spotlight 121
 A Pryor Engagement 122
The Task Force on Prescription Drugs 124
 Research, Findings, and Recommendations 125
 Drug Benefits for the Aged 126
 Quality of Care – Drug Use Process 126
 Economic Issues 127
 Professional Education/Proficiency 127
 Government Regulatory Duties 127
 Federal Policy 128
 The Dunlop Report on the Task Force 128
Conclusion 130

4 Legislators and Legislation 133
Introduction 133
Laws and Policy 135
Bills and Sponsors 140

The Process 146
    The Waxman–Hatch Law 146
    The 1962 Drug Amendments 148
    The Orphan Drug Act 149
    Medicare Catastrophic Coverage Act (1988) and Repeal of Same (1989) 149
    "Hillary Care" and "Obamacare" 150
    Narcotics and Other Drugs of Abuse 151
    State Laws 151
Conclusion 151

5 Regulators and Regulations 153
Introduction 153
The Food and Drug Administration 154
    Safety and Effectiveness 156
    Labeling and Promotion 159
    Manufacturing 164
    FDA Remedies 164
Other Regulators and Regulations 165
    Federal Trade Commission 165
    Federal Communications Commission (FCC) 166
    Drug Enforcement Administration (DEA) 166
    Centers for Medicare and Medicaid Services (CMS) 167
    Patents and Trademarks 167
    State Regulations 168
Drug Names 168
Conclusion 170

6 Non-Government Influence 173
Introduction 173
Self-Regulation 173
    Medicine 173
    Pharmacy 174
    The Congress 174
    Press and Other Media 174
    Drug Industry 175
Third Parties/Managed Care Controls 175
Formularies and Prescription Limitations 178
Lawyers 178
Advocates and Adversaries 179
Mail-Order Pharmacy 180

Pharmacy Benefit Managers and Outcomes Management 180
    Services Provided by PBMs 181
        Claim Adjudication 181
        Claims Processing Standards.. 181
        Pharmacy Network Management.. 181
        Community Pharmacy Networks 181
        Mail-Order Services... 181
        Specialty Pharmacy Services... 182
        Formulary Management 182
    Controversies in the PBM Industry... 182
    Future of the PBMs 183
Conclusion.. 183

7 The People and Their Drugs 185
Introduction... 185
The People as Patients 185
    Demographics 186
    Needs and Wants 186
    Beliefs or Knowledge?.. 188
Health Belief Model 189
A Case – Health Belief Model 190
Attitudes and Evaluation of Drugs 193
The Sickness Career... 195
    Significance of the Change 197
    Need for Help... 198
    Type of Help Needed.. 198
    Appropriateness of a Particular Treatment or Type of Setting 199
The Sick Role 201
    Health Behavior.. 202
    Illness Behavior 202
The Sick Role in Acute and Chronic Illness....................................... 204
    Rheumatoid Arthritis.. 207
    Ulcerative Colitis.. 208
    Emphysema 208
Compliance with Medication Regimens.. 209
A Case – Sick Role and Compliance 214
Other Influences on Medication Use 217
What to Do.. 218
Death or Maybe Not 219
Conclusion.. 219

8   Response of Big Pharma 221
- Introduction 221
- Response to Government 223
  - Not Guilty 224
  - Counterattack 224
  - Guilty 225
- Big Pharma Speaks 226
  - An Alternative View 228
- Response of Big Pharma to the People 232
- Some Ideas for Big Pharma 232
  - Public Perceptions of Pharmaceutical Marketing 232
  - What Pharmaceutical Marketing Is and Does 232
  - What Drives Product Development? 233
  - Marketing Exerts Downward Pressure on the Price of Medicines 234
  - Communicating with Prescribers Linking Products to Patient Needs ... 235
  - Cost Savings through Marketing Directly to Patients 236
  - Pharmaceutical Marketing Stimulates Demand – Good for the Health Care System 237
  - Tell the People 238
- PMA Monographs 239
- Statesmanship 240
  - Maybe We Can Help 241
- Conclusion 242

9   Little Pharma and Friends 243
- Introduction 243
- Generic Pharma – Not So Little 243
  - Appearance and Labeling of Generics 244
- Big Bio 245
- What Is Special about "Specialty Drugs"? 246
- Little Boutiques 247
- Back to the Future – Compounding Pharmacists 247
- Friends 248
  - Advertising Agencies 248
  - Market/Marketing Research 249
- Conclusion 251

10   Greedy Big Pharma 253
- Introduction 253

Two Parts of Greedy 253
AARP and Greedy Big Pharma 255
Congress and Greedy Big Pharma 256
Risk versus Reward 258
Greedy Big Tech 259
Conclusion 261

11 Whence the Drugs? 263
Introduction 263
Origins of Drugs 263
   Search for New Drugs in Medical Folklore 264
   Advances in Allied Sciences 265
   Biochemistry 265
   Enzyme Inhibition 265
   Clinical Medicine 265
   Serendipity 265
   Exploration of Natural Products 266
   Modification of Existing Drugs 266
   Planned Programs of Chemical and Biologic Research 266
   Random Screening 266
Drug Product Development 267
Marketing in the Last Century 269
   Product 269
   Price 271
   Place 272
   Promotion 274
   Environmental Developments 276
Invention, Discovery, and Development 277
Curiosities and Surprises 279
Recommended Reading 280
Conclusion 280

12 Drugs of the Future 283
Introduction 283
But Seriously 284
Drugs in an Aging Society 284
Future Drugs for the Aged 285
Lifestyle Drugs 286
Conclusion 290

13 The Non-Prescription Products – Market-Profits and Public Health in Conflict – W. Stephen Pray, PhD 293

Introduction 293
Patent Medicines: Once Popular Nonprescription Products 295
    Characteristics of Patent Medicines 295
    Patent Medicine Manufacturers: The Proprietary Association 296
    The Fight against Patent Medicines 298
Laws That Regulated Nonprescription Products 299
    The 1906 Pure Food and Drugs Act 299
    The 1914 Harrison Narcotic Act 300
    The 1938 Food, Drug, and Cosmetic Act 301
    The Durham–Humphrey Amendment 304
    The 1962 Kefauver–Harris Amendments 306
FDA's Review of OTC Products 306
    Genesis of the FDA OTC Review 306
    Organizing the Review 307
        Phase 1 307
        Phase 2 308
        Phase 3 310
        Benefits of the FDA OTC Review 310
    The OTC Label 310
    Criticism of the FDA OTC Review 312
    Nonprescription Products Not Reviewed 312
    OTC Manufacturers and the Review 313
The Prescription-to-OTC Switch 314
    Methods by Which Switches Occur 314
    Factors Considered in Approving an Rx-to-OTC Switch 316
    Types of Switches 317
    Examples of Rx-to-OTC Switches 317
A Third Class of Drugs – Opposition from OTC Manufacturers 318
Quackery – Nonprescription Products and Devices Lacking Proof of Safety and Efficacy 325
    What Is Quackery? 325
    The Conspiracy to Legitimize Quackery 326
    The Nutrition Labeling and Education Act of 1990 328
    Establishment of the National Center for Complementary and Alternative Medicine (NCCAM) 328
    L-Tryptophan – The 1993 FDA Report 329
    FDA Accelerates Its Anti-Quackery Activity 329

    The 1994 Dietary Supplement Health and Education Act (DSHEA) 330
    FDA and Quackery Post-DSHEA – Defining Fraud 331
    Pharmacy Codes of Ethics Change to Embrace Quackery 332
    Pharmacy Textbooks Endorse Quackery 333
    Pharmacy Journals Endorse Quackery 334
Quackery – New Names Confer False Respectability 339
Conclusion 340

14 Issues and Studies in Pharmacoeconomics 341
Introduction 341
The Emergence of Socioeconomic Research 342
    Definition of Socioeconomic Evaluations 342
    Types of Socioeconomic Evaluations 343
The Cost of Illness 345
Quality of Life Assessment (QOL) 346
The Economics of Non-Compliance 349
Economic Epidemiology 351
Conclusion 354

15 On Drug Prices – Dr. E. M. "Mick" Kolassa 355
Introduction 355
Pricing – The Forgotten "P" 356
    The New Product Dilemma 357
    Market Segments 358
    Fear of Pricing 358
    Managed Care Myopia 359
    The Need to Price on Purpose 361
The Growing Importance of Pharmaceutical Pricing 361
Prices, Politics, and Problems 363
    A Pharmaceutical Pricing Philosophy 364
        Willingness to Pay 364
        Pricing on Purpose 365
Pricing Terminology 365
    Important Terms in Pharmaceutical Pricing 366
What Is a Pharmaceutical Price? 366
    AWP 367
Price Decision-Making 369
    Key Factors in the Pricing Decision 369
    Competition 371
    Patient Characteristics 372

　　　　The Decision-Making Process 373
　　　　Disease Characteristics 373
　　　　Company Needs 374
　　　　Company Abilities 374
　　　　Public Policy Considerations 375
　　The Value of Pharmaceuticals 375
　　The Future of Pharmaceutical Pricing 377
　　　　The $100,000 Prisoner's Dilemma 379

16　Summary, Ruminations, and Apologia 383
　　Introduction 383
　　Ruminations 386
　　Trends 386
　　　　Immortality 388
　　　　Slow or Stop the Aging Process 388
　　　　A Council on Drug Policy 389
　　　　Other What Ifs 389
　　Apologia 391
　　Author's Notes 392
　　　　Post Script 393

Appendix A – Annotated References and Cross Index 395

Appendix B – Some Useful Quotes 447

Appendix C – The Saga of Vitamin B_{13} – A Pharmaceutical Triumph 455

Authors 461

Index 463

Preface

Where to begin? I know! "It was the best of times, it was the worst of times". One simply can't beat Dickens for an opening line. He went on, of course. "It was the age of wisdom, it was the age of foolishness, it was the epoch of belief, it was the epoch of incredulity…". Dickens might very well have been describing the atmosphere that pervades today, and has for more than a century, in the Congress and in Big Pharma, both, ostensibly, for the People.

"It was a dark and stormy night" had already been used. I could legitimately have used, "Last night I dreamed I went to Manderly again". There *is* a Manderly in my home state of Mississippi. It is one of the most outstanding plantation homes in the South according to Wikipedia.

In some ways, this Book had its origin in 1964 when my employers at Pharmacia Laboratories (then a very small incursion into the U.S. market by the Swedish Company) very generously allowed me to go one morning a week to Rutgers to teach a course in pharmaceutical marketing. At that time, there was no textbook. I was inspired to write one, and, did, *Principles of Pharmaceutical Marketing*. Now, more than a score of Books later, at what my lawyer insists on describing as "advanced age", I have constructed what will surely be my final Book.

Friends have asked me, "How long did it take you to write this thing"? My answer to them and to you, the Reader, is the same….all my life. Well, more than half of it. At the risk of what someone in the *Wall Street Journal* has called "humble bragging", I can offer a few credentials: many years practicing pharmacy in St. Louis and in small towns in Mississippi, employment as a Marketing Manager for a Drug company, consultant to more than a dozen members of Big Pharma, testimony and consulting with, and to, the FDA, FTC, Congressional Committees, and the World Health Organization. Most important to me was 40 years in the classroom attempting to explain to Pharmacy students their pivotal role in the Health Care system.

Throughout I have tried to keep the Reader foremost in mind. I know full well that many of you will know far more than I, about some of the topics. On the other hand, I believe that some of what I recount will be comparatively new. I have tried to see this as a (one-sided) conversation that might be held during a lengthy commute, in front of a cozy fire, or during the weekly coffee club meetings at the Beacon in Oxford, Mississippi.

I have cited my own works and those of colleagues and former students, many (perhaps too many) times. But with 400 published papers and a score of Books (translated into five languages), I hope it is permitted.

A reviewer of one of my Books described my writing as "breezy". I am comfortable with that but hope never to see "windy" in a review. With the remarks out of the way, I offer several caveats to the Reader:

- This work is, in the main, a history. Lord Acton has written: "Advice to persons about to write a history: Don't". I have ignored that very excellent advice. For half of the century under study, I have lived it, read about it, and written about it. There are some few comments about contemporary events, especially in Chapter 16. During the time of this writing, and even during the few months between submission of the manuscript and actual publication, there will have been sometimes dramatic developments. Avorn (234) acknowledged this problem in the introduction to the updated version of his Book, *Powerful Medicines*.
- Pronouns. I have expropriated Herrari's (455) practice of using the feminine gender in my writing but have not changed pronouns or applied a "sic" when using quotations by others. Generally, I refer to myself, "the Author", but sometimes that's just too stuffy and I resort to "I". I have done the same thing with you, the Reader.
- Bias. The subject and its players are rife with bias. An effort has been made to identify implicit bias by the parties involved. Sometimes the Reader will identify bias by the Author, mostly unintentional, but there, nevertheless. The Reader will find them, of course. Perhaps the Book will help the Reader identify their biases (a "pre-existing condition" in the vernacular of Health insurance). Or perhaps it will only reinforce them! We are all only human (unless, of course the geniuses in the field of artificial intelligence have already come up with a device that will read, digest, and produce unbiased opinions). Or, perhaps, Big Pharma will find a new "bias reducing" drug with which Congress and Big Pharma might be compelled to be vaccinated. But I digress.

The Book contains a plethora of definitions, references, and pithy quotes which, the Author hopes, will provide a remedy.
- The "bottom line" (yet another term often misused by those with a proverbial axe to grind) is that the aim of the Book is to provide the Reader with a better understanding of Congress (whatever that is) and Big Pharma (whatever that is), and, of course, the issues between them. If the Reader does detect an occasional bias that may have crept in, some of their own biases will serve as a protection against mine.
- Drug Abuse is not *per se* one of the foci of this Book. Reference is made to the problem where appropriate and necessary. Clearly, abuse of licit and illicit Drugs remains an enormous problem, and solutions seem hard to come by. Marijuana and the opiates are two very different examples.
- References. Quite a large number are provided, often with a comment by the Author. Actually, sometimes, opinions do creep in. There are an amazing number (plethora? surfeit?) of sources available on the subject of this Book. Certainly the Reader may be aware of some that I overlooked. The references in Appendix A do not always contain the complete, academically correct information. My rule of thumb has been to assure that the Reader can find them.
- Quotations. Here again, they were selected by the Author, and the influence of the Author's bias and opinion may be identified in their having been included.
- Time Span. This Book is, in the main, historical in nature. No claim is made that it will offer insights right up to the publishing date. It is current in that many of today's and tomorrow's controversies, conflicts, mistakes, and successes can be seen in the past (Yes, Groundhog Day). In any case, there is the well-known dictum that "one who does not remember history is doomed to repeat it" (that should have been in the Quotations!). Or there is Lily Tomlin – "Maybe if we listened, history would stop repeating itself."
- The Book Title. Government is used to mean *all* aspects of Government (or "the Gummint" as we say here in Mississippi). Big Pharma is used to mean the pharmaceutical industry, of which both terms defy definition.
- BTSB. This is the most important caveat, an acronym, for "beyond the scope of the book". The Reader will find it often. *Encyclopedia Britannica* would be hard-pressed to fit this story, with all of its conceivable elements, into their thousands of pages. I could only try.

With the Reader's assumed permission, I offer.

A Courtroom Analogy

Although a bit imperfect, the Dynamic Tension, which I describe, gave rise to this courtroom analogy. For the Prosecution, we have the Government, presumably representing the People (the Jury). For the Defense there is Big Pharma. In fact, the case will probably be known as The People versus Big Pharma.

Witnesses for the Prosecution will be individuals and their collective advocates. Witnesses for the Defense will be individual members of Big Pharma and their collective advocates (trade associations). Both sides will call economists, physicians, scientists, and a host of other "expert witnesses". The trial will go on and has gone on for years. (Jarndyce and Jarndyce in *Bleak House* comes to mind.)

The charges are two:

1. That Big Pharma did, knowingly and willingly, take money from sick People.
2. That Big Pharma did so with malice aforethought. (Greedy)

To the first charge, Big Pharma may find its defense very limited. They may find some relief from pointing out that the bread industry takes money from hungry People. Or that the auto and oil companies take money from People who need transportation.

To the second charge, we can expect Big Pharma to offer descriptions of how the money they receive is used, to support the research to find new Drugs that are even safer and more effective, and sometimes to find cures for illnesses for which there is little hope of financial return.

The trial continues as I write this. And as a surrogate court reporter/journalist, it is hard to keep up! Jerry Avorn in his remarkable Book, *Powerful Medicines* (234) expressed this dilemma very well in describing the "string of dramatic drug-related events that instantly brought its subject matter to the center of public awareness and debate", in the year following publication of his first edition. I faced the same dilemma.

My efforts are greatly enhanced by the contributions of my collaborators! Dr. Steven Pray, author of the chapter on nonprescription Drugs and a Book on the subject, and Dr. E. M. "Mick" Kolassa, who brings to the chapter on pricing, his expertise on that subject from his work as a member of, and consultant to, Big Pharma.

And, finally. In November 2018, I lost my wife of 58+ years. She died just before her eightieth birthday, *with*, but not *of* dementia. Prior to being affected with this dreadful condition, she was intelligent, affectionate, vital, and adventurous. Nothing Government or Big Pharma could do to fix it. Millions of patients and caregivers know this story all too well, as they hold onto the urgent, agonizing hope for a "breakthrough". A jaundiced view of Big Pharma would call it a "blockbuster", and that term is appropriate as well.

This Book is about the struggles of our Government to control the economic costs to the Public of "blockbusters" without harming the possibilities of "breakthroughs". The Reader should have little trouble finding someone to agree with the idea that, "Drug prices are too damn high". Finding someone to agree with, "Today's drugs are no damn good" might be more difficult.

Acknowledgments

To acknowledge all who have played a part in the execution of this Book is simply BSTA (Beyond the Scope of the Author). Omissions in no way exclude their presence in my mind and heart. So –

- Shelia Goolsby, without whose masterful interpretation of my mostly illegible handwriting and mastery of the publisher's requirements, a manuscript would not have been possible
- Jen Blakeley, as my "Certified Literary Agent" who flawlessly dealt with copyrights and correspondence
- John Bentley, who made available resources of the Ole Miss Department of Pharmacy Administration – still the best of its kind – and for his many personal kindnesses to me and my family
- Dr. Leonard Schifrin, for a treasure trove of Congressional Proceedings
- Dr. "Mick" Kolassa, the Prince of Pricing and now, the Baron of Blues

Also

- Keith Moore, my "Professional Driver" cum Philosopher
- Leslie and Susan at UPS for thousands of copies
- Julie Fisher, as Managing Editor of my three journals over many years and my "go to" person with questions of style and language
- The hundreds of authors whose works I have quoted and referenced
- Dr. Charles Hartman, my first "boss" whose influence continues now – 60 years later
- To Sister Mary Cafeteria (fictitious name), third-grade teacher who introduced me to the joy of reading and to the Classics through the painless medium of *Classic Comics*

- To the makers of Perdemo Cigars, whose fragrance is a sure cure for writer's block
- Dr. Hind Hatoum, for friendship and inspiration

And Finally

A geriatric physician/author has listed four items as a recipe for a good old age – "good genes, good luck, enough money, and one good kid, usually a daughter". The doctor got that right!

Chapter 1

Introduction

What follows is a description of an advertisement that appeared on the front cover of *The Pharmaceutical Journal,* February 1961, the official organ of the Pharmaceutical Society of Great Britain. The illustration depicts a small child looking into an open prescription container. The text reads: This child's life may depend on the safety of "Distaval". The text continues:

> Consider the possible outcome in a case such as this-had the bottle contained a conventional barbiturate. Year by year, the barbiturates claim a mounting toll of childhood victims. Yet it is simple enough to use a sedative and hypnotic, which is both highly effective... and outstandingly safe. "Distaval" has been prescribed for over three years in this country, where the accidental poisonings rate is notoriously high: but there is no case on record which even gross over-dosage with "Distaval" has had harmful results.

Distaval was the trade name for thalidomide. As some of the Readers probably know, thalidomide was the centerpiece for one of the most tragic stories in the history of the Drug industry. What most probably *don't* know is that thalidomide was available without a prescription! The United States barely avoided being a major victim of this tragedy. Thalidomide was a terrible, horrific tragedy. There have been others, smaller, but no less tragic. I will speak more about them later.

In fact, any death as a result of any kind of Drug misadventure is no less tragic. If there is one issue on which all the players in this narrative are of one mind, it is to prevent Drug-related tragedies, whatever the cause.

But how can one safeguard against such terrible anomalies, without stifling the often wonderful results of the process of Drug research and development?

What kinds of policies are needed? What Legislation and regulation can the People look to for a proper balance between danger and achievement? How can such balance be attained? That struggle is described in the pages which follow. It is a struggle which affects us all and, in which, individually and collectively we can all play a part. And we must!

I chose to begin the Preface with the "Thalidomide Incident" for two reasons. First, my informal polling convinces me that very few Americans under the age of 50 have ever heard of the Drug, and if they *have* heard of it, their understanding is vague at best. Just as with Pearl Harbor and the Alamo, thalidomide *must* be remembered. The second reason is that the story embodies many of the issues described in this Book.

The human elements of the thalidomide event have been chronicled by many writers. One of the best is that by Hilts (368).

As we shall see, there have been other, perhaps less traumatizing, Drug misadventures, but none raised the degree of Public awareness of the potential hazards of medication use than did this one. Despite the earnest and best efforts of Government and Big Pharma, the ever-present threat of the unforeseen always looms. What follows in this chapter is an overview of most of the topics covered in this Book. Each will surface many times and will be examined in much more detail.

Health

Having begun this introduction with a dramatic and tragic episode in history, let us turn to some problems of definition, in this case, Health. In 1948, the World Health Organization (WHO) defined Health as "a state of complete physical, mental and social well-being, not merely the absence of disease or infirmity". WHO has held steadfastly to that definition, in spite of efforts to induce some modifications.

Sartorius (377) noted that the WHO definition may be inadequate to the task. He added two alternative definitions. The first definition is "a state that allows the individual to adequately cope with all the demands of daily life". The second States that Health is "a state of balance, or equilibrium that an individual has established within himself, and between himself, and his social and physical environment". Regarding the Health of an individual, it is the physician (or other health care provider), whose responsibility it is to determine, the presence or absence, of disease or disability. The individual is not truly involved in that decision. *Others* are.

The second definition requires a direct quote from Sartorius: "Health would thus be a dimension of human existence that remains in existence regardless of the presence of disease, somewhat like the sky that remains in place even when covered with clouds".

Sartorius brilliantly observes that by his definition "He (the healthcare provider) must explore how individuals who have a disease feel about it, how the disease influences their lives, how they propose to fight the disease or live with it". Surely, he notes, this would "improve the practice of medicine and make it a more realistic as well as humane endeavor". His eloquent paper continues with a description of implications for health Promotion and health Policy. It is well worth reading in its entirety.

From the foregoing, one can see that Health is a relative and elusive concept. Perhaps a (very) personal description of the "Health" of the author will serve to illustrate. At the age of 81, at the time of this writing, I consider myself to be, and in the expressed opinions of significant others, "healthy" – "for my age". The qualifier is always used.

I am relatively mobile, although I have given up driving an automobile (for the sake of the safety of others on the road). I still travel, although finding airlines troublesome. But that difficulty is certainly not the province of the elderly alone. I remain interested in national and world affairs. I read voraciously good stuff – biographies, history, Churchill and Dickens, as well as a healthy (?) dose of trashy mysteries and thrillers. My social networks are intact, and I take care of matters of nutrition, exercise, and hygiene. I believe my writing is reasonably coherent. (The Reader will be the judge!) *But*, I have carpal tunnel syndrome (CTS), neuropathy, recurrent minor episodes of skin cancer, a balance problem, and a bit of difficulty with names. You get the picture.

As well as others my age, and older, I have concerns, even fears, about the future. Not so much of dying, but of *not* dying. What if I succumb to dementia as did my wife? What about a lingering, painful illness? The various concerns, these and others, are laid out in Chapter 7. All of this, and more, is real and relevant to the struggles of the various parties involved in the Dynamic Tension which is the subject of this Book.

Woman as a Biological and Social Entity

Without being schizophrenic, each of us is, at the same time, many things. We are first of all individuals, and the kind of individual affects our responsibility and response to illness.

In addition, to our individual characteristics and behavior, each of us has other identities as parts of ever larger groups, including family, various formal and informal communities, and finally the total society. There is some value in understanding the Parallels illustrated in Figure 1.1, which shows the dual position of woman in nature. Just as woman as the entire organism must often take action to correct disruptions at the lower levels of the mental, physical organization, so the total society must frequently initiate programs to correct health problems among its individual members.

Dubos found in earlier writings of famed medical scholar Virchow further justification for studying society in order to study health care (226). In Virchow's words, "Epidemics resemble great warnings from which a statesman in the grand style can read that a disturbance has taken place in the development of his People, a disturbance that not even a carefree Policy can long overlook". Thus, according to Virchow, the treatment of individual cases is only a small aspect of medicine. More important is the control of *crowd* diseases which demand social and, if need be, political actions. In this light, medicine is a social science.

The study of a society and its goals is imperative for anyone who intends to operate in the health system which the society has developed. For, in

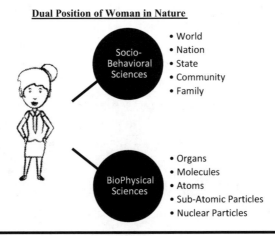

Figure 1.1 Dual position of woman in nature.

spite of its failure to reach unanimity of purpose consistently, society does on occasion Act as one organism: setting priorities, defining goals, choosing methods. When *society* is the patient, it decides how much health care it will seek and who will provide it.

A Different Paradigm

It is instructive to review comparative paradigms regarding assumptions underlying different medical models. Ferguson's ideas, even though some are 40 years old, are still relevant today. They appear in Table 1.1.

Table 1.1 Assumptions Underlying Different Medical Models

Assumptions of the Old Paradigm of Medicine	Assumptions of the New Paradigm of Health
Treatment of symptoms	Search for patterns and causes, plus treatment of symptoms
Specialized	Integrated, concerned with the whole patient
Emphasis on efficiency	Emphasis on human values
Professional should be emotionally neutral	Professional's caring is a component of healing
	Pain and disease are information about conflict, disharmony
Pain and disease are wholly negative	Minimal intervention with "appropriate technology", complemented with full armamentarium of non-invasive techniques (psychotherapies, diet, exercise)
Primary intervention with Drugs, surgery	Body seen as dynamic system, context, field of energy within other fields
Body seen as machine in good or bad repair	Emphasis on achieving maximum wellness, "meta-health"
Disease or disability seen as thing, entity	Disease or disability seen as process
Emphasis on eliminating symptoms, disease	Patient is (or should be) autonomous

(*Continued*)

Table 1.1 (*Continued*)   Assumptions Underlying Different Medical Models

Assumptions of the Old Paradigm of Medicine	Assumptions of the New Paradigm of Health
Patient is dependent	Professional is therapeutic partner
Body and mind are separate; psychosomatic illness is mental, may be referred to psychiatrist	Body-mind perspective; psychosomatic illness is province of all health care professionals
Mind is secondary factor in organic illness	Mind is primary or co-equal factor in all illness
Placebo effect shows the power of suggestion	Placebo effect shows the mind's role in disease and healing
Primary reliance on quantitative information (charts, tests, data)	Primary reliance on qualitative information, including patient's subjective reports and professional's intuition; quantitative data an adjunct
"Prevention" largely environmental: vitamins, rest, exercise, immunization, not smoking	"Prevention" synonymous with wholeness work, relationships, goals, body-mind-spirit

Source: Excerpts from *The Aquarian Conspiracy* by Marilyn Ferguson. Used by permission of Tarcher, an imprint of Penguin Publishing Group, a division of Penguin Random House, LLC, all rights reserved.

Health Care and Rights

Anyone interested in the tortuous path taken by "Health" to achieve status as a right should read the comprehensive history by Chapman and Talmadge. According to their review, the first mention in the Congress of the right to health was in 1790 as part of a States' rights debate on who might impose quarantine. "The right to preservation of health is inalienable", said Lymon during the debate. Although the concept of health as a right continued to crop up, it was 150 years before it came into its own as a part of President Franklin Roosevelt's Economic Bill of Rights (331).

There have been some important landmarks along the way. The American Medical Association House of Delegates passed, in 1969, a resolution that said in part: "It is a basic right of every citizen to have available to him adequate health care". The American Public Health Association has made this concept a part of official Policy, and the Federal Government has taken steps which indicate some sort of commitment to this principle.

The phrases *right to health* and *right to health care* have too often been used interchangeably and, therefore, incorrectly. *Right to health* implies the existence of health as a definable entity, a condition which does not exist. The term also implies an ability to confer health, once the right is assumed. Certainly, this is and can only be an empty promise in many situations, even if given in good faith. Perhaps the only concept of *right to health* which can be generally acceptable to all is as a right not to have one's existing level of health impaired or threatened by others – for example, through unsanitary cooking, spreading disease, or blowing smoke in another's face.

The phrase *right to health care* is deceptive as well, implying as it does that if care is available, better health will result. Medical science has proven over and over, to our chagrin, that this is simply not the case. Indeed, those who are "deprived" of health care may sometimes be deprived of future suffering.

Complicating defining health is the increasing view that Medicine, the arbiter and gatekeeper of health-related matters, has promoted, or at least allowed, the extension of its boundaries to include a growing area of social and psychological problems. As Daniel Callahan, director of the Hastings Center has noted:

> One major feature of individualism in our society is that it knows no limits: anything may be aspired to, anything may be hoped for, anything may be sought. A very loose concept of health, then, allows people to trade upon the fact that with minor ingenuity any desire can be seen as a health need; and any health need can be legitimated in the name of the right to health. The political system cannot make all the people happy all of the time, but it is just possible that physician-prescribed psychotropic drugs can. If all of us have a right to define happiness in our private terms, why should we not call upon medicine to give us what other institutions cannot?
>
> *(332)*

It is entirely appropriate that social goals should have become more and more clearly identified and more and more forcefully pursued. The social changes which have been occurring so rapidly have had a serious impact through creation of both psychological and physical-environmental hazards. Individual health needs quickly become community health needs – more numerous, diversified, and complex. More community participation is required to provide the comprehensive services necessary for resolution and/or prevention of the multiplication of problems.

Health professionals frequently express concern over an increasing Government role in the financing and direct provision of health care. What is sometimes overlooked in these concerns is the fact that the Government is, in theory at least, expressing the will of the People.

Whether we are ultimately to have socialized medicine in the United States will be determined to a large measure by the answers which our society finds two questions:

1. Is health care a right? And, if so,
2. What system of health care delivery and financing is most likely to assure this right?

In 1977, Dr. George Pickett, then President of the American Public Health Association, distinguished between rights and privileges. "Privileges are rights granted as special favors and are inherently private matters. Rights, on the other hand, are privileges granted to all, and therefore public matters" (379).

Under these definitions, there is a Public duty for the Government to protect rights, and in the case of health, this would mean assuring access to needed health care. The implications are enormous. Depending upon how "health" is defined, the steps which might be necessary to guarantee that right could be far-reaching indeed.

There is some question of practicality. As Callahan notes, the right becomes meaningless when that which is demanded in the name of rights is impossible to achieve in either a real or plausible world (380). He points out that the right to *available* health resources leads logically to a right to demand that medicine *develop* new resources to achieve whatever is desired in the name of health. He contends that "health" is meaningless if it cannot limit its boundaries. If "health" is used to bear on everything to do with human well-being, then the right to health care becomes tantamount to a right to happiness – a right which could be espoused, but hardly guaranteed" (even the Declaration of Independence refers only to the *pursuit* of happiness).

The courts have recognized some of the potential conflict between rights and practicalities. In 1976, a Federal judge in Georgia noted that the Medicaid Regulations required that Drugs provided be "sufficient in amount, duration, and scope to reasonably achieve their purpose". However, in handing down a ruling on the legality of a formulary limiting the availability of certain Drugs to Medicaid patients, he also noted that use of federal funds was allowed "for the purpose of enabling each state, *as far as practicable* (italics added) under the condition of such state to furnish Medicaid and, therefore, expressly recognize financial matters as relevant considerations in fashioning Medicaid programs".

This rather obscure, but legally binding, decision would hint at an atmosphere where "health is a right as long as the money holds out", and indeed, this is a real consideration.

If we return again to our picture of woman as both a biological and a social entity, it may help in understanding what the future actually holds. As an individual, man rationally attempts a State of health for all parts of his body. In fact, however, the teeth may be neglected in favor of the heart, preventive care in favor of acute care. Decisions are sometimes, but not always, rational and are often influenced by ignorance, stupidity, economic, and cultural concerns. So, too, society seems likely to *want* to take care of all its members. Practicalities may be somewhat different.

Donabedian (159) has noted that medical care needs are almost limitless, while our resources have definite limits. If there are no restraints on the use of medical care, who will decide what is enough – even in the extreme of a National Health Service? The answer, according to Donabedian, is the same as it has been in education – for we do have a National Education Service, locally administered – through political (social) decisions that set limits on the total resources to be made available. This total would then be reallocated within the system as productively as our wisdom and political and economic realities will allow. "Everyone has equal access to medical care that is equally good or, for that matter, equally bad".

It is not possible to predict the outcome of these attempts to alter health care delivery and financing. It *is* possible to predict with certainty that change lies ahead.

Drugs and Their Role in Society

What, exactly, is a Drug? We go to our handy dictionary first. "Drug: a substance used as a medicine or in making medicines" or "a narcotic substance or preparation". Let's try "medicine": "a substance or preparation used in treating a disease", or "something that affects well-being".

In fact, the term "Drug" can have a variety of meanings, and Drugs can have many functions as shown in Table 1.2.

For this Book, we will be referring to the therapeutic function. In this sense, there are two classes of Drugs: "legend" Drugs, so called because they bear the legal "legend", "Caution: Federal law prohibits dispensing without a prescription", and nonlegend Drugs, referred to as nonprescription or O-T-C (over-the-counter) Drugs.

Drugs come from a variety of sources as detailed in Chapter 11. "Drug" is often used in a pejorative sense as in Drug Abuse. Most of our attention will be devoted to the legitimate use of Drugs as medications, although some serve cosmetic (Rogaine) and social functions (Viagra, "The Pill"). The various functions of Drugs and problems associated with their discovery are development, marketing, pricing, and use, which make up much of the contents of this Book.

Reviewing Table 1.2, it can be observed that many of the functions of Drugs are recognized by some as non-legitimate. There is a growing concern that some of the "legitimate" uses of Drugs may not be in the best medical tradition. This is particularly true in the area of the psychologic determinants of Drug use. The psychologic determinants of Drug use have

Table 1.2 Functions of Drugs

Function	Example
Esthetics	Use of marijuana by jazz musicians
Aphrodisiac	Mostly folklore
Ego disruption	LSD, other hallucinogens
Ideologic	Use of peyote by anti-white Indians
Political	Use of opium by Japanese in attempt to demoralize Chinese in the 1930s
Psychologic support	Tranquilizers
Religion	Marijuana in Jamaica, Peyote in Native American Church
Research	Behavioral studies
Social control	Peyote "confessions"
Therapeutic	Any medical application
War and other conflicts	Biologic warfare

Source: Table constructed based on narrative in pages 168–185 of Bernard Barber's *Drugs and Society*, Russell Sage Foundation, 1967.

been widely discussed. They are too complex, and there is as yet a lack of consensus, so that an elaborate discussion here is not appropriate. However, a word should be said on psychologic determinants and effects of the use of Drugs in the formal structure of the physician's prescription blank. Lennard and his associates (272) have described a psychologic component in the prescribing of a Drug – any Drug.

> Prescribing a drug, such as a minor tranquilizer, legitimizes the doctor-patient relationship. Through giving a drug the physician sets a patient's comfort as legitimate, and he agrees with the patient's definition of himself as being sick. Through prescribing a drug, a physician also reduces a patient's anxiety by implying that he has defined the problem and can alleviate the complaint.

Motives for the use of Drugs have been identified by Svarstad (384) and are shown in Table 1.3. This along with Table 1.4 provides adequate evidence of the ubiquitous role played by Drugs in the lives of everyone.

A final word about the *prescription*, by which the legend Drugs, are obtained. The latent functions of Table 1.4 are not necessarily intended nor recognized by the prescriber and/or the patient. They exist, variably, nevertheless. This is in contrast to the manifest (recognized and intended) functions: method of therapy, legal document, record source, and means of communication. There will be much more on these in Chapters 2 and 7.

Drug Policy

"Health Care Delivery System" is, at best, an oxymoron. A useful analogy might be a million-piece jigsaw puzzle. Some of the pieces are missing, and some just don't seem to fit. The Reader will find scores of references to the efforts of, usually well meaning, scientists, economists, politicians, and others attempting to put the puzzle together. Some try to find missing pieces. Others try to force ill-fitting pieces into a space (square peg in a round hole).

Still others offer solutions – what the picture will look like if we can just solve the puzzle. Unfortunately, there are some players also who will hide some of the pieces or disfigure some of them.

"System" is, in itself, a euphemism. The dictionary defines it: "a regularly interacting or interdependent group of items forming a unified whole".

Table 1.3 Human Motives and Functions of Drugs

1. Prevent, treat, and cure disease; relieve pain and discomfort	Therapeutic function
2. Relieve feelings of personal failure, grief, stress, fear, loneliness, sadness, or inferiority	Psychological function
3. Relax and enjoy the company of others; experience pleasurable sights, sounds, tastes, smells, and feelings; satisfy curiosity or desire for new and unusual experiences	Recreational function
4. Relieve fatigue and improve academic, athletic, or work performance	Instrumental function
5. Manage or control the behavior of demanding patients, disruptive children, political dissidents, and other persons	Social control function
6. Beautify the skin, hair, or body image	Cosmetic function
7. Gain social status, approval, or prestige	Status-conferring function
8. Express feelings, values, preferences, interest, or concern	Expressive-symbolic function
9. Seek religious meaning, salvation, or transcendent experiences	Religious function
10. Gain knowledge and understanding of human behavior	Research function
11. Allay hunger or control the desire for food	Appetitive function

Source: B. L. Svarstad, "Sociology of Drugs", In, A.I. Wertheimer and M. C. Smith Eds., *Pharmacy Practice*, Third Edition, Williams and Wilkins, 1981, with permission.

Another definition: "harmonious arrangement or pattern bringing order out of confusion". "Regular?" "Unified?" "Order out of confusion?" Sorry! "Mosaic" doesn't work either.

Health Care *Policy*? Again: "Prudence or wisdom in the management of affairs". So far, at least, that hasn't appeared to everyone's satisfaction. Anyone with the temerity (your humble Author included) to attempt to explain the extant system or Policy faces a forbidding task. Of course there is plenty of temerity around as the Reader will easily discover in the pages that follow.

Implementation of a Drug Policy might go roughly like this. Government, with influence from a variety of sources, identifies problems and opportunities affecting the People. A thorough Investigation often follows with the ultimate goal of Legislation. This takes the form of Acts and Bills. Although these documents are very detailed and may run to scores of pages, they, too,

Table 1.4 Latent Functions of the Prescription

Visible signs of the physician's power to heal (Drug)
Symbol of the power of modern technology (Drug)
Sign that the patient is "really" ill (Drug)
Legitimizes the long-term illness without cure
Concrete expression that physician has fulfilled his contract
Reasonable excuse for human contact with physician
Satisfactorily terminates the visit
Fits the concept of modern man that he can control his own destiny
Expression of physician's control
Indication of physician's concern
Medium of communication between physician and patient
Source of satisfaction to the physician
Identifies the clinical situation as legitimately medical
Legitimizes sick role status (see Chapter 8)
Symbol of patient stability
Symbol of patient control
Excuse for failure
Means of patient goal attainment
Evidence of physician as an activist
Evidence of pharmacist's activity
Research source on utilization and treatment
Political tool
Medium of exchange
Sampling medium
Method of clinical trial
Method of differentiating legal Drug status

are often broad, leaving it often to the Regulators to work out the details. (Here's what we want done – handle it.) The Stakeholders then respond pointing to flaws and shortcomings, and the Dynamic Tension begins or continues.

Is there a U.S. Policy on medications? If such exists in written form, I have not seen it. I suggest that such Policy could take the form of the following:

> With diligence and intelligence to assure the availability of safe and effective medications to meet the legitimate needs of every citizen with due regard to the science of medicine and economics.

Perhaps a policy should include reference to the *rights*, accorded to the citizenry, by the Declaration of Independence and the Bill of Rights. But nowhere in these documents is there mention of a right to health or to health care (of which medication is an integral part). Arguments on this subject can be found elsewhere in this Book. "Health", too, is a relative term and in any case cannot be guaranteed. "Life" (as in "life, liberty, and the pursuit of happiness") certainly has medical implications, but that, too, can hardly be guaranteed.

Moynihan (252) has warned that a lesson to be learned is that Government intervention in social processes is risky, uncertain, and necessary. It requires enthusiasm, but also intellect, and above all, it needs an appreciation of how difficult it is to change things and People. Persons responsible for such programs who do not insist on clarity and candor in the definition of objectives, and the means for obtaining them, or who will settle for a short and happy life in office, do not much serve Public interest.

Avedis Donabedian wrote, in 1973, the definitive work on medical care organization (159). His Book, in his own words, was

> constructed around the simple notion that the medical care administrator is often faced with certain responsibilities that he must discharge or tasks that he must perform. He may find it necessary, for example, to define his objectives, to assess the need for service, or to decide whether or not resources are adequate.

Society's efforts to affect a viable Drug Policy have included the following:

- **Legislation** was passed to provide financial assistance in acquiring drugs for special groups (Medicare, Medicaid).
- **Legislation** was passed granting expanded powers to regulatory agencies to require proof of effectiveness as well as safety in drugs (1962 Drug Amendments).

Regulations were promulgated by the Food and Drug Administration requiring, among other things, full disclosure of facts about drugs in their promotion.

Investigations (notably those of Senators Kefauver and Nelson) were held to inquire into structural characteristics in the drug industry which might result in artificially inflated drug prices and other problems.

These efforts have been helped along by Public opinion, consumer advocacy groups, and indirectly in the voting booth.

One problem with the Government procedures (about which you can read much more in Chapters 3 and 4) is that any objectives constitute the moral and legal basis of a program. They give it legitimacy. Governmental programs generally rest on statutory provisions that give the general intent of the program and the rough outlines of its structure and function. A more detailed specification of all these features, including objectives, is a task for regulatory and sometimes judiciary, interpretation, not to say surmise (386).

The goals of our society, which should form the basis for any Policy, and accordingly the actions of the legislative and regulatory bodies, are reflective of its values. Our American society places a high value on technical progress and the advancement of knowledge. This value affects the medical care complex to the extent that vast sums of money, from both Public and private sources, are expended each year on basic and clinical research into the causes, effects, and cures of disease and disability. The attitudes and values of our society dictate that this progress will be stimulated and its results implemented through a pluralistic rather than a monolithic social system. Throughout the nation and in its States and communities, a variety of mechanisms for organizing and financing health services are sanctioned under private, voluntary, and governmental auspices.

Our society does value the principle of equality of opportunity. Attempts are made to insure that health services of an acceptable standard of quality are made universally available that communities are assured a supply of health personnel, health facilities, and health financing appropriate to the needs of their populations.

Our society values efficiency and economy in the use of its resources. It is hoped that the resources allocated to the medical care complex will be used in the most efficient manner possible, consonant with humanitarian goals. At times, of course, the goal of efficiency may conflict with other social goals. Ideally, however, our society feels that advances in knowledge gained through research should be readily and widely applied; that unmet needs or duplication of services should be minimized; and that the use of services should be appropriate in quantity and quality to the need for them (271).

Many of our problems are relatively new: urbanization, increased population density with its pollution of all kinds, automation, industrialization, and depersonalization. Successful functioning in isolation is no longer possible as the components of the intensely complex society have of necessity become interdependent.

Our society has become better informed on health matters, and its stated goals reflect a more knowledgeable Public. Freedom from disease has been expanded to include the desire to live in a State of well-being. The Public no longer regards medical care as only a means of restoring health; this care is now considered to include the means for maintaining good health. It is now expected that the highest quality of medical protection should be available and accessible to all of the People when they are sick or when they are well.

Federal Government Policy, with respect to the development of new Drugs, is not describable as a single item but, rather, is a collection of policies. Moreover, the Government not only entertains a Policy statement or point of view but at times also throws itself into the arena as an active participant. That is, it not only has *Policy* but also has *programs* for which it spends Public funds.

Big Pharma

As with other sectors of the economy, the U.S. pharmaceutical industry is undergoing profound changes that influence how it develops and markets products. These changes have come about in response to a number of factors including the globalization of the pharmaceutical industry and its markets, the consolidation of the U.S. Health Care industry, the explosive growth of managed care arrangements, and greater sophistication on the part of the People.

The pharmaceutical industry is, as Pollard (387) characterizes it, "rooted in the soil of innovation; new products, preferably patentable, are *its cash crop*". Within the past decade, pharmaceutical products have become a much more potent element in modern medical intervention but have achieved visibility with policymakers primarily because of attendant high costs. Manufacturers counter criticisms by advancing the argument that the development of new Drugs is a costly and risky enterprise, pointing out that only 5 of about 5,000 substances screened in preclinical studies actually progress to human testing. Of these five, only one makes it to the Pharmacy shelves. Thus, the Prices of "successful" Drugs must compensate also for the costs of the research and development of the "unsuccessful" Drugs, i.e., those that do not make it to the marketplace.

The loudest voice of Big Pharma is certainly the Pharmaceutical Research and Manufacturers Association (PhRMA), formerly the Pharmaceutical Manufacturers Association (PMA). Their members represent the largest number of brand name (and more recently some Generic) Drugs. The insertion of *Research* into the name represents their continued assertion of the importance of their members' research in the discovery and development of a continuing supply of new therapeutic entities.

The pharmaceutical industry, in all of its aspects, is, in fact, much more than the members of PhRMA. But it is the members of that organization to which the media and industry critics refer when they use the term, Big Pharma. And it is truly *Big*. The organization is comparatively new by historical standards having been organized only in 1958.

The PhRMA has a mission statement which reads: "To conduct advocacy for Public policies that encourage the discovery of important new medicines for patients by pharmaceutical companies". Started just about the time Senator Estes Kefauver began his Administrative Prices Hearings (Chapter 3), it was a timely beginning. As of 2017, the organization had more than 50 members and assets of 455 million dollars. Of that, 128 million was reported to have gone to lobbying efforts. More will be discussed on that in Chapter 8. In 2019, Ken Frazier, CEO of Merck, was on record suggesting a new, different organization with only a dozen or so members, presumably to represent only *really* Big Pharma.

Big Pharma is a comparatively new appellation. It is a handy catch-all and smacks a bit of shadowy practices. (You won't hear industry executives use it.) In early days, the industry recognized that the Congressional Investigators had, and have, a bully pulpit. Needing a pulpit of their own, they sought professional help in the form of Public relations. They employed Public relations firms, notably Hill and Knowlton, just as they had secured the expertise of pharmacologists, chemists, and other scientists. Their efforts continue to this day.

Drug-Related Problems

Drugs, for all their many benefits, are also prey to a great many shortcomings. Strand (181) has made an ambitious attempt to catalog the categories of Drug problems as shown in Table 1.5. These are problems related to the medical or personal use of Drugs for therapeutic purposes.

There are, of course, other non-therapeutic problems by no means the least of which are economic in nature. Notable is the Price/cost of Drugs. In the first 10 years of this century, the FDA approved Drugs with such Price tags as Chlolar at $34,000 a week and Provenge at $93,000 for three infusions. The first of those treats childhood leukemia, and the second was used to treat advanced prostate cancer. Is the Price too high? And there is evidence that more Drugs with similar Price tags are on the way.

Other dilemmas rear their ugly heads throughout this history. All parties are affected at some time or the other and in some way or another. Consider just one.

Table 1.5 Categories of Drug-Related Problems

1. *Untreated indications*: The patient has a medical condition that needs Drug therapy but is not receiving a Drug for that indication.
2. *Improper Drug selection*: The patient has an indication for Drug therapy but is taking the wrong Drug.
3. *Subtherapeutic dosage*: The patient has a medical condition that is being treated with too little of the correct Drug.
4. *Overdosage*: The patient has a medical condition that is being treated with too much of the correct Drug.
5. *Adverse Drug reaction*: The patient has a medical condition that is the result of an adverse effect or Drug reaction.
6. *Drug interactions*: The patient has a medical condition that is the result of a Drug-Drug, Drug-food, and Drug-lab interaction.
7. *Failure to receive Drugs*: The patient has a medical condition that is the result of his or her not receiving a Drug, perhaps due to psychological, sociological, cultural, and/or economic reasons.
8. *Drug use without indication*: The patient is taking a Drug for no medically valid indication.

Source: L. M. Strand, et al., "Drug Related Problems: Their Structure and Function", *DICP Annals of Pharmacotherapy*, Vol. 24, 1990, with permission.

The thalidomide tragedy resulted in a heightened awareness of the changes of teratogenicity. No one wants to risk birth defects or other dire consequences of Drug use during pregnancy. But how would one test the possibility without clinical trials? Does anyone want to risk the consequences? Or should we simply warn against *any* use of a new Drug during pregnancy, thus depriving women of new, possibly better therapy? Looking up dilemma in the Dictionary, one is referred to "predicament". *Indeed*! Admittedly this example, while real, is, however, over-simplified, and ways have been found to solve this particular dilemma but not absolutely.

An additional Drug problem has been the existence of a "Drug lag". Simply stated, it refers to delays in the approval of new, potentially valuable Drugs because of over-stringent FDA Regulations. The term was used frequently during the course of Congressional Hearings by, especially, Big Pharma. Campbell (371) wrote, at the time (1976), the definitive treatise on the subject appropriately titled *Drug Lag*. She concluded that a Drug lag still existed in the United States "in some therapeutic areas" and called on the FDA to enlist more economic study such as cost-benefit analysis instead of relying only on biological risk. Drug lag is likely to continue to be a theme.

Much more will be written in this Book about the problems associated with Drug use, misuse, and non-use. Taking medicinal Drugs is a risky business. Even though medicines have become increasingly efficacious, there is always a chance that any given Drug will fail to cure a condition or will induce an adverse reaction. As the chief justice of the California Supreme Court put it, "Ill health offers adventure; no one has a better chance to live dangerously than the ill who must take their medicine" (390).

Temin (49) has identified three distinct, albeit intertwined, risks in using medicinal Drugs. There is the risk of overpaying for a Drug, either because the Price is high or the quality is low. There is also the risk of getting sick or dying as a result of taking a Drug. In the language of the trade, this is the risk of an adverse drug reaction. And once sick, from whatever causes, there is the risk of not getting well. People can fail to recover because no suitable Drug is available, because they take the wrong Drug, or even because they take too much or too little of an appropriate Drug.

Drug products themselves are inanimate objects – powerful tools with great potential to do good or to cause harm. How they are used is of ultimate importance. Harmful adverse results cannot legitimately be blamed on Drugs if they are prescribed inappropriately, any more than computers can legitimately be blamed for errors caused by inappropriate programming.

The People

In the many Books written over the years about the events, issues, and controversies which make up the subject of this Book, the People (consumers, patients, victims) have too often, I believe, been given less than adequate attention. Their beliefs, knowledge, attitudes, and fears often take a backseat to the machinations of the Government and Big Pharma.

In his introduction to Norman Couzins' *Anatomy of an Illness*, Rene Dubos, author of the perfectly titled and brilliant Book, *Mirage of Health* (226), notes that every person must accept a certain measure of responsibility for his or her own recovery from disease or disability. The key words here are "certain measure".

Donabedian (159) tells us that the model of the free market postulates a "sovereign" consumer who, by deciding whether to buy or not, what to buy, when and where, calls the tune to economic activity and, ultimately, bends the entire economy to his will.

The ability of the client to control and manipulate her demands on the market is clearly diminished by the great extent to which illness is involuntary and unpredictable. These characteristics are what justifies health insurance and makes it actuarially feasible. The fact that, in most cases, medical care is a necessary and urgent need imposes additional constraints on the capacity of the consumer to manipulate demand.

If the consumer/patient is effectively to accept that measure of responsibility suggested by Dubos, that person would need the knowledge necessary to do so and some degree of rationality in using that knowledge, as Donabedian puts it.

> The success of the market in satisfying not only the individual's whims and desires but also, to a reasonable extent, his own welfare and the welfare of society at large, depends on choices by a reasonably well-informed and rational consumer. The ability of the consumer to act in this manner with regard to medical care is severely hampered by (a) limitations in knowledge, (b) the deferred consequences of present choices, and (c) the non-pleasurable nature of most medical care services.
>
> *(159)*

Underlying all of this is a very consumer-sensitive issue. In a paper aimed at pharmaceutical marketers, Smith and Kolassa (192) described a situation that is very relevant to the People. (Bear in mind that the paper was intended for a readership of pharmaceutical marketers.)

> How much do you enjoy buying car insurance—or gasoline? How about deodorant and lawn fertilizer? What about bug killer?
>
> In the stuffy terms that academics are fond of using, these are "negative goods". A well-accepted definition is "products/services seen by customers as an unpleasant necessity bought to avoid some disutility". Disutility is something you don't want to happen to you, such as an automobile accident, the house burning down, or dying from a heart attack—a major disutility. You who are charged with the marketing of pharmaceuticals should understand that medications are "negative goods" by this definition. There are exceptions, maybe, such as Rogaine (minoxidil), Viagra (sildenafil), and other lifestyle-enhancing drugs, but even these are used to overcome problems. Generally speaking, you are charged with marketing products that most people do not want.
>
> Your challenge, however, is even worse, at least with regard to prescription medications. Absent DTC (Direct to Consumer) promotion, you are the mercy of an intermediary prescriber—usually a physician. The fact is, for the majority of the population, a visit to a physician is also a negative experience. Thus, the patient has to pay for a "negative service" that in turn usually leads to a "negative good"—your product. Your business resides at the tail end of this string of negative experiences.
>
> One of the most obvious implications of the marketing of a negative good is the effect on pricing. *The price of a negative good will always be far too high.*

More depth and detail of the role of the People in their own pharmacologic care will be found in Chapter 7, where, among other subjects, we will discuss "cultural lag" as it applies to the People and their Drugs.

What's Ahead

In Chapter 2, we introduce the classic "Four P's" of the marketing mix with examples and applications to Big Pharma.

Chapters 3–5 describe the sequence of events wherein the Government Investigates (Congressional Hearings) sometimes enact Legislation based on the Hearings, and the Regulations (by FDA and others) which, over time, changed the nature of the Drug discovery and distribution processes.

In Chapter 6, other types of *non-governmental* controls are examined including insurance programs, consumer advocacy groups, and professional organizations. Chapter 7 brings us to the People in all their diversity, attitudes, beliefs, misinformation, fears, age effects, buying habits, and especially compliance and non-compliance with medication regimens.

In Chapter 8, we will see the many ways in which Big Pharma has responded to the pressures brought to bear on them – their performance during Investigations, Public relations efforts, and lobbying. A bit of internecine maneuvering is also described.

Chapter 9 highlights the Generic Drug industry primarily from a historical perspective as the borders between the "brand names" and Generics are increasingly hard to define. "Boutique" companies are described as well as the biologic arm of the industry.

"Greedy" Big Pharmacy is limned in Chapter 10. This widely used sobriquet is examined on its merits, and a brief Parallel to "Greedy" Big Tech is offered.

In Chapter 11, the origin of Drugs is surveyed from animals, plants, and laboratories. It is followed by Chapter 12 which offers prognostications for the future – some probable, some fantasy.

Dr. Steven Pray brings his expertise to Chapter 13 on "Over-the-Counter" or "NonPrescription" Drugs. The author of *A History of Non-Prescription Drug Regulation*, Dr. Pray provides a necessary addition to the other chapters which focused mostly, but not entirely, on prescription Drugs.

In Chapter 14, I have tried to include some issues and studies in pharmaeconomics that we may have missed before.

In Chapter 15, Dr. E. M. "Mick" Kolassa provides an insider's perspective on Drug Prices and pricing practices. A former Drug industry executive and pricing consultant to the industry, Kolassa is widely acknowledged as an authority on the subject.

The Final Words in Chapter 16 are an attempt to tie a ribbon around the package as well as a few words about what seemed to be going on at the time this Book was being constructed.

There are three appendices:

A. Annotated references with cross index by author/sources.
B. Some useful, but random, quotes.
C. A satire: "The Saga of Vitamin B_{13}".

Conclusion

This introductory chapter began with the thalidomide tragedy. The horrible nature of the incident cannot be overemphasized. The risk of an event of this magnitude has been minimized by succeeding events in the hands of the Government and of Big Pharma itself. In spite of the extraordinary efforts of good-meaning and often brilliant People, the risk of catastrophe still lurks.

While many writers lean a bit on the side of "viewing with alarm" the many problems in the health care system (an oxymoron as I have said), a number have offered "solutions". Some of these solutions, which, perhaps, leave much to be desired, are frequently brought to earth by realities. Nevertheless, thoughtful exploration of the problems is in the best interest of us all.

Regarding the People, there is a continuing undercurrent – "Why doesn't somebody *do* something about (fill in the problem of your choice)?" The fact is a myriad of "somebodies" have spent more than a century trying to *do* something. And there have been some notable successes. The 1962 Drug Amendments resulted in Regulations requiring that a Drug actually *works*. That seems elementary in retrospect, but it took more than half a century to reach that point (of course many of the old Drugs were "safe" simply because they didn't do much of anything.)

The continuing struggles to invent an equitable Drug discovery and distribution system beg for clichés, "Don't throw the baby out with the wash water" comes to mind as does Shakespeare's "Striving to better, oft we mar what's well". This history is rife with examples of "solutions" which gave rise to new and unforeseen problems. So we're not going to run out of problems anytime soon.

I close this chapter with a strong recommendation to the Reader of Rene Dubos' *Mirage of Health* (226). First published in 1959, the Book is even more relevant today. Dubos' brilliant and eloquent exposition of Health in the human milieu beggars encapsulation. It requires reading in its entirety. Dubos' narrative makes the issues described in my Book seem almost petty. Yes, he's that good! Consider my few quotes herein as merely an appetizer for the feast which Dubos prepared. Here is one.

> The earth is not a resting place. Man has elected to fight, not necessarily for himself. But, for a process of emotional, intellectual, and ethical growth that goes on forever. To grow in the midst of dangers is the fate of the human race, because it is the law of the spirit.

I will use a thread throughout this Book – sometimes explicitly, sometimes implied – incorporating the term "dynamic tension". Older Readers may remember it, as I do, from their "comic book days". Simply put, it refers to a body-building technique which "pits muscle against muscle" with the result of overall fitness. While "Dynamic Tension" is a registered trademark of Charles Atlas, Ltd. in the context of instructional booklets for isotonic exercises, this book will use the term strictly for editorial and descriptive purposes with regard to the efforts of all three parties highlighted in this history to use their respective "muscles" with the aim of a robust medication delivery system. One that is "fit".

> This book is an independent publication that is not affiliated, associated, authorized, endorsed by, or in any way connected with Charles Atlas, Ltd., or any of its subsidiaries or its affiliates.

Chapter 2
The "Four P's"

Introduction

In this chapter, we will describe the four elements which comprise the considerations used by Big Pharma, in taking a medication from the laboratory to the patient. The "Four P's" have been widely used as a framework for understanding a company's strategy and tactics. That is what we hope to offer here, along with a theoretical framework. Thus, this chapter is about Big Pharma and how it goes about its business.

Pharmaceuticals represent only one element of the Health Care system, and their appropriate use is based on many factors. Proper diagnosis, prescribing, manufacture, distribution, and patient use all combine to determine the extent to which patients benefit from pharmaceutical therapy. Essentially, pharmaceutical marketing must strive to inform a technically sophisticated audience about dramatically changing product and service mixes in a climate of constant governmental Regulation, Public scrutiny, and industry competition.

The pharmaceutical industry touches every member of the population at one time or another. It deals in products which People would prefer not to buy and over which they often have no control as to choice. As a consequence, the industry tends to be subject to wide-ranging criticism each time the activities of the industry come under Public scrutiny. A particularly vulnerable area of pharmaceutical activities comes under the general umbrella of marketing practices. This is partly attributable to the fact that a substantial portion of the cost of the Drugs, as borne by the consumer, is composed of marketing elements at the manufacturers' level as well as throughout the chain of distribution.

The firms comprising the pharmaceutical industry occupy a special position within the American business community. Every business firm has a responsibility to the consumers of its products. However, firms within the pharmaceutical industry have a third responsibility not encountered by other business enterprises – a responsibility to the members of the Health professions who prescribe and dispense their products. Each firm's responsibility to the Public and to the members of the Health profession is somewhat analogous. In both cases, their responsibility is to provide products which are both safe and efficacious. In discharging their responsibility, manufacturers are monitored by the Food and Drug Administration (FDA) in addition to meeting all the tests of the marketplace experienced by every business firm.

It is well to establish here that this Book deals mostly with the marketing of *prescription* medications and my position is that good marketing and good medicine are not only compatible, they are inseparable as well. The Reader is urged to view this chapter as a sort of Marketing 101, as we lay out the components of the "Marketing Mix", a term often used synonymously with the "Four P's". I rely on some marketing theory, but such theory is quite basic and understandable.

The efforts of marketing practitioners to match as closely as possible the marketing mix of their companies, with the needs of the consumer, have led to the development of a way of thinking known as the "marketing concept". The marketing concept States that what seems obvious now, but was not always practiced, that it is easier to change the products and activities of the individual manufacturer to fit the market, than it is to convince the entire market to use the products and services, as the individual marketer prefers them. The marketing concept further requires that all of the resources of the firm be organized into a total system aimed at meeting the needs of the customer.

Marketing as an Actualizing Process

Discussion of marketing may be done from the perspective that marketing is a *process* by which markets are actualized. Because markets may be viewed as gaps that separate parties interested in an exchange, marketing, as a discipline, is a study of how various gaps or separations between parties interested in an exchange are anticipated and removed. Consequently, the process of market actualization requires that various activities (called marketing activities) remove the gaps between parties interested in an exchange. Some of these points require careful examination.

The essence of marketing is exchange. The existence of a market is the *foundation* for an exchange and not a *substitute* for it. Every exchange requires that (1) there are two or more parties who (2) are interested in satisfying their unfulfilled desires, (3) have something of value to offer to each other, and (4) are capable of communication and delivery. The widely used term "zero-sum game" comes into play here.

As used, the term means that two parties to an exchange benefit equally because each wants what the other has, and thus, both parties benefit from the exchange. The producer gets the money and the customer gets the product. But there is a flaw when applied to prescription Drugs. As noted in Chapter 1, the customer (patient) does not really *want* the Drug. What she wants is the result of *using* the Drug. Who *really* wants a drill? You want *holes*! Under these circumstances, Drug Prices will always be too high!

Marketing plays a key role, influencing or directing activities from the manufacturer to the patient. And the patient, it should be noted, stands at the peak of the marketing pyramid. It is her characteristics which determine which goods will be sold or, more correctly, which goods will be produced. Any firm that wishes adequately to serve its market would therefore strive to direct marketing activities, so the right product is sold, in the right quantity, at the right place, at the right price, at the right time.

The Marketing Mix – The "Four P's"

The Right Product

Few industries feel so keenly the need to have their products meet such rigid specifications as does the Drug industry. A few micrograms difference in the composition of the active ingredients of a tablet may not only injure the sales curve but the patients as well.

One of the most desirable developments in recent years in the pharmaceutical industry has been the increased role played by the marketing department in the development of the right product. The specific subdivision of marketing, which bears the major responsibility for aiding in this development, is market research. This functional area is charged with the determination of not only the therapeutic activity needed in diseases with an incidence (which also must be determined) but also the dosage form and package which is likely to be most acceptable to both physician and patient.

The Right Price

Price is an integral part of the marketing mix, even though needed Drugs will probably be purchased regardless of Price, within limits. Insofar as there are other products that are substitutable, a product that bears an excessive Price tag may find itself without a market.

As we shall see throughout this Book, one of the many unique characteristics of the Drug industry is the undesirability of its products, i.e., with few exceptions patients would prefer not to purchase a prescribed Drug. They would prefer to purchase a new dress, a ticket to a movie, a dinner in a fine restaurant. Further, they are often ill when the prescription is necessary. These factors combine to make prescription Drugs unpopular and their Prices even more unpopular. As a consequence, the Prices of Drugs are regularly publicly criticized. Sometimes the community pharmacist receives the complaint. At other times, the industry as a whole is criticized. In this context, there is no *right* Price – only a "too high" Price.

Obviously, if Drugs are to continue to be produced by private industry, there will have to be a charge for them. Regardless of whether they are paid for by the patient, by an insurance company, or by a Government Agency, it is part of the task of the marketing department to determine what that charge should be. In practice, not one Price but several Prices will be set for a given product.

The Right Place

For prescription Drugs, the problem of place would seem to be an easy one. Prescription Drugs must be dispensed by physician or pharmacist; therefore, the place is pre-chosen. It is not that simple, however. Efforts toward fulfilling the requirements to distribute prescription Drugs as efficiently as possible have been the reason for the development of the complex distribution channels that include wholesalers, retailers, hospitals, clinics, and Government installations. These establishments are influenced by both the needs and desires of the patient. Further, the location of the patients, and the establishments in the channels of distribution, will affect plant location, warehousing, development of sales territories, and transportation of the product.

Availability of the Drug product *when* it is needed is a further responsibility of marketing management and is closely related to the place function. The injection must be available in the hospital emergency room when the patient is there, not several hours later.

Spreading the Word – Promotion

Even though marketing succeeds in its basic task, which we defined to include right product, quantity, place, price and time, it is still theoretically possible for the product to fail as a marketable item. The potential area of failure could be described broadly as communications. The part of the marketing communications process which may be most familiar to us is Advertising. This is the most visible and perhaps most exciting form of communication. However, if marketing is performing efficiently, communication will be a two-way process.

The minimum amount of information that must be communicated by the manufacturer is the *availability* of a product. Obviously one does not purchase a product that she does not know exists. The physician is engaged in what the late Wroe Alderson called a "vicarious search" (323), i.e., with a knowledge of the needs of her patient, she searches the characteristics of available products for the patient (who is not equipped to judge) for that which most closely approximates the answer to the patient's problem. Even though the physician is engaged in this relatively active and educated search process, there is a strong possibility that she will not become aware of a given product unless someone (usually, but not always, the manufacturer) has made a formal effort to communicate to her its availability. With the foregoing in hand, we will examine each of the "Four P's" more thoroughly and individually.

The Pharmaceutical Marketing System

As stated above, pharmaceutical marketing, as a subspecialty of marketing, can be defined as a process by which market for pharmaceutical care is actualized. It encompasses all of the activities carried out by various individuals or organizations to actualize markets for pharmaceutical care. Let us examine this definition closely.

The emphasis in pharmaceutical marketing is on pharmaceutical *care* and not just on Drugs. Any article, service, or idea needed to anticipate and to remove gaps in pharmaceutical care should be included in the discussion of pharmaceutical marketing. The marketing of many clinical pharmaceutical services and programs is as much a part of pharmaceutical marketing as is the marketing of Drug *products*. In other words, pharmaceutical marketing is not synonymous with, and is significantly broader than, the marketing of pharmaceuticals.

Any party interested in the exchange for pharmaceutical care may undertake pharmaceutical marketing activities. Hospital pharmacies, community pharmacies, third-party insurance companies, consulting pharmacies, and many other organizations and individuals, in addition to pharmaceutical manufacturers and Drug wholesalers, are involved in pharmaceutical marketing.

The actualization of markets for pharmaceutical care requires that all activities involved in anticipating, enlarging, facilitating, and completing or removing gaps in pharmaceutical care are within the scope of the field of pharmaceutical marketing. In other words, pharmaceutical marketing is not a static passive process but a *dynamic, active* process.

If pharmaceutical marketing is viewed as a part of the Health Care marketing system, it can be depicted as a simplified network of relationships between various institutions and their attributes, leading to actualization of markets for pharmaceutical care through exchange flows and marketing functions within the bounds established by external systems.

So, to summarize, the "Four P's" are defined as follows:

Product

The *benefits* or positive *results* that markets derive out of doing business with the company using the products you offer in the way you offer them.

Price

The total cost components that markets must bear in order to use the products offered.

Place

The distribution channels and physical distribution practices that make it possible, easy, or difficult for markets to use the product.

Promotion

What and how markets are informed of the firm's product, place, and Price. The interaction of these components makes up the marketing mix.

Before continuing, it should be noted that the Government has examined and taken action with regard to *each* of the "Four P's". Product is the everyday purview of the FDA. Price has been the bull's-eye at which many, many Investigations have aimed. Place was specifically affected by the Durham–Humphrey Amendment (Chapters 4 and 5) and Promotion has likewise been found in the sights of the investigators. Thus, the Dynamic Tension has been made manifest by the efforts of Big Pharma to actualize this marketing mix and the attempt by the Government to control these efforts.

Since coined by E. Jerome McCarthy (526) in 1960, the Four P's of marketing – Product, Place, Price, and Promotion – have been a standard for organization in developing marketing strategies. However, the current constraints of the pharmaceutical industry, including less physician access, promotional tool restrictions, and increased pricing pressures from payers, make marketing using the classic P's a challenge.

The foundation of the marketing mix – indeed, the most important element in it – is the Drug itself. All medications on the market are FDA indicated for a specific condition or disease, and pharmaceutical companies can legally market a product only for the approved indications.

Price is uniquely set in the pharmaceutical industry. In most other categories, the producer or manufacturer is in control of Price, subject to normal market constraints. This is not the case in the pharmaceutical industry, where companies have limited time to recoup development costs, and, in most cases, the end user is not the ultimate payer. Pharmaceutical product Prices are also constrained by managed care organizations and Generic pressure.

Although the distribution system of getting a medication from point A (manufactured) to point B (pharmacy/end user) has remained relatively the same over the years with the role of the wholesaler, community pharmacies, and, more recently, mail-order pharmacies, the flow of *information* to the ultimate end user of prescription medications, i.e., the patient/consumer, has drastically changed.

Although much is made of the impact of the evolution of direct-to-consumer (DTC) Advertising, Promotion in the pharmaceutical industry was once relatively simple. A company would hire sales representatives, train and educate them on product attributes, and arm them with product samples. These "reps" would then directly promote the Drug to doctors. Until 2009, sales representatives enjoyed enormous freedom in Promotion to professionals. In 2009, a new set of voluntary industry standards were introduced by the Pharmaceutical Research and Manufacturers of America (PhRMA), which considerably reduced the flexibility of the sales representative's independence in the Promotion process.

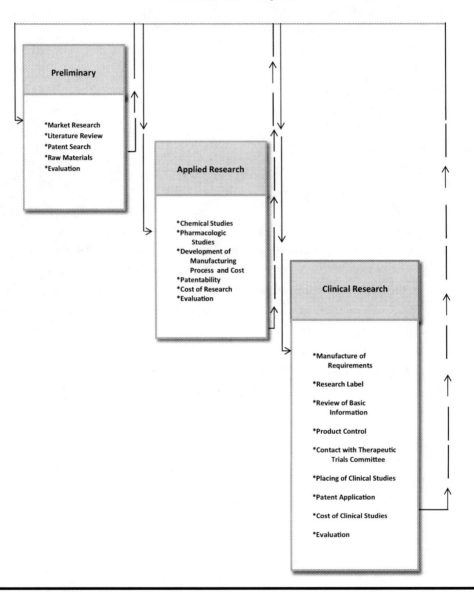

Figure 2.1 Product development committee.

Product

Figure 2.1 portrays, in very elementary form, the product development process. The "product" of Big Pharma would seem obvious – tablets, capsules, liquids, and patches. But for the consumer, the product may more realistically be seen in forms of the outcome of using it.

Big Pharma understands this. The majority of DTC ads on television imply the presumed outcome of a products use – a visit to a butterfly farm, attending a grandchild's graduation, or happily mowing the lawn. There are exceptions…ease of use, comparative effectiveness, etc. (See Promotion below.)

In the case of the prescriber, at least in the outpatient environment, "the Product" can take on different characteristics. For example, the prescriber may often not even *see* the physical product. Even samples are usually pre-packed, so, again, this "Product" in the prescriber's eyes is likely to be viewed for the results. Thus, the approach to the prescriber will rarely involve a physical description (although the "little blue pill" has made its way into the vernacular).

The actual physical characteristics of a Drug are only *sometimes* relevant to the prescriber. Such would be the case, for example, with injections. But they become relevant through Reports from patients – "hard to swallow", "tastes bad". Any patient complaint calls into question the rationale behind the prescriber's choice.

The importance of Big Pharma's vaunted research and development (R&D Programs) are, from the patient's point of view, the "D" that is most directly affecting. It is nice to know that Big Pharma's research is vast and successful, but such mundane matters as to taste, smell, and frequency of use are *very* relevant in the consumer's mind. So, of course, is Price.

From Medicine to Your Mouth (or Wherever)

Discussions of product seldom include the process of production. A very excellent primer on the subject, understandable by laymen, is *Modern Pharmaceutical Industry* by Jacobson and Wertheimer (25). A few items will be noted here.

The first, or at least early, stage in product development is the selection of a dosage form. Options include: solid/oral (pills, capsules, gelcaps); parenteral with options of intravenous (IV), intramuscular (IM), and subcutaneous (SC or "SubQ"); ophthalmic; topical; oral liquid; aerosol; and others. The choice must be made very early as the ultimate dosage form must be available for clinical trials and that includes any placebos. It is easy to overlook such developments as the invention of the soft capsule by the Eli Lilly Company around the turn of the twentieth century. It had enormous impact on prescription preparation.

Dosage form decisions, in addition to conditions dictated by patient considerations and the nature of the condition to be treated, result in a wide range of choices. A partial list would include: stability; container closure systems; dissolution factors for oral solids, shelf life, special storage conditions, if any; and the site of Drug action in the body. The list could go on. The reference cited above (25) offers an outstanding and thorough coverage of the subject.

Most attention in discussion of Drug research and development is given to the chemists and pharmacologists. It should be noted that other areas of science also play a pivotal role. "Pharmaceutics", which is the study of issues such as those briefly described, is a doctoral level of study in a number of schools of pharmacy. Quantitative analysis is a specialty area essential to Generic Drug products especially over-the-counters (OTCs) where the patient expects the Listerine "wannabe" to look, taste, and smell like its brand name counterpart. Animal biologists, too, play an essential role in preclinical trials even to the point of cultivating transgenic or "knockout mice" (25). Our library offers a 400-page Book entitled, *Mouse Ear Models and Their Pharmacologic Applications*!

Molecular Modification

This term, most often used in the pejorative, is a kind of "tinkering" with initial chemical substances. There is nothing necessarily bad about this activity. Indeed, the practice is usually engaged in hoping for more effectiveness, a lower needed dose, with fewer side effects.

There have been some notable successes from educated tinkering. Occasionally, such a modification has yielded a major new type of Drug, sometimes of breakthrough importance, as in the change from cortisone to prednisone, or in the apparently minor modification of the early antihistamines that led to chlorpromazine, the first phenothiazine tranquilizer. Of course molecular modification has often been used by a competitor to create a competing product which may, or may not, offer therapeutic advantages. Critics charge that this practice has resulted in a flood of "me too" products with a concomitant flood of promotional activities. Similarly, the originator of a successful product will almost certainly continue "tinkering" as Patent expiration looms and Generic competition lurks on the horizon.

Generic Products

Generics have a rich and sometimes troubled history. Because of economic and market considerations, they were frequently the subject of Congressional

Investigations. There were turf battles revolving around prescribing and the pharmacists dispensing.

In 1967, Sadove, a pharmacist and a physician, submitted a lengthy statement during the very first session of the "Nelson" Hearings (Chapter 3). He titled it "What is a generic equivalent"? Sadove and two physician collaborators described at great length the kinds of considerations necessary in determining generic equivalence. Things such as salts, vehicles, pH-stabilizing agents, and contaminants were cited as potential barriers to equivalence. The conclusion reached by the author was "that generic equivalence is frequently a fable without basis in fact: chemical equivalency of the primary agent, or agents, is not necessarily clinical or pharmacologic equivalency" (123).

Now, more than 50 years later, after years of wrangling, bioequivalence has become the standard for approval of a Generic product. The history is played out in several subsequent sections of this Book.

Generic Drugs have had a checkered history. Early on, there were charges that some pharmacists "substituted" Generics for the brand name product without the prescriber's knowledge. Pressure was brought to hear on that practice, and over time, many States adopted control measures to allow the physician to get engaged. Special prescription forms with a "Do not substitute" warning allowed the physician to specify her wishes.

The FDA's solution to the nomenclature problem has been to require all print and OTC Promotions to include the Generic name in type at least half the size of that of the brand. It is difficult, of course, to impose such a restriction on the detailer. With quality considerations essentially solved by the Waxman–Hatch Legislation and subsequent FDA Regulations, Generic Drugs have become completely legitimate. A number of firms now market both Generic and branded versions of the same Drug. Pfizer, in fact, effected a merger with Mylan, a major Generic supplier, to market its line of "off patent" Drugs.

Generic Drugs, for all the controversy of the past, are now a permanent and legitimate part of the offerings of Big Pharma.

Place

In a 1992 article (81), I tried to put "Place" in its place. The prescription Drug industry is a great industry by almost any standard. Its products, in spite of their often-cited problems, are remarkably effective. Perhaps most important of all, the distribution system has been beautifully efficient.

Of all the components of the Health Care system, pharmaceuticals have been the most accessible. There are pharmacists in almost every hamlet, and they have made a way of life of having any prescription Drug available when it is needed. Whereas one might have to travel miles to obtain cobalt therapy, orthodontist services, even a pediatrician, the odds are that in any town of more than 1,500 People, nearly any prescription Drug will be available.

Pharmaceutical products do not automatically find their way to pharmacy shelves. A vital, but seldom discussed, function of pharmaceutical marketing is the development and maintenance of a system for the physical distribution of medicines. Marketing has created in the United States one of the most efficient and cost-effective medication distribution systems in the world.

This system allows for the rapid distribution of lifesaving new medicines immediately after they are approved for marketing. Following FDA approval, the availability of an important new medicine can be communicated immediately to all practicing physicians in the United States and the product shipped to every pharmacy in the country within forty-eight hours.

This distribution system also enables a rapid, corrective response to bad news, by informing doctors and pharmacists about important, newly discovered adverse effects. If quality control or tampering problems are discovered, batch designations can be quickly traced to locate and recall products from individual pharmacies.

The availability of virtually any prescription medicine in any town in America documents the success of this effort. This distribution system was developed mutually by the manufacturing, wholesaling, and retailing segments of the pharmaceutical industry. This system is virtually invisible to consumers.

The wholesaler segment of the pharmaceutical industry makes a special contribution to efficiency and cost savings. Wholesalers select, purchase, and store goods in close proximity to pharmacies. Wholesalers provide economic savings by concentrating goods, dispersing them in economic quantities, and then transporting these goods to pharmacies. This sorting function reduces the number of transactions required, thereby saving the system considerable costs.

For legend Drugs, "Place" will almost always involve a pharmacist in some capacity, drugstore, hospital, nursing home, etc. Manufacturers rely on an interdependent system of distribution to assure that their products arrive at the right place and at the right, sometimes critical, time.

For OTC Drugs, "Place" is virtually *everywhere*! One can find these products in grocery stores, department stores, and gas stations. One can often find antacids at the cashier's counter in restaurants. (That's enough to give one pause with regard to the proprietor's confidence in the cuisine!) Read more in the chapter on OTC Drugs.

In the case of prescription Drug products, it is not unrealistic to suggest that the "P" of Place be replaced by the "P" of Pharmacy inasmuch as the pharmacy is the place where virtually all prescription Drugs finally, physically reach the patient. (There are notable exceptions – mail order for one.) Raymond Gosselin, architect of the famous Gosselin Prescription Survey, called the prescription counter "the last 18 inches in the channel of distribution". Not everyone agreed however.

Mail-Order Prescriptions

Full disclosure first! As a pharmacist, I am strongly opposed to mail order. I have no financial stake in the issue. My concerns are strictly professional. Indeed, I published a small editorial, years ago, in the *Pharmacy Press* entitled, "Mail Order Pharmacy is Unethical" (528). My argument was based on the Code of Ethics of the American Pharmacists Association (APh.A.).

My biggest concern is the destruction of any pharmacist–patient relationship. Continuity of care is compromised. Both of these things are also true when patients "shop around" for prescriptions and doctors. These issues represent a flaw in the Health Care system. Again, my bias, but the traditional pharmacist/patient relationship, even though it is not uniformly exercised, is a goal to be vigorously sought.

The Wholesaler

The wholesaler is the classic "middleman" (or middle person) in the channel of distribution. The long-standing issue involving potential conflict is whether the pharmacist should "buy direct" from the manufacturer or use the services of a wholesaler. The manufacturers' have their own considerations. Thus, the wholesaler is truly "in the middle", essential to the needs of the independent pharmacy and to the smaller manufacturer.

New distributive mechanisms have sprung up, including the need to safely accommodate the sophisticated requirements of new biotech pharmaceuticals. Some Drug manufacturers have sought out disease specialty pharmacies to ensure that laboratory-monitoring services, needle disposal, or counseling take place. Others, selling products for conditions with a small number of sufferers such as hemophilia and cystic fibrosis, seek to limit costs associated with selling products on a national scale. The new group of Specialty Drugs often require immediate distribution to the site of use.

As a result of pricing, insurance coverage and patient expectations are all affected, depending on whether the medication is available locally, through the mail, in the physician's office, or by accessing Internet-based sole-source vendor pharmacies.

Price

Probably no aspect of business is more complex and less understood by the general Public than that of Prices. This is particularly true of the Prices of pharmaceuticals.

Drug Prices have been and continue to be the subject of one Congressional Investigation after another. Although they represent only a part of total medical care costs, it seems much easier to find the "villain" in the Price of Drug products than for the Prices of other elements of the medical care market basket.

The subject of Drug Prices rears its ugly head throughout the pages of this Book. Chapter 15 is devoted entirely to this topic. Unfortunately, the Price of Drugs requires consideration of a variety of concepts, many of which are given too little attention. Among them are: cost, value, need, desire, worth, justice, and profit.

The fact is that from the patient's perspective, the Price of Drugs is too high – and it always will be, for Drugs are "negative" goods, as we have seen. The frequently heard declaration, "When it comes to my health, money's no object" often doesn't hold true for long.

When Drug Prices have been investigated, headlines such as "7,000% markup", which characterized the Kefauver Hearings, grab the Public's attention. That particular charge was based completely on the cost of *ingredients* of the Drugs. The idea that the cost of ingredients is the only cost incurred in getting the Drug into the patient's medicine cabinet was disingenuous at best.

After canvassing the many references used in research for this Book, notably Kolassa (10), McEvilla (66), and Weston (342), it was possible to construct Table 2.1. The Reader will note the complexity of the Drug Price issue. It constitutes a far cry from the simplistic listing of the cost of ingredients as Senator Kefauver (see Chapter 3) was fond of doing.

One cannot discuss pricing practices in the pharmaceutical industry without including in the discussion some attention to the subject of competition. While Price is only one form of competition, and while Price competition has not always, in the past, been the major form of competition in the

Table 2.1 Summary of Factors Influencing Drug Prices

A. Demand	
1	Product characteristics defined by (a) acceptability, (b) efficacy, and (c) absence of side effects
2	The therapeutic qualities of a Drug in relation to other products
3	Classes of physicians who are the most likely prescribers
4	Price Schedules for related products
5	Daily dosage quantity and expected donation of patient therapy
6	Dosage or treatment costs in a Health Care program
7	Effects on related costs in a Health Care program
8	Extent and characteristics of probable users, considering age group, income levels, etc.
9	Elasticity of demand with respect to Price
10	Cross elasticities of demand with respect to Price and product qualities
11	Elasticity of demand with respect to income
12	Probability and timing of appearance of new competing products
13	Projected volume at various Prices
14	Duration and pattern of probable product life cycle
15	Extent of use of prepayment plans, insurance plans, and Government programs in paying for Health Care and Drugs
B. Supply	
1	Number and types of competing products
2	Number and types of competing companies
3	Rate of future prospective development of competing products
4	Research, production, and quality control requirements expressed in required investments and cost levels
5	Nature of distribution systems required for effective marketing
6	Size, forms, and strengths of products to be marketed
7	Expected shelf-life of products
8	Patent position of the firm in relation to other products and firms

(Continued)

Table 2.1 (*Continued*)   Summary of Factors Influencing Drug Prices

9	Other products produced by the firm and their prospective Prices, costs, volume, and returns
10	Ease of imitation or improvements by others
11	Location of production in relation to markets served; domestic versus exports
12	Sources of raw materials
13	Differences in required associated services to the medical profession
14	Tax patterns
15	Government Regulations and procedures required for certifying Drugs
16	Sources and costs of capital
17	Types of scientific and technical capabilities required
18	Production and quality control supervision by regulatory agencies
C. General Environment	
1	Size of the economy
2	Percentage of income spent on Health Care
3	Nature and expectations toward Health Care systems
4	Consumption habits and patterns with respect to the use of pharmaceuticals
5	Standard of living in the economy
6	Size and distribution of gross national product
7	The political party in power
8	Role of Government in payment for Health Care
9	Role of Government as regulator and inspector
10	Rate of growth of the economy
11	Economic instability or stability
12	Patterns of Price changes in the economy as a whole
13	Import, export, foreign exchange Regulations
14	Antidumping Regulations
15	Laws with respect to patients
16	Laws and administrative policies with respect to compulsory licensing
17	Licensing Regulations
18	Comparative licensing Regulations among different countries

prescription Drug industry, it is nevertheless true that the pricing policies of this industry have been the subject of far more attention by the Public and the Public's representatives in the Congress than have the other forms of competition.

Pricing policies have as their object to establish the right Price for the product. The "right price" may be determined by cost influences, the nature of the market, the nature of the competition, and a variety of other factors. The pharmaceutical industry has been criticized for: having the same Price for the same products; having different Prices for the same product; having different Prices for different customers for the same product; and for having too high Prices.

There are *social* issues. What is an equitable profit? At what point do the obligations to society loom larger than those to the stockholders? Should the manufacturer of a full line of pharmaceuticals price those products which are more useful to the elderly so as to yield a lesser profit than those used to aid in dieting?

Prices are, of course, inextricably linked with *profits*, which have been the subject of Government scrutiny for well over half a century. Topics such as Price controls, Price ceilings, and excess profit taxes are frequently raised.

The Government has mostly avoided any Draconian measure with regard to Prices of anything. During World War II, there was a Price ceiling on food. There was also rationing. (Both of these measures led to some black market activities.) In 1973–1974, the United States Cost of Living Council limited Prices on oil and gasoline, leading to shortages. President Nixon tried a Price freeze for ninety days – a political, but short-lived, success.

There are various methods to address Drug Price issues. In 2019, the Department of Health and Human Services (DHHS) proposed a new Policy known as the International Drug Pricing Index. The Index would set certain Drug Prices based on an international benchmark. Primarily aimed at Medicare Part B, it would be implemented by the Centers for Medicare and Medicaid Services (CMS) and was supported by the Administration.

Price Listing in Direct to Consumer Advertising

The Government has attempted to require Price information in DTC Advertising of prescriptions. But, what kind of Price – per dose, per week, per regimen (which varies)? This would result in confusion in the patient's mind and at the prescription counter. The practice could certainly result in "shopping around" resulting in damage to continuity in pharmaceutical care. The effort was ultimately withdrawn but may resurface.

Retail Pricing

Manufacturers' Prices, while they reflect what is ultimately paid by the patient or a third party, are actually borne first by an intermediary – a wholesaler or a pharmacy. The Prices/costs imposed by pharmacies deserve some attention.

Until roughly the 1960s, prescription pricing at the pharmacy or retail level was ordinarily a markup process. This process played a special role in two ways. For the pharmacist, it assured a uniform gross profit on any prescription. For the patient, it imposed a double dip. A high manufacturer's Price also meant a high pharmacist Price. A simple hypothetical example:

Rx Drug A		Rx Drug B
Manufacturer's Price	$10.00 →	$20.00
Pharmacist Markup	2.00 →	4.00
Patient Pays	$12.00 →	$24.00

Thus, the patient pays double the cost of dispensing the prescription for the same pharmacy function. A similar disparity can be found in this example:

Rx Brand Name		Rx Generic Name
Manufacturer's Price	$20.00 →	$10.00
Pharmacist Markup	4.00 →	2.00
Patient Pays	$24.00 →	$12.00

In this case, the pharmacist receives only half as much for dispensing the Generic as for the branded Drug. The implications for the Generic Drug industry are obvious.

Enter the Professional/Dispensing Fee. McEvilla (66) was among the first to explain the rationale and to espouse the concept. The American Pharmaceutical Association (APhA) supported it. Plus, it was attractive to the emerging third-party payers who could now concentrate on the manufacturer's Prices *and*, through negotiations, establish a uniform professional/dispensing fee. Of course, problems remained. How much would third parties pay for the ingredients? They could, and did, simply *decide*. A maximum allowable cost (MAC) could be arbitrarily established and so, too, the average wholesale price (AWP). The largest third party, Uncle Sam, was directly involved in both, which are examined in detail in Chapter 15.

Note that a dispensing fee, while it ensures a uniform return on every prescription, does *not* result in a uniform percentage return on inventory investment in the Drug products. It should also be noted that the large retail chains are in a much better bargaining position vis-à-vis the manufacturers than one of the independents.

Hospital Pricing

Drug Prices to hospitals are a different matter than in the case in pricing to retail pharmacies. Hospitals and hospital pharmacists operate in a different environment. Through restrictive formularies, hospital pharmacists have virtual control over the selection and use of medication in their institutions. Usually with the help of formulary committees, which typically include physicians and administrators, they are the final word on which Drugs will be used in their hospital. Although physicians are to different degrees involved in the process, they have somewhat less control over such things as use of generics and the number of Drugs available in a given therapeutic category. Hospital budgets, if not paramount, are extremely important, and there is some evidence that the decisions of pharmacy directors are influenced by the fact that their personal compensation is tied to budget performance (191).

Typically, Drug charges are buried in hospital billing. Patients no longer can complain that "they charged me ten dollars for an aspirin!"

The monolithic character of some hospital chains makes them a formidable bargainer with any Drug company. At the smaller, local level, formulary decisions are also likely to have at least some influence in prescribing decisions in their community outpatient practice.

Promotion

> Let us begin with the words of the late, great marketing genius, Wroe Alderson (310): "The informational content of advertising has been grossly understated by both friend and foe. That is because this judgement generally starts from some technical or ethical conception of information and not from the limited requirements of the consumer of the advertising message. Information provided by advertising is only one incremental addition to what the consumer

already knows but this may be enough to establish the identity of the product which will satisfy his need".

Communication by and information from the manufacturer takes many forms as we shall see. To better appreciate the role of Advertising and Promotion, attention to the basic goals of these activities is necessary. (Advertising and Promotion will be used as equivalent terms here.)

Advertising originally was designed to merely inform the potential buyer of the availability of a product; Promotion was more concerned with persuading the buyer that she needed the product by showing her how it would or could contribute toward achievement of her objectives. Persuasion was accomplished by describing the various positive attributes of a product in terms the potential buyer could understand. The ultimate goal of Promotion, of course, is an increase in sales.

Promotion practices of the Drug industry have been the target of several influential groups for a number of years. The Kefauver Senate Hearings of the late 1950s were mainly concerned with the high cost of Drugs and the relationship between Promotion and cost. Beginning in 1967, Senator Nelson's Subcommittee on Competitive Problems in the Drug Industry succeeded in keeping the promotional practices of the industry in the limelight. Representative Fountain served the same purpose in his role as Chairman of the House Subcommittee on Intergovernmental Relations. Senator Edward Kennedy's Senate Subcommittee on Health, whose Hearings received widespread publicity, focused more intensely on promotional practices at the retail, wholesale, and manufacturer levels.

John Wanamaker said, "Half my Advertising is wasted, if only I knew which half". He could certainly have been talking about Big Pharma. Marketers refer to "waste circulation" in the print media meaning that many of the dollars spent reach People for whom they have no relevance. The same is true of DTC television. (So far, I have not personally seen a prescription Drug ad that applies directly to me. One wonders how many more of us there are!)

Criticism of Drug Promotion takes second place, after Price, in the continuing criticism of Big Pharma Cost (which is a part of the Price). Biased information and even the possibility that Promotion may result in irrational prescribing are among the charges.

Of course, there are problems. Marketing managers are human and will not always be faithful to a farsighted view of the benefits of completeness of information. Some will be too eager for sales to be able to refrain from excessive claims. But Drug Promotion must convey correct and reasonably complete information to be credible and thus effective.

This view runs contrary to one which regards Drug Promotion as essentially misleading and uninformative. The latter view holds that Drug Promotion consists largely of numerous repetitious messages which tell little about each Drug, contain outright lies, and avoid mention of any unpleasant side effects. Moreover, the story goes, what little information is conveyed to doctors is done inefficiently and entails enormous waste. The Drug firms unload on doctors thousands of pieces of mail which provide the same message and send around hundreds of detailpersons who make the same pitch.

But this negative view disregards the *information* service provided by promotional activities in the Drug industry. The elimination of all Drug Promotion would result in greater demands on doctors to spend time learning about the qualities of Drugs and probably in a reduction of the information which they acquire. Busy practitioners, who are the ones who write a relatively large number of prescriptions, are unlikely to devote the required time to learning about Drugs in the event of a reduction in promotional efforts. So let us examine the various forms taken by Big Pharma in Promotion.

Personal Selling – Detailing

The term "detailman" was for many years common parlance. It is no longer politically correct nor is it accurate. The gender mix in the field is not known exactly, but there are many, many "detailwomen" in the field. Medical Representative (Rep) is widely accepted. Salesperson is not. I chose to use the term, detailer, for convenience, although Medical Service Representative is more formal. "Drug Rep" or "Sales Rep" is used in day-to-day conversations.

Detailing is a tough job. In rural areas, there may be considerable travel. In the cities there is traffic and parking. And there is *waiting* – to see the prescriber. Physicians deal with detailers in various ways. Some few simply won't see them. Others have designated hours or days. Some welcome them. Some tolerate them.

The detailers' first job, then, is to somehow make herself welcome. There are a variety of ways to do that. Samples (see below) can help. Co-opting office nurses is sometimes possible. (Some provide an occasional lunch for staff but this has been widely criticized.)

The best strategy is to bring *value* to the visit. There is an opportunity cost involved for the physician. She could use the time instead with a patient. A physician, testifying during the Nelson Hearings, put it this way:

> I still believe the detail man has a minor but important place in the well balanced continuing education program of the practicing physician. Those detail men I spend time with who bring information about drugs—sometimes new drugs of major import, sometimes ones I will elect to forget, and he brings it in person. So I can challenge him and his company. So I can ask for and receive additional information quickly. Please don't send me any small bore detail men.

In order to avoid sending any "small bore" detailers out in the field, most firms offer extensive training for new hires. They receive training in sales techniques, of course, but also in the traits of the Drugs they are promoting, as well as any competing products.

On one occasion, I had the opportunity to speak before a hundred recruits at the Pfizer facility in Arrowwood, New York, and to several individually. I found them bright and eager. My message to them was that in their duties they were, in effect, buying the time of the physician – time that could have been spent, and financially rewarding, with patients. I have no idea what they were told by Pfizer but I feel sure that was at least a part of the corporate message.

Some detailers are specialized in congruence with their company's products. There are "hospital reps" familiar with formularies and charged with establishing a good professional relationship with the pharmacy director. It should be noted, however, that some hospital pharmacy directors refuse to allow detailers to work in their institution. It is essential in any setting for the rep to establish rapport and credibility as a trusted source of accurate product and disease-state information while demonstrating socially engaging and professional interpersonal skills.

Recognizing the demanding nature of this career, a credential service was launched in the early 1960s. The Certified Medical Representative (CMR) was to be styled after the Certified Life Underwriter in the insurance business.

Print Media

The primary print medium for Big Pharma is journal Advertising followed by direct mail. Both have been heavily criticized and sternly regulated.

FDA shares Advertising Regulation duties with the Federal Trade Commission (FTC), which monitors for "false and misleading" violations and the Federal Communications Commission (FCC), which shares with FDA oversight of television Promotion.

The print media are created by specialized Advertising agencies, which abound. These agencies must be conversant with all the Regulations and somehow remain creative. No easy task! When I was serving as marketing manager for Pharmacia Labs, we once were required to "pull" ads for our product because the type size of the product's Generic name was a millimeter smaller than half-size of the brand name of the product!

There are scores of State and national journals, requiring attention to the informational needs of the Reader and the promotional goals of the company. Drug Advertising is an important source of revenue for the organizations to which they are sent and this has caused suspicion and criticism from some quarters. A number of national journals are, in fact, sent free, supported entirely by Advertising revenue.

Under FDA Regulations, advertisements that mention a product's name and indication are required to include a "brief summary" of the Drug's adverse effects, contraindications, and effectiveness. Typically, this brief summary includes a reprinting of these sections of the labeling for the product in the print advertisement. However, manufacturers found it difficult to meet the "brief summary" requirements particularly in broadcast (e.g., radio, television) advertisements. In guidance, the FDA stated that broadcast advertisements could include information about the major risks of the advertised Drug (often referred to as the "major statement") in either the audio or audio and visual parts of the presentation, and instead of presenting the "brief summary" information, the manufacturer could make "adequate provision" for the dissemination of the Drug's approved labeling.

Direct mail Promotion has likewise been widely used both by those citing the cost and by the recipients who are "inundated" (the word most often used) by them. As most of this material is discarded, often without even being seen, the potential for waste is obvious. Marketers cite the "reminder" element when even as a mailer goes toward the trash, the prescriber might at least notice the product name.

Other Forms of Promotion

It is not possible to list/describe all of the promotional efforts of Big Pharma. Some anatomical models, education posters, and patient reading materials for the prescribers' offices are more ingratiating than frank selling. There are pens, calendars, and other "gimmicks" to keep a product or company name in front of the prescriber. Less reputable are lunches brought in for office staff, pre-printed prescription pads, and other outright gifts. In the face of continuing criticism and Regulations, these activities are generally kept in check.

Meetings and Exhibits

Professional meetings/conventions continue to be an important part of Big Pharma Promotion. Typically, they involve an exhibit/booth in an exhibit hall contiguous to the site of professional meetings. The booths are generally staffed by detailers, some local and sometimes People from upper levels of sales administration. These events provide an opportunity to meet with and "detail" scores of physicians in a single day. There is always ample printed material available perhaps including reprints of favorable scientific papers. Companies often support symposia on a subject relevant to their product(s) and sometimes samples are distributed. The exhibits can be impressive. A famous example was a full-scale Japanese Tea Ceremony occupying hundreds of square feet in the center of the exhibit hall at the annual meeting of the American Medical Association.

Meetings are held by virtually all medical specialty groups as well as State associations. (Pharmacy and other Health professions do the same.)

Samples

Samples, normally brought by a detailer, serve several purposes. The most obvious is for the prescribers' own "clinical trials", especially for new products. They can be used to "get a patient started on a drug". They can be, and often are, used to soften the economic blow to the patient. In many cases, they may be the only opportunity for the prescriber to actually see the product apart from photographs in print media. Misuse of samples was excoriated during the Kennedy Hearings (Chapter 3).

Direct-to-Consumer Advertising (DTC)

DTC Advertising of prescription Drugs is generally believed to be a relatively new phenomenon. That is largely true, but this transcription of a radio ad by Squibb about 1942 shows that it is not brand new:

> Just as thrilling as tracking down some fabulous treasure is the search for the unknown which goes on unceasingly in the Squibb Research Laboratories. For that is the search that leads to discovery of new life-saving drugs and new life-saving uses for existing drugs. Streptomycin is one of the newest products of research. In the new field of medicine opened up by penicillin, Streptomycin, still in the testing states shows great promise against additional enemies of mankind. That is why Squibb scientists are working night and day to unlock the secrets of Streptomycin, to improve the strain, to find and test all the ways in which it may be used in the conquest of disease. It is this same questing spirit, this refusal to stop anywhere short of perfection, that inspires all endeavors of the house of Squibb. It is one reason why, wherever you come across it in the service of human health, Squibb is a name you can trust.
>
> *(235)*

Another example is this ad by (then) Schenley Labs, who were also on radio.
   This commercial appeared on an episode of "The Doctor Fights", June 19, 1945. The show starts with this week's star, Robert Montgomery, reading from the Hippocratic Oath. This particular program was written by Arthur Miller.

> Schenley Laboratories voice the wish of all Americans that victory in the Pacific soon will be ours. When that day comes, this war will end for most of the men fighting today, but for some of those now serving on the battle front, their fight will never end. These men are America's physicians for whom the battle against disease goes on endlessly. No development in recent medical history has given the doctor such aid in his fight both in war and civilian use as penicillin. The story of how this drug, so difficult to produce in sufficient quantity, was first produced for the army and navy and then finally in enough quantity for most civilian needs is a tribute to the twenty-two great industrial companies who turned their facilities to the demanding task of penicillin production. Schenley Laboratories is indeed proud to have been among those firms permitted to produce penicillin!
>
> *(235)*

DTC advertisements have encouraged millions of consumers to talk with their doctors about medical conditions or illnesses they had never discussed before seeing advertisements about them. Consumers with general positive perceptions of DTC Advertising have a greater likelihood of using ad-conveyed information during their health care decision-making process. Recent reports suggest that nearly one-third of a study population talked to their doctor about the prescription Drug they saw advertised, and nearly half of these respondents even received a prescription for the Drug they requested.

Historically, physicians, the most influential providers in the Health Care environment, have held negative attitudes toward DTC Advertising. Results from earlier studies indicate physicians viewed DTC as causing problems for both themselves and their patients, such as confusing patients, increasing demand for the advertised Drugs, and even leading patients to challenge a physician's authority. Most of the family physicians surveyed thought DTC ads were not a good idea, impaired the patient–physician relationship, and even discouraged the use of alternative Generic Drugs. Further, they said that they felt pressured by their patients sometimes to prescribe a medication that was not their primary choice. Physicians also believed that DTC ads did not provide risk and benefit information about the Drug in a balanced manner, and that they created unreasonable expectations among consumers.

"Off-Label" Information

The FDA Modernization Act of 1997 added provisions to the Food Drug and Cosmetic Act that allow for manufacturers of Drug products to disseminate information about certain "unapproved" uses under certain conditions. Such dissemination was previously prohibited.

The FDA issued final Regulations in 1998 implementing these provisions of the Act. The Regulations described the type of content of information a manufacturer could disseminate. In general, the information was required to be in the form of a peer-reviewed article and include a statement that the information concerned a use not yet approved by the FDA. The Regulations established the procedures for submission of the information to the FDA before it could be disseminated. Manufacturers must also agree to submit a supplemental application for the unapproved use within a specified period of time (generally 6–36 months after dissemination of information, depending on whether any studies have been completed).

Social Costs and Benefits of Promotion

A final, but perhaps overriding, issue with regard to Drug Advertising revolves around the costs and benefits to the patient, since it is the patient who ultimately pays for the Advertising – either directly or through taxation. Critics imply or state outright that Advertising does not provide complete information of the type needed to make a rational choice – either between alternative Drugs, or between Drug and non-Drug therapy. Two concepts are basic to a discussion of this issue. The first revolves around the "agent" role of the prescribing physician. The second, the economics of information, follows and builds upon the first.

A pedestrian, but widely held, view of why the patient visits a physician is so that the physician will "do something". A more enlightened view would describe the physician's role as determining whether something should be done and then doing that which is appropriate. Because the patient is ill-equipped to do so herself, she hires a physician as her agent in the search for acquisition and application of knowledge, until the point at which the physician actually performs a physical task (surgery, bone setting, etc.). It is knowledge, more than anything else, for which the patient is paying, and that payment includes three elements:

1. The core knowledge acquired during medical school,
2. The new knowledge gained following graduation through all-the information-gathering activities of the physician, and
3. The application of that knowledge through discriminatory judgment of alternatives.

The physician is a knowledge or information agent of the patient and her fee is in large part based on this function. The patients, individually (as "customers") and collectively (as society), have a right to be concerned with whether they are getting the most for their money from the information-gathering activities of these agents.

Surprisingly, the economics of the information search activities of a physician (as patient agents) have received little formal attention. Indeed, only two authors seem to have made a serious attempt to examine the issue to date.

Schwartzman (343) adapted the economic theories of Stigler (427) and Nelson (428) to an analysis of promotional expenditures by the pharmaceutical industry. Schwartzman concluded that: "…from the standpoint of the benefits of information to doctors and patients, a reasonable case can be made for the position that the expenditures on promotion by the industry have been inadequate rather than excessive".

In the process of reaching his conclusion, Schwartzman made several other observations which weakened his argument somewhat. He noted, for example, that Advertising will not include the advantages of competing products. (He does not note that they will also usually omit the advantages of non-Drug therapy.) The physician, therefore, has a complex information task. Finally, Schwartzman observed that "some patients (those with informed physicians) are overpaying and others are underpaying" for the cost of getting Drug information to physicians. He dismissed the problem by stating that there is no way of avoiding it.

A problem with Schwartzman's arguments, which *support* Promotion, as well as with the arguments of many negative critics, is that *both* start from a position of industry responsibility, when, in fact, the responsibility for information lies with the information expert – the physician. The heart of the matter may lie in Schwartzman's observation:

> The elimination of all drug promotion would result in greater demands on doctors to spend time learning about the qualities of drugs and probably in a reduction in the information which they acquire. Busy practitioners, who are the ones who write a relatively large number of prescriptions, are unlikely to devote the required time to learning about drugs in the event of a reduction in promotional efforts.

Peltzman (121) has prepared the other serious economic evaluation of Drug Promotion, although he limited his considerations to the benefits, excluding the costs, of what he termed "diffusion" for pharmaceutical innovation. Further, he did not evaluate the relative efficiency of other possible methods of increasing the rate of diffusion of Drug innovations.

Within the constraints listed, Peltzman presented a strong argument for as rapid as possible (stimulated by Promotion if appropriate) adoption of certain pharmaceutical innovations. He used tuberculosis Drugs and tranquilizers to illustrate his contention that economic savings could be realized by early adoption. Without the cost analysis, however, one is left only with potential benefits of Promotion, and the magnitude of the potential is cloudy since measures of promotional efficiency and effectiveness, particularly relative to other information sources, are lacking. Similarly, but perhaps less obviously, lacking are considerations of non-Drug interventions such as prevention, in the case of tuberculosis and psychotherapy, or early counseling in the case of the tranquilizers.

It is worth noting that if arguments hold true, journal Advertising would hold little attraction for the physician aside from any value as a dissonance reducer (460) and the preferred form of Promotion would be the Drug sample. It is also worth noting that because of the physician's agent role, she is in effect deciding to "try" Drugs on her patients with her only personal cost being patient dissatisfaction (or at its extreme, liability suits). Such dissatisfaction is, of course, a real cost only in a competitive market in which the loss of a customer (patient) is a real concern. In fact, in most medical markets this does not hold true, and there is no reason for active search efforts. The physician can learn how to use the Drugs by trial and error.

What is largely missing from all of the foregoing discussions is a statement by the patient. At which point does patient input, either individual or collectively, become a part of the equation? Since the patient, or a surrogate, ultimately pays the bill, it does not seem illogical to suggest that she have some input into the information gathering decision, for example, would the patient prefer to pay a higher price for the Drug including an information component for advertising and other forms of Promotion or (perhaps) a somewhat higher price for the services of a physician who (possibly) must spend more of her time in gathering, assessing, and acting upon information gathered?

Peltzman (121) has argued persuasively that, at least for conditions which require Drug treatment, the costs of *not* getting the information to the physician may far outweigh the costs of Promotion. He suggests the alternative of charging separately for the Drugs and for the information but admits that few customers are likely to gamble in advance on the value of information.

His economic arguments include the position that the benefits from diffusion of an innovation may rival the benefits from having the innovation in the first place. He also pointed out that the ability of manufacturers to treat promotional expenditures as tax deductions may effectively be a tax subsidy to subsidize dissemination of information.

What to Do

Sadusk (430) defined the purpose of a journal advertisement as follows: "To acquaint the physician with the fact that we have available a specific product for him to use in accordance with labeling and his own medical knowledge". More to the point, he noted:

> The need for careful diagnosis is basic and is a matter for the physician, the medical community, and his professional organizations to consider. The responsibility of the manufacturer is to place safe and effective drugs on the market. The physician is the person who decides whether or not he will use these drugs.

In an editorial in the *New England Journal of Medicine*, Ingelfinger (431) says: "Advertisements should be overtly recognized for what they are – an unabashed attempt to get someone to buy something, although some useful information may be provided in the process". These remarks were preceded by the statement:

> Unfortunately, the FDA and its practices solidify the illusion that pharmaceutical advertising is educational. We are aware that some years ago some elements of the drug industry were trying to pass off advertising as education, but the industry learned its lesson. We thought certainly that medicine had too. Surely no physician really believes that the ads are *purely* educational.

During one meeting in England, the Director of the Office of Health Economics (the office is an extension of the British pharmaceutical industry) asked rhetorically: "Are we not generally agreed that the medical profession gets the advertising it deserves? Is it not up to the profession to bring pressure to bear on the pharmaceutical industry to make changes (432)"?

An answer was unintentionally supplied at the same meeting by a physician-researcher:

> As I look at the current advertisements for these drugs I cannot but feel some shame; partly because I am disturbed that the pharmaceutical industry should use advertisements more suitable for cosmetics than for drugs, but mainly I am ashamed that such advertisements should be successful in influencing members of a learned profession.
>
> *(433)*

The degree of complexity in the Drug Advertising issue was exemplified in the published conclusions of a Panel organized by the National Council of

Churches of Christ. One conclusion of the Panel was that: "Given no real evidence to the contrary, we are persuaded that there is a link between the promotion of legitimate drugs and drug misuse and abuse". It seems only slightly overdrawn to suggest the following paraphrase: "Given no evidence of innocence, we are persuaded that there is guilt". I am convinced that it is not unreasonable to suggest that the "link", if one exists, must clearly be the prescribing physician.

If one accepts some indeterminate level of guilt associated with Drug Promotion, "fair balance" requires at least a mention of some of the other factors which may be involved. I suggest the following as a partial listing:

1. Failure of the FDA adequately to "police" the advertisements.
2. Failure of the Congress to provide the FDA with the budget necessary to staff its policing activities.
3. Failure of pharmacists to exercise their responsibilities in Drug use control, particularly with regard to refills.
4. Failure of hospital administrators to back up or encourage Drug use control functions of pharmacists.
5. Failure of the physician to take the time to get the necessary lab work before prescribing.
6. A system which fails to provide sufficient physician manpower, of the types and location needed, to obviate the "need" for telephone prescribing without seeing the patient.
7. Legal pressures which lead the physician to practice "defensive medicine", i.e., it's easier to use antibiotics on everybody than to risk an infection which may result in a malpractice suit later.
8. A greedy Public which makes it attractive for lawyers to seek such opportunities.
9. Physicians who are willing to take their chances with industry information because it is accessible and palatable.
10. Organized medicine and medical education, which seem willing to admit that the Drug industry can supply the information needed by physicians easier and better than they can.

Government and the Four P's

A recent commercial for a dishwasher detergent has a little girl plaintively asking, "What does a dishwasher *do*"? One is moved to ask the well-known question, "If the opposite of 'pro' is 'con', what is the opposite of 'progress'?"

Yes, that's cynical, but as comedian, Lilly Tomlin, has famously said, "No matter how cynical you get, you still can't keep up".

So what does Congress *do*? Congress has its own Four P's.

Product

The Constitutional "Product" of the Congress is Laws, hence the term "Act of Congress". In order to formulate these laws, the Congress does its own manner of research and development. These activities are revealed, as they relate to Big Pharma, in Chapters 3 and 4.

Price

When referring to Price, with regard to the Government, we really mean cost in terms of taxpayer dollars. These Parallels between the Price of Government and the Price of Big Pharma are many. Remembering the concept that Drugs are "negative goods", how about some of the laws and especially the Regulations? The costs resulting from the latter are really the Prices we pay, either directly or indirectly through higher Prices for regulated goods and services. How much does a law cost? Or the Kefauver Hearings? At least one law, the so-called "Catastrophic Drug Act" was "withdrawn from the market" a year after it became law. How much did *that* "law recall" cost? The simple fact is that the customer (taxpayer) has very little idea, except in broad, general terms how much the specific products of their work cost, i.e., their Price.

Place

Congress' Place is, of course, Capitol Hill, for the President, the White House. But members of Congress are expected to and mostly do spend considerable time at home with their constituents – their "grass roots". They are also known to visit foreign lands for a variety of reasons. (Cynics have been known to refer to some of these visits to, e.g., Bali, as junkets.)

Another aspect of Place is the absolutely essential cliché, "both sides of the aisle" (No TV commentator should be without it). The term refers to where members sit (sometimes on their hands if the opposition is speaking) in the two Houses. Thus, Democrats sit on one side and Republicans on the other.

What about the few independents? Where do they sit? Is there assigned seating? How is it assigned? This needs looking into!

Promotion

Congress, as such, engages in little Promotion. The individual members are a different matter (Rhetorical questions: Does the Reader own a television? Have Twitter? Watch "talk shows"?) Individual members of Congress are literally everywhere. Much of this unfortunately is ritual, but Promotion nevertheless.

The Government doesn't run any Advertising campaigns as a body. Most of the promotional efforts tend to be self-Promotion. Members do have their "Advertising agencies" in the forms of their respective political party national Committees (DNC and RNC). Regulators use Promotion, but their promotional efforts tend to lean toward Public service announcements "Don't text while driving", "Eat nutritiously", "Alcohol and smoking can be harmful". Presumably such messages redound to the People's regard for the regulatory agencies.

The House of Representatives has a "Speaker". Rarely, it seems, does the Speaker speak for the entire House. The same can be said in the Senate where the spokesperson is the Majority Leader. Both of these seldom reflect the views of "both sides of the aisle", but their views often appear to be Promotion of the views of the party in the majority.

Congress has now for decades employed its Four "P's" in Dynamic Tension with the Four P's of Big Pharma, as we shall see in Chapter 3–5. Each of the "P's" has been the subject of one or more Investigations and Legislations.

Conclusion

In this Chapter, I have attempted to provide some appreciation for the marketing activities of Big Pharma using the classic "Four P's" framework. Such appreciation is essential to any sort of understanding of how the industry tends to operate and why. Other players were identified whose activities are an integral and usually integrated part of the process which results in medications in the nation's medicine cabinets. The Reader will find examples of how the process works and some of the reasons for the Dynamic Tension when it doesn't.

Chapter 3

Investigators and Investigations

Introduction

Emphasis in this chapter will be on those Congressional efforts by Estes Kefauver, Gaylord Nelson, David Pryor, Edward Kennedy, and others. The Kefauver Investigation is probably the best known and the first of its kind to receive live television coverage. Gaylord Nelson took the reins after Kefauver's death and he, too, received considerable media attention. The Investigations by Pryor, Kennedy, and others, which we will describe, were not quite as celebrated, although Senator Kennedy seemed to draw considerable attention, regardless of the subject matter.

The amount of material contained in the various Congressional Proceedings is, in a word, massive. It required the Library of Congress 111 pages to summarize the Hearings on just *psychotropic* Drugs, although much of that material deals with illicit Drug use as well.

In this chapter, we offer some basic characteristics of most of the earlier investigative activities of the Congress, as they regard to the Drug industry. We have identified the major themes – monopoly, Drug use by the Public, marketing/Advertising practices, and, of course, Drug Prices.

In his written statement to the Kefauver subcommittee in February, 1960, Austin Smith, President of the then Pharmaceutical Manufacturers Association (PMA) offered this, "The relations between the Pharmaceutical Industry and the government in the United States have been aptly described as a living example of the free enterprise system working **reciprocally** (emphasis added) with free government!" One might find it difficult to reconcile this statement with the often bitter exchanges between Government and Big Pharma and, indeed, between some of the members of the Government themselves. Perhaps "reciprocally" should have been replaced with "hopefully".

The late, great, economist Leonard Schifrin favored me, upon his retirement, with box loads of the Proceedings from the Hearings. Many, to my good fortune, were filled with his own marginal notes. Included was a detailed listing of Hearings before 1996. There were more than 60 on the list, as well as numerous Reports to Congress. Dr. Schifrin was personally involved as a witness and by his writings in many of these Hearings and I regret the limitations, which prevent me from giving a full and complete treatment to all of the material. That would require several Books.

Much of this activity took place over a comparatively short period, but the Drug industry (Big Pharma) has been the target of Congressional Investigations for more than 60 years. The person-years spent, not only during the Hearings themselves but also in background work, exhibits, and prepared statements (for the record but usually not read) are inestimable. In addition to the members of Congress (sometimes only the Committee Chair and one or two others were present), the Drug industry representatives, individual companies, their trade organizations, individual physicians and their professional organizations, consumer advocacy groups, and even individual citizens were called to testify. I am not leaving out the Food and Drug Administration. They were represented not only by the Commissioners (26 between 1907 and 2020 – see Chapter 6) but also by their legal Counsel (for years Peter Barton Hutt) and a variety of other staff.

Accounts presented here may sometimes seem adumbrated. That is a fair charge. Such was necessary given the exigencies of time and space on the part of the author, as well as consideration for the perceived level of interest of the Reader. The goal, as noted in the Book's Preface, is to provide evidence of the intent (if such is clearly stated in the transcripts), scope, and flavor of a few. Where conclusions were reached, I have provided them. The same is true of any resulting Legislation. The relationship between Legislation and Regulation is often tenuous, reflecting judgment on the part of Regulators. Sometimes the Regulations have been found to go too far, sometimes not far enough. Indeed, FDA itself has been the subject of Hearings.

Recent years saw some decline in activity by Congressional Investigators. Nevertheless, there are Hearings under way as this is being written and more can certainly be expected, especially with regard to the Drug Prices. A few of the Hearings presented here received scant Public attention and have seldom, if ever, been discussed by other authors on the subject. Investigations still to come will certainly receive their share of attention given the explosion of media possibilities.

The Reader will appreciate that it would not be possible to provide all the substance of all the Investigations in a single chapter – or in several Books. With this caveat, we will begin with the "**big one**", Senator Estes Kefauver and his Hearings on Administered Prices.

The Hearings

The Grand Inquisitor – Estes Kefauver (124)

In the eyes of Big Pharma at least, Senator Estes Kefauver was the Torquemada of Investigations of the Drug industry. A one-time Presidential hopeful who campaigned wearing a coonskin cap, Kefauver had honed his skills in the bread and steel industries. The genesis of his choosing Drugs as a target is not clear. His interest was piqued, certainly in part, by the "Wonder Drugs" – antibiotics – which were just becoming a factor in therapy. Patients were amazed – and appalled – by the Prices – 50 cents a dose (!). Comedians were fond of saying, "I 'wonder' how to pay for it".

The impending Hearings were certainly the reason for the Drug industry to form a somewhat united front and become Big Pharma. The PMA was then founded in 1958. The Senator's Hearings began in July, 1957, published 26 volumes and 16,504 pages.

In his final Report from the Subcommittee of the Senate on Antitrust and Monopoly, Senator Kefauver noted that, like steel, automobiles, and bread, which the Subcommittee had also studied, Drugs were critically important to America's way of life. He also uttered the now famous, "He who orders does not buy; and he who buys does not order" (more than once).

Members of the Subcommittee included Senator Roman Hruska (Nebraska) and Phillip Hart (Michigan). Senator Hruska represented the Minority and was quite outspoken during the Hearings. Senator Hart would conduct Hearings of his own later.

The Hearings were controversial and contentious. Well-known physician, Henry Dowling, described the atmosphere this way (393).

Naturally these revelations attracted headlines, which Senator Kefauver did not discourage and in fact probably aided by the timing of the testimony. The public was aroused. That he was soaked and his doctor was duped was the message, right or wrong, that reached the man on the street.

The drug industry was horrified; its pride was injured; its purse was threatened. It sprang to the defense. It tried to justify its profits on high risks, on its contributions to the nation's health, on its record in research, on its part in educating the physicians. It paraded its own witnesses – economists, physicians, laboratory scientists (including Nobel Prize winners). During the first round of hearings, it made a poor showing, probably because of the haste in which its case had to be prepared, but after Senator Kefauver had introduced a bill and hearings were held (from July 1961 until February 1962) the industry presented its case more effectively.

The lay press displayed its usual divisiveness depending on its conservative or liberal leanings. But the Press did cover it. Kefauver was charged with "leaking" stories on Friday afternoon, giving his opponents no chance to rebut until after the weekend. (See also the Minority view below.)

News stories could be captivating, especially in reporting verbal exchanges. I include a few to give the Reader some of the flavor of the dialogs (and sometimes monologs). These are essentially random in order.

Practicing pharmacists had expressed concern about the tenor of the Hearings. Dr. Smith, in his testimony, placed into the record articles from State Pharmacy journals. In the *Missouri Pharmacist*, Virgil Phillips, President of the State's Pharmacy association, wrote in January, 1960.

> The adverse publicity which has filled press, radio and television during the past few weeks, as a result of the United States Senate Antitrust and Monopoly Subcommittee's investigation of Drug manufacturers' pricing policies, is being felt across the nation at the retail level. Too many customers believe some of the margins of the manufacturer which have come under sharp criticism apply at retail, and that we druggists are robbing the public on prescription medications.
>
> Retail druggists across the nation could well be smeared by this probe, and the standing of pharmacy as a profession is at stake. The time is now to marshal our forces against the unjust

criticism we are experiencing and which will most likely become more severe. The failure to do so could result in injuries which are irreparable. Each of us must do his share in his own way for the good name of all druggists and all pharmacy.

Senator Everett Durksen, whose Minority views will be presented later, had this exchange concerning Promotion.

> **Senator Dirksen:** Well, Doctor, I just want to observe that certainly a country doctor would welcome any information that comes along. You can call it what you like. I don't think this question of how much mail a doctor receives is world-shaking in its importance. And I have an idea that if he has time between patients, he likes to take a look at some of these circulars, advertisements; it keeps him abreast of the drugs. Senator Kefauver was probably not too happy with the statement of economist Fred Thompson of the PMA.
>
> The research which has led to the development of so many tremendously useful drugs since World War II is already behind us. The much more difficult research, the research where risks of failure are greatest, lies ahead. Cancer and other important diseases give rise to prodigious research problems. One drug manufacturer already has expended over $7 million in the search for a chemical that might be useful in the treatment of cancer, with no marketable product resulting. If the manufacturers' increasing chances of loss are coupled with new penalties for success, it is hard to see how the consumer can gain. To condemn an industry or a firm for its ability to maintain profits through successful new product development will not only discourage profits, but much more importantly the unique efforts that have produced these profits.

On February 23, 1960, Senator Kefauver's Subcommittee, meeting at night, had received the testimony of Austin Smith, then President of the PMA. Senator Kefauver and Senator Dirksen were the only Senators present. The Senators determined that Dr. Smith's salary was $45,000 per year.

A few excerpts from Smith's lengthy written statement follow, but before that, the Reader may find this exchange amusing:

> **Dr. Smith:** Some time ago, Mr. Dixon kindly called my office to inform me that I could appear before your Subcommittee on

February 23, and I appreciated Mr. Dixon's call, but I was without voice then. Unfortunately, the pharmaceutical industry had not yet found a treatment for laryngitis.

Senator Dirksen: If you find it let me know, will you?

Dr. Smith also preferred a "real world" example of PMA's position.

I believe though, Mr. Senator, that perhaps, I could lend some emphasis to some of the points that I would like to make if I could place before you two bags. These are doctor's bags. The one on the left is a bag that is outfitted as a doctor 25 years ago would carry it.

The one on the right is outfitted with the drugs that are used today. This is most significant because in this bag of 25 years ago, there is not one drug that is life-saving. They are all palliative, and in here you will find things ranging from castor oil to the old fashioned remedies that we might rub on our throats or our chests. And in this other bag you will find tablets and injectable preparations which are not only effective in reducing suffering and lessening the cost of dying, but these also are economic aids as they put people back to work more quickly and lessen the drain on the community and on the family budget.

Excerpts of Austin Smith's prepared statement follow. It is notable as the first occasion on which PMA attempted to explain Big Pharma to the Government, represented by the Senator and, of course, to the People. Smith's statements were a virtual dissertation on his industry, a pre-emptive apologia. Edited excerpts follow:

There is, as you know grave danger of misinforming the public when attention is directed toward the single product of a single company – toward the isolated price charged by another company – without relating these to the many thousands of products produced by the entire industry. As a matter of fact, the industry has an outstanding record of low prices maintained in an inflationary period when prices of other commodities have climbed at the faster rates.

In my testimony today, I will demonstrate that the competitive pharmaceutical industry in America has played a role unparalleled elsewhere in the world in reducing human suffering in helping to eradicate diseases which have crippled mankind for centuries.

Further, I will illustrate the fact that the profit incentive in the drug industry has served the public interest by driving prices down to the lowest levels that can be maintained while supporting the future growth and discovery.

In fact, Americans today would be paying a billion dollars a year more for drugs if the price of medicine in the past few years had gone up only as much as the total cost of living.

On the basis of the record, I shall explore, I know of no other American industry that has contributed more from its resources to the public welfare –

Through research on problems that affect the lives and health of every individual;

Through effective and constructive use of profits for discovery and growth;

Through mammoth tax savings to the public by reducing the cost of public health services;

Through maintenance of a reasonable price level in an inflationary period;

Through cooperation with Government in working toward the highest standards of quality, purity, and control of its products;

Through creation of a distribution and information network unrivaled anywhere else in the world to make available the newest and the best life-giving and pain-relieving medicines whenever and wherever they may be needed; and

Through efforts to solve the challenging health and welfare problems still confronting us.

The record will show, Mr. Chairman and Senators, that no other American Industry has devoted a greater proportion of its resources to provide such great social benefits for the vast majority of our citizens.

On Patents

The patent system works to provide incentive for the many companies, owned by Hundreds of thousands of Americans who have invested their savings in drug concerns, to risk the enormous sums required in the gamble that one research project out of thousands will produce a result of benefit to mankind.

***

On Competition

Any examination of the record of the drug industry must be undertaken, if it is to serve the public interest, in the light of the need for preserving the many-faceted, never-ceasing and highly costly explorations which have brought past gains, and which hold so much promise for the future.

These discoveries, the progress of recent years, can be attributed – more than to any other factor – to the intense competition which exists within the drug industry. This is a matter of primary interest to this Subcommittee, vested with responsibility for investigations, in this field. On the basis of the record, this Subcommittee will have to conclude that the ethical drug manufacturing industry is one of the most competitive it has ever examined.

***

On Promotion

Doctors are highly trained scientists who are not subject – and should not be subject – to commercial pressures. But they have high professional interest in ascertaining the value of new drugs and studying the circumstances under which they should be prescribed. The detail man is also a professional in his field. Most have college degrees in pharmacy or other sciences. All are thoroughly schooled by the companies they represented. Throughout their careers they received on-the-job training, followed up by rigid written examinations.

Doctor surveys have shown that medical journal advertising is the American physician's second chief source of new drug information, and in many ways this advertising complements and supplements the work of detail men. Some doctors have already read new prescription drug advertising in medical journals before the detail man arrives, and can therefore, devote the later face-to-face interviews to obtaining further information and close questioning on dosage, side effects, toxicity, and other technical aspects of the new product.

***

Ours are about the only ads in America that tell not merely the good things about our product but deal exhaustively with the bad ones as well. Toxicity, side effects—all must be exposed in full detail. Some, of course, are "reminder" ads, intended to recall to the reader's memory the more extensive clinical findings he has seen earlier.

But the most important advantage of medical advertising is that it brings new product information to the doctors' attention almost as soon as the new drug has received approval by the Food and Drug Administration. This is not true of scholarly articles which appear in the editorial content of medical journals. The time lag here ranges between 6 months and a year.

***

Advertising, supported by detailing, is the fastest means our free enterprise system has produced to guarantee that the lag between availability of a drug product and its use in treatment is held to a minimum.

***

On Brand Names

Fundamental to the successful system of education and distribution is the industry practice of using brand names rather than the generic names of its formulations. There are compelling reasons for this practice. First, and most obvious, is a fact indigenous to the American enterprise system. Unless a manufacturing industry gives a name to its products, it cannot hope to meet competition and maintain its sales, let alone to improve them.

***

Behind brand names lie the reputation, reliability, and skill of the manufacturer. By brand name prescription, too, the doctor orders for a patient a specific product in which he has absolute knowledge of quality, purity, and any side effects that might have importance for a particular patient. In the case of combination formulations, brand names stand not only for the active ingredients, but also for special excipients, vehicles, and bases, frequently developed by costly research to be non-allergenic, specially buffered to promote tolerance, sugar-free for the obese and diabetic, and many other important variations for individual patient needs. So-called generic equivalents often do not.

***

On Profits

Much has been said during these hearings about profits. In the same way that many disparagers of the of the industry have argued illogically that the industry is both too concentrated and too competitive, some witnesses have indicated with the same degree of illogic that the drug industry has made "enormous contributions" to American life but that its profits should be reduced.

But it is ridiculous to expect, in our system of private industry which depends upon the profit motive for progress, that the cause of medicine could be well served if the drug industry were not profitable.

***

On Prices

None of my original testimony on the general subject of prices has been refuted, but I will briefly summarize it:

Because of my work with a trade association, I cannot comment on the discussions of individual drug prices that have taken place during earlier hearings. But there is ample evidence in my previous testimony, that even the costliest new drugs, which may represent research investments as high as $20 million, are reduced in price under the impact of competition and increasing production. Many specific examples are in the records of this hearing. Any attempt to prove excessive markups is doomed to failure because the profit picture in the prescription drug industry, while healthy, is competitive with other industries.

Austin added, in comment, on the relationships between Government and industry.

> The pharmaceutical industry is subject to an unusually high degree of Government regulation. Its relationship to the Government has not, however, been limited to that required by statute regulations. Joint action has taken place promptly and voluntarily wherever it has appeared to be in the public interest. The relationships have been characterized by a high sense of public responsibility on both sides and, whether voluntary or involuntary, have been carried forward in an atmosphere of mutual respect.

Senator Kefauver had the last word in his Summary Report issued in May, 1961. The Senator's Report occupied 253 pages of testimony including 40 tables and 16 charts, as well as an 8 page Appendix.

Kefauver's Report was, in essence, a "snapshot" of the 26 volumes and 16,505 pages of Proceedings of the Hearings. As would be expected, the Report contained highlights of the various exchanges during the Hearings themselves. The condensation of 16,000 plus pages into 253 is every bit as memorable as that done with the first 17 volumes of the "Nelson" Hearings (see following). The author of the Report is not identified per se although credit is given to a few staff members.

The introduction to the Report provided some clues as to what lay ahead. A few excerpts from the Report follow:

> The importance of drugs lays not so much in the overall size of the business (which, however, with annual sales of $2.5 billion is hardly, negligible) but more in its crucial relationship to health and indeed life itself.

***

> A unique characteristic is the difference between buyer and the one who orders; in the words of Chairman Kefauver, "He who orders, does not buy; and he who buys, does not order". Or, as one witness observed before the Subcommittee, the physician acts as "purchasing agent" for the consumer. Regardless of how well

intentioned, the physician may be, another party can never be expected to be as interested in price as the individual who has to spend his own money.

The drug industry is also unusual in the extent to which the demand for its products is inelastic, i.e., unresponsive to changes in prices. The fact that demand is inelastic means that one of the checks which might serve as a possible constraint upon corporate price policies is absent in ethical drugs. When demand is elastic, prices may become so high as to result in a significant reduction in sales volume. Appropriately, the Report begins to set the stage for future legislation:

***

In competitive industries what would generally be accepted as a reasonable profit rate and a reasonable relationship between costs and prices is brought about automatically by the very force of competition itself. High profit margins in a given competitive industry may be enjoyed temporarily, but since they serve as a lure to attract new resources and new firms which enter the industry and compete on a price basis, excessive prices are soon driven down. Unfortunately, this possible restraint on price has been conspicuous by its absence in the ethical drug industry.

Concluding, the introduction calls, if not for a Public outcry on Drug industry abuses, then at least Public support for Government action.

Surely if enlightened management could be relied upon in any industry to adopt pricing policies which reasonably reconcile management's drive for profit with the Public interest, it would presumably be Drug manufacturing, owing to its crucial relationship to the Public Health. If in this industry the "Public consensus" has been rather ostentatiously ignored, as might logically be inferred from the data on profits and margins presented in Part I, this constraint would appear to be a slender reed on which to rely for the protection of the Public interest in administered price industries generally.

Minority Views

A lengthy dissent (105 pages) was included in the Report prepared by Senators Roman Hruska and Everett Dirksen, both of whom had been active and vocal throughout the Hearings. Individual views of Senator Alexander Wiley were also included. Well prior to the remarks included in the Report, there was ample evidence of a kind of internecine conflict. Issues were raised from timing of the meetings to bias in selection of witnesses. These occurred many, many times, and, while they often included obligatory courtesies, they could verge on vicious. Here are just a few:

Senator Dirksen made a comparison between the Chairman's statements on Drug markups and those of the bread industry which Kefauver had previously investigated:

> If this committee should ever become a laughing stock of the country, and its objectivity should be successfully assailed, then I think we will have to evaluate the usefulness of the investigator's technique and to a considerable extent the usefulness of the committee.

***

> Now, if I am in error, I am always glad to publicly confess my error. But if on the other hand, I am correct, and if the research as made by my own staff people have come up with the fact that those are the comparisons, then I must assert with all the vigor at my command that that is an unfair technique, and that I cannot tolerate it, and I shall not tolerate it with respect to the witnesses who will be appearing before us now.

***

> Now I think the testimony shows that the manufacturers who came before the committee showed a profit according to their statements of some 12 to 16 percent on sales. That is a far cry from an alleged 1,118 to 7,000 percent markup.

***

> Mr. Chairman, I just point out here that that looks to me like a completely un-objective approach and this committee cannot put itself in the position of impeaching one of the great industries of America, meaning the manufacturers, the druggists, the distributors and all of those laboring in the interests of the health services of the people.

***

Senator Hruska also had some comments:

> Mr. Chairman, as a new member of this Subcommittee, I have attended only three or four sessions, although two of them were of the past-midnight variety, which I hope will not be repeated.
>
> ***
>
> After this brief experience, however, and after reviewing some of the record made in these hearings, I am greatly disturbed by what I have seen, heard, and read.
>
> ***
>
> In these few sessions, I have witnessed a performance of un-objective, unfair, and distorted proceedings used in this committee room against a vast and important industry and its officials. It is an industry which has done much to advance the safety, health, well-being, and security of our Nation and its citizens by reason of the jobs it provides and the taxes it pays. It may have its share of individual and isolated bad actors, as any larger sector of our economy may have. But, as a whole, it is respected and has done much good.
>
> In other hearings I have followed within the Senate Judiciary Committee, the usual and approved format has been to invite and hear the heads of the Federal agencies having jurisdiction over the matters involved; then, the heads or official representatives of the industries or companies involved, and the labor leaders whose unions are interested parties; then, the National, State or Regional trade associations, retail and wholesale groups, or professional associations, whether they be medical, legal, engineering, or other. And then such other witnesses who desire to be heard individually and who are within reason and balance as to number and as to non-repetition.
>
> ***
>
> Such a pattern, however, has been thoroughly disregarded and avoided here. No federal agency officials have been called so far, with the exception of Dr. Austin Smith of the Pharmaceutical Manufacturers Association, no professional or trade groups have been allowed to appear. No broad and competent basis has been laid for those hearings and for this inquiry.

Author: (Because it is so damning in its language, I have added a bit more:)

> In fact, Mr. Chairman, an observer of these hearings has suggested that those in charge of conducting these hearings, being unable to find any support for pre-conceived views and beliefs from any official, representative, or truly authoritative sources, are forced to resort to the use of witnesses, who, in the main, have a personal "ax to grind", who are non-conformists, who are not representative, often lacking qualified vantage point or competence in the field in which they undertake to testify, and who do not hesitate to recklessly attack constructive efforts of persons with responsibility. It was suggested further that perhaps the lack of such support might also account for the resort to sensationalism, headline seeking, misrepresentation and distortion reflected in much of the testimony and many of the exhibits.

Senator Kefauver rebutted:

> I must say it is a matter of great regret to me that my colleagues, Senator Dirksen and Senator Hruska, have elected to take this position about the work of this committee. As a member of the House and the U.S. Senate, I have been on investigating committees for a long, long time, including some very difficult ones. I have always, to the best of my ability, tried to conduct them on a non-political, fair and impartial way.

***

> In this hearing, it has been specifically charged there have been statements misrepresenting the facts and accusing the Chairman of a deliberate attempt to misrepresent, and to present biased, distorted, and untrue statements. I have seen statements made publicly quoting these charges at meetings of pharmaceutical associations.

***

> I have reluctantly come to the conclusion that there is no way that these investigations can be conducted to satisfy my colleagues unless the testimony is going to be a whitewash of the pharmaceutical manufacturing industry. So long as I am chairman, there is not going to be any whitewashing of any industry or of any group.

Senator Dirksen had a bit more to say:

> Now, Mr. Chairman, speaking for myself and my colleague Senator Hruska, we are not interested in pleasing or non-pleasing statements or facts or anything else. We are just interested in objective truth and nothing more. We don't care, the tail can go with the hide so far as I am concerned, but I don't know if you would like to have us be candid and speak our minds or sit here like frogs on a log and let this thing go on without registering a protest.

Senators Dirkson and Hruska had left little doubt, in their opening Preface, of what was to follow:

> The majority's views in the report on administered prices in drugs do little credit to the Subcommittee for there is no attempt whatsoever to be objective and constructive through judicious evaluation of all the testimony and exhibits presented during the course of the hearings. On the contrary, a reading of the voluminous 500-page mimeographed monstrosity, which was submitted to the minority for comment and analysis, appears to be nothing more than a calculated review of choice quips, statements, and exhibits presented by biased witnesses whose views were well known to the majority at the time they were called to testify. Thus, the majority's views would appear designed toward misleading, and erroneous statements rather than a judicious evaluation of all of the evidence presented.

During the course of the debate on February 8, the Chairman stated:

> I think it should be pointed out also that sometimes the exploration of an issue, even though the result is that no bill is reported, may be of greater service to the public than would be the case if some legislation resulted.

***

> If this were the primary function of this Subcommittee, we could not in good conscience justify expenditures of public funds and the enormous demands upon private individuals who must prepare material for presentation to the Subcommittee. It is to be hoped

that American citizens will follow all congressional debates and
hearings with interest and understanding, but every hearing must
have a legislative purpose and cannot be justified on the basis
that it is essential to widen the knowledge of the American people
respecting our economic system and its strengths and weaknesses.

Especially interesting in light of my comments in Chapter 2 was the following:

Singularly enough, questions of the cost of these investigations to
all concerned are seldom raised. Responsible and busy executives
with their staff assistants are immobilized for days on end when
they should be actively engaged in their own private and productive enterprises for the well-being of the country.

The two Senators proceeded to provide "a number of basic economic facts" in order to "set the record straight". Their 11 points, severely edited, follow. In each case, they were supported by excerpts from Hearings to Testimony, as well as new information.

Point 1 – The position in the majority's report that the drug industry has had a price, profit, and cost structure that was uncompetitive, is unfounded and erroneous.

Point 2 – The position that the industry has a permanent control of the market is "unjustified, erroneous, and unfounded.

Point 3 – Also "erroneous and unfounded" is the position that the patent system has not operated effectively in the drug industry.

Point 4 – The position that contributions by American industry to American research are "negligible, erroneous, and unfounded". (Author's Note: *Since the majority positions were deemed, by the minority, to be "erroneous and unfounded", I will continue with a simple listing of the offending (to the minority) positions.*)

Point 5 – That foreign prices of drugs are more advantageous to consumers than those here in the United States.

Point 6 – That there have been substantial economies for the American taxpayer's in purchasing drugs abroad.

Point 7 – That selling prescriptions, and that promotional/advertising expenses are excessive.

Point 8 – That drug manufacturers do not operate in the normal competitive economy.

Point 9 – That inelasticity of demand exists for drugs under present marketing arrangements.

Point 10 – That new, specialized medical preparations are over-rated and do not meet the needs of the patients.

Point 11 – That the use of trade names, in lieu of generic names, (Author's note: *Seems incomplete but the meaning is obvious*).

The Senator concluded as follows:

> Our citizenry is entitled to a true balanced and complete picture submitted in a timely, understandable way". So far, this has been denied them.

***

> In fact, up till now there has been a deliberate attempt, in my judgement, to inflict devastating and irreparable damage upon an indispensable business by trying hard to shatter public confidence in it upon the basis of a biased, distorted, and incomplete record.

***

It is one thing to make a constructive effort to improve an industry or its operation. But to lead the Public erroneously, to condemn a necessary industry, without any hope of gaining a workable or acceptable replacement for it, is a catastrophe which should not be visited upon the men, women, and children of America.

Senator Alexander Wiley, in his independent view, took a special issue with the subject of "Reasonable Price".

> Our Federal antitrust laws are not generally concerned with the question of price reasonableness. The belief is inherent in our free enterprise philosophy that prices are best adjusted and determined by the free operation of the forces of supply and demand in the marketplace. It is only when these forces are unreasonably restricted by monopolistic practices that the Government must step in. Consequently, the real question before this subcommittee at all times must be the factual determination as to the existence of illegal restraints of trade—not the speculation as to whether prices are reasonable or unreasonable. It is obvious that

once we undertake to substitute Government judgment of what is reasonable or unreasonable for the free play of prices in the marketplace—the final product would be a general Government price-fixing program.

FDA under the Microscope – A Resignation and a Whistle Blower

Seldom mentioned in accounts of the Kefauver Proceedings because of the focus on pricing, Promotion and other industry concerns are two elements which occupied a considerable time of the Subcommittee.

The first was the case of Dr. Henry Welch. The importance attached to this issue is evidenced by the 1,400-page Appendix added to the many pages of actual testimony and exhibits presented during the course of the Hearings.

The second incident resolved around the testimony of Dr. Barbara Moulton, a former member of the staff of the Bureau of Medicine in the Food and Drug Administration.

Dr. Welch

Dr. Henry Welch had resigned on May 19, 1980, not quite 3 weeks before the Hearings. As he was ill, he was never called to testify.

The issue was Dr. Welch's editorial activities, for pay, with several medical publications. The first question was whether this was permitted under the rules of employment. And the second question was whether there were any possible conflicts of interest existing, as Dr. Welch was serving in an editorial position with two journals – *Antibiotics and Chemotherapy* and *Antibiotic Medicine and Clinical Therapy*. Would he be put into a position where he could influence the content of articles applying to products of companies that advertised in these journals, while also serving as Director of the FDA –Antibiotics Division?

It was never alleged that the activities of Dr. Welch ever did, in fact, result in materials unduly favorable to the products advertised in the journals in which he had editorial interest. The only charges which were clearly demonstrated were that he violated Health Education and Welfare (HEW) rules and lied about it.

On June 6, 1960, just 3 weeks after the Welch Investigation was opened, the FDA was in for more grief in the person of Dr. Barbara Moulton.

Dr. Barbara Moulton

Dr. Barbara Moulton, at the time of her testimony, June 2, 1960, apparently between positions, had resigned from the Food and Drug Administration the previous February. Previously she had been on the staff of the Bureau of Medicine at the FDA. By her own account, she had planned to remain there permanently saying that "the avowed aims of the Agency are ones with which I am in complete sympathy". In her resignation statement, she stated that she was no longer in sympathy with the Bureau policies and, "to a certain extent with those of the Administration". (It is not clear to which Administration she referred.) Specifically, she cited trends in the FDA "which to me represent a deliberate neglect of the interest of the consumer, and an unwillingness to make Policy decisions honestly on the basis of scientific fact".

Her resignation became Public and resulted in an article in the *Pink Sheet*, an industry newspaper. The article described an "epidemic of resignations" at FDA including that of her former boss a few days before her.

Dr. Moulton quoted from a letter she had written (but never sent) to George Larrick. At that time, he was head of the FDA Commission. Most striking in her lengthy letter is this: "The Food and Drug Administration should request of Congress authority to pass on efficacy, as well as safety...." That is exactly what happened in the 1962 Drug Amendments. Obviously, someone was listening!

It is obviously not possible to give a complete account of the Welch and Moulton episodes – as fascinating as they are. Certainly the FDA came away from both more than a bit diminished.

Congressional Hearings, which make up much of this chapter, make fascinating reading, although reading and absorbing just all the testimony from the Hearings could take a lifetime (as the author will attest). The exhibits, written statements, charts, and graphs amount to thousands of pages alone.

The dialog was sometimes obsequious, although sometimes the sincerity was subject to some doubt. On a few occasions, participants engaged in ad hominem remarks. A good example follows.

Senator Kefauver (129) remarked....

> Some days ago when I was in Paris attending the NATO Parliamentarians meeting, a copy of a speech by Senator Hruska delivered to the New Jersey pharmaceutical companies at Far Hills Inn, Somerville, N.J., on November 16, was sent to me. It is a caustic and somewhat vitriolic attack upon the majority of the

committee particularly upon the staff of the committee, and particularly upon me as its chairman. This apparently was delivered to a small audience. I won't comment on it other than to say that I think it is unjustified, the hard time that is given the staff, the majority members, and myself. I think it is proper that this speech be made a part of the record so that anyone who is reading the speech and reading the record can come to their own conclusion as to whether the criticisms were justified or not.

Senator Kefauver then dutifully entered a copy of the speech into the Record noting, "I am sure Senator Hruska would want wider dissemination of his address". Excerpts of the offending speech follow:

This is not a partisan exercise. It is neither Republican nor Democratic. It is, however, political. It concerns a most disturbing aspect of the relationship between Government and business. If I had given the talk a title, it might be called "The Anatomy of Congressional Investigations" or "The Disillusionment of a Senator".

I am, of course, that Senator. I am the man who stands before you, stripped of his pristine respect, not for an old and established congressional process itself, but rather for the way in which that process has been perverted, distorted, and abused.

***

But in other than the most scrupulous hands, the congressional investigation can be a very dangerous thing. If those who use it are wooly headed, or undertake it cynically and selfishly, it can be evil. It ceases to be an investigation. It can more accurately be called an inquisition.

***

Why? Why all this heavy concentration of fire on the drug makers? To understand the motive behind these investigations is to see the reason. It's quite simple. The primary idea is not to make laws but to make news. There's more appeal to the professional bleeding hearts in the subject of health than in asphalt roofing. In terms of headlines, there's more emotional mileage in an antibiotic than in an automobile, in the cost of a tablet than in the price of a tail fin.

***

> To play politics with medicine, to tamper with the segment of free enterprise that has led us steadily toward better health and longer life, to jeopardize the odds that our children will live in fuller freedom from disease, is an intolerable form of mischief.

The full text of Senator Hruska's remarks can be found on pages 2393–2399 of the Proceedings (129).

Yet another small clash had occurred when the industry news publication, *Pink Sheet*, ran a story with this headline "Dr. (Austin) Smith's P.R. to Rid Pharmaceutical Field of 'Kefauverrea'". Not surprisingly, this was not well received by the Senator who apparently attributed the term to the PMA President!

Conclusion/Kefauver

Estes Kefauver died in 1963. His mark on the history of the Government and Big Pharma is secure. The Senator never saw any sort of direct Legislative influence on the subject of his Hearings, Administered Prices. Nevertheless, the Hearings may be said to have: established the central role of the Food and Drug Administration; marshaled the organization of an entire industry in opposition; and informed physicians, pharmacists, and the People. Certainly the single-most important outcome of all this effort was the passage of the Kefauver–Harris Amendment (1962 Drug Amendment) which transformed the Drug-approval process by requiring proof of efficacy.

Many have noted the role played by the Thalidomide tragedy in the passage of the "62" Amendment, and that is undisputed. Nevertheless, the spotlight turned on the Drug industry by the Kefauver Hearings (for all their controversy) was certainly the genesis.

By the 1990s, the "feeding frenzy" inaugurated by Estes Kefauver had somewhat died down. The major heirs: Fountain, Dingell, and Pryor had moved on. By 2020, with an election looming, the Drug industry is again very much in the spotlight. Media coverage is not as intense as in earlier days, in part because there were so many other issues – immigration, climate control, China, Iran, and North Korea. However, that definitely does not mean that Investigations will go away. Drug Prices are very much on the minds of the People, and politicians are busy nailing that plank into their platform.

John Gardner, founder of Common Cause, in the July 23, 1973, issue of the *New Yorker*, gave this warning:

As I listen to people listing all the great problems they intend to solve, I think of people sitting in an ancient automobile by the side of the road. The tires are flat and the steering wheel is broken and the drive shaft is bent, but they're engaged in a great argument as to whether they should go to Phoenix or San Francisco, or the Oregon coast. And in my imagination, I am standing by the road saying, "You're not going anywhere till you fix the god-damn car".

Gaylord Nelson – Son of Torquemada (123)

Senator Gaylord Nelson (Wisconsin) chaired the Subcommittee on Monopoly during much of his Hearings but succeeded Alan Bible as Chair of the Select Committee on Small Business of the Senate in March, 1975.

The Nelson Hearings in many ways outdid even those of Kefauver, both in length of time and pages of Proceedings produced. Nelson provided himself with some scope by styling the Hearings as "Competitive Problems in the Drug Industry". Senator Nelson had served previously as Governor and was acclaimed as founder of Earth Day. His efforts on behalf of the environment were widely praised and forecast the "Green" movement of today.

Senator Nelson had occupied a front-row seat while Kefauver held sway. He must have realized that Kefauver had essentially failed in his stated purpose to alter the practice of Administered Prices and uncover telling evidence of monopoly or at least oligopoly. (See Chapter 14.) The Senator, anticipating and already experiencing criticism of his plans, offered up pre-emptive comments as he opened the Hearings on May 27, 1967:

> Since it was announced, this committee would conduct hearings in the drug field, numerous articles and columns have appeared in the press and trade journals, speculating about the hearings. Since I have not discussed the scope of the hearings with the press or trade journals, all commentary has been no more than speculation. Some articles have already attacked the committee for what they think it might do or questioned the wisdom of conducting hearings at all. Others have revived attacks on the late Senator Kefauver for the hearings he conducted several years ago. I have already received numerous letters attacking the idea of holding any hearings and suggesting that this field is not of public concern. I do not agree. This is public business and important matters of public

interest are at stake. Since everyone is going to have ample opportunity to present his case, there is no valid reason for opposition to the hearings.

The late Senator from Tennessee, Estes Kefauver, listed three important characteristics which tend to distinguish the Drug industry from other industries:

- The first is that Drug products are not conveniences or luxuries or even ordinary necessities. They are involved in problems of Health and are often matters of life and death.
- The second characteristic is that the demand for Drugs is not elastic. That is, demand is not very responsive to changes in Prices. In most industries, Prices react to the supply and the demand of a product. Conversely, consumers tend to buy more or less of a product depending on how high or low Prices are at a certain time. Such restraints are absent in the Drug markets, and so the incentive to lower Prices also tends to be absent.
- Thirdly, in the words of Senator Kefauver: "He who orders, does not buy and he who buys does not order".
  The Nelson Hearings were wide-ranging and covered a number of specific Drugs.

***

Other Drugs and Issues

Special attention in the Hearings was given to three products: MER-29, chloromycetin, and "The Pill". For the Reader interested in detail on the examination of the three Drugs, I suggest Mintz: *The Therapeutic Nightmare* (211). Although Mintz describes it as a Report on the "irrational and massive use of prescription Drugs that may be worthless, injurious, or even lethal", his Book, agenda aside, is filled with considerable detail; although oddly, his General Index does not list Senator Nelson.

In addition to the three Drugs already described, the Nelson Hearings also targeted: anti-obesity Drugs; oral hypoglycemic; clindamycin and lincomycin; antibiotic combinations; vibramycin; and Indocin.

Drug Patents were also considered. Senator Nelson tried to make a point regarding Patents:

Senator Nelson: Research is an important issue. Is there any industry in the country that you can think of that will say you should really buy our more expensive product, say a lawnmower, than the equivalent lawnmower that was put out after our patent expired, because we did the research?

The purpose of the patent, which the Congress gives to any company which comes up with an original product, is to allow them 17 years to get back all their R & D costs, and to get back ample profit from their products.

Why should the monopoly privileges extend beyond the expiration date for only one industry in America? There is no argument about affecting research and development when their patent runs out. They have gotten all the money they are entitled to, and then a competing product that is equivalent ought to be purchased by the public, and in every other product, except drugs, that happens.

You do not see anybody going into a hardware store buying a lawn mower that is equivalent to the original innovation developed by some company 17 years before, on the grounds that the purchaser thinks it ought to pay twice as much because that company was good enough to come up with a good idea.

Using the lawnmower example, Big Pharma might have offered the following responses. The lawnmower inventor didn't necessarily have to show that it worked – effectively. Nor did the investigator need to establish safety in use, and certainly not, with different population segments—obese, elderly, infirm, etc. The lawnmower maker people would likewise not be required to use "fair balance" in their advertising-warnings, contraindications, and interactions (for example: a couple of beers in the operator). To the author's knowledge, Big Pharma never used that particular sort of response.

Conclusion/Nelson

Nelson offered up a smorgasbord of issues at one time or another, focusing on "misdeeds" by Big Pharma in all of the "Four P's". The Hearings continued, off and on, for more than 12 years and filled 17,000 plus pages of testimony, exhibits, and "prepared" statements. The latter were dutifully included in the Record but were seldom, if ever, read aloud. It was the "give and take" which was most often reported and which usually was the most interesting. Minority views were heard, notably by Senators Hruska, Dirksen, and Dole, about which we will learn more later.

The Fountain Hearings (130)

Congressman L. H. Fountain (NC) began a series of House Hearings in 1964, hard on the heels of Senator Kefauver and shortly before Senator Nelson began. Fountain's Intergovernmental Relations Subcommittee was eventually to meet more than 30 times.

These Hearings marked the first time detailed attention was given in Hearings to the role of hospital Pharmacy and Therapeutics Committees and Hospital Formularies. What would emerge as a major role in Drug therapy was described in detail by representatives of hospital Pharmacy.

Fountain in his opening statement explained the role of his Intergovernmental Relations Committee as "determining the economy and efficiency" of Government Operations at all levels. In this case that meant the FDA.

With Drug safety as part of its charges, the Subcommittee was particularly interested in adverse reactions to Drugs. The American Medical Association described its Registry of Adverse reactions. Their representative noted the usual caveat that "There is no such thing as an absolutely safe drug".

In his first appearance before the Subcommittee, New FDA Commissioner, Dr. Goddard, too, felt the need to echo Kefauver; "He who orders does not buy; and he who buys does not order". Why that was apropos in the context is not clear. What *is* clear was that the intention to follow on Kefauver's work on Drug Advertising. Dr. Goddard laid out his position.

> The movement of the drugs that are prescribed—and, Mr. Chairman, I would say, therefore, the quality and power of the advertising message that gets through to the prescribing physician who is, frankly, under siege in my opinion. He is under siege from magazines, from direct mail, from movies, from unsolicited and frequently unwanted samples, from symposia sponsored by drug companies, from printed reports of these captive symposia, and from the manufacturer's own detailers who visit the doctor's office one after another, day after day.
>
> The Kefauver Hearings on administered prices first placed drug advertising and other promotional practices under the lens of public scrutiny. This investigation, which was concerned with the range

of costs of prescription drugs, embraced drug advertising because such high-cost advertising clearly affected the pricing of pharmaceutical products. It was built right in. Before the hearings were completed, they had exposed a number of advertising practices that cried out for reform.

The Federal Trade Commission (FTC) was also represented at these Hearings in the person of the Chairman, Paul Rand Dixon. Probably speaking for us all he noted:

> There is a substantial amount of advertising today, especially on television, which occasions complaint from the public but which has not been found false and misleading. I refer particularly to commercials which are in poor taste, or which irritate the viewer, or which many people say are just plain silly and insult their intelligence. Personally offensive to some as such advertising may be, it seems that it sells to others.

Senator Kennedy Joins the Fray (131)

Senator Edward M. "Ted" Kennedy convened the first session of his hearings, *Examination of the Pharmaceutical Industry*, on December 18, 1973. This was hard on the heels of the long efforts of Senator Nelson, and Nelson was, in fact, a member of Kennedy's Subcommittee.

The stated purpose of the Subcommittee Hearings was to study "Legislation amending the Public Health Service Act and the Federal Food Drug and Cosmetic Act". The Legislation was contained in Senate Bills 3441 and 5966. They were, respectively, the National Drug Testing and Evaluation Center Act (from Nelson) and the Drug Utilization Improvement Act (from Kennedy).

Although the Kennedy Hearings covered much of the same territory as did Kefauver and Nelson before them, Kennedy focused more on two types of Promotion, detailing and samples, than had his predecessors as we shall see. But in the opening round, there were several interesting exchanges between the Senator and Joseph Stetler who had succeeded Austin Smith, as head of the PMA. The first example dealt with Generics, always a popular topic.

> Senator Kennedy, quoting Casper Weinberger, then Secretary of HEW......

He states in his article, which I will make part of the record that was based on many years of experience with this program he is confident there is no significant difference between generic and brand named antibiotic products on the American market. Any antibiotic offered for sale in the United States has met the same standards of FDA.

Mr. Stetler: Based on long experience, we say that is wrong.

Senator Kennedy: He says it is right.

Mr. Stetler: That is not where it ends.

Kennedy wanted to know how the doctor was served by brand name ads for the same, identical, generic drug. Stetler pointed out that the generic name was required to be in every ad.

Senator Kennedy: Exactly, but it is awfully small. I mean you can see the name Bactrim and then you see what illnesses it is indicated for, but the generic names are rather small, and the same thing is true with this one. This is a little bit bigger. But you are really talking about advertising two of the same product, which would be like advertising two Fords, not a Ford and a Chevy, except you have a Ford that is called a Ford, and a Ford that is called something else.

Mr. Stetler: Again, a doctor has a little more knowledge—a good deal more knowledge than you would find in those ads. We think, rather than this being a bad thing; it certainly does enhance competition. On one hand we are accused of being noncompetitive. Certainly, if you only had one manufacturer of that drug, he would have a monopoly. Here you have two manufacturers with drugs that compete.

The conversation turned to pricing in Promotion.

Mr. Stetler: But if the point is: Should doctors have specific price information, our answer is: "Yes, he should, and he should look at it and pass that intelligence on to his patient".

Senator Kennedy: Why is it so difficult in terms of pricing? Why can't you develop a standardization on that?

Mr. Stetler: Just as an example, you might have, say, several brands or several makers of tetracycline, and there may be—and there are—some variations at wholesale in those prices. That does not necessarily mean that at the retail level those same differences are going to be reflected in the retail price. They may, they may not, but what is important to the patient and the customer is, first that you get a good quality drug, but also, it is what price he pays the pharmacist.

If there is some way to communicate that information, the doctor should know in the area in which he practices what competing prices are. That would be of some value to him, but just to know the barebones of wholesale pricing, that is not translatable necessarily into what the consumer or the customer pays.

Mr. Cutler from the PMA recalled.....

3 years ago, a recommendation to Secretary Wilbur Cohn that one of the requirements for qualifying prescription drugs under Medicaid-Medicare be that for a pharmacy to be eligible for reimbursement, it had to provide price lists for the leading prescribed drugs to the doctors in that community, or in that neighborhood, wherever the pharmacy was, and also that manufacturers, to be eligible for reimbursement, had to supply lists of their wholesale prices to doctors. And we think that would go a long way, and we have always thought that, to convey useful competitive pricing information to the physicians and patients. But it was not carried out.

Senator Kennedy: That would at least appear to me to be a very constructive step.

Mr. Stetler: We agree with what they are trying for completely.

Senator Kennedy: What happened to that recommendation, Mr. Stetler?

Mr. Stetler: Nothing.

Kennedy was particularly interested in Drug detailers, which we covered in Chapter 2. Called as witnesses, were three former detailers. One of them, formerly with Merck, took pains to aver that he was not a "disgruntled former employee". He took strenuous issue with an article in the *Pink Sheet*, which had described him and his fellow witnesses as "defectors, seeking to confess our own misdeeds".

The second promotional technique to which Kennedy gave attention was that of Drug samples to physicians. Drug samples have been a time-honored method of Drug Promotion. They cannot be divorced from the detailer who usually serves as the delivery person.

Samples have varied degrees of acceptance by presenters. As noted in Chapter 2, some welcome them as a method of clinical trial for new patients. Others use them as a means of lessening the Price burden for some patients. Others see them as a nuisance.

The PMA informed the Subcommittee of their view of the role of sampling. Their printed overview is too lengthy to include here but a few relative points will be given.

Two independent research projects found that physicians want and use samples because they:

- Permit clinical evaluation of a product by a physician to see if he finds it of value in his practice.
- Allow evaluation of a specific product to see if the patient tolerates it and if it has the desired effect before the prescription is filled and the patient's money is spent.
- Allow the physician to start therapy immediately.
- Allow the physician to help low-income or indigent patients, many of whom are not covered by Health or welfare plans.

Two issues arose involving the *pharmacist* vis-à-vis sampling. The first was the occasion of physicians giving or selling these samples to a pharmacist who would then put them in stock bottles for resale. Ethics aside, this raised questions in the case of recalls (lot numbers, etc.). The second issue arose from complaints by pharmacists that samples cost them revenue for a first prescription. A few companies initiated programs whereby the physician could give the patient a coupon redeemable for a free first prescription (a "sample" as it were) after which the pharmacist could submit this to the manufacturer for a kind of rebate.

The pharmacist, too, came under scrutiny. The issue of Price-posting by product name in the Pharmacy was discussed and had been tried but found to be impractical.

Conclusion/Kennedy

As is the case with all of these Hearings, it is not possible here to give a complete account of all that transpired. Consumers were represented by the well-known Ralph Nader and Sydney Wolfe. Minority views were expressed by Senators Javits, Hruska, and Dirksen.

As a result of the Hearings, new restrictions on detailing and sampling were imposed. Nothing of real substance was done about Drug Prices. Price posting in the Pharmacy was considered, again. Testimony by Gregory Stern, who was representing consumerist, Betty Furness, was given:

> I will say that price posting is neither a placebo nor panacea in its field. Many stores do not post the signs in a clear and conspicuous manner. They are out of the way, behind the counter, too high or too low. For a second thing, even with price posting, many people are unable to make comparisons and judgments. There is a long list. It is like a telephone book on a wall of 115 drugs, being priced in various sizes.
>
> So only your most discriminating consumers are going to be able to go up to a store, to walk in, to point out the price, and then to go into another store. In many cases, people are afraid of, intimidated by their neighborhood pharmacist. They view the pharmacist as a learned person—to an extent he is. Especially in some communities they know if you leave the store without buying, you may earn the enmity of the pharmacist. They do not want to get on his bad side.

Senator Kennedy remained very active in the Drug field, advocating national Health insurance, working with Senator Hatch on the "Orphan Drug Act", supporting the Food and Drug Administration Modernization Act (see Chapter 4), and worked with Big Pharma to bring in Drug benefits under Medicare.

Small Business Problems in the Drug Industry – Dingell (139)

While Senator Kennedy was busy in the Senate, John Dingell had been equally busy in the House of Representatives. Dingell died in 2019 and was the longest serving (59 years) member of the House. His Subcommittee on Activities of Regulating Agencies met from 1967 to 1968 for a total of 16 sessions.

Considerable time in the Hearings was given over to discussing the pros and cons of the Robinson–Patman Act, not surprising as Wright Patman, whose name is on the Act, was also former Chair of the House Committee on Small Business of which Dingell's Subcommittee was a part.

Congressman Patman was the first to testify, noting that his Act had been in place for 35 years. He called it the "Magna Carta of Small Business" and urged that it be enforced in a manner that fully carried out the intent of the Bill. Patman's concern was that the small business person was "under attack on many fronts" because "the big corporations and monopolies get bigger and bigger".

Specific to the Drug industry, Congressman Patman singled out the National Association of Retail Druggists (NARD) for attention.

> The National Association of Retail Druggists represents most of the 40,000 corner drugstores in the United States. It is the largest segment of small business remaining in this country. I know their losses have been many, but few in comparison to other groups of small businesses.
>
> I believe it is the largest group proportionately, I am sure that is true, of any group, of small businesses in the United States. They have been able to withstand the rugged competition of the national chains. It is a great tribute to them that they were able to do that.
>
> But they were selling something in addition to products in their drugstores. Most all of them are public spirited civic minded citizens in the community where they live and where they have stores. They have influence in every way in their communities, and they are looked upon as leaders.

It was clear that Patman was not happy with the role of the FTC in the enforcing of his Act.

> The FTC majority, I am convinced, remains solidly behind the basic principles of this act. I am sure of that. But, I was frankly amazed last August when an FTC Commissioner devoted most of a 64-page speech to an attack on the Robinson-Patman Act. The major points of the speech were apparently drawn from the legal defenses put forward through the years by the principal violators of the Act.

Patman then cited conglomerate mergers, vertical integration, dual distribution, and increasing economic concentration as "new perils to the survival of smaller firms". Differential pricing and promotional allowances were also examined.

In the course of the Hearings, Public attention was finally focused on the pharmacist's professionalism. Prescriptions have long been priced on some sort of markup based on the cost of ingredients. Professor Joseph McEvilla (66) had explained the basis for the concept years before, but the Dingell Hearings gave it a forum.

The witness for the professional fee was Dr. William Apple, head of the American Pharmacists Association (APhA). Apple was speaking to the Subcommittee, but he also had inserted in the record an article which he had written explaining the fee to pharmacists and encouraging its use.

> To the pharmacists, Apple had written:
> Stated in simplest terms, the professional fee is the difference in dollars and cents between what the patient is charged for the prescription and what the pharmacist actually paid for the drug dispensed. This is true regardless of the system or formula (fee, mark-up or combination) you use to arrive at the charge to the patient. Rent, heat, light, advertising, insurance, salaries and all of the other expenses incurred in providing the professional service obviously must be paid for from the dollars realized as the professional fee. Dollars for taxes and return on educational and capital investments likewise must come from the same source.
>
> With the increased participation of third parties (including government) in the payment for pharmaceutical services, the profession collectively is being called on to justify the cost (professional fee) it claims as the essential minimum required to provide safe and timely professional service. It can be expected that initially third parties will be interested in the dollar value pharmacists are currently receiving—not what pharmacists think they deserve—from the public for professional services in dispensing a prescription. Obviously the first yardstick to be examined will be the "average" professional fee nationally. The actual current "average" professional fee by geographical region or service area will then be scrutinized.

Apple was proven right of course, and third parties do not only recognize the professional fee but usually impose it.

Drug Efficacy Problems – Fountain (145)

These Hearings, which might have been called "Son of Chloramphenicol", were conducted by L. H. Fountain of North Carolina. Congressman Fountain had concluded after the first session of Hearings that the FDA's "lack of vigor in enforcing the law and protecting the public, appeared to border on indifference".

These were difficult days for Herbert Ley, who was the FDA Commissioner, even though accompanied by General Counsel and six other members of the FDA scientific community. Dr. Ley had been informed by hand-delivered letter that he was to appear at a Hearing on April 17. The letter was dated April 4.

In his letter, Fountain listed three serious problems:

1. It appears that hospitals, physicians, or other interested parties have never been appropriately advised of the FDA's decision that there is not adequate evidence that Chloromycetin Succinate is effective by the intramuscular subcutaneous routes of administration. These routes were recommended in the previous labeling but were deleted from the labeling approved in September 1968 as a result of a study by the National Academy of Sciences.
2. It appears that there has been no recall, from hospitals, pharmacies, or other trade channels, of Chloromycetin Succinate which bears the old labeling and became mislabeled as a result of the September 1968 revision.
3. It appears that the FDA has taken no action to assure that the large volume of Chloromycetin Succinate bearing the old labeling, which is only now being recalled from Parke Davis' widely scattered warehouses, is in fact being appropriately labeled or destroyed.

These and other issues formed the basis for discussion during the Hearings.

Commissioner Ley, in his prepared statement, provided Fountain with a detailed description of FDA's actions regarding the Drug beginning with the isolation of the substance in 1947 from a soil sample in Venezuela and to the present. It was a lengthy and unusual history of the Drug from dirt to the patient.

Chairman Fountain was far from satisfied with Ley's account:

> I think your statement could have been more explicit in a number of places in spelling out the connection between agency actions and events. And, I would hope that future statements to this Subcommittee would be more explicit so that hopefully all of us can spend less time in the hearing room, because a good portion of our time is taken up in questioning you about some of the statements which were made in your prepared statement.
>
> And in the light of some of the statements which have been made here today, I would hope that you and your staff would

take a very careful inventory of not only your present procedures and regulations but of the law, to see if the law itself is adequate to enable you to do what needs to be done to protect the public interest.

A few days after the close of the Hearings, Ley sent Chairman Fountain a letter stating, among other things, "With respect to our regulatory powers, as a result of the information brought out in the Hearings, we are re-evaluating our entire Drug control procedures to determine how it can be improved". In addition, Dr. Austin Smith, then President of Parke Davis, provided Chairman Fountain with a long, detailed list of remedial measures to be taken by his firm.

Moss on Drug Abuse (135)

Senator Frank Moss (Utah) convened his Consumer Subcommittee in September 1970. The topic was the *Relationship between Drug Abuse and Advertising*. Considering the fact that the Hearings were held a half century ago, it is troubling to know that virtually everything discussed is still in the headlines today.

Here is what Chairman Moss said to open the Hearings:

> Drug abuse by the young has become a social cancer of hideous proportions. There are today 100 million young Americans under 25. At least 12 million young Americans have experimented with marijuana and the stench of hard-drug abuse permeates the culture of youth.
>
> And as the curtain of our ignorance is drawn back, we see, enmeshed in this trap, first the tragic ghetto youth and the criminal psychopath and now, unmistakably, our children—the children of middle America.

Much of the testimony centered on ads for OTC Drugs. As Moss said: "Certain kinds of advertising stand accused of seducing the young to drug-dependency, and creating vulnerability to drug abuse."

Chairman Moss adjourned the Hearing with news of a House Report leading to House approval of the Comprehensive Drug Abuse Prevention Control Act of 1970.

Fountain Redux (141, 146, 147)

Congressman Fountain was back again in 1970–1971 with three sets of Hearings:

- Regulatory Policies of the Food and Drug Administration (147)
- Prescription Drug Advertising
- The safety and effectiveness of new Drugs.

The first of these, spotlighting the FDA, found the Agency with a new Commissioner, Charles C. Edwards. It was his first experience with this Subcommittee. Edwards began with a lengthy prepared statement which essentially provided his view of what the Agency does. As part of that statement, he included reference to a proposed patient package insert (PPI) for oral contraceptives.

Congressman Fountain commented:

> **Mr. Fountain:** Doctor, I don't know whether the insert should be long or short and I don't feel qualified to say what it ought to contain, although I do have some slight opinion as a result of what I have read about it and briefing by the staff. I am concerned that a woman who uses these pills, other than the general warning which you give her in the short statement, has to rely completely upon a doctor for adequate advice. I am not so sure any woman is completely justified in relying exclusively upon her doctor for advice. Doctors are so busy these days, and unless she knows to ask him for this pamphlet, she may not get it. Also, what about the woman who is not under medical supervision, about whom you have spoken so strongly, and where there is no doctor-patient-relationship—where, in your language, the doctor-patient- relationship is nonexistent! I am concerned about that.
>
> I don't think people today are as naïve as you may think they are. They can read and have a pretty good understanding. It seems to me that language that is more explicit would alert a woman to ask more specific questions of her doctor than she will under the general language which you now have. The doctor is there to give that information, but I have come away from my doctor many, many times realizing that I was either too timid to ask him or he was too busy to tell me information I needed to know. I think that

happens time and time again because we are so busy. The very fact that the old-time doctor-patient relationship doesn't exist, the one we were all so proud of, is an indication of how busy they are. People are going to doctors for more and more ailments for which I guess they are still in many instances prescribing aspirin as a means of satisfying those patients who feel they must have some kind of prescription.

The dialog continued for some time with both Congressmen Clarence Brown and Fountain asking some very practical questions. Again, there is simply too much to include here.

Finally, recalling Commissioner Ley's letter to Congressman Fountain, Commissioner Edwards' remarks are telling indeed:

In 1970, the Food and Drug Administration has pursued these serious tasks with diligence. Seven months ago the prognosis would have been less than optimistic.

When we arrived at FDA on December 15, 1969, we found the agency with strong scientific competence, but this competence was poorly marshaled. There existed a clear imbalance between scientific and regulatory responsibilities. The decision making environment was disorderly. Professional talent was stifled, poorly directed, and unmotivated. Planning was shockingly myopic.

The very next month, Fountain held new Hearings on Prescription Drug Advertising (146). Particular attention was given to "Dear Doctor" letters in which the FDA informs prescribers of any inaccurate or misleading elements in the Promotion of a Drug. (**Author's note:** *There are many types of prescribers in today's marketplace. One wonders if such a practice is in any way practical.*)

Congressman Fountain's next venture was into the land of the Safety and Effectiveness of New Drugs (141). Much of the Hearings were devoted to the subject of "fixed combination" Drugs. There was a companion Hearing, Marketing of Fixed Combination Drugs and Unapproved New Drugs and Advertising and Promotion (148).

Fixed combination Drugs are products with two or more active ingredients in "fixed" proportions. A very old example would be the product from the 1950s, Milprem, which combined meprobamate with Premarin (conjugated estrogen). The logic of that product was rather sound for use in menopause – the estrogen the body needs and the minor tranquilizer that conventional wisdom says every menopausal woman needs.

There are some real potential advantages to fixed combos: patient convenience, economy, and better adherence to medication – taking schedules. But there are disadvantages, too: lack of flexibility for physicians to adjust dosages of each component to patients' needs, possible exposure to unnecessary Drugs when one Drug would be effective alone, and increased risk of adverse reactions.

The FDA Policy proposed at the time of the Hearing for fixed combos set several criteria for new Drugs coming to the marketplace as combinations and for old combination Drugs remaining on the market. The FDA would approve combinations where there was proof that each active ingredient contributed to the effects claimed for the fixed combinations. Each added ingredient would have to enhance:

- Effectiveness of the Drug by increasing potency or prolonging its effects; or
- Safety of the Drug by decreasing or reducing severity of adverse effects; or
- Prevent possible misuse or abuse.

When two or more Drug components are given, instead of one, the advantages of the combinations would have to apply for Schedules and durations of use as recommended.

Congressman Rogers on Transition (150)

Paul C. Rogers was Chair of this House Subcommittee formed to plot the progress made in implementing the 1962 Drug Amendments passed nearly a decade before. Rogers chose to revisit the "fixed combo" issue which Fountain had just reviewed. He found considerable support in the medical community for the idea, with prescribers citing convenience and reduced expense as leading reasons for this support.

Dr. Julius Michaelson, representing the American Academy of General Practice, opened his remarks with strong words in defense of his colleagues in medicine.

> First of all, I would like to take advantage of this opportunity to dispel a myth or two about the family physician and the specialist,

too, for that matter. They are far too busy to take time away from sick people to respond to a lot of nonsense about their competence and performance. It has become fashionable for nonmedical sources and some academic sources, to castigate us for something called "irrational prescribing, poor prescribing, overprescribing, et cetera."

Most of us appear to be glibly categorized as little more than a collective band of medical semi-illiterates who have learned little and know even less despite lifetimes of study and experience in medicine. If we practiced as badly as some of these critics claim, the Nation would have so many sick people that it could hardly go on about its business.

I'd like to assure you that the great majority of doctors do practice conservative, responsible, scientific medicine. We prescribe drugs cautiously with close surveillance of the results. We are not unduly persuaded by detailmen from drug firms. Nor do we accept every promotional effort as gospel.

PMA joined in, in the person of Bruce Brennan, General Counsel. Brennan brought with him results of a research study by the R.A. Gosselin Company, a well-known market research firm. They looked at 71 combination products and concluded that, if prescribers had prescribed the two ingredients separately, the increase in cost to the consumer would have been 443.2 million dollars or nearly 60% more than the consumer would pay for the "fixed combo".

The FDA in a proposed Policy statement on fixed combos cited five disadvantages to their use:

1. Lack of flexibility to adjust the dosage of a compound to individual patient's needs.
2. Increased possibility of adverse reactions without increased efficacy.
3. Increased risk of Drug interaction about which little is known.
4. Exposure of patients to unnecessary Drugs if one Drug alone would be effective.
5. Possible difficulties in defining the responsible agent if a Drug allergy results.

Returning to the Hearing title, remember that the 1962 Amendments required proof of effectiveness for the first time. Mr. Preyer of the FDA identified a kind of "tight rope" imposed on the FDA. The FDA general Counsel began the dialog:

> **Mr. Goodrich:** Yes. There is one other factor I should have mentioned. Where you have a relative efficacy issue tied in with safety, you know one drug is just so much more dangerous than the other and they both do the same thing, then relative efficacy comes to bear on it. But those are the two situations.
>
> **Mr. Preyer:** I think the legislative history of the 1962 amendments is very clear, in fact it is very explicit, that it was not the intention of those amendments that the Food and Drug Administration should get into the business of saying "this drug is more effective than some other product", but to say this drug is safe and effective. Is that your understanding of the intention of the 1962 amendments?
>
> **Dr. Edwards:** Yes.
>
> **Mr. Goodrich:** I was there when then Secretary Ribicoff made that statement. What he said was that we would have no business evaluating relative efficacy and precluding a drug from the market, that if the drug worked for a limited patient population where another one worked for a wider population, there was room for both of them on the market, but that the claims would have to be fully supported by adequate proof of effectiveness.
>
> Now, these are two different things. One is precluding the product from the market and the other one is holding it to its claim. Relative efficacy is a factor in the latter but not the former.

Senator Humphrey and the Literature (168)

This Report, *Drug Literature*, was actually a part of the Hearings on Inter-Agency Coordination. The Report was compiled by the National Library of Medicine (NLM) and was entitled *A Factual Survey on the Nature and Magnitude of Drug Literature*.

The findings of the survey are important as they show the significance of the printed word which lies behind and influences so many of the decisions made on the road to a Drug Policy. Because the Author believes the importance of the literature is often underestimated, this Report underlined its vastness and proliferation.

There was a monumental amount of work behind this Report and it is appropriate to recognize Winifred Sewell, Deputy Chief, Bibliographic Services of NLM, at the time. She and her staff provided an invaluable reference source for those with the good sense to use it. Senator Hubert Humphrey (later, of course, Vice President) headed up the Senate Subcommittee on Government Operations to which this Report was directed.

The Report was for more than just a simple listing of sources. There was analysis. Case studies were presented on two Drugs – vinblastine and chlordiazepoxide. In the latter case, it demonstrated how rapidly Drug literature would grow. Accessing the Roche Library of 528 entries in October, 1962, the following progression was found: in 1959, 2 papers; in 1960, 96 papers; and in 1961, 314 papers. While 270 papers of the 528-paper Roche Collection were from the United States, 21 other countries were home to one or more papers. The difficulty for scientists to keep up is obvious, and don't forget the practicing prescriber.

A bonus in the Report was the inclusion of a "World List of Pharmacy Periodicals". That was as of 1963. The mind can only boggle at the size of such a list today.

The final words of the Report place the problems in context.

> The New York Academy of Medicine Committee on Public Health states:
> Skepticism has its place in the early stages of judgment, but it should create a desire for more facts. What the practicing physician needs is an honest and comprehensive basis for forming critical judgments, and information adequate to meet this need is not always supplied to him.

In discussing changes in attitudes toward Drugs as new information develops, says:

> All of us covet the security of advice and guarantees of safety and effectiveness from the sources available to us—pharmacology and therapy text-books and reliable medical journals, etc. But this security is not to be had. Every physician, when he administers a drug, faces the necessity of using his own best judgment. He cannot escape the responsibility of being well informed and ready to change his mind on the basis of new information.

(170)

A Newcomer – Congressman Lionel Van Deerlin (144)

Congressman Van Deerlin was new to the Drug Hearings and must have had a problem with geography as the Hearing was held in San Diego. In his opening statement, Van Deerlin stated, "At the retail end, although price differentials can be as great as several thousand percent among similar products...." Clearly the Senator from California had been paying attention during the Kefauver Hearings.

Van Deerlin's Hearings, which were billed as, *Prescription Drug Advertising and Price Advertising*, were specifically tied to a single piece of proposed Legislation. H.R. 884 – in the Author's opinion – was one of the most unrealistic pieces of Legislation ever contemplated in the field of Drug Legislation. A Mr. Price, whose affiliation I have not determined, introduced the Bill. If he (whoever he was) ever spoke with any pharmacist before introducing the Legislation, I can only assume that the pharmacist thought he was joking.

The Bill required, among other things – Posting (in a form which the FDA would explain some day) a list of the "prices of the one hundred prescription Drug products that had the highest dollar volume of retail sales" (in a period that the FDA would determine – someday). The obvious question is: What Price? The Price the pharmacist actually paid or some arbitrary Price to be determined – someday? This very question remains today and has given rise to a covey of new acronyms – average wholesale cost (AWC), actual acquisition cost (AAC), maximum allowable cost (MAC), average manufacturers price (AMP), etc. These are all discussed along with their definitions in Chapter 17.

And how often would the Price posting need to be changed? Every time there is a change in the Price of a single product? And where would this "price poster" be placed? A suggestion was made of a loose-leaf binder available for patient review, but that is not "posting".

What about the professional fee which was espoused and explained at length during the Hearings by "Bill" Apple, head of the American Pharmaceutical Association? Such a fee appears nowhere in the Bill. The reason for that may be the word "professional". The authors of the Bill apparently did not recognize Pharmacy as a profession. Hence, from the Bill, "The term 'drug retailer' means a person who is engaged in whole or part in the business of *selling* (emphasis added by the Author) prescription drugs at retail". "Bill" Apple should have pointed this out. Instead, he called for the elimination of brand names.

The Bill and the Hearings held in support of it were, at best, unrealistic and at worst foolishly ignorant of the "retail" practice of Pharmacy.

Senator Fountain "One More Time" (177)

By the time of this Hearing, Alexander Schmidt was FDA Commissioner. The subject of these Hearings was the use of Advisory Committees by the FDA. This is an important topic as such committees supply the outside and objective information used by FDA staff to make decisions on a whole range of existing or proposed Regulations. This Hearing was unusual and helpful in providing insight into how such a committee works.

Dr. Goldberg was concerned that a Panel might be "intimidated from adopting their own independent position by questions concerning whether their own scientific judgment will stick or whether FDA may have some problems". He was concerned that the Panel would be concerned about possible litigation which might be brought against FDA if the Agency adopted a Panel recommendation. Commissioner Schmidt responded:

> **Dr. Schmidt:** There is a purpose to this whole thing. The panel does not wish to spend a year, 3 days at a time several times a year, plus immeasurable hours at home going over these data, they do not wish to waste their time. They do not wish to be irrelevant. We do not wish them to be irrelevant to the purpose of this whole process. I heartily disagree with your implications and your conclusions.

Before adjourning, the Chairman had one final comment:

> I think today marks the last official appearance of Mr. Hutt before this subcommittee as General Counsel of the FDA. While his appearances have at times been stormy, I think we can all agree he has conducted himself in an extremely competent fashion.
>
> The Congress and the Administration are currently working on the whole question of regulatory reform. While it is not within my competence to predict what will happen, I think a lot of the reforms you have brought to the Food and Drug Administration will in substance be transposed to the other regulatory agencies.

(**Author's note:** *As recorded above, Peter Barton Hutt would retire after these Hearings. Anyone familiar with the many times he was involved in these proceedings (as I am) can only applaud the way he represented the FDA as Counsel and the interests of the American People. Deferential when he needed to be but firm in his convictions always, he fit perfectly the title of Public Servant. The same is true for Dr. Mark Novitch, who was involved in this and other hearings. His contributions to the deliberations were very significant. It was my privilege to host each of these men as classroom speakers in my graduate program at the University of Mississippi. Each distinguished himself there as well.*)

Senator Kennedy Returns (151)

These Hearings, entitled "Pricing of Drugs, 1977", were aimed at just what the title suggests. In Kennedy's opening remarks, he made it clear that Drugs for the elderly would receive special attention:

> Drug prices in the United States, already the highest of any nation in the world, are going up. The burden of this, at the retail level, falls on senior citizens. Although they comprise only 11 percent of the population, the elderly fill 25 percent of the prescriptions.
>
> How are drug prices set? What is a reasonable rate of return for a health- oriented industry? What degree of profit is necessary and justified to sustain an effective research and development program for new drugs? When do profits become unjustifiable? What effect does the patent system have on drug prices and on industry profits? How does the patent system effect the competitive nature of the industry?

Four members of Big Pharma were present, as were the American Association of Retired Persons (AARP) and the National Retired Teachers Association (NRTA). The administrator of the new Health Care Financing Administration (HCFA) was also present. Big Pharma got a grilling.

> **Sheldon Kilgore** of Pfizer took the lead:
> I guess I was sort of surprised that Mr. Derzon was surprised that there seemed to be such wide-ranging variations in price between actual prices and Red Book prices, and why there seemed to be so much in the way of vigorous discount activity. We spent a

lot of time calling that to the attention of HEW back beginning in 1973 and it is a matter of public record. I guess I wasn't surprised that you were unsurprised, because I am sure you recall the Pfizer testimony here in 1974 that pointed out many of those same things.

Senator Kennedy: The point he felt was of such concern, so much so, that he recommended that the Federal Trade Commission have an opportunity to examine it, is that there are different groups that do not have the same information in terms of pricing policy. They also draw that conclusion in terms of the disparity of pricing.

They are not saying or do they reach the conclusion, and while Mr. Derzon is still in the room, I don't want to misstate it, that the companies themselves are trying to rig this. They just draw the final conclusion that there are these disparities without any kind of pattern of practice, and with really no explanation that they can logically reach on it. So really, what I would like to ask you for is for your explanation on this whole question. Otherwise, I think one possible interpretation would be that, at the same volume, some deals are available to some pharmacists that are not available to others, and that does raise questions about the application of the Robinson-Patman Act. I think that is the question that I would like to have particularly addressed.

Dr. Kilgore: Yes; we have studied this very carefully, and our view is that a market price structure that is bottomed on quantity discounts, published deals for one reason or another, and specific instances where competitive prices are being met, is consistently within the law and allowable under Robinson-Patman. We have been assured of this by inside and outside counsel.

Senator Kennedy: Does this mean the same price is available to each pharmacy throughout the country?

Dr. Kilgore: It is, if they have a competitive offer.

Senator Kennedy: How do they know what offer to make?

After some back and forth during which Dr. Kilgore referred to "ferocity" of Price competition in the market, he returned to a familiar theme – the effect of Price competition on R&D funding.

I guess the great concern that all of us have is that as more patents expire, and this type of price competition develops on what were formerly sole source drugs, where there are not enough new drugs coming through the pipeline, innovative new drugs to replace them, the money that exists that allows us to fund our research and development, and present physician education programs, and consumer education programs, and all the other things in the public interest, will no longer be available. So we will have to stop these programs, because we sure as heck cannot fund them out of these fiercely competitive multisource drug markets.

The backdrop to this had been opening remarks from the Minority in the person of the venerable Strom Thurmond of South Carolina. Thurmond's remarks were a thinly-veiled warning to Kennedy.

> **Senator Thurmond:** Mr. Chairman, as we begin oversight hearings on pharmaceutical drug pricing, it is my hope that the hearings will prove to be objective and constructive as we evaluate the testimony, statements, and other evidence on this important subject.
>
> ***
>
> The reason these points are raised at this juncture goes back in time to 1959 when this same subject was considered by the Subcommittee on Antitrust and Monopoly through 1962.
> I welcome the witnesses who are here today to testify. Our country is a leader in pharmaceuticals. The history of the drug industry reveals progress in producing drugs which save many lives and cure or control many illnesses to permit fruitful and gainfully employed lives. The efforts of the drug industry have certainly extended the life span of many people. In our free enterprise system, the industry is entitled to a fair profit. It could not be otherwise if these companies are to remain in business.
> On the other hand, we must insure that those people who need drugs to cure or control illnesses are able to have access to them. Our senior citizens, those on lower incomes as well as the more affluent, must not be denied the means of curing and controlling illness.

Without mentioning him by name, Thurmond wanted to be sure that no one had forgotten the controversy that Kefauver had aroused 15 years before.

The case for the elderly consumer was brought first by Fred Wegner representing both AARP and NRTA. He, and they, were enthusiastically in support of the Hearings. He began:

> We hope this subcommittee will conduct a far-reaching and in-depth investigation into such questions as compulsory licensing, non-competitive practices in drug retailing and manufacturing, high administered prices protected by patent monopolies, differential drug product pricing by manufacturers which is unfair to pharmacists and patients alike, a national drug formulary and compendium, the economic waste of brand name advertising, promotion, and prescribing, whether excessive prices paid by sick Americans for new drugs are an ethically and economically acceptable method of financing drug research and development, and whether a health-oriented, patient service industry, reaping profits twice the average of other U.S. manufacturers, is adequately accountable to the public interest.

Wegner brought with him to the Hearings a number of elderly persons to provide accounts of their own "high personal expenditures for drugs" (Wegner's words). Their accounts were predictably moving.

Shortly before the end of the day, Senator Thurmond raised an issue which was to re-surface in 2017–2018, the cost of Federal Regulations.

> **Senator Thurmond:** I will ask a question, and I will be glad for different companies to answer it. It is not directed to this issue, but it concerns every business in America.
>
> I am deeply concerned about all of the regulations that our Government is imposing upon business people today, and I just wondered if you had any estimate as to how much money does it cost your company to comply with the maze of Government regulatory requirements.
>
> **Senator Thurmond:** We have about 80 regulatory agencies, employing over 100,000 people, costing the Government over $4 billion a year, and costing the consumer $130 billion, and I was just stunned when I read those figures.
>
> Would you each mind supplying for the record just what it costs your company to meet your requirements?

Senator Kennedy: It will give you a little more paperwork. (Laughter). The purpose in getting this paperwork is to try to reduce your paperwork permanently.

Senator Thurmond: That is what we would like to do.

Senator Kennedy closed the Hearing with a few remarks.

Senator Kennedy: We have heard earlier today, during the course of the hearing, matters about which, I am sure, you are very much aware of, and you would have to be aware of, and that is the cost of drugs probably falls heaviest on our elderly population. All matters are going up in terms of their purchase price, but our elderly are the most affected by this.

This is the most important difference in the quality of their lives.

Then we heard a different kind of analysis from HEW, and from the companies. We are not marketing experts, and we are not scientists on this committee, we know that HEW has done this study, and raised some very important kinds of questions.

We want to extend the Medicare coverage in terms of the drugs, and in order to develop a viable policy in that area, we are going to have to know more about the allocations of costs. Meanwhile we also want to insure the strength and research capability and capacity of our pharmaceutical companies, which I think all of us are agreed, are clearly the best in the world. Obviously, we want to insure them a reasonable rate of return, so that it has this type of incentive, but we must protect the public in terms of the cost in these areas.

FDA under the Microscope Again (138)

In 1979, it was the Food and Drug Administration's turn on the hot seat. FDA had yet another Commissioner, Donald Kennedy (they're everywhere!) PMA, too, had a new leader, Lewis Engman. With Committee Chairman George E. Brown, they made an interesting trio. Kennedy, with a Ph.D. in biology, served 2 years at FDA before becoming President of Stanford; Engman had previously been Chairman of the FTC and had never been a member of any Big Pharma company; and, Congressman Brown, long active in science affairs of the Congress, among other things, established the Environmental Protection Agency.

Oversight, as defined by the Congress, is what might be called the "watchdog" role. The Oversight Committee could investigate anything "within their jurisdiction". And they did. There is a long list of their responsibilities – postal service, paperwork reduction, even holidays.

The Hearing was titled *Oversight: The Food and Drug Administration's Process for Approving New Drugs.* The Proceedings ran for 1,300 pages with 426 pages of actual testimony. At the outset, Chairman Brown turned over the Hearings to Congressman James Scheuer (NY), who presided thereafter.

Chairman Scheuer opened with some context and it became clear that the "drug lag" would be very much a topic. Noting that FDA approval of a new drug could take 2–12 years and $30–$850 million, the Congressman stated.

> I don't want to prejudge the outcome of this hearing but we suspect this must have a stifling, or deadening effect on the zeal and enthusiasm with which innovations would be made in the decision making process in the drug industry. How about the individual chemist with a brilliant idea? How can he possibly cope with the mountains of paperwork and the tens of millions of dollars of experimentation? It just seemed to us that there was a real threat of deadening, of a terrible deadening effect. Now this raises the whole question of the costs and the benefits of the Federal regulatory process.
>
> Behind all of our deliberations and thinking hangs the Spector of another Thalidomide. We have absolutely no intention whatsoever of impinging on the safety or the efficacy requirements that it is FDA's legislative mandate to forward. We don't want drugs that won't work and we don't want drugs that aren't safe. This morning, we heard that the Supreme Court of the United States has ended the process of deliberation over a drug—laetrile—that our society has said is neither efficacious nor perhaps safe. So, we intend to stick with that. But, within those parameters of safety and efficacy, surely, something can be done to diminish the extraordinary burdens of the 8 or 10 or 12 year time period and this $30 to $50 million cost of getting a new drug into the stream of commerce and into use by 220 million Americans.
>
> Sophisticated, advance countries with standards of health care quite equal to our own have enjoyed the use of drugs for years before they have been approved in this country. I think all of us would like to know why.

Dr. Barbara Moulton, who had made prior appearances, in other Hearings, was back. After establishing her impressive credentials at FDA and elsewhere, she stated that she was "the only person to testify before this Committee who has ever had the responsibility for reviewing and approving new drug applications". After establishing the several benefits of FDA actions, she wanted to be sure there was no rush to judgment on the question of whether drug approval took too long.

> I shall attempt to show that in all likelihood more lives have been lost than saved by the release in other countries of the very drugs which are usually cited in an attempt to prove that FDA restricts lifesaving drugs at the cost of lives. Additionally many other patients have been subjected to increased pain or deformity and to life-threatening episodes which they managed to survive.

In his statement prior to handing over the Chair to Scheuer, Brown had offered his own thoughts (he noted that it was actually Congressman Scheuer who had requested the Hearings).

> An issue of concern to all of us is the health of the American public: Safe and effective drugs have made a significant contribution to the health of our people and in a number of cases, have reduced the costs over other forms of therapy. However, the apparent slower drug approval process in the United States has brought charges of a "drug lag". We hope to learn about some of the significant drugs available in other countries and reasons for their delay in this country. Also, the role of technology transfer of medical research and development information and the worldwide acceptance of scientific data are issues of interest to this subcommittee.

The Proceedings could be a bit contentious. Commissioner Kennedy obviously felt the need for strong language. He called attention to the requirement by law that "effectiveness be demonstrated not by testimony but by experiment".

> I think that it is a terribly important provision. It provided for American medicine the first universally applicable, formal, quantitative mechanism of outcome evaluation that it has had. That mechanism of outcome evaluation resulted in the most quantitative formal

outcome of any evaluation of any medical practice that exists anywhere.

And the Congress clearly meant to establish it, and did so by strong language.

The statutory standard for substantial evidence is adequate and well-controlled investigations by experts qualified by scientific training and experience to evaluate the effectiveness of the drug involved under the conditions of use.

That language is not the language of a regulation-happy bureaucrat. It is the language of the Congress of the United States.

Now, there are other nations that do it differently. There are other nations that have adopted a kind of position consensus procedure for new drug approval. And I think myself that the benefits of our method enormously outweigh the cost. That is a subject for another debate on which I and others have written.

But the Congress established clearly that what we were to do is experiment not take testimony.

And so it continued. Not exactly acrimonious but tense. These Hearings were especially important as they were certainly a factor in the ultimate passage of the Waxman–Hatch Bill (Chapter 4).

Kennedy – Not Too Tranquil (167)

In September, 1979, Senator Edward Kennedy called to order a Hearing on Use and Misuse of Benzodiazepines. Joining him on the Subcommittee on Health and Scientific Research were Gaylord Nelson, an old hand at these Hearings, and Orrin Hatch, whose name would appear on Legislation with great impact on the Drug industry (see Chapter 4). Hoffman-LaRoche was nationally represented as the pioneer with benzodiazepines.

It should be kept in mind that these Hearings were being held nearly two decades after the two Drugs were manufactured, Librium in 1960 and Valium in 1963. Because of the other resources available, cited above, we will provide only a glimpse of the Proceedings.

Senator Kennedy lead off by citing his opinion that Valium and Librium had about become "household words".

> For many Americans, these drugs and other minor tranquilizers have brought needed relief and assisted in prompt recovery.

> For others, these drugs have produced a nightmare of dependence and addiction (sic), both very difficult to treat and to recover from.
>
> The purpose of this Hearing is to set the record straight on Valium and Librium; to try to understand the reasons for overuse and misuse of these drugs; to try and alert the American people to the consequences of misuse and abuse; to try to see what can be done to assure appropriate use.

As in other Hearings, a series of witnesses were brought to testify to their problems with, usually, Valium. In addition to a Catholic priest, there was a medical doctor from California. The physician testified that before he went "cold turkey" he was taking 200 and 300 mg a day. (At the normal dose of 5 mg that is 40–65 tablets a day.) No one seems to have thought to ask how he obtained, or even swallowed, that many. Notwithstanding that, his description of the suffering during withdrawal was riveting.

Testifying for the FDA was Dr. Richard Crout, Director of the FDA Bureau of Drugs. He described "psychological dependence" with the Drugs, not addiction, noting that they have helped millions of People and, "given this wide use they have a remarkable safety record". He did add, however:

> More recently it has become clear that all of the marketed benzodiazepines can also produce physical dependence. Symptoms of withdrawal include agitation, insomnia, sweating, tremors, abdominal and muscle cramps, vomiting and even convulsions. The symptom complex is similar to that associated with barbiturate or meprobamate withdrawal, although it is relatively less common with the benzodiazepines than with these drugs.

Dr. Crout cautioned:

> We must be sensitive to the fact, however, that these drugs can also be instruments of harm. The dependence they can produce when used in high dosages for long periods of time is very real. They can also be lethal when taken in high doses along with large amounts of alcohol and other drugs, such as propoxyphene. Health professionals and the public all have an obligation to understand the risks, as well as the benefits, of these important drugs and to use them with the care they deserve.
>
> Mr. Chairman, I would be pleased to answer any questions.

Senator Kennedy: What is basically your own conclusion, or the position of the FDA, about the use of Valium in stress situations? I think you commented in a general way in your testimony about it. Is it the conclusion of the FDA that it is appropriate to use or to have doctors prescribe Valium for the sort of everyday kinds of stresses that the average citizen faces, whether they involve the family or job or financial matters, parenting?

Dr. Crout: It is a difficult question. We have permitted in drug labeling the prescribing of Librium and Valium for that use. Basically, we have recognized that these transient situations of life can, in certain people, create a sufficient amount of anxiety that it is appropriate.

What about the prescriber?

Whether benzodiazepines are, in fact, overprescribed relative to medical need, however, is a question that cannot be answered with scientific certainty. The fundamental reason for this difficulty is that because of differing value judgments on how best, to treat patients with anxiety or tension, there is no consensus on how to establish the optimal medical need for these drugs. The problem is further complicated by imprecision in the diagnosis of psychoneurotic disorders and lack of good epidemiological data on the extent and duration of benzodiazepine use in various subgroups of the general population.

Kennedy put on the record, copies of instructions to Roche detailers, that put Roche in a bad light and said to Roche President, Robert Clark, "At some point, I expect to see an ad saying that if your morning newspaper is not on your doorstep you can take a Valium".

The federal Government had proposed control of Librium and Valium under the provision of the Drug Abuse Control Amendments of 1965. This action was contested and remained in the courts until March, 1973. Both Drugs were then listed as Schedule IV of the Controlled Substances Act.

Senator Howard Metzenbaum (Ohio) believed that some physicians were complicit in the problem as a whole:

Senator Metzenbaum: Mr. Chairman, the misuse or abuse of any drug in our society is reason for concern and action, but the misuse and abuse of the most frequently prescribed drug in the United States calls for serious questioning of drug company responsibility, physician prescribing practices, and the quality of information provided to patients.

In my discussions with physicians on this matter, I was convinced that there is a serious problem with the misuse of Valium, as I am sure today's witnesses will confirm. However, I do not believe that the fact of abuse should be an indictment of the drug itself. Rather, I believe that it is an indictment of a medical care system that will resort to long-term treatment of symptoms instead of taking the time and effort to determine the source of the problem.

Michael Halberstam, a Washington, D.C., internist, was concerned about the tenor of the Hearings. "I think the thrust of these hearings so far is to add an additional burden of *guilt and anxiety* (emphasis added) to these People who are genuinely albeit temporarily overwhelmed". He added, "It is a fallacy....to believe that merely by talking with patients you can relieve their anxieties".

Halberstam went on to say,

> The people whose marriages were saved by the use of Valium, whose jobs were helped, who were tied (sic) over through tremendously traumatic periods in their lives through the use of these drugs, did not appear (at the Hearings) today, but they are in the overwhelming majority.

On the final day of the Hearing, Robert Clark, Roche's President, was allowed to be heard. He went on at length, of course, and provided a lengthy prepared statement. Clark quoted the findings of Dr. Mitchell Balter, Director of a National Institute of Mental Health (NIMH) in a study. "This widely held belief that (the drugs are overused) is not borne out by the data in our national study".

Conclusion/Kennedy

It is difficult to discern any concrete result of these Kennedy Hearings. They did, certainly turn a spotlight, yet again, on this class of Drugs.

> Dr. Halberstam had some final words. They were discussing a Valium ad.

Dr. Halberstam: Senator, could I say something, because I am the person to whom this is addressed? I believe I am the only practicing general practitioner or internist here today. That ad is addressed to the practicing physician who is confronted with patients who come to his or her office who already cannot cope with these stresses.

We do not go out and drag people off the streets, if they are having trouble with their jobs or if their husbands or wives are giving them problems or if they have got a sick relative. If they can handle it, they are at home. They come to us because they are overwhelmed and because they cannot cope.

I think the thrust of these hearings so far is to add an additional burden of guilt and anxiety to these people who are genuinely, albeit usually temporarily, overwhelmed. I think that advertisement, although crude in a sense, as most advertisements have to be, teaches the physician something that he was taught in medical school; that symptoms that are severe enough to bring a patient to a doctor—abdominal pain or funny chest pains—are often the result of anxieties.

It is a fallacy, and a fallacy that I think is supported by the medical literature, to believe that merely by talking with patients, you can relieve their anxieties.

Gore on Pharmaceutical R&D (152)

This Hearing in April 1981 was notable for two reasons. The first is its focus, which for the first time, was on Research and Development. The second is the Subcommittee (on Investigation and Oversight) Chair, future Presidential Candidate, "Al" Gore. Congressman Gore must have been encouraged at the outset by the words of Congressman James Scheuer (NY), who praised Gore for "his high intelligence, his thoughtfulness and his insights".

The "drug lag" was again a main topic and Scheuer noted that:

> Today's Hearings will focus on breakthrough drugs. Some of these have already been approved for use in the United States, while a number of other important ones still await final regulatory approval. We look forward with great pleasure to hearing from our distinguished panel of scientists today on what the latest advances in pharmacology promise us, and the kind of reforms

and improvements in the regulatory and approval process of drugs which will speed the day when they're available for enhancing the health prospects and the quality of life for the 226 million American health consumers.

He then deferred to Gore who opened with what would be the general thrust of the Hearing. He planned a series of "joint efforts" (presumably with Scheuer) to spotlight the strengths and deficiencies of the Federal Drug-approval process.

> I can think of no more propitious time to begin than with the inauguration of a new Commissioner of Food and Drugs. The message of this hearing—that the FDA needs to improve its new drug approval process—should be carried loudly and clearly to Dr. Hayes and to the new administration.
> We must insure that potentially lifesaving new discoveries reach the market in the shortest possible time. The prevention and treatment of disease must go hand in hand; the American people deserve no less. There is no reason, why our Government cannot be efficient in dealing with drug applications, at the same time that it is effective in carrying out its health protection mandate.
> In this context, I think that an examination of some potentially important advances in drug therapy is timely. Not only will we hear about the cutting edge of American science, but we will be able to take what we learn to the FDA and ask that some of those new discoveries be given priority treatment. FDA has already instituted some new procedures, and the agency needs to know that we will be following the progress of these drugs very closely.
> But it is not enough merely to deal with Drugs on a case-by-case basis. In the future, the Investigations and Oversight Subcommittee will be examining some important structural issues that affect research and development in the pharmaceutical industry. For example, we will want to examine whether the FDA relies too little on the advice of its scientific advisory committees in approving new Drugs.

(**Author's Note:** *This issue had been thoroughly explored during the Fountain Hearings, above.*)

Gore's statement captured the tone and the context of the Hearing that followed. While not exactly "old wine in new bottles" what followed had been heard, in various ways, in other Hearings. Gore did allude to the work of Henry Waxman on Patent term restoration, which ultimately led to the Waxman-Hatch Bill (Chapter 4).

The Minority was heard from in the person of Congressman William Carney (NY), who raised, again, the issue of too much Regulation in general. After the obligatory pleasantness, Carney testified:

> I believe that changes are needed in the way the nation develops new drugs and approves them for public use, as the chairman has so aptly described in his statement. However, the problem regarding this aspect of regulation of the pharmaceutical industry is only one element of the overall regulatory morass we have allowed ourselves to develop in the United States. There are numerous instances where we have permitted too much regulation, and we are now paying the penalty. I personally support the regulatory reform efforts proposed by the Reagan administration, and believe that nowhere do they have as much potential for direct benefit to people as they do in the issue before us today.

Congressman Carney posed an extremely provocative question to Dr. Gilbert McMahon, a witness from the Tulane Medical School. The question had not been raised, to the Author's knowledge, at any prior Hearing. His answer, along with Congressman Walker's (PA) quick question, is compelling.

> **Carney:** If aspirin were unknown to the medical community today, and someone found or discovered aspirin in a clinical atmosphere in one of our leading universities, attached to a research medical facility, could you project how long it might be before aspirin would be put on the market or if, indeed, it would ever get on the market?
>
> **Dr. McMahon:** I think it's a classical question, and I'll give you the classical answer. It may surprise you. Yes, I think it would get on the market, but it would be for which claim? If you want to prove it lowers fever, you would get it on the market in 7 to 10 years and spend $50 million. If you want to prove it relieves pain in arthritic patients, that would be double those costs. If you want to get the claim that it is anti-inflammatory, you do the studies all over in inflammatory disease like rheumatoid arthritis. If you want to prove its antiplatelet adhesiveness properties diminish coronary

artery disease, you might be spending billions of dollars, I think, and virtually no one can afford to do those kinds of studies, that indeed people are benefited by taking two to four aspirin tablets a day after having had a single heart attack, which many doctors in this country believe. I think the FDA now believes the data and has made this concession to the aspirin manufacturers.

So I think it would be a very difficult thing, but I think it really would get on the market, yes, sir, sooner or later.

Mr. Carney: That's amazing, though, when you consider the cost and the time involved in that, to get that drug on the market.

***

Mr. Walker: Just one follow-up question, if I could, on that. How much would aspirin likely cost the consumer after going through that whole process that you described?

Dr. McMahon: Fifty cents a pill, as a guess. It would be outrageous.

Mr. Carney: And they're 89 cents for 250.

Dr. McMahon: The patient ultimately pays. With the continued studies necessary, you're only hurting patients in the long run. You're hurting sick people.

And so it continued. Surprisingly, the FDA was not represented. Big Pharma provided testimony from Upjohn and from Hoffman-LaRoche.

The Roche representative, Richard Faust, ended his prepared statement with what was the industry's consistent position:

> If we recognize that the drug development process now ranges from 7 to 10 to 13 years, depending on the drug substance, that means that for any new pharmaceutical to emerge during the decade of the eighties, if we are to have a breakthrough in the eighties, that compound must be in the development stream, in the development process, today.

***

Oftentimes at these hearings and in other discussions, we talk about those who are the stakeholders in the process, and whether we're talking about the geriatric population or the orphan drug population or other groups, it occurs to me that there is frequently

one stakeholder that is never mentioned. That is the stakeholder
represented by your children's children and their children; in
other words future generations. I think we have to preserve the
incentives within the private sector to maintain and develop basic
exploratory research programs which are now under pressure in
many pharmaceutical firms. We need to preserve this investment in
basic research so that we will have the drugs of the future, which
as you know sometimes take as long as 15 to 20 years from the
time of the original research until the final product emanates from
the laboratory.

Congressman Gore adjourned the Hearing with the hope that, "We can
come up with sensible recommendations that will improve the process at
the FDA".

Senator Fountain Again (136)

Senator L. H. Fountain continued the theme of Congressman Gore's
Hearing, in his own Hearing, "The Regulation of New Drugs by the Food
and Drug Administration: The New Drug Review Process". (*The Reader is
reminded that this Hearing was held 20 years after passage of the 1962 Drug
Amendments. [Chapter 6]*)

This time the FDA was there in force with Dr. Arthur Hull Hayes, the
new Commissioner, his Deputy Chief Counsel, Dr. Frances Kelsey (The
"heroine" of the thalidomide tragedy), and two other FDA directors.

> Congressman Fountain set the stage:
> Since 1964, the subcommittee has periodically examined the
> performance of the Food and Drug Administration, FDA, in pro-
> tecting the public from unsafe or ineffective new drugs. Few
> governmental activities affect the public's health more than those
> involved in determining whether powerful new drug products are
> safe and effective human use.
> Today the subcommittee begins oversight hearings on the Food
> and Drug Administration's current policies and procedures for
> regulating the clinical investigation of new unapproved drugs and
> for evaluating applications for marketing new drug products.
> The perception of how FDA exercises its responsibilities
> in this area is analogous to the proverbial blind man describing

an elephant. Those interests favoring the quick approval of newly developed drugs tend to view FDA as a timid or obstructionist bureaucracy, and sometimes allege the existence of a "drug lag" in the United States as compared with other countries. On the other hand, those concerned by the adverse effects of powerful new drugs or the prescribing of expensive new products which are no better than drugs already on the market may view FDA as overly anxious to please the medical community or business interests.

Commissioner Hayes began with a listing of new and planned improvements in the Drug-approval process and pointed to recent (1979) Legislation designed to "streamline" the approval process. Despite the Hearing's title, testimony seeped over into other areas giving rise to some interesting testimony. The issue was Promotion of Drugs, still in the IND stage, as "safe and useful for purposes under which it is under investigation". Dr. Peter Rheinstein who was with the FDA Bureau of Drugs was present and quoted the Regulation:

> This regulation is not intended to restrict the full exchange of scientific information concerning the drug, including dissemination of scientific findings and scientific or lay communications media. Its sole intent is to restrict promotional claims of safety or effectiveness by the sponsor while the drug is under investigation to establish its safety or effectiveness.

It had been reported that one Drug had been favorably mentioned in a film shown at a convention cocktail party.

> **Mr. Fountain:** This said that it was safe and effective, and this was prior to the drug's approval. That was at the cocktail party.
> **Dr. Rheinstein:** Right. That was at the cocktail party. That was part of a meeting of the ARA, the American Rheumatism Association. If the presentation had been part of the giving of a paper by the investigator, we clearly would not have objected. Now you start to make gradations of that. How about if the statement is made as part of a separate meeting which is immediately adjacent to the American Rheumatism Association which is included in the program of the American Rheumatism Association? Does that bring it within the purview of FDA regulation? There are numerous

meetings of that type which discuss a particular product and which are sponsored by a particular company held as part of scientific study meetings.

How about if you serve wine and cheese? How about if you go a step further---

Mr. Fountain: I do not know how big a cocktail party it was or how many people were there.

The Congress works in mysterious ways!

These Hearing's Proceedings, with testimony, exhibits, and letters, occupied nearly 700 pages. The final day was marked by Commissioner Hayes' statement that this was his first Hearing but would probably be his last. He left in September 1983, and he was replaced in 1984 by Dr. Frank Young.

Claude Pepper for the Old Folks (142)

This Hearing was the work, jointly, of both the House and Senate Committees on Aging. Congressman Pepper served as Chairman of the Subcommittee on Aging and Long-Term Care. Pepper, from Florida, was long active in affairs dealing with the elderly. The late John McCain (AZ) and the late John Glenn (OH) served on the various committees, as did David Pryor (AR), about whom we will hear more. Also, on the Subcommittee was Congresswoman Geraldine Ferraro, one-time candidate for Vice-President.

Big Pharma was absent, having declined an invitation. Their absence was noted on several occasions during the Hearings by Pepper. FDA's Mark Novitch described some of the problems with drugs for the elderly.

> I appreciate this opportunity, Mr. Chairman, to discuss an issue which is of deep concern to all of us, and that is the safe use of drugs in older Americans. I would like to discuss four major areas in which FDA is playing an active role in improving the use of drugs in the elderly. In each of these areas, FDA has already taken what I think are important steps to deal with existing problems and to identify and deal with future ones.
>
> The first is increasing our knowledge of the effects of drugs in the elderly. That problem has two aspects. One is the participation of elderly subjects in drug investigations. We need to be sure that any drug with potential usefulness in the elderly is, in fact, studied in that population, and that special parameters, such as decreased

kidney function, which is common in the elderly, are appropriately evaluated. Second, we need to be sure that this information is included in drug labeling, so that physicians who treat the elderly will have it available to them.

***

Novitch described efforts to improve the Drug knowledge of the elderly:

There is a third activity which we believe can also promote the safer use of drugs in the elderly, and that is patient education. We are just beginning a new approach to provide drug information directly to the elderly. In July, in fact, next week, an FDA patient education insert will accompany all social security checks that will reach as many as 36 million people. The insert will alert these people to the kinds of information that they should have about prescription drugs, and will advise them to ask their physician or pharmacist about their medication. The insert also offers a free brochure, entitled, *"Here Are Some Things You Should Know About Prescription Drugs"*, if the patient writes to the Government's Consumer Information Center.

Of course, the patient or her caregiver had to write to get the information. That is not the same as a PPI which the patient would receive with the prescription.

Dr. Novitch had been at pains to explain the reasons that the FDA was not pursuing the PPI idea. Chairman John Heinz (PA) was not satisfied.

Chairman Heinz: All right. Well, Dr. Novitch, you are clearly a very bright and able man. I have to tell you, I think there probably is more that you could be doing—I am not saying you are not doing anything. I do question the judgment of you and your associates, however, in abandoning totally even an attempt to test the pilot program on patient package inserts. But you have been forthright enough to say that you will get back to us with a policy decision on whether or not you will test that. I would strongly urge you to do so. I think your position of simply dropping it without any better analysis than you have given is totally indefensible, and at real variance with a lot of tests that we have made, in other very difficult public policy areas.

Novitch quickly responded that the FDA was neither opposed to PPIs nor had they abandoned the idea.

Unusual testimony was provided by Dr. Jerome Avorn, a Professor of Social Medicine at Harvard. He described a Harvard program of "undetailing" and "unadvertising" in which an attempt was made to provide physicians, as he put it, "to provide a neutral voice in the cacophony of claims that reach physicians". More revolutionary was his suggestion that physicians receiving medical reimbursement be required to pass "a rather simple, straightforward test" to demonstrate knowledge of the particular Drug needs of their elderly patients. Dr. Avorn acknowledged that in the past, such a requirement would be "unthinkable". He got *that* right!!

The Hearing was adjourned, as T S. Elliot wrote in *The Hollow Men*, "not with a bang but a whimper."

Zomax in the Spotlight (179)

This Hearing, under the Chairmanship of Congressman Ted Weiss (NV), was devoted exclusively to Zomax, its competitors, and narcotics. The Proceedings are notable for the eloquent discourse on pain provided by Dr. Ellen Bernstein, a practicing ophthalmologist and herself a cancer victim. She was a fan of Zomax.

> In February 1981, I had a mastectomy for breast cancer. The disease had spread to local lymph nodes so I was treated with chemotherapy for one year. Up this point no pain, no ZOMAX. Two months after the chemotherapy was complete, I leaned over to pick something up and felt like I had been knifed in the back. Over the next few months, I developed more main in the back, as well as pain in one hip, my shoulders and several ribs. Various x-ray studies revealed that all of these problems were due to the spread of the cancer.
>
> Pain is something everyone has experienced whether it's a headache, a toothache or a Charlie horse. How an individual reacts to the pain and what is needed to treat it depends as much on the reason for the pain as on the severity of the pain. A backache you have after a Sunday spent raking the lawn, reminds you of a job well done; you've earned an evening with your feet up and a pain pill that makes you a little sleepy.

A Pryor Engagement

David Pryor headed the Committee on Aging, having followed Senator Harris into that position. He chaired two Hearings in July and November, 1989. The umbrella term for the two sessions left little doubt over what to expect, "Skyrocketing Prescription Drug Prices". The individual sessions were named, respectively, "Are We Getting Our Money's Worth" and "Turning a Bad Deal into a Good Deal".

Big Pharma, remembering, perhaps, the days of Kefauver was represented by only a single company – Amgen. Pryor noted right away that 17 other companies (which he named) had been invited but declined. Pryor expressed indignant surprise over their absence. Nevertheless, Gerald Mossinghoff, now President of PMA, was an active participant.

Pryor used the "no-show" of the Drug companies as an opportunity to castigate them in their absence during his opening statement. One company had declined saying, "We believe that a hearing is not an appropriate forum in which to elucidate the many complex issues you raise". Pryor wondered "what the proper setting might be?"

Pryor listed the "usual suspects", with charts: "me too" Drugs, Price increases, and differential Prices for different customers. He illustrated the latter point with some comments on Motrin (which was then still prescription only). He also had a folksy note about the pharmacist.

> [Demonstrating bottle of Motrin.]
> **The Chairman:** Here's what Medicare would pay for that Motrin: $29. Here's what the hospital pays, $8 for the same bottle. Here's what the Department of Veteran's Affairs pays, $5. So we see a vast range of price variation between the various prices that the drug manufacturers charge to these prospective customers.
> Let me also state that the local pharmacist at the local drug store, the person who is out there in the trenches every day, in the foxhole, *selling drugs* to Aunt Minnie and Cousin Joe and whoever, this druggist is the one who has to almost on a weekly or monthly basis tell those consumers that their prices are going up yet once again. Now, why is it that we're seeing those tremendous price increases when the druggist himself, as we will see later in another chart, is receiving only a few pennies, only a few cents more, for a prescription which is backed up by Medicare and other governmental programs?

Congressman John Warner (VA) was worried.

> **Senator Warner:** I'm still concerned about the uniqueness of this marketplace. What about foreign competition? We've watched the American television industry. We started it, we built it, and we lost it. Automobiles—we started, we built it, and we darned near lost it. We're getting it back. Now, we've got a great industry here, before Congress gets in and meddles around perhaps with laws and regulations. I'd hate to see us lose the quality that we're getting. Maybe the price isn't good, but nobody's arguing quality, are they? We've got the best in the world.

Pryor had made a point in his "me too" statement of the FDA's classification system for new Drugs. Class A represents a "significant contribution to existing therapies", Class B is a "modest contribution", and Class C is "little or no contribution", to which Pryor added – "except to the bottom line of a profit and loss statement". He noted that, between 1981 and 1988, 84% of new Drugs were classified as "C" Drugs by the FDA.

Mossinghoff had a strong rebuttal on that point.

> **Mr. Mossinghoff:** First, I would respectfully submit, and it's with great respect, Mr. Chairman, that the me-too factor chart is pretty misleading. The ratings of A, B, and C are set by the Food and Drug Administration. A *priori,* when a drug comes in, they set that and it determines how it paces through the FDA.
>
> In the C category are whole new classes of drugs: ACE Inhibitors, for example, approved during the 1980's and Calcium Channel Blockers, which could very well obviate very expensive bypass surgery. On one of your charts that I saw, you had Zantac, and well you should, because that's the highest volume drug sold in the world. That was a 1-C drug when it went to the FDA. So I would submit that although your figures are obviously accurate, they are based on this *priori* rating set at the beginning of the time before they've had any serious review, and they don't recalibrate it, because all it is a method for pacing drugs through. These so-called drugs, and that's clearly something of a pejorative term that is used, have enormous differences in terms of side effects and profiles. Many people can tolerate one drug in a certain class, but not another. So I don't think the medical profession would regard

these "me-too" drugs as anything like a superfluous addition. They'd regard them as a valuable part of the armamentarium.

The Hearings were a bit unusual in that the majority (11 of 18) of the Committee members made opening statements. Notable names, still around at the time of this writing, were: Harry Reid, "Chuck" Grassley, John Warner, and Bill Bradley. Two statements referred to the Medicare Catastrophic Care Act which had just been passed. Congressman Grassley noted that there were reassessments of the Act because of potential Drug costs. The Congressman expressed hope of repeal. In fact, it *was* repealed (see Chapter 4).

The first session of the Pryor Hearings (July 18, 1989) had called only eight witnesses, as did the second session on November 16. This session included testimony from two representatives of the Belgian Consumers Association to explain Price differentials between Europe and the United States. Two elderly citizens described briefly their difficulties with Drugs and their Prices. The Executive Director of the People with Aids Health Group detailed problems with Drug Prices affecting their members.

I want to conclude this with an observation. The two sessions of the Pryor Hearings lasted, respectively, three hours and forty-three minutes and two hours and fifty-one minutes – a total of about six and half hours. Yet, these two sessions generated 800 pages of Proceedings. I leave it to the Reader to ponder just what this signifies. The Pryor Hearings are not different from the other Investigations in this regard.

The Task Force on Prescription Drugs (395)

The foregoing has provided, I hope, a good feeling for the nature, findings, politics, and results of an array of Congressional Hearings in the middle and late twentieth century. There were more, and as of this writing, Hearings on Drug pricing are underway under the Chairmanship of Congressman Isaiah Cummings (MD). That there will be more seems certain. But a chapter in Drug Investigations would not be complete without an account of the work of the Task Force (TF) on Prescription Drugs. A Book-length description including details of the TF Investigations and conclusions is available in *Prescription Drugs under Medicare* and *The Legacy of the Task Force on Prescription Drugs* edited by this Author (7). Also available are six publications of the TF:

- Final Report
- Approaches to Drug insurance design
- American and foreign Drugs
- Drug makers and Drug distribution
- Drug prescribers
- Drug users

The collection totaled 667 pages and was edited by Dr. Milton Silverman, a well-respected economist, and was said by Dr. T. Donald Rucker to "represent a singular achievement both as a conventional effort and as an accomplishment within the Federal Bureaucracy".

It *was that*! And the late Dr. Rucker should know! Rucker, a Ph.D. economist and later Pharmacy academician, came to the TF on detail from the Social Security Administration where he had been examining Drug insurance design. In many ways, Don Rucker was the "architect" of the Report or at least the construction foreman.

In September 1968, Dr. Philip Lee had presented the Interim Report of the TF to the Nelson Subcommittee. In February 19, 1969, he announced in a written statement that the TF Report was complete. He wrote that the charge to the TF had been "to determine whether it is both necessary and feasible to include prescription Drugs as a benefit in the Medicare Program". The answer, he wrote, was "an unequivocal yes". Dr. Lee, who had served as Chairman of the TF, submitted a written statement as he was leaving his job as Assistant Secretary for Health and Scientific Affairs at HEW to assume the post of Chancellor at the University of California Medical Center.

Readers will note that there was consensus, following such extensive study, that a Medicare prescription Drug benefit plan was both needed and practical. But no such benefit plan was provided. It was not until 1988 that Congress passed Legislation providing the long awaited benefit program. The Medicare Catastrophic Protection Act of 1987 included prescription medications. In 1989, the Medicare Catastrophic Coverage *Repeal* Act was passed. The story of this extraordinary set of actions by Congress could fill a Book.

The TF provided 48 "Findings" and 25 "Recommendations". A summary of the TF Research, Findings, and Conclusions follows.

Research, Findings, and Recommendations

The call for a comprehensive study of the problems associated with prescription Drug benefits led the TF to examine many related issues as well.

Consequently, a total of 48 findings and 25 recommendations was put forward. These pertained to Drug coverage, the quality of care associated with prescribed medications, the economic use of resources, professional education and proficiency, regulatory considerations at the federal and State level, and federal Policy pertaining to pharmaceuticals in general. In short, the TF recognized that optimal Drug benefit design could not be realized within the context of the insurance model and that analysis of the complex infrastructure underlying the role of prescribed medications in our society was also necessary.

Drug Benefits for the Aged

The TF reported that many persons 65 years of age and older lacked financial resources to pay for prescribed medicines. Therefore, a need existed for an out-of-hospital insurance program under Medicare. Moreover, such a program "has been shown to be economically feasible in many countries", although "no single method will by itself guarantee program efficiency, but without at least two features – reasonable formulary restrictions and effective data processing procedures – program controls will be ineffective".

Although some 28 findings pertaining to a Drug benefit for ambulatory patients under Medicare were put forward, the TF failed to make a formal recommendation to this effect. Only the transmittal letter from Dr. Lee to the Secretary specified "that such a program be instituted". However, the TF did recommend that more effective methods be found to determine the AAC of pharmaceutical products.

Quality of Care – Drug Use Process

The TF found that prescriber decisions were often suboptimal and believed that cooperation among Health professionals, suppliers, and Government could contribute to more rational prescribing. In addition, it clarified the distinctions between chemical, biological, and clinical equivalents and reported that "lack of clinical equivalency among chemical equivalents meeting all official standards has been grossly exaggerated...." Moreover, the TF enumerated certain criteria for implementing a sound formulary while noting that the exclusion of "certain combination products, duplicative Drugs, and noncritical products from federal reimbursement would "contribute significantly" to both rational and prescribing and reduced program cost.

Economic Issues

The TF observed that much of the Drug industry's research and development activities appeared "to provide only minor contributions to medical progress". The economic sequelae associated with this result include a waste of skilled resources and a confusing proliferation of Drug products that combined to produce a burden on patients or taxpayers who ultimately must pay the costs. Further, the exceptionally high rate of profits attained by large manufacturers was not accompanied by excessive risk or the inability to attract capital.

Use of low-cost chemical equivalents, when of high quality, could yield savings of approximately 5% at the retail level. Finally, cooperative efforts on the part of professional associations and consumer groups are needed to help patients obtain better information on local prescription Prices.

Professional Education/Proficiency

The inability of most physicians to question their competency in making therapeutic judgments was lamented by the TF. It recommended development of curricula in medical and Pharmacy schools to train pharmacists as Drug information specialists on the Health team. It stressed the desirability of strengthening Pharmacy education along with preparation of Pharmacy aides to provide their professional superiors with more time to engage in clinical functions. HEW should strengthen the teaching of clinical pharmacology in medical schools and support continuing education for physicians regarding rational prescribing.

Government Regulatory Duties

The TF recommended that all products licensed for distribution in interstate commerce be subject to the quality control standards established by the FDA and that this Agency be provided with adequate financial resources to command internal and external expertise to exercise its scientific and regulatory responsibilities. In addition, it recommended that the FDA establish intramural clinical and laboratory research capabilities to help attract and retain the best scientific personnel. It also specified the need to study whether three classifications – new Drugs and "not new" Drugs, certifiable products, and biologics – were appropriate to ensure uniform quality. Finally, the TF recommended that HEW support studies on pharmacist licensure and reciprocity to facilitate expanded functions for these professionals and to ensure, rather than impede, fair competition.

Federal Policy

The TF found that a permanent mechanism is needed at the federal level to collect, analyze, and exchange information and to provide effective coordination of Drug-related activities, such as uniform standards of quality, among the agencies involved. However, it found no need to centralize all Drug-related functions within the department. As a result, the regulatory, discovery, manpower, and scientific information divisions of HEW would remain largely as organized.

The TF recommended establishment of a Federal Interdepartmental Health Policy Council to coordinate all federal prescription Drug purchase and reimbursement programs. It also recommended adoption of a standardized Drug Code (to facilitate efficiency in processing prescription Drug claims) and surveillance of Drug costs, prescription Prices, and rug use by the Social Security Administration.

The Dunlop Report on the Task Force

As the *Final Report* of the TF was being issued, a new administration took office in Washington. On March 24, 1969, Secretary Robert H. Finch asked a diverse group of 17 leaders from outside the Government to assist him in determining the course of action regarding selected aspects of the TF's work.

Within a period of 4 months, and without staff support, Dr. John T. Dunlop, Professor of Political Economy at Harvard, had elicited a response from each of his Review Committee members covering four basic questions: (1) the feasibility of adding prescription Drug coverage to Medicare, (2) federal Policy pertaining to chemical/biological/clinical equivalency, (3) economic matters related to Drug manufacturing and distribution, and (4) methods for improving the flow of information regarding Drugs to practicing physicians.

With only one dissent, the Review Committee concluded that the Medicare program should be expanded to include Drug benefits and that HEW should develop more detailed plans concerning program Regulations, data processing procedures, and cost computations necessary for legislative consideration. However, the Committee noted that (1) limitation of benefits to chronic disease treatments was neither advisable nor administrable, (2) age limitation above 65 was undesirable, (3) a deductible should be avoided because of the record-keeping burden it placed on patients, (4) copayment was preferable to coinsurance, and (5) only a "purely advisory national formulary...might possibly be appropriate". The Drug program should be built around copayment (with perhaps an annual ceiling beyond which the patient could be reimbursed), vendor payment based on a flat dispensing fee, coverage under Part A, and utilization review.

When the Review Committee confronted the major economic questions, there was general agreement that (1) pharmaceutical manufacturers' profits are high, relative to other industries; (2) a study should be made of Price differentials that exist when products are sold to various types of buyers; and (3) patients need better information about prescription Prices. The Committee recommended that the department support research to improve the efficiency of community and hospital Pharmacy operations and generally prohibit reimbursement of physician-owned repackaging companies. However, there was less agreement among Committee members regarding the TF finding concerning duplicate and wasteful research by Drug manufacturers.

The work of the TF represented the first systematic attempt by the administrative branch of the federal Government to define and evaluate major Public Policy issues associated with Drug use and insurance beyond the traditional regulatory matters pertaining to product purity, safety, and efficacy. In this endeavor, the TF made available the first national profile of Drug use among the elderly; defined rational prescribing; documented the prevalence of irrational prescribing; and stressed the contribution that Drug utilization review could make, first in reducing inappropriate prescribing and second in controlling program cost. The TF also put forward a number of innovative proposals, such as the idea that exclusive rights to a product's trademark should last no longer than the Patent, that Drug program design should be simple enough that the patients do not become unduly burdened in obtaining benefits, and that Drug programs under Medicare and Medicaid be coordinated.

The Dunlop Report added credence to the TF Report. Nevertheless, Dr. Rucker, the "insider" on the TF, highlighted a number of flaws in the TF studies and conclusions. These are discussed in his chapter of *Prescription Drugs under Medicare* (7).

Dr. Lee himself left the Subcommittee with a lengthy written statement in which he expressed his personal concerns gained from his leadership of the TF, finishing with –

> In conclusion, Mr. Chairman, I would like to state my conviction that the problems facing the medical profession in the use of prescription drugs must be solved by doctors themselves. We can benefit greatly from the attention that has been drawn to the problems of drugs in our society. But I doubt that any solution that comes from outside of the profession, or that lacks the understanding and support of physicians can produce the changes that are urgently needed in medical education, prescribing practices, and the protection of the American people.
>
> But there is growing evidence that physicians—and medical students—are deeply concerned, and I expect that this concern will be evidenced in support of measures both public and private to help assure that the medical profession—**not the makers and sellers of the drugs**—will retain its critical responsibilities in this area.

Conclusion

The Congress has seen fit to investigate many aspects of Big Pharma and its products. The printed Proceedings run to upward of 100,000 pages. I am fortunate to have hard copies of many of them and they make interesting reading. They are by turns fascinating, sometimes boring, and often repetitive. They are filled with political posturing, defensive arguments, and a good deal of acrimony. As this is being written, there are more underway or planned (threatened).

I have focused on a few of the more well-known Investigations, but noted others. Obviously it is impossible, in this space, adequately to summarize all of the testimony and exhibits contained in the printed Proceedings. Faced with that impossibility, I provide some of the flavor of the Hearings as well as any resulting Legislation and subsequent Regulations. Many others have addressed these "goings on" and they are referenced, as are each of the Hearings on which I have touched.

As I stated at the outset of this chapter, its contents are by no means a complete account of every Congressional Investigation of the Drug industry.

Hearings were not so numerous in the final few years of the twentieth century. Some of the most vigorous investigators had died. No Kefauver or Nelson had emerged, but, as noted, the new century seems certain to find new and vigorous Investigations. In Chapter 4, we will show the lines between Legislation and these Investigations – their Constitutional precursors.

In Mark Antony's eulogy for Julius Caesar, Shakespeare has him say, Four times, that Brutus "is an honorable man". There is frequently such irony in exchanges in the Hearing Room.

Laid upon the Congressional Record are myriad exhibits, formal written statements, and letters intended to buttress the give and take of the testimony and questions. One can only wonder to what extent they are ever read. Certainly the Honorable Members don't have the time. Perhaps the staffers do.

Chapter 4
Legislators and Legislation

Introduction

Not all Investigations lead or led to specific laws. Some of them cited specific targets. For instance, S-105, H.R. 210, was cited. Some never achieved their original goal (Kefauver being an obvious example) and certainly many pieces of Legislation were not preceded by specific Hearings.

Perhaps a couple of quotes will serve to set the stage:

> If it is not necessary that there be a law, it is necessary that there not be a law.
>
> *(Lord Acton)*

And,

> Laws are like sausages. It is better not seeing them made.
>
> *(Otto Von Bismarck)*

May as well, add another:

> Lawyers are the only persons whose ignorance of the law is not punished.
>
> *(Jeremy Bentham)*

Oh, well, one more:

> First thing we do, let's kill all the lawyers.
>
> *(Shakespeare – Henry VI)*

Of course not all members of Congress are lawyers, far from it. But all, at one time or another, must vote on the laws. And, as Avorn (234), observed, there was so much litigation to finally find that the Drug, Bendectin, was *not* a teratogen (birth defects), it was definitely a *tortogen*.

The general process by which a law is finally enacted is thoroughly and concisely outlined in Fulda and Wertheimer (56). The laws which directly affect the Drug industry, the Drugs themselves, and those that prescribe and use them are many. Some, more general, laws affect virtually all business.

An incomplete, but representative, listing of Federal laws affecting business in general and the Drug industry specifically is contained in Table 4.1. Before discussing some of the specifics, some general comments can be made.

Alderson has pointed out that "despite our tradition of a free market, a very large portion of all the goods of commerce involves some kind of interference with market forces, interference either tolerated or created by government agencies" (322). No segment of marketing activities is untouched by some sort of legal or quasi-legal controls.

In addition to the more formal controls of Law and Regulation, our society has found additional informal means of imposing its will upon any recalcitrant industry. Separate texts could be (and have been) written on the subject of these external controls alone. The treatment here will have

Table 4.1 Federal Laws Affecting the Drug Industry

Legislation	Year Passed
General applicability	
Sherman Anti-trust Act	1890
Federal Trade Commission Act	1914
Clayton Act	1914
Robinson–Patman Act	1936
Miller–Tydings Act	1937
Wheeler–Lea Act	1938
Lanham Trademark Act	1946

to be, because of the breadth of the subject matter, more descriptive than analytical – and, limited.

A great deal of Legislation and resulting Regulation has been enacted to affect business. Much of this affects marketing at least indirectly. For example, the laws of incorporation have such an indirect effect. Some Legislation and Regulation are specifically aimed at control of *marketing* activities. Thus, we see laws affecting advertising, pricing, and types of competition. Finally, there are legal controls which affect specifically the Drug industry and some which are aimed directly at pharmaceutical marketing practice.

Drugs are among the most regulated of commodities in the United States and in most other countries. Drugs are regulated through various and diverse laws at the national, State, and local levels. Laws result in Regulations that affect the activities of manufacturers, growers, and consumers. They also control the intermediaries which exist between consumers and producers of Drugs or Drug components. Often these laws duplicate, overlap, and are in conflict with each other. They may sometimes seem incomprehensible and lacking in general governing principles. Closer examination shows, however, that general principles regulating Drug supply and demand *do* exist and that the system also tolerates many exceptions to the overall plan of Regulation and control.

Laws and Policy

A country's Health Care laws can be assumed to reflect its Policy. Thus, a review of the laws affecting the role of Drugs in the nations should logically mirror its Policy even though that Policy is not explicitly stated. (Whether or not it does so is addressed elsewhere in this Book.) Likewise, that Policy should reflect the wishes of the People.

There is a social overlay that affects society's views and goals in Health. Historically, People have tended to be satisfied with medical care of the curative or "crisis" type. Medicine has been importantly affected by major discoveries that have allowed a shift in emphasis from an almost exclusive concentration on diagnosis and treatment to a much broader approach that includes the prevention of disease and rehabilitation from its effects.

Our society has become better informed on Health matters, and its stated goals reflect a more knowledgeable Public. Freedom from disease has been expanded to include the desire to live in a State of well-being. The Public no longer regards medical care as only a means of *restoring* Health; this care is now considered to include the means for *maintaining* good Health. It is now expected that the highest quality of medical protection should be available and accessible to all of the People when they are sick or when they are well.

A further comparison of patients as individuals and in the broader social context is provided by the data I have compiled in Table 4.2. These data reflect responses of more than 10,000 People (221) regarding what individual patients and their responding Health Care systems should do in an ideal system. Although the two lists are not incompatible, obviously compromises are needed.

The ultimate test of a business or its industry is its social relevance. Clearly, the pharmaceutical industry is socially relevant. The relevance of an individual firm or its individual products is ultimately determined by those in the marketplace.

In the final analysis, it is society itself that controls all marketing activities. The principal means of control resides in the decision to buy or not to buy. This is the most potent form of Regulation. Since the People elect the legislators, they do, indirectly, enact the laws as well. In fact, control by Regulation is probably the farthest removed from the People.

The average layperson does not, of course, have sufficient information to decide the merits of all of the controls imposed on marketing. In many cases, she does not even have enough knowledge to appraise the value of the products that this marketing activity brings.

Table 4.2 What Patients and the Health Care System Should Do

What People Believe Patients Should Do	What People Believe the Health Care System Should Do
Responsibility	
Risk-related behavior: be responsible for the consequences of their own lifestyle *Personal responsibility*: offer Rx compliance *Financial obligation*: pay for elective care	*Civic issues*: offer support for unexpected crises *Financial obligation*: pay in the event of a crises
Fairness	
Convenience: have Health Care services close and information readily available	*Universal access*: offer care of equal quality *Community issues*: give sense of caring and support *Convenience*: make services accessible

(*Continued*)

Table 4.2 (*Continued*) What Patients and the Health Care System Should Do

What People Believe Patients Should Do	*What People Believe the Health Care System Should Do*
Affordability and Efficiency	
Cost/benefit/value: have information about the cost and effectiveness of treatment *Prudence*: recognize the limits of their care *Simplicity*: have understandable information	*Accountability*: identify good performers *Cost/benefit/value*: benefit the whole *Productivity*: minimize waste *Prudence*: Act intelligently for personal and national interests *Affordability*: Price services affordably *Simplicity*: make the system more consumer friendly
Dignity	
Caring: receive emotional support from providers *Compassion*: receive understanding and patience *Trust/honesty*: be able to cultivate personal relationships with providers *Respect*: have providers accept wishes	*Humaneness*: help patients avoid pain and suffering *Caring*: view its caregivers' role as "healers" rather than "doctors" *Compassion*: understand patient etiology *Trust/honesty*: offer accurate, honest, information.
Choice	
Information: be allowed more individual decision-making with patients *Control*: have some control over Health outcomes *Informed consent*: be given the opportunity to investigate in advance of decisions *Personal responsibility*: be permitted a choice, such as to accept or reject treatments	*Information*: make decisions in cooperation *Control*: cede some control to patients *Informed consent*: give patients full information for Health Care decisions *Personal issues*: allow patients to select providers *Autonomy*: allow patients to make decisions
Quality	
Quality of life: maintain their quality of life *Quality of care*: receive the best individual care and attention *Technical excellence*: have access to the best and latest technology. *Healing/caring*: have providers who are understanding and supportive	*Quality of life*: make quality paramount *Quality of care*: give the best care possible and offer a hospitable environment *Technical excellence*: adopt techniques that improve *Healing/caring*: make system more approachable

The laws which lead to regulating Drugs in this country, regardless of their level (federal, State, or local), can be categorized under several general kinds specifically designed to relate to Drugs and Drug-related products:

1. Laws governing the record of movement of Drugs and related items through various distribution channels.
2. Laws governing the information content of Drug labeling.
3. Laws defining the qualifications of persons responsible for both the movement of Drugs through the various distribution channels.
4. Laws defining the scope of the legal duty owed by the various practitioners involved in the provision of Drugs and Drug-related services.
5. Laws regulating the quality and nature of a Drug and its container.
6. Laws defining the punishment and/or civil penalty for non-compliance with medication law.
7. Laws affecting the supply and demand of Drugs by direct and indirect controls on internal and external competitive practices.
8. Laws directing that certain categories of the Public be provided with Drugs dependent only on their categorical membership.

This discussion will only indirectly and peripherally consider the fundamental question of why Drugs have been selected and isolated for their intensity of Regulation. However, some brief comments about this fairly modern State of affairs have been and will be made.

With regard to the Durham Humphrey Amendments (see following), there was a basic question of the Government's right to restrict access to a commodity – "legend" Drugs. Drugs are not the only commodity so limited. Various State laws prescribe age limits on access to alcohol, for example.

The question here was not whether this vast reclassification of legend Drugs should be undertaken but what degree of individual control is to be exchanged for some increased measure of Health. Ultimately, the ends which can be achieved through current technological means may not be those which a society should strive toward. Friedson has succinctly and lucidly summarized this point (102).

> A profession and a society which are so concerned with physical and functional well-being as to sacrifice civil liberty and moral integrity must inevitably press for a scientific environment similar to that provided laying hens on chicken farms—hens who produce eggs industrially and have no disease or other cares.

The fact is that laws have been, and will be, passed which affect Drugs: those who make them and those who use them. We will examine only a few as a comprehensive treatment of all as it is definitely BSTB (Beyond the Scope of the Book). A list of specific Legislation is provided in Table 4.3.

Table 4.3 Selected Legislation Specific to the Drug Industry

Legislation	Year Enacted
Food and Drug Act	1902
Harrison Narcotic Act	1914
Federal Food, Drug and Cosmetics Act	1938
Durham–Humphrey Amendment	1951
Drug Amendments of 1962 (Kefauver)	1962
Drug Industry Anti-trust Act	1962
Physician Ownership in Pharmacies and Drug Companies	1964
Drug Abuse Control Amendments	1965
Medical Restraint of Trade Act	1967
Controlled Substances Act	1970
Food and Drug Administration Act	1972
Drug Regulation Reform Act	1978
Patent Term Restoration Act	1981
Orphan Drug Act	1983
Price Competition/Patent Restoration Act	1984
Drug Export Amendment Act (Waxman–Hatch)	1986
Medicare Catastrophic Protection Act	1988
Repeal of Medicine Catastrophic Protection Act	1989
Prudent Pharmaceutical Purchasing Act	1990
Prescription Drug User Fee Act	1992
Prescription Drugs in Social Security Act	1993
FDA Modernization Act	1997
Medicare Prescription Drug Improvement and Modernization Act	2003
Comprehensive Addiction Act	2016
Prescription Drug Cost Reduction Act	2019 (pending)

Bills and Sponsors

In the previous chapter, we highlighted some of the major Hearings which ostensibly are held to gather information necessary for informed Legislation, when Hearings result in Legislation proposals. The latter takes the form of a Bill. Such Bills are quite detailed.

Senate Bill 255 was proposed during a Hearing on April 30, 1981. Senator Strom Thurmond (SC) chaired the Committee on the Judiciary before which the Hearings were held. It is notable that Senators Orrin Hatch and Edward Kennedy were members of the Committee, but neither were in attendance at the Hearing. It is also notable that, just before the end of the Hearing (then) Senator Joseph Biden asked that his name be added as a co-sponsor.

The Hearing lasted only three and one-half hours but generated 304 pages of testimony, prepared statements, and exhibits. Late in the Hearing, Senator Grassley (IA) wanted each of the witnesses to state their position.

> S.255 provides a regulatory review period to be calculated for each product and then an equal amount of time is to be added to the life of that product's patent. In your opinion, when should their regulatory review period begin and when should it end?

Within the 2 weeks during which the Hearing record was kept open, all of the 12 witnesses had responded in writing. An additional 20 comments were received for sources not represented as witnesses. Some few responses were simply an endorsement of the Bill as written, but most had specific suggestion too detailed to recount here. There was testimony from two witnesses, however, which bear specific attention.

The first is the testimony of William F. Haddad representing the Generic Drug industry. The reason for its inclusion here is found in his own words.

> If you will, permit me a moment of total candor and a little impertinence.
> My reaction to these hearings, Senator, can be summed up in the thought that came to me when I was writing this testimony. If the late Senator Kefauver could hear of these proceedings, he would turn over in his grave.
> You are being blandly presented with the identical, discredited arguments that Senator's Kefauver and Long effectively fought 5 years ago, 10 years ago, 15 years ago, and 20 years ago.

> Over the 20 years since the Congress last acted, all attempts to help the small entrepreneur to keep drug prices reasonable have been swept aside with a force that is difficult to understand and comprehend.
>
> After all these long years, the many congressional hearings and the comments of Senators Long, Nelson, Kennedy, Mathias, and others, when contrasted to the economic commercial reality of the generic industry today. I can only tell you that this legislation, along with what I am about to say, is forcing competition and innovation out of the marketplace, exactly the opposite of what you are trying to do.
>
> Actually, you should have Defense Secretary Casper Weinberger here as a witness, not Bill Haddad. He did more to end the myths of the pharmaceutical manufacturers association than anybody else. He put an end to some of the nonsense that went on previous to his tenure at HEW.
>
> The hard truth today, Senators, is that 9 out of every 10 Americans—conservatively, 8 out of every 10—is paying 4 to 10 times as much for prescription drugs as they should or could pay. Price was and is a major prohibition to good medical care.
>
> There are reasons for this tragedy and travesty. The Congress has yet to act on a national formula of interchangeable drugs which now exists administratively, largely the result of State initiative.

Haddad concluded his remarks which were, in fact, rather brief with this:

> Finally, thank you for your willingness to hear my somewhat strident statements, which I hope you will understand are underlined by 20 years of frustrating experience with the pharmaceutical industry and watching them time after time pervert the truth, turn fact into fiction, and frighten great and courageous men into silence.

Haddad continued to be the voice of the Generic Drug industry on Capitol Hill and was a major player in the ultimate passage of Waxman–Hatch.

The other unusual bit of testimony came from Dr. Sidney Wolfe, representing the Citizen's Health Research Group. Dr. Wolfe was a frequent witness in Congressional Hearings. What he proposed was revolutionary – to limit the rights to trademarks or brand names to the life of the Patent.

Thus, when the Patent expired on Valium for instance, any producer of diazepam could call its product "Valium". He argued that such a move would be helpful to the prescriber who often couldn't remember or even pronounce the Generic name. Wolfe had other suggestions without the passage of which he would oppose S.255.

In Table 4.4, we have listed Drug-related Hearings and resulting Bills for just the ninety-third, ninety-fourth, and ninety-fifth Congresses. Where known, the names of the Congressional sponsors of the Bills are supplied. Two things are notable from the table. First, some Hearings result in multiple Bills. In such cases, resolution can be achieved through Amendments and compromise. Also apparent is the fact that most of the Hearings did not result in the introduction of Legislation. This is not to say that Legislative proposals did not subsequently occur.

Table 4.4 Drug-Related Hearings Ninety-Third, Ninety-Fourth, and Ninety-Fifth Congress

Hearing Title	Bill Numbers and Sponsors
Quality of Health Care – Human Experimentation, 1973 Legislation relating to biomedical research technology human experimentation.	S. 878 – Javits S. 974 – Javits S. J. Res. 71 S. J. Res. 86 S. 2071 – Kennedy S. 2072 – Kennedy H. R. 7724
Barbiturate Abuse in the United States, 1973 Examination of the use of barbiturates in the United States.	None
Psychosurgery in Veteran's Administration Hospitals Examination of problems resulting from patients being subjected to untested and experimental surgery and medical devices.	None
Medical Device Amendments, 1973 To protect the public health by amending the Federal Food, Drug, and Cosmetic Act to assure the safety and effectiveness of medical devices.	S. 2368 – Kennedy and related Bills S. 2368 passed Senate but died in the House S. 510 – 94th Congress – became public law 94–295.

(Continued)

Table 4.4 (*Continued*)   Drug-Related Hearings Ninety-Third, Ninety-Fourth, and Ninety-Fifth Congress

Hearing Title	Bill Numbers and Sponsors
Examination of the Pharmaceutical Industry, 1973–1974 Legislation amending the PHS Act and the Federal Food, Drug, and Cosmetic Act regarding pharmaceuticals.	S. 3441 – Kennedy S. 966 – Nelson
Brand Names and Generic Drugs, 1974 Examination of the Office of Technology Assessment report of the Drug Bioequivalence Study Panel.	None
Food Supplement Legislation, 1974 To amend the Federal Food, Drug, and Cosmetic Act to include a definition food supplements. To amend the Federal Food, Drug, and Cosmetic Act to promote honesty and fair dealing in the interest of consumers with respect to the labeling and advertising special dietary foods, such as vitamins and minerals, and so forth.	S. 2801 – Proxmire S. 3867 – Nelson
Regulation of New Drug R&D by the FDA, 1974 Examination of new drug research and development by the FDA.	None
Shortages of Prescription Drugs, 1974 Examination of shortages – current and impending – of prescription drugs in the United States.	None
Food and Drug Administration Practice & Procedure, 1974 Examination of the history of FDA's regulatory efforts with the Dalkon Shield and the procedures they use in considering various drugs given to animals that may be consumed by the American people.	None
Regulation of Diethylstilbestrol (DES), 1975 To amend the Federal Food, Drug, and Cosmetic Act to prohibit the administration of the drug DES to any animal intended for use as food and for other purposes.	S. 963 – Kennedy Passed Senate
Preclinical and Clinical Testing by the Pharmaceutical Industry, 1975–1976 Examination of the process of drug testing and FDA's role in the regulation and conditions under which such testing is carried out.	None

(*Continued*)

Table 4.4 (*Continued*)   Drug-Related Hearings Ninety-Third, Ninety-Fourth, and Ninety-Fifth Congress

Hearing Title	Bill Numbers and Sponsors
Biomedical and Behavioral Research, 1975 To amend the PHS ACT to establish the President's Commission for the protection of human subjects involved in Biomedical and Behavioral Research and for other purposes.	S. 2515 – Kennedy Passed Senate
Oral Contraceptives and Estrogens for Postmenopausal Use, 1976 Examination of the increasing use of estrogens, both as a means of contraception and as a treatment for the effects of menopause.	None
Basic Issues in Biomedical and Behavioral Research, 1978 Examination of public policy in the area of biomedical and behavioral research.	None
Oversight of Food and Drug Administration Examination of the quality of animal test data submitted to regulatory agencies; testimony of past and present FDA employees, many of whom had testified before the Subcommittee previously.	None
Recombinant DNA Research and the NIH Guidelines Examination of the nature and extent of Government and industry-sponsored recombination DNA (genetic engineering) research and its relation to the proposed NIH Guidelines; discussion of potential benefits and risks of this controversial research area.	None
Ninety-Fifth Congress	
Biological Testing Involving Human Subjects by the Department of Defense, 1977 Examination of serious deficiencies in the Defense Department's efforts to protect the human subjects of drug research.	None
Preclinical and Clinical Testing by the Pharmaceutical Industry, 1977 Examination of the process of drug testing and FDA's role in the regulation and conditions under which such testing is carried out.	None

(*Continued*)

Table 4.4 (*Continued*)   Drug-Related Hearings Ninety-Third, Ninety-Fourth, and Ninety-Fifth Congress

Hearing Title	Bill Numbers and Sponsors
Banning of the Drug Laetriles from Interstate Commerce by FDA Evaluation of information on which the FDA based its decision to ban the drug laetrile from interstate commerce.	None
Pricing of Drugs, 1977 (Joint hearing by the Subcommittee on Health and Scientific Research of the Committee on Antitrust and Monopolies of the Committee on the Judiciary.) Examination into the areas of how drug prices are set, what is a reasonable rate of return for industry, what profits are justified, and how the patent system affects the competitive nature of the industry.	None
Food, Drug, and Cosmetic Act Amendments of 1977 To amend the Public Health Services Act to provide for a National Center for Clinical Pharmacology, to provide support for the study of clinical pharmacology and clinical pharmacy, and to provide for review of drug prescribing; and to amend the Federal Food, Drug, and Cosmetic Act, as amended, to provide for the continuation and expansion of existing authority through the establishment of an appropriate mechanism to be known as the Federal Food, Drug, Cosmetic, and Devices Administration; to provide for additional regulation of the pharmaceutical industry; and for other purposes.	S. 1831 and related Bills
Human Drug Testing by the CIA A continuation of the examination of biomedical and behavioral research conducted by the Central Intelligence Agency.	S. 1893
Drug Regulation Reform Act of 1978 Hearings on legislation to revise and reform the Federal law applicable to drugs for human use and to establish a National Center for Clinical Pharmacology within the Department of Health, Education, and Welfare	S. 2755

The Process

The Durham–Humphrey Amendment of 1951 changed forever the nature of the Drug distribution and medicine-taking systems. As we have noted elsewhere, the Amendment established a class of "legend" Drugs. Prior to that, many Drug manufacturers had self-classified some of their products as "prescription only". But that provision did not have the force of law, and in any case, there was really no way a patient could have access to or even know about many Drugs. The indirect but enormous effect was to really increase the power (and the workload) of the FDA.

The Waxman–Hatch Law

This piece of Legislation is important for being touted as a "win-win". Big Pharma brand names now found it possible to receive an extension of a Drug Patent life (unprecedented in Patent law history). The Generic producers could now file an Abbreviated New Drug Application (ANDA), vastly decreasing costs and time to market. There were major implications for Drug Prices as well. This Legislation was largely responsible for the size and scope of the Generic Drug industry today. It also transformed the Price structure of the industry, and this requires some elaboration.

New uses for old Drugs may be patentable where the new use is not obvious. This is referred to commonly as "ever greening", i.e., the practice of using Patents to block competition by discovering new uses for old Drugs. A classic example of "ever greening" occurred with Epogen, where the Drug was actually approved as an orphan product with a very limited indication and now enjoys many indications and is considered a blockbuster Drug.
A more limited type of "ever greening" is where a pharmaceutical manufacturer looks for new indications in different patient populations, for example, pediatric patients. However, Patent term extensions are not granted for new uses or dosage forms of previously approved Drugs (133).

The importance of the Government in pricing decisions for pharmaceuticals is threefold. There is the routine interest in Price fixing and Price discrimination which may affect any industry. In addition, the Government is a major and growing purchaser of pharmaceuticals.

Finally, the Prices of Health-related goods make great political material, and the Drug industry in the United States, for example, has been the subject of Price Investigations by the Congress almost unremittingly, since the mid-1950s.

An illuminating example of Government effects, both overt and subtle, on industry pricing is the relationship of the Waxman–Hatch Act and the Catastrophic Drug (Medicare outpatient) Bill (2006). The thread of continuity tying the Waxman–Hatch law to the Catastrophic Coverage Drug Provision was Rep. Waxman, the co-sponsor of the Patent Restoration/ANDA law and one of the architects of the Medicare outpatient Drug Legislation. Over the past decade, Waxman had become the most important legislator on Capitol Hill on matters relating to FDA and the Drug industry. As Chairman of the House Energy and Commerce Committee Health Subcommittee, Waxman had jurisdiction on all Health-related legislative matters coming through the House of Representatives.

Waxman used his position to gain a thorough knowledge of the Drug industry. His legislative initiatives in the Drug area included the Patent Restoration/ANDA Bill that bears his name, the Orphan Drug Act, and the Drug export law. In oversight Hearings, he also kept a close watch on FDA operations and developed a firm understanding of the Agency's complex regulatory mechanism.

Waxman championed the interests of the Generic segment of the U.S. Drug industry, aiding the American consumers of prescription Drugs by making more low-cost Generic Drugs available. After enactment of the law, Waxman followed up on the Drug Price issue in two major Hearings, one in 1985 and the second in the spring of 1987, as the Catastrophic Care Legislation was moving through the House.

In both of the Hearings, Waxman asked the Pharmaceutical Manufacturers Association (PMA) spokesmen and representatives of individual brand name companies to explain why pharmaceutical Price increases were continuing at record high rates. The response from the industry on both occasions was the same: the Price increases were necessary if industry is to continue funding research programs to discover medically important new Drugs.

Another cause of continuing high rates of Drug Price increases paradoxically can be traced to the Waxman–Hatch law itself. The Legislation achieved its primary goal of dramatically expanding the pool of multiple source Drugs, reducing cost to consumers through Generic substitution. The Price competition, however, had secondary effect of putting sudden, intense pressure on the revenue streams of many research-based companies.

Faced with precipitous declines in market share because of Generic Price competition, those companies tended to respond in kind; where possible, they raised Prices to try to retain revenues. For example, as a single source product neared the end of its Patent term, a company would sharply increase the Price and keep it high, even after the Patent expired, relying on sales and marketing to sustain volume. Prices of single source Drugs with significant Patent life remaining were also routinely raised to compensate for the actual or expected loss of revenue on a Drug coming off Patent. The defensive Price increases may have offset the Price reductions achieved through the competition introduced by the Waxman–Hatch law and certainly led to the charge of "Greedy".

Given his continued involvement in Drug Price issues, it was no surprise that in 1987, as the Catastrophic Coverage Bill began to gain momentum, Waxman stepped forward as a leader in the effort to add an outpatient Medicare Drug benefit provision to the Legislation. The law provided both an opportunity to extend Drug benefits to the elderly and a new approach to the Drug Price question. Waxman saw a possible connection between a catastrophic coverage initiative and the addition of an outpatient Drug benefit.

Some estimates suggested that the Government would become the purchaser of as much as 30% of all pharmaceuticals in the United States. With that buying power, the Government has the leverage to change the structure of the Drug industry in the same way that the hospital and medical products industries were changed by the implementation of the prospective pay system.

The Pharmaceutical Manufacturers Association, representing brand name Drug companies, was put in a difficult position. The Drug benefit was supported in Congress because of its popularity with the elderly, and to oppose the law would create an image problem for the industry. The law was also good for business, at least in the short run, because it would result in a significant expansion of the market for prescription Drugs. On the other hand, PMA recognized that the new business would be with a single, notoriously difficult customer, the Federal Government.

The 1962 Drug Amendments

As described in detail in the Chapter 3, these Amendments were the direct result of the Kefauver Hearings with the result, not Kefauver's target, of requiring proof of efficacy for approving any new Drug. This had the effect again of increasing both the power and workload of the FDA.

While the concept of the Amendments can hardly be argued against – everyone wants her medicine to work! The new law was responsible for the putative, but vigorously argued, "Drug lag". Peltzman (150) analyzed the economic effects of the "62 Amendments" and found evidence of four kinds of downsides. First, there was the number of new chemical entities reaching the market that was cut in half but was not combined with a concomitant decline in Drug problems from inefficacious Drugs. Second, the amount of new data required for clinical and other studies necessary for approval doubled the cost of developing and bringing of a new Drug to market. Third, the marketplace now dictated focusing on R&D for Drugs, with a high likelihood of success eventuating in higher profits, which in turn would lead to higher Drug Prices. Fourth (quoting another economist), the new law may result in "more risk of adverse reactions and less safety". The background detail for Peltzman's conclusion is provided in the reference.

The Orphan Drug Act

This 1983 Legislation was passed after years of deliberation to incentivize research on Drugs with limited market potential, i.e., to treat conditions which affect a comparatively small part of the population.

Incentives provided to the Drug company under the Orphan Drug Act were these:

1. Exclusive marketing rights for 7 years, after approval of the Drug, and this applies whether or not the Drug is patented.
2. Tax credits for clinical testing.
3. Grants and contracts to support orphan Drug research.
4. Flexibility and assistance in the regulating processes. This includes authorization to physicians to administer the Drug prior to approval to patients even if they are not involved in clinical trials – a "compassionate" IND.

Medicare Catastrophic Coverage Act (1988) and Repeal of Same (1989)

In 1988, Congress enacted the Medicare Catastrophic Coverage Act to provide protection for catastrophic medical costs and to add a limited long-term care benefit. Because President Reagan refused to consider a tax increase to pay for this benefit, and the laws then in effect required any new program to not increase the deficit (called PAYGO), Congress required the beneficiaries, particularly those with high incomes, to pay for the benefit.

The beneficiaries, including the low-income beneficiaries who would receive the Drug benefit without added premiums, rebelled, and Congress repealed the benefit in 1989. It was yet another of those curious meanderings to which Congress is sometimes prey. And, it costs money to pass a Bill and then legally to change one's mind.

Rovner (286) describes the effect of the debacle as a result of "politics not substance".

> The real story of the rise and fall of the Medicare Catastrophic Coverage Act sends several ominous messages about the state of Congress and our political system, but the power of the senior citizens' lobby is not one of them. Those who lived through this nightmare instead learned a lot more about the power of direct mail, the ease of manipulating the public with information that is simply wrong, the resistance recipients of federal entitlement programs feel toward change, and the lack of knowledge Americans have about programs that so directly affect their lives.
>
> (316)

Finally in 2003, President Bush signed the Medicare Prescription Drug Improvement, and Modernization Act (MMA). Unlike the Medicare Catastrophic Coverage Act of 1988 and the Health Security Plan of 1993, there was virtually no strong political opposition to the MMA, except initially from the AARP. This new Medicare Part D would be financed in the same manner as Part B, namely, with 75% of its financing coming from the federal general tax fund and 25% from premiums paid by senior citizens. As mentioned earlier in this chapter, seniors were unhappy with what they perceived to be the lack of generosity in the benefit structure of the MMA but were reassured when the AARP vowed to fight for more generous benefits in the future. The pharmaceutical industry continued to voice its fears about eventual Price controls in the Medicare Program. Their fears were justified.

"Hillary Care" and "Obamacare"

In 1984, President Bill Clinton proposed a new program of "affordable" (sound familiar?) Health Care for all. The First Lady was appointed to head a Task Force on National Health Care Reform. Criticism began at once. There had been no "Hearings", and secrecy was charged. To make matters worse, polls found that nearly 50% felt there were people better qualified than Hillary to head the Task Force. The proposed Legislation was declared dead in September 1994.

In contrast to Clinton, President Barack Obama left the details of his proposed Legislation to Speaker Pelosi and Senator Harry Reid. The President was not involved publicly in the details – "You can keep your plans. You can keep your doctor" – and, as noted, Speaker Pelosi hadn't read it either, but as of this writing, it is still Law and calls for its repeal seem to be replaced by suggestions for modification.

Narcotics and Other Drugs of Abuse

While this topic is certainly fascinating and especially timely, it is definitely BTSB. Starting with the Harrison Narcotic Act of 1914, there has been a myriad of legislative, investigative, and regulative attempts to deal with this multifaceted problem. The opioid crisis is a clear and present danger and the Chinese Opium Wars of so long ago tell of the age of the problems. New Drugs, the products of legitimate R&D, have found their way into the abuse category. Marijuana is going through some sort of evolutionary process of acceptance, but the votes are by no means all in on that subject.

State Laws

Each of the States has its own Pharmacy Laws. The variations are many. Licensure laws for medicine, Pharmacy, and other professions are uniform in their ubiquity but characterized by their diversity. We visit these issues in Chapter 5.

Conclusion

Again, volumes have been written on the subject of this chapter. More to come, I feel surely, for this most investigated, legislated, and regulated industry. Stay tuned.

Chapter 5
Regulators and Regulations

Introduction

There are many Federal Agencies which promulgate Regulations. For purposes of this text, the most important, by far, is the Food and Drug Administration (FDA). It is well to remember that Federal Regulations once enacted have the force of law. Once the Regulations are formulated, there is a period for Public comment and, presumably, changes may be made. Ultimately, the approved Regulations become part of the Code of Federal Regulations (CFR). Unless you are an attorney, I would not even go there.

It seems certain that no industry is subject to as many forms of Regulation as is the Drug industry. Certainly this is appropriate for an industry with such great potential for harm and which affects such a large portion of the entire population. As with all other major industries, pharmaceutical manufacturers must cope with the regular business laws such as antitrust, Federal Trade Commission Regulations, Interstate Commerce Regulations, and pricing Regulations. In addition, however, the pharmaceutical industry has been given the responsibility of living up to special restrictions on every segment of the industry from the manufacturer to the retail outlet. State Agencies regulate the practice of Pharmacy in community pharmacies and hospitals as well as distribution of prescription products by wholesalers. Federal Agencies require registration of manufacturers, limit the methods by which prescription Drugs can be distributed, and oversee every phase of Drug development and marketing.

The Food and Drug Administration

The FDA was originally a part of the Department of Agriculture but was moved in 1940 to the Department of Health Education and Welfare, now the Department of Health and Human Services (DHHS). It is a part of the Executive Branch of the Government, which means that the President appoints the Commissioner.

As society and marketing activities have grown increasingly complex, the lawmakers are finding it more and more difficult to write Legislation to a degree of specificity sufficient to cover a given industrial situation. Alderson describes the development of law for the Regulation of marketing as going through the following three stages (322).

1. Crystallization of the Policy issue through debate (Hearings).
2. Assignment of responsibility for solution to the enterprise sector of the Public sector, involving the reconciliation of ideologies.
3. Developing an effective mechanism for efficient performance of the regulative function.

The original charge to FDA was a simple one – to protect the People from unsafe and ineffective Drugs. That mandate certainly sprang from the excesses of the "Patent medicine" era of the early twentieth century. Note that it was not until passage of the 1962 Drug Amendments that *effectiveness* was formally addressed.

Bezold (375) argued that the FDA's Generic charter should have included the *Promotion* of the development of safe–effective new Drugs. As he observed, "the well-intentioned narrowness of the FDA's charter produces a number of unintended, undesirable side effects that should be reviewed. It may be time to direct the Agency to actively encourage the development of new safe and effective drugs". (One effort in this direction was made in a version of Title I of the proposed Drug Reform Act of 1978, which stated "...it is in the interest of the American People...to encourage...the discovery and development of safe and effective drug products...and maintain optimum freedom for scientific investigation".)

Variations of this theme are at the heart of the "Drug Lag" which is discussed later in this chapter and elsewhere in the text.

FDA has had what might be called a "checquered" history. At times, it has been charged with being too favorable to Big Pharma who, in return, has been harshly critical of Regulations they considered onerous. At one point there were unsuccessful efforts to dismantle the FDA (1996). But in 2015, a group of former Commissioners called for elevation of FDA to a Cabinet position. That did not happen either.

This probably is a good place to mention FDA leadership, which takes the form of a Commissioner. The first FDA Commissioner was Harvey Wiley, who served from 1907 to 1912. All prior Commissioners are listed here, in order, to demonstrate their usually comparatively short tenure. Given the complexity of the issues faced by FDA, it seems that any Commissioner was required to be a "quick study", especially in view of the amount of time spent testifying to Congress. (Of course, the respective Commissioners were usually accompanied by expert staff as well as Counsel, such as the redoubtable Peter Barton Hutt.) In any case, here they are:

Harvey Wiley, 1907–1912
- Carl Ashberg, 1912–1921
- Walter Campbell, 1921–1924
- Charles A. Brown, 1924–1927 (The first African American, appointed by President Coolidge)
- Walter Campbell, again, 1927–1944, appointed by both Hoover and FDR
- Paul Dunbar, 1944–1951
- Charles Crawford, 1951–1954
- George Larrick, 1944–1965, appointed by three presidents – "IKE", "JFK" and "LBJ"
- James Goddard, 1966–1968
- Herbert Ley, 1968–1969
- Charles Edwards, 1969–1973
- Alexander Schmidt, 1973–1976
- Donald Kennedy, 1977–1979
- Jere Goyan, 1979–1981, the only pharmacist Commissioner to date
- Arthur Hayes, 1981–1983
- Frank Young, 1984–1989
- David Kessler, 1990–1997
- Jane Henney, 1999–2001
- Mark McClellan, 2002–2004
- Lester Crawford, 2008, forced to resign due to conflict of interest. The only veterinarian to date
- Andrew von Eschenbach, 2006–2009
- Margaret Hamburg, 2009–2015

Scott Gottlieb, 2017–2018
Norman Sharples, April 2019–October 2019
Stephen Hahn, November 2019

These, then, are the men and women who have directed the FDA since its inception. It would be folly to describe in detail all that the People at FDA do, so a broad brush will be used to describe the major areas of FDA Regulations. The FDA has 17,000-plus employees.

Safety and Effectiveness

A major, perhaps the *most* major, activity of the FDA today is to assure that any new Drug that is developed has been proven to be both safe and effective for its intended use. For Big Pharma, this is a major nexus of Dynamic Tension. In 1993, the U.S. Office of Technology Assessment produced an outline of the regulatory process for a new Drug. (See Table 5.1.)

There has been much "fine-tuning" since then. The Waxman–Hatch Legislation led to the FDA Regulations allowing makers of a Generic product to "piggy back" on the NDA of the origination, an abbreviated New Drug Application (ANDA). In addition, the Generic producer must prove "bioequivalence" to the original, meaning that the Generic essentially has the identical effects in the body as the original. The manufacturers of Generic products have become very adept at this process.

We should return here to a theme which recurs throughout this Book, "safe" and "effective" are relative terms. No Drug is 100% of either. Understanding that principle leads naturally to the conclusion that any FDA decision on safety/effectiveness is, in essence, a value judgment, based on good science, of course.

While "New" Drugs occupy most of the FDA's approval process today, the FDA found itself with an extra burden after 1962. The 1962 Kefauver–Harris Amendment required proof of efficacy in addition to proof of safety before a Drug product could be introduced into interstate commerce. The issue of how these provisions should be applied to Drugs approved between 1938 and 1962 was controversial.

In 1966, the FDA commissioned the National Academy of Sciences/National Research Council to evaluate Drug products introduced between 1938 and 1962. Some 16,000 claims for 4,000 Drug products (15% over the counter [OTC] and 85% prescription) were reviewed, and 14.7% were reported to be *ineffective* (i.e., lack of substantial evidence of effectiveness),

Table 5.1 The FDA Regulatory Process for a New Drug

1. For a given disease State, the Drug company evaluates 100 compounds and finds that only one of them shows any promise.
2. The company then does animal studies (mostly higher order animals, e.g., dogs and monkeys), using an FDA protocol to test for, among other things, toxicity.
3. If these studies indicate that the Drug has no undesirable characteristics for use in animals, then the company applies to the FDA for an IND (Investigative New Drug) clearance for testing on human subjects.
4. If the FDA grants an IND for the Drug, then the company performs three successive phases of clinical trials on humans.
    a. Phase I: the Drug is administered to a small group of humans who do not have the disease and are healthy (usually volunteers or prisoners).
    b. Phase II: the Drug is administered to a larger group of individuals who do have the disease.
    c. Phase III: the Drug is administered to a much larger group of individuals who do have the disease.
5. If the Drug appears to be both safe and effective in human beings, the company submits all of the data that resulted from the three phases of the clinical trials to the FDA and applies for an NDA (New Drug Application).
6. The FDA evaluates the data.
7. If the evaluation of the Drug is favorable, the FDA grants the NDA, and the company can now legally market the Drug to the general population.
8. During the next 3 years, the company and the FDA do post-market surveillance of the Drug (the so-called "Phase IV").
9. If there are any safety or effectiveness problems, the company must remove the Drug from the market and be legally liable for any damages that the Drug caused. The FDA does not bear any legal liability.

Source: Office of Technology Assessment, 1993.

34.9% were reported to be *possibly effective*, 7.3% were reported to be *probably effective*, 19.1% were reported to be effective, and 24% were reported to be "effective, but ..." Subsequent to the 1966 studies, other efficacy studies were ordered.

The FDA initiated an action to remove from the market those Drug products that lacked proof of efficacy. This process was known as the Drug Efficacy Study Implementation (DESI) project. The process took a number of years (until 1984) and had a profound effect on the science of Drug development. The NDA was henceforth center stage.

The complexity and difficulty of achieving approval of an NDA are in a word, enormous. It can also be fraught with ethical dilemmas. Before the NDA, however, comes the Investigational New Drug (IND) Application. It is the legal ticket to ship an unapproved Drug in interstate commerce; in other words, to begin clinical (human) trials. The IND will provide evidence from animal and in vitro studies demonstrating that the Drug is "safe" for use in a limited number of humans.

The New Drug Application is the culmination of what may be years of clinical studies. The applicant does not have to labor in hope and isolation. Frequent meetings with FDA scientists are necessary and valuable. In actuality, it is in the interests of both parties that a successful outcome be achieved. Obviously, it is particularly vital to the patients who will ultimately receive the new "breakthrough".

Equally obvious is the fact that clinical studies are not simply a matter of "let's try this stuff on a few patients and see if it works". Some of the questions to be asked immediately include what dose to use. Remember, that, so far, the Drug may have been tried only on mice, monkeys, and pigs, which are all different species from Sapiens. There is the question of dosage *form*: oral, injectable (IV or IM), rectal, topical, or inhalant? The list goes on and ultimately the dose and form tested will/must be the one for which the application for approval will be based.

Double-blind studies were not always the rule but certainly are now. Simply put, neither the investigator nor her patient is to know whether the Drug being administered is a placebo, the real McCoy, or even a similar effective Drug (comparative trials). Controls on double-blinding are extremely tough to be certain that they are truly "blind".

Simply setting up clinical trials is both an art and a science. There are a host of factors to consider. What other Drugs is the patient taking? Can diet be a factor? Will the patient be compliant? The amount of detail and rigor required to mount a successful clinical trial is far beyond the limited space available here for details.

When all goes well, a successful NDA should be the result of open communication between the applicants and the FDA. The goal of the applicant is to see a safe and effective (and competitive) product to market. Philosophically, that should be the same goal of FDA (minus the "competitive").

A brief footnote – the Treatment IND. Such a submission is based on two reasons: (1) to facilitate the availability of promising new Drugs to desperately ill patients as early in a Drug's development as possible, and (2) to define conditions under which the manufacturer can charge a fee for the Drug under study. The Treatment IND has been reported to have some favorable consequences, including streamlined procedures for proposing and conducting clinical studies (34).

Labeling and Promotion

Clearly, it should be the responsibility of a Government protecting Agency to be sure that a product was so labeled as to ensure its safe and effective use. No one quarreled with that, but as the FDA continued to expand its definition of labeling, things became a bit troublesome.

We start with the official language. The FDA Regulations differentiate between the terms "label" and "labeling". Label means the printed, written, or graphic material that is literally affixed to the container of the Drug. Labeling means the printed, written, or graphic material that is enclosed with or accompanies the Drug once it enters interstate commerce and is put up for sale after shipment.

Much of the authority of the Food, Drug, and Cosmetic Act, over the manufacture and distribution of food, Drugs, medical devices, and cosmetics, is through the labeling requirements of the FDA Regulations implementing the statute. To violate the labeling requirements of the Act and the FDA Regulations is to violate the essential spirit and letter of the law governing the purity, safety, and efficacy of food, Drugs, medical devices, and cosmetics. Under the authority delegated by the DHHS, the FDA promulgates Regulations dealing with specific labeling requirements. In addition, the FDA issues labeling requirements pursuant to the authority of the Fair Packaging and Labeling Act, which concerns truthfulness in labeling as applicable to *consumer* packaging (e.g., defining "economy size," "king size").

The package insert is the part of a prescription Drug product's approved labeling directed to Health Care professionals. It is the primary mechanism by which the FDA and Drug manufacturers communicate essential, science-based prescribing information to Health Care practitioners.

Under the Regulations, the package insert labeling must contain a summary of essential scientific information that is needed for the safe and effective use of the Drug. The labeling must be informative, accurate, and neither promotional in tone nor false or misleading. The labeling must be based, whenever possible, on data derived from human experiments. Implied claims and suggestions for Drug use may not be made if there is inadequate evidence of safety or lack of substantial evidence of effectiveness. Conclusions that are based on animal data are permitted if they are necessary for safe and effective use of the Drug in humans; however, they must be identified as animal data.

Troubles have arisen in regard to labeling with two issues – the patient package insert (PPI) and Promotion.

The PPI has been the subject of considerable wrangling before the FDA shelved the idea. One reason was the basic assumption behind the use of the information by the patient.

- The patient can read.
- The patient will read it.
- The patient will heed what she reads.
- Reading and heeding will change the patient's Health status for the better.

These rather shaky assumptions were elaborated upon by Gibson (27). Among the considerations he postulated were:

- Some drugs can be used properly only on the advice of experts.
- Some drugs can be used properly without the advice of experts.
- Some drugs can be used properly with only the information provided on the package label.
- Drugs produce inseparable desired and undesired effects.
- Observing relevant precautions will decrease the likelihood of experiencing adverse effects from a drug.

To these somewhat faulty assumptions was the very real problem of where and how the pharmacist was supposed to store and distribute PPIs for every medicine in his/her inventory. Added to that was the possibility of causing unnecessary concern by the patient and interfering with the prescriber–patient relationship. This was an idea whose time has come and gone.

Once Promotion had been included by FDA as labeling, the problems became interesting and continue. Regulation of Drug Promotion had been the responsibility of the Federal Trade Commission until 1967, when it was moved to the FDA. It is fun to conjecture what sort of chaos there might have been, had that separation been allowed to stand.

There was chaos aplenty anyway as the FDA struggled to adapt to its new responsibility. An Agency steeped in a science-based tradition now had to come up with Regulations of a whole new kind. And, of course, they did!

The Regulations on pharmaceutical Promotion were revolutionary. In addition to policing any false and misleading claims of a Drug benefit, the FDA wanted to do more. They now required all advertisers to exercise "full disclosure", i.e., to include statements about side effects, contraindications, and the like in their ads. In other words, the advertiser was paying for the privilege of saying bad things about the products. And that wasn't all! The FDA also required "fair balance" in the ads meaning giving significant space to both the good and the bad.

One Regulation which seems hard to justify as a protective action is the requirement that the Generic name be included in type at least half as large as the brand name. This was clearly the result of the long-standing controversy over the economic and clinical issues of Generic prescribing. It was certainly intended that the prescriber be regularly reminded of the Generic name should she wish to prescribe generically. There is no overt evidence that the Generic Drug companies played a serious role in the genesis of this Regulation.

In all the print and TV media, the FDA is constantly challenged by the creativity of the drug advertising agencies. The illustrations in the ads are particularly troublesome and require vigilance at the very basic level by the FDA. The degree of such vigilance is illustrated by a couple of examples. One Drug ad showed a group of "patients" including one African-American. The FDA investigator found that no African-Americans had been involved in the clinical trials. The ad had to be re-done. In this case, the FDA did not require either a remedial ad or a "Dear Doctor Letter", but they had the *authority* to do so and *did* 22 times in 1- to 2-year period.

The other example, from the Author's personal experience concerned our product, Azulfidine. A new, enteric-coated form was being introduced to lessen the gastrointestinal symptoms which it often produced. A new ad campaign was produced featuring a picture of the new tablet and a headline, "The Tablet with a New Profile". FDA objected to the use of the word "The", arguing that it implied some sort of exclusivity. New, costly, ads had to be produced with the "The" excised. Sharp eyes at the FDA!

Commissioner James Goddard on his arrival in 1966 made it clear that "there was a new sheriff in town". In a speech to the Pharmaceutical Manufacturers Association (PMA), he told company executives, "I am very uneasy....I will be quite candid with you...the pharmaceutical industry as you and I know it today may be altered significantly, altered beyond your present fear".

The gauntlet lay on the floor by the podium.

After noting the "hand of the amateur is evident" in too many INDs, Goddard focused on Advertising using a specific example – a Drug for which FDA had suggested a label which read, "WARNING – DANGEROUS DRUG". The company instead had used "unusually effective" along with "unparalleled potency". Goddard was not happy. "The effect was clearly promotional rather than precautionary. This is the language of advertising, not the language of danger. This is not in the spirit of science".

The next year *FDA Papers* featured what would probably be described as a polemic, "Medical Advertising, State of the Craft and Regulation". If it was not actually written by Goddard, it certainly bore his imprimatur because it effectively foretold FDA Advertising Regulations for the next 60 years and I quote extensively.

> The year 1967 will mark the fifth anniversary of the Kefauver-Harris Drug Amendments to the Federal Food, Drug and Cosmetic Act.
>
> During the extensive investigative and legislative hearings which preceded the passage of the Amendments, a great deal of attention was paid to advertising as a primary source of medical information for the physician. It was shown that busy doctors frequently must rely on the claims made by the pharmaceutical manufacturers about various new or established drugs. Congress decided that medical advertisements lacked a balance of information about possible bad effects as compared with the claims for benefits from use of the drugs. "The physician," Congress said, "must have the whole truth about therapeutic usefulness."
>
> The recent history of medical advertising practices shows a disappointing level of industry compliance with the spirit and letter of the Kefauver advertising amendment. There have been formal charges of violation of the advertising amendment and consequent legal actions. Additionally, FDA spokesman have informally told advertisers, in general and specific terms, that journal advertisements and other Rx drug promotion do not meet the requirements of frank and fair disclosures called for by the regulations.
>
> The regulations do require that medical advertisements fairly show the effectiveness of the drug for the condition for which it is advertised and list all those side effects and contraindications which are pertinent for the uses recommended in the ad as well as other uses for which the drug is commonly prescribed. The law allowed this information to be presented in "brief summary" form.
>
> To make the customary "brief summary" useful to the physician, there has to be at least mention of all the warning ideas in the official package insert, although the small size of an ad might limit the total amount of information to be presented.

(64)

Table 5.2 Common Failings in Medical Advertising

1. Extension or distortion of the claims for usefulness beyond that approved in the product's final printed labeling
2. A quotation from a study intended to imply improperly that the study is representative of much larger and general experience with the Drug
3. The selection of research papers of questionable quality that are favorable to the product and omission of contrary evidence derived from much better research
4. Prominent citation of data previously valid but made obsolete or false by subsequent findings
5. Quotation out of context from a seemingly favorable statement by an authoritative figure, but omission of unfavorable data from the very same article
6. A favorable quotation from an obviously authoritative source, but no quotation from other differing experts in the same field and of equal standing
7. Data from papers that report no side effects and omission of Reports on side effects in other papers published contemporaneously

Source: 64 – FDA Papers.

(The industry was warned to avoid the common failings [Table 5.2], which FDA had observed up to that time.)

> As a result of these regulations, it seemed, by January 1964, that medical advertisements had distinctly improved. The typical layout of many ads showed that some attention had been paid to the fair balance between indications and warnings; the "brief summary" was more explicit than it had been earlier; some ads even showed a more discriminate use of the graphic arts.
>
> It soon became evident, however, that the changes in medical advertising had more shadow than substance. There was an appearance of more careful adherence to the formal requirements of the regulations, but too often it was mere appearance. Careful perusal of many advertisements during 1966 indicated that some were more unreliable and misleading than ever.
>
> The graphic arts made noisy declarations, unwarranted claims, and unproved implications. Suggestions were made that drugs which may have excellent validity in selected areas were applicable to a vast spectrum of medical problems. These and other violations were the basis of FDA charges made during legal actions taken in 1966.

***

While internal discussions continue, the FDA is also continuing its dialog with industry representatives and the advertising profession.

> Several meetings have been held to discuss new proposals for voluntary compliance with the present regulations. The participants in these discussions have taken cognizance of the industry's *failure to live up to its code of advertising and of the problem facing an industry when competitive facts impoverish the richest code.*
>
> *(Emphasis added)*

In the 50 years that followed, Promotions, especially detailing, were to come under continued scrutiny as we saw in Chapter 3.

Manufacturing

In addition to Regulations governing Drugs in use, the FDA is charged with monitoring the Drugs in process. Manufacturers are required to comply with Current Good Manufacturing Practices (CGMP), which are enforced by plant inspections. Rigorous quality control procedures must be followed. Packaging is included in the FDA jurisdiction. As one would expect, the Regulations on manufacturing are many and technical, and, BSTB.

FDA Remedies

The FDA has the Regulatory authority to remedy Drug industry transgressions. A few are listed here:

- Drug Recall – An action imposed on a manufacturer to remove a product from the market that is defective. In 2019, OTC medicines containing ranitidine were removed because of levels of a possibly cancer-causing ingredient.
- Corrective Advertising – A company may be required to run Advertising to correct a prior ad which was found by FDA to be false, misleading, or incorrect.
- Off-Label Promotion – More than 30 such cases had been handled by 2020. They are subject to both criminal and civil actions.
- Corrective Action – To "improve a company practice". This was applied in a DTC Promotion for the product, Yaz, incorrectly claimed to treat premenstrual tension.

- Debarment to prevent individuals from working in Drug development who have been involved in criminal conduct in Drug R&D.

There are, of course, others.

Other Regulators and Regulations

Federal Trade Commission

As noted above, the Federal Trade Commission (FTC) was at one time responsible for regulating Drug Promotion. But the FTC had played an important role in the early evolution of the Drug industry. The route from FTC to Kefauver Hearings was circuitous but fascinating. Hilts in his Book, *Protecting America's Health* (444), and quoting Richard Harris in the *Real Voice*, describes the characters and actions as follows:

1. Walton Hamilton, a D.C. attorney, learned in a routine visit that three antibiotics all were priced the same. He was suspicious because he was married to…
2. Irene Till, economist, formerly with the Federal Trade Commission and now with the Senate Subcommittee on Antitrust and Monopoly, where her former boss at the FTC …
3. John M. Blair was chief economist. Senator Kefauver had finished with steel, bread, and automobiles and was seeking other targets, so he asked…
4. Blair for ideas and he turned to …
5. His wife, Irene Till, who reportedly responded without hesitation, "Drugs".

And the rest, as they say, is history.

The FTC was established in 1914 and uses the slogan, "Protecting America's Consumers for over 100 years". Simply put, the mission is consumer protection and stopping anticompetitive practices. The Clayton Act reinforced the FTC in its work against monopolistic practices. The FTC has authority over OTC Drug Advertising and other Agencies such as the Consumer Product Safety Commission (CPSC) also worked in the area of consumer protection.

Federal Communications Commission (FCC)

The Federal Communications Commission (FCC) was established in 1934 just in time for television. FCC has jurisdiction over all forms of communication but especially radio, television, and telephone. The latter means that FCC is responsible for regulating "robo calls". (We're still waiting for more relief from this form of harassment.) Interestingly, the FCC is funded entirely from fees assessed on those being regulated.

The FCC works closely with the FDA on direct-to-consumer Rx Drug Advertising. Little recognized is the FCC's responsibility in the area of national defense and the enforcement of non-discriminatory (race, creed, etc.) Regulations.

Drug Enforcement Administration (DEA)

The Drug Enforcement Administration (DEA) was established in 1973 under the Nixon Administration. Its basic charge is to prevent the distribution of illegal narcotics. Toward that end, the DEA works with FBI, ICE, Customs and Border Protection, and the Department of Homeland Security.

At the community Pharmacy level, the DEA is responsible for a Federal "Schedule" of Drugs with abuse potential. The Schedule affects prescriptions by refill limitations and requirement of written (not telephone) prescriptions.

It is worth including here the controlled substances Schedule. This is adapted from the DEA Pharmacist's Manual.

> **Schedule I** The substances in Schedule I have a high abuse potential and no accepted medical use in the United States. This is the only schedule that includes drugs that are not available for prescribing, dispensing, or administering. Heroine is on this list as has been marijuana, although the recognition of "medical marijuana" suggests change including legalization, already the case in some states.
>
> **Schedule II** Substances in Schedule II have a high abuse potential with severe psychological or physical dependence liability, have an accepted medical use in the United States, and are available for practitioners to prescribe, and administer. Morphine, Codeine and Amphetamines are examples.
>
> **Schedule III** These substances have less abuse potential than those in Schedule II and more than those in Schedule IV. How

that is determined is definitely BSTB. Examples are products containing less than 15 milligrams of hydrocodone or not more than 90 milligrams of codeine per dosage unit.

Schedule IV You guessed it! It has more abuse potential than III and less than V. The benzodiazepines fall into this Schedule.

Schedule V This scheduling is primarily dose-related. Ingredients typically are found in cough medicines and anti-diarrhea medicines.

Centers for Medicare and Medicaid Services (CMS)

Formerly the Health Care Financing Administration (HCFA), the CMS is at the heart of anything to do with the economics of Health Care in its control. Not only do their policies directly affect Medicare and Medicaid patients, they indirectly affect policies of other third-party payers, and, ultimately, Drug economics for everyone.

The Medicare program, without Drugs, was begun in 1966 among Public fears of "socialized medicine". Medicaid was quietly enacted without much fanfare and quickly paid for prescription Drugs. It was years later that Medicare incorporated a prescription Drug benefit (see Task Force on Prescription Drugs in Chapter 3).

It is the job of CMS to administer both programs which include paying for part of the eligible patient's medication.

Patents and Trademarks

Patents and trademarks are highlighted many times in this text. They are at the heart of the Generic Drug issue, as well as the "Drug lag". The Patent Restoration Act (Waxman–Hatch, Chapter 5) was a revolutionary event as, for the first time in history, Drug Patent rights could be extended – another example of the uniqueness of this industry.

The Patent and Trademark Office administers the Regulations and most agree that they embody the American capitalistic system. Some infer, incorrectly, that Patents give the Patent holder the right to bring their product to market. Not so. There is another regulatory agent (FDA) which can only confer that right. Patents simply prevent someone *else* from marketing a product identical to that of the Patent holder. Court battles over Patents have been the rule over the decades after the Patent Office and Patent System came into being.

State Regulations

So far we have concentrated on Federal Regulations in play in the marketplace. But there are 50 States with an interesting diversity of ideas about what and how to affect Drug distribution. Sometimes a given State's Regulation is at odds with Federal Regulations. Marijuana is an example.

Consider the list in Table 5.3 of State Regulations in existence in the mid-1960s. Not every State had all or even any of them, but some are remarkable for their lack of reality in the marketplace. In many, maybe most, cases, they almost certainly reflect pressure by Pharmacy interests. The implications of some of the listed Regulations are explained in detail by Cady (372). Few of those listed would be enforceable today. The single most important Regulations promulgated and enforced by State Boards of Pharmacy are those related to licensure of pharmacists and pharmacies.

The Reader should note that the "police powers" of the Boards of Pharmacy are, constitutionally guaranteed by the Tenth Amendment, often quoted, which says that powers not specifically granted to the Federal Government are reserved for the States. The spirit of the Tenth Amendment is observed in some ways – there is no Federal licensure for pharmacists – but there are numerous Federal Regulations affecting Pharmacy practice in the 50 States. They include Regulations regarding Medicare/Medicaid services, controlled substance requirements, and others.

Drug Names

Before getting into Drug nomenclature, a few general observations are in order, for names take on a special significance in the world of business, especially as regards to trademarks. We have our arm of the Government specifically charged with checking with the issue – the Trademark Office (above).

In fact, when a Drug reaches the market, it has three names – the Generic name, usually unpronounceable, the chemical name, and the brand name. The first two are immutable but brand names proliferate.

Generic names are produced by the U.S. Adopted Names Council (USAN), a non-governmental Agency, with representatives from American Medical Association, American Pharmaceutical Association, the FDA, and the U.S. Pharmacopeia (USP). The latter is also non-governmental and more than 200 years old. The USP is also the name of a compendium of Drugs which,

Table 5.3 Some Regulations Enacted by State Legislation and Boards of Pharmacy

1. Ownership prohibitions
   - Physician ownership of pharmacies prohibited
2. Ownership requirements
   - Pharmacist ownership of pharmacies required
3. Merchandising prohibitions
   - No Pharmacy permit for a general merchandise store
   - No Pharmacy permit for a "fair trade" violator
4. Limitations on outlets
   - Limitation on the number of pharmacies in a State
5. Physical requirements
   - Physical separation required of prescription department in a general merchandise store
   - Separate entrance mandatory for prescription department in a general merchandise store
   - Entrance to adjoining store prohibited
   - Floor space of prescription department of a minimum site
   - Self-service for nonprescription products prohibited
   - Minimum prescription inventory rule (as a percentage of total inventory)
   - Ban on "closed door" operations
6. Advertising restrictions
   - Outdoor signs controlled
   - Prohibition from implying discount prescription Prices in Advertising
   - Advertising of prescription Drug Prices prohibited
   - Promotional schemes (e.g., senior citizens discount) prohibited
7. Pharmacist restrictions
   - Pharmacist manager requirement
   - Pharmacist on duty whenever Pharmacy is open
   - Specification of hours a pharmacist works
   - Specification of the number of pharmacists to be employed
   - Specification of operating hours for Pharmacy
   - Prescription dispensing rules
8. Regulation of competing distribution methods
   - No prescription agents allowed
   - Mail order Drug sales prohibited
   - Ban on sale of nonprescription Drugs in vending machines

Source: Derived and modified from narrative in F. Marion Fletcher, *Market Restraints in the Retail Drug Industry*, University of Pennsylvania Press, 1967.

along with a companion compendium, the National Formulary, contains a "description, method of preparation and dosage for virtually all drugs". Both are accepted worldwide. At one time, some States required every Pharmacy to maintain a current copy of both the USP and NF. No more.

If the Reader is confused, here's all you need to know. The chemical name will be dictated by the molecular structure, which only chemists care about. The Generic name, once decided on, becomes part of the IND and NDA, ultimately also being required in Promotion as we have seen. The brand name can be invented by the manufacturer but only with FTC and FDA approval. There are restrictions. You can't use a brand name such as "No Pain" for an Rx analgesic. Drug firms are said to maintain computer banks of brand/trade names for potential future use.

Naming Drugs is crucial for the prescribers as regards to spelling and pronunciation. They are also important for OTC television ads. How is the potential user to follow the advice "Ask your doctor if ---is right for you", if she can't remember or pronounce it. Drug names can be a challenge for the creative Advertising teams who may want to use it in a "jingle".

Conclusion

Regulations are the site of the real action. The Legislation typically establishes the various bureaus, agencies, and the like, defining their duties and authority. They, in turn, issue Regulations which, once promulgated, have the force of law. The Regulations are the home of the details wherein lies the devil. Thus, it is the Regulations that rule. It is ultimately the "bureaucrats" who finally run things. That is not necessarily bad in spite of the "bad rap" bureaucrats often receive. Regulations are much like the little girl with the curl in the middle of her forehead.

A glance at the Code of Federal Regulations (CFR), wherein all Federal Regulations are compiled in excruciating detail, will demonstrate how busy the Regulators have been; a possible portent for the future. There is currently no legal basis for the FDA to analyze the cost-effectiveness of pharmaceuticals. However, some in Policy circles have suggested that the FDA conduct such analyses. This interest is still largely academic. Adding cost-effectiveness criteria to the already long and cumbersome regulatory process would likely be a problematic and controversial step.

Big Pharma operates under a complex system of Regulations, developed over many years. It has been built not from abstract concepts but by continuing efforts, statutory and regulatory, to deal with the problems of a complex system of producing and distributing safe and effective human Drugs. There is thus a logical and historical necessity underlying the system which defines each change. As one examines the individual regulatory requirements covering different aspects of the development, manufacture, and distribution of human Drugs, it is apparent that most of the regulatory requirements are basically reasonable and fulfill a legitimate purpose. It is certainly possible, however, to criticize various specific regulatory requirements and to suggest ways of improving them or eliminating them entirely.

Even the broadest legitimate criticisms, however, do little more than scratch the surface in affecting the overall regulatory burden on the development and production of human Drugs. Regulatory reform and other efforts can improve the system to some degree, but they cannot change its basic nature. Unless the American Public is willing to forsake completely the protection of its Drug supply provided by this system, which it assuredly is not, major changes in the overall regulatory burden associated with production and distribution of human Drugs cannot be expected. Moreover, unforeseeable Public Health disasters, occurring with distressing frequency, will most likely preclude any change in the Public attitude in this regard and may even lead to more stringent regulatory requirements.

For the Reader who would like a Book-length insight into the FDA, I highly recommend Philip Hites' *Protecting America's Health* (475). Similarly, Steven Pray's, *A History of Nonprescription Drug Regulation* (475) provides just what the title promises. Dr. Pray also contributed Chapter 13 on that subject.

Finally, I want to emphasize just how extraordinarily difficult is the job of the FDA. The Agency has been blamed for a "Drug Lag" but also at times for being "too cozy" with Big Pharma. Consider their task. Throughout the world, scientists work feverously finding new remedies and often creating new kinds of science. All of these are laid, sooner or later, at FDA's doorstep. The FDA staff is faced with a constant learning process. Even with advisory councils and consultants, the resources of the FDA pale in comparison with those arrayed against them.

The FDA is constantly faced with politics, unforeseen Drug misadventures, even dishonesty by Drug product advocates. New challenges occur regularly. The emergence of DTC Promotion of prescription Drugs required a new set of rules requiring a balance of judgment in considering creativity and fair speech. A whole new skillset was needed. The FDA probably does not receive nearly the credit the Agency deserves.

Chapter 6
Non-Government Influence

Introduction

Having spent the three prior chapters detailing the activities of various Government entities in an attempt to shape Big Pharma and those with whom it deals, it seems helpful to briefly mention some of the non-governmental efforts toward effecting a sound system of pharmaceutical care delivery.

Self-Regulation

While I don't remember the exact words, or the source, an observation, paraphrased, was "self-regulation has rarely been successful in anything from personal evacuation to international trade". Nevertheless, the various parties often do set rules for themselves, sometimes in the form of Codes of ethics.

Medicine

The American Medical Association (AMA) has the Hippocratic Oath which can be seen, framed, in many physicians' offices. In addition, AMA has a formal Code of Ethics adopted in 1947 and expanded to fit the times since. The Code consists of a number of "Principles", explained in the chapters as follows (paraphrased):

- Patient–physician relationships
- Connection with the community and decision-makers
- Privacy and confidentiality

- Genetics and reproductive medicine
- Care at the end of life
- Organ procurement and transplantation
- Medical research and innovation
- Professional self-regulation
- Intra-professional relationships
- Financing and delivery of Health Care

Pharmacy

The American Pharmaceutical Association has its own Code consisting of nine general areas, again paraphrased:

- Establishment of a covenantal relationship
- Promotion of good, caring, compassionate, service
- Respect for autonomy and dignity
- Acting with honesty and dignity
- Maintaining professional competence
- Respect for values and autonomy of other professions and colleagues
- Service to community and societal needs
- Seek justice in Health resource distribution

Various professional sub-specialties of medicine, Pharmacy, and other professions such as dentistry and nursing likewise have their own Codes specific to their professional spheres.

The Congress

While not "non-governmental", the Congress is also involved in self-regulation. The House has a Code of Official Conduct including 19 items, with details, ranging from "behaving at all times in a manner that shall reflect creditably in the House" (I guess that doesn't include televised Hearings unless I misunderstand "reflect creditably"), to consulting and lobbying.

Press and Other Media

Unquestionably the press, television, and social media have a major impact on the events that unfold every day in this fascinating example of the

Dynamic Tension which we can observe and in which we can participate on a daily basis. One can find an entire spectrum of opinions and learn via the various polls what others profess to believe and want. Nowhere is the First Amendment so brilliantly exemplified.

Drug Industry

The Pharmaceutical Research and Manufacturers Association maintains a Code, as does the Pharmaceutical Marketing Council, which consists of Advertising and other functions which serve the industry.

Many Drug companies publish their own Codes. Perhaps the most elaborate of these is *The Blue Book*, a 50-page monograph from Pfizer, with sections dealing with: integrity, the industry generally, and company relations with colleagues, the community, and the Public.

Third Parties/Managed Care Controls

Since the establishment of Medicare and Medicaid, they, and a wide variety of other third parties offering Drug benefits, have imposed a laundry list of controls affecting a range of activities from the manufacturer down to the dispenser. Especially important is their effect on pricing.

As managed care plans use their substantial buying power to alter purchasing patterns in the marketplace, an area of potential backlash against these arrangements is evident in a series of legislative and court battles over unitary pricing (referred to as "anti-discriminatory pricing" Bills by supporters and "anti-discount pricing" by opponents). These proposals typically require that pharmaceutical manufacturers and distributors offer their products to all retail purchasers on the same terms and conditions.

A close relationship with a managed care organization can help a Drug maker carve a niche in the developing field of disease management because of the need to focus on patient populations rather than individual patients. Such programs require "the development of clear clinical guidelines, agreement on the part of providers and patients to participate, a sophisticated information architecture, well-designed and tested interventions and a logical measurement plan for the collection of outcomes" data – all tasks within the purview of managed care (445).

Central to the arena of third party managed care are the Pharmacy Benefit Managers. (See below in this chapter.) A Report by a Department of

Health and Human Services Panel described Pharmacy Benefit Management services as falling into three categories as shown in Table 6.1.

PBMs have been and certainly will continue to be controversial especially because of various kinds of vertical integration. Various forms of vertical integration between pharmaceutical manufacturers and Pharmacy Benefit Managers have been achieved. These alignments take a variety of forms, ranging from acquisitions to contractual agreements that cover collaboration on patient and physician education programs, joint development of patient compliance strategies, or the formation of new companies to develop disease management protocols. Especially troubling to independent pharmacies is the role of chains (e.g., Rite Aid and CVS) who own PBMs. Similarly, some PBMs own and operate mail-order pharmacies. The continuing evolution of the issues is BTSB, as is "Managed Care", a term which is inextricably linked with third-party programs.

Managed care has been described or defined in a variety of ways, but the essential attributes generally consist of (1) contractual arrangements with selected providers, such as pharmacies and pharmacists, who furnish a package of services to enrollees for a predetermined fee (capitation); (2) imposition of criteria for selection of providers, such as board certification or accreditation; (3) application of quality assurance, utilization review, and outcome measures; (4) use of financial or program coverage incentives or penalties to direct enrollees toward certain providers and away from others; (5) provider participation in risk-sharing; and (6) management of providers to assure that enrollees or members receive "appropriate" care from a cost-efficient mix of providers.

A number of managed care organizations agree with consumer advocates on the need for national standards for managed care to eliminate what has been called a "crazy quilt" of Regulations at the State and federal level. In September 1997, for example, managed care providers Kaiser Permanente, New York's HIP (Health Insurance Plans), and the Group Health Cooperative Puget Sound joined with the consumer advocacy groups, Families USA, and the American Association of Retired Persons (AARP), in calling for 18 principles of consumer protection to be embodied in national standards. The principles cover assured choice of Health plan and of primary care physician, as well as "prudent layperson" language that would require coverage of emergency care when a patient reasonably believes it is needed. The principles specifically call for an objective process to review new Drugs, devices, and therapies (447).

Table 6.1 Types of PBM Services

1. *Basic services*, which are composed of system management functions. These include:

    Claims processing, involving processing individual prescription claims for payment. This may involve confirming the patient's eligibility and the conformance of the Drug with the plan's formulary.

    Online Pharmacy networks, which employ an electronic link between independent pharmacies and the PBM for the transmission of claims, as well as to adjudicate eligibility and payment decisions on behalf of a given Health plan.

    Mail service pharmacies, which involve dispensing of prescriptions for chronic conditions by mail service pharmacies rather than through traditional retail Pharmacy settings.

2. *Intermediate services*, which harness the economic leverage of the PBM and its capacity to screen large databases of prescription chains against utilization and quality criteria. Such services include:

    Drug use review services involve scrutiny of individual prescriptions and overall prescribing patterns in comparison with predetermined cost and/or quality criteria. *Prospective review* screens individual prescriptions before they are filled to identify quality or utilization problems. *Retrospective review*, which occurs after prescriptions are filled and the claims submitted for payment, involves screening large numbers of claims to identify patterns of inappropriate prescribing or dispensing, potentially fraudulent activity or patient compliance problems.

    Formulary development and management services involve using the PBM to evaluate and select the Drugs to be included on the Health plan's lists of preferred Drugs (formularies). In such cases, the PBM decides which Drugs to include in the formulary, as well as the relative preference ranking for each Drug. In some cases, PBMs also actively manage prescription Drug formularies on behalf of Health plans. In this role, they typically handle requests for prior authorization; manage limits on the frequency or number of prescriptions or refills allowed; and enforce guidelines for Generic or therapeutic substitution programs.

    Educational interventions involve contact with physicians, pharmacists, and patients to alter product selection, consumption, and related practices.

3. *Enhanced services*, which are the most recently developed, involve PBMs in directly managing patient care. They include:

    Disease management practices, which are designed to manage the treatment of groups of patients who are grouped by diagnosis. Disease management is particularly popular in the management of chronic conditions, in which Drug therapy is expected to be needed on a long-term basis.

    Outcomes/cost-effectiveness research which uses the PBM's database for research on the cost-effectiveness or outcomes of Drug selections and therapies.

Source: 446 – Office of the Inspector General.

Formularies and Prescription Limitations

Formularies, when they are restrictive (and they usually are), affect the market place in a variety of ways. Hospital formularies, for example, limit the Drugs available for use in the hospital. Thus, the choices available to the physician are limited. Decisions on including a Drug, especially a new one, are usually made by a formulary Committee where the physicians can make their case for a Drug's inclusion. The hospital Pharmacy director (backed by the administrator, with her eye on the budget) is in a position of considerable power. She can, and does, argue on the basis, not only of economics but also on the literature extant, for inclusion or exclusion of any Drug as well as for Generic substitution. Essentially the hospital is a closed market (to the frustration of detailers to whom many hospitals limit or even forbid access.)

Every State has its own Medicaid Formulary, as does virtually every supplementary Medicare insurance provider. There are a variety of other restrictions in this marketplace such as requiring pre-authorization for prescribing certain Drugs and refill restrictions (both the number and frequency). For the patient, various restrictions limit Drug availability and affect the amount which she must co-pay. From personal experience as both a pharmacist and as a patient, I can attest to the amount of confusion that exists. This can be exacerbated when the prescriber, is not familiar with all of the formulary restrictions, prescribes a new "breakthrough" Drug (the detailer having just left her office and leaving samples) and the patient having driven across town to Walmart only to find that the Drug is "not covered". At whom should she be angry? The pharmacist? Not her fault! The physician? Maybe her fault. Perhaps she should have asked that detailer if the Drug was covered. (To their credit, many prescribers *do* make that a practice.) To the nameless/faceless People who decide these things? Or to Big Pharma, because "Drugs are too damn high"? All of the above?

Lawyers

Apart from their role in Investigation, Legislation, and Regulation, the legal profession is very much a factor in a variety of ways. The most visible are the attorneys encouraging the TV audience to explore how to get "substantial compensation" because of a Drug misadventure about which the drug manufacturer should have known or, worse yet, covered up. Understand that I am in no way opposed to a patient receiving damages for a condition or even death caused by a failure in the drug testing, production, or distribution system. I am often affronted by the content and tone of many of the TV ads especially, not on behalf of the drug industry, but mostly by my own perception of what I believe to be the advertiser's perception of the viewer's intelligence. But that's my rant. In any case, the legal profession does exert a certain level of control on the drug industry outside of the Government.

Advocates and Adversaries

There are many number of consumer advocacy organizations which have been vocal in their advocacy on behalf of their constituencies. Quite visible during Congressional Hearings has been the AARP, especially as they have given up the pretense of representing only retired persons. AARP is on record and in print of calling Big Pharma "Greedy". (See Chapter 10.) Consumers Union, which has published *Consumer Reports* since 1936, and *Public Citizen* are among the better known organizations.

The title Consumer Advocates suggests organizations created to support the needs and wishes of consumers who could do little as individuals. More than one such organization has been targeted as not really listening to those that they represent. A case in point is the AARP, by every account the largest of such groups.

In August, 2019, the *Wall Street Journal* reported that AARP had "fought a proposal….that would likely have lowered drug costs for its members". Why would AARP do that? As the movie said, "Look for the money". According to the article, membership dues amount to about $300 million, but *AARP* received more than twice that from United Health in royalties paid for an *AARP* endorsement.

Many *AARP* members certainly pay their relatively modest membership fee in order to receive various discounts on various goods and services. An unknown percentage certainly do belong in the hope and belief that *AARP* is looking out for them. In any case, the original Government proposal to end a rebate system with resulting lowering of Drug costs was withdrawn. The author of the *Wall Street Journal* "op ed" finished – "If *AARP* won't act in its members' best interest, maybe it's time seniors look elsewhere for the advocacy they need".

Mail-Order Pharmacy

The author is on record here and elsewhere for his opposition to mail-order prescriptions. The basis for my opposition is that it deprives the patient of the opportunity for complete services by a pharmacist. I take this position with full knowledge of the fact that not every community pharmacist provides the full measure of services which are now accepted.

In conjunction with the National Association of Boards of Pharmacy (NABP, an accrediting organization), Verified Internet Pharmacy Practice Sites (VIPPS is trademarked) was established in an effort to eliminate "rogue" mail-order pharmacies. Such accreditation is either recognized or required by more than 20 State Boards of Pharmacy (see also "Place" in Chapter 2).

Pharmacy Benefit Managers and Outcomes Management

(**Note:** A comprehensive treatment of the complicated role of PBMs can be found in Refs. 56 and 553.)

Pharmaceutical benefits managers (PBMs), or as they are sometimes classified, pharmaceutical benefits administrators (PBAs), represent a widely diverse business sector that serves as an operational intermediary to the Health insurance industry for the processing of prescription Drug claims in insurance benefits. Some PBMs offer a wide option of services, ranging from claim processing to clinical intervention programs, whereas others are more focused on limited services. PBMs offer services to insurance companies, as well as to governmental programs or directly to self-insured employers.

The anticipated goal of a quality pharmaceutical benefits management program is to control cost of Drug treatment and increase the safety and quality of care beneficiaries to the program. To facilitate these services, employers, Health plans, and government benefit programs will often contract with pharmaceutical benefits management (PBM) firms, organizations that specialize in Pharmacy claim and distribution services. PBMs typically offer their potential clients a variety of clinical and administrative services, but the services offered and administration methods vary significantly across PBMs.

Services Provided by PBMs

Claim Adjudication

The primary function of the PBM industry has historically been, and continues to be, the industry's ability to provide electronic claim processing services to clients. Claim processing functions are similar across the industry and provide the single greatest source of administrative efficiency to the Health insurance industry with regard to Pharmacy benefit administration. PBMs typically charge their clients a claim processing fee.

Claims Processing Standards

Pharmacy claims are processed electronically in accordance with standards that have been established by the National Council for Prescription Drug Programs, Inc. (NCPDP). NCPDP is a not-for-profit ANSI-Accredited Standards Development Organization that creates and promotes standards for the transfer of data within the Pharmacy sectors of the Health Care industry.

Pharmacy Network Management

One of the primary services that is provided by the PBM industry is the provision of a Pharmacy network that will provide prescription services to designated beneficiaries. All major PBMs offer a wide variety of network options, including both chain and independent community Pharmacy and mail service (home delivery) Pharmacy.

Community Pharmacy Networks

PBMs offer community Pharmacy networks that are very broad or fairly restrictive, depending on the client's needs and the desired cost of the Pharmacy services. Typically, PBMs offer a wide network that includes most community pharmacies nationwide.

Mail-Order Services

PBMs often offer mail Pharmacy services as a convenience to the client's beneficiaries and to provide added savings to the Pharmacy program.

Typically, the PBM will contract with a single mail-service vendor in an exclusive arrangement that offers deep discounts on the purchase of pharmaceuticals.

Specialty Pharmacy Services

Recently, several PBMs have focused significant efforts on the acquisition of specialty pharmacies as a product extension. Specialty pharmacies limit their Drug-dispensing activities to those medications that require unique handling or patient monitoring.

Formulary Management

The PBM industry provides formulary management as a basic component of the services that it provides to its clientele. A formulary is a list of medications that is preferred for use in a patient population. Based on recommendations used by hospitals and required by the Join Commission for the Accreditation of Healthcare Organizations (JCAHO), PBMs utilize the service of Pharmacy and therapeutics (P&T) Committees for the development of the formulary.

Controversies in the PBM Industry

The PBM industry has been under considerable scrutiny with regard to their business practices. Although many clients contract with PBMs under the expectation that the PBM is acting on behalf of the client, recent disclosures regarding the industry suggest that this may not always be the case. As a result, Investigations into PBM business practices and litigation against the industry have been common in recent years.

The shifting of corporate revenues from plan sponsors to manufacturers has raised significant concerns regarding the intended focus of PBM business practices. These Drug interventions may provide savings to a plan sponsor, but it is also quite possible that the interventions could result in decisions that are not in the interest of the health plan, particularly when the activities are a significant source of the PBM's profits. The inherent conflict of interest within the industry became apparent. Furthermore, many of these relationships were not disclosed by the PBM when contracting with a client.

Historically, the PBM industry has been largely free from regulatory oversight. Although a Pharmacy operation is subject to State Pharmacy laws and any publicly traded companies were subject to Securities and Exchange Commission (SEC) Regulations, the actual business practices of the PBM were not subject to Regulation. Unlike a Health insurance company that is subject to considerable regulatory oversight, the PBM industry, as a claim processor, was viewed as a service vendor, subject only to contractual obligations to its clients.

Future of the PBMs

As with the entire Health Care industry, considerable change is occurring within the PBM industry. Changes in electronic capabilities, enhanced oversight, and industry competition will all play a role in the scope of services offered by the industry in the future. Finally, overriding concerns about prescription drug prices will lead to a revised emphasis in evaluating PBM performance.

Without a doubt, the electronic capabilities of the industry are essential for efficient adjudication and payment of claims in the Health Care industry. This capability will increase. By electronically transmitting prescriptions, physicians will be able to identify other medications that the patient is receiving, regardless of the source of this prescription. Feedback regarding cost-effective alternatives and clinical literature will be available to the prescriber when initiating the prescription. Information regarding patient compliance and potential Drug interactions will also be made available. Clinical information and diagnosis can be captured during the prescription transmission, providing the dispensing pharmacist with valuable clinical information regarding the patient for the purpose of counseling patients regarding their Drug therapy.

Conclusion

This is not an exhaustive listing of influences by forces outside the Government. The ballot box certainly qualifies, but it serves to demonstrate, again, the Dynamic Tension that can exist in a free enterprise-based democracy.

Chapter 7

The People and Their Drugs

Introduction

While the Government and Big Pharma are hard at work flexing their respective Dynamic muscles, the People are hard at work: ploughing furrows, assembling autos, teaching reluctant children and combative college students, giving care to the ill, writing Books, being ill, and dying.

In my research for this Book, I found little evidence that either the Government or Big Pharma has spent much time trying to understand the People. Evidence is the operative word. Big Pharma certainly does explore the behavior of their potential customers, especially in the over-the-counter (OTC) marketplace, but their findings are rarely published – for obvious competitive reasons. Big Pharma tends to focus on the prescriber, the Government, and on the voter.

What *is* published tends to be the work mainly of academics. Sociologists have been primarily keen observers of what the People do, and psychologists focus on why they do it. The work of both disciplines forms the basis of much of what follows in this chapter. Some of the material may seem a bit abstract, but good sociology, especially, results in explanations of phenomena we already know but perhaps had not thought about.

The People as Patients

In fact, all of the People are real or potential patients. Patienthood can be professionally conferred or self-conferred. People can be ignorant (treatable) or stupid (not treatable). People can fear illness or seek it (hypochondriacs, malingerers). People fear death or, in some cases, seek it. People may be insensate, disabled, or debilitated. They can be plagued or sustained by their own beliefs, attitudes, knowledge, social status, age – the list can go on. People find their hopes buoyed or destroyed by any or any combination of these and other factors. In short (too short), "patienthood" can be ephemeral or permanent – imprecise, when the patient needs and desires precision. And, of course, the patient may not believe or trust the precision even when it exists.

Demographics

The Public consists of several easily identifiable groups, although the borders between the groups are often a bit fuzzy. Of interest to the players are such obvious categories as: age, gender, race, religion, marital status, occupation, political party (by the time this Book is published, the 2020 election will be history), and many, many others of differing relevance. Exploration of the *relevance* of each is BTSB, but the elderly deserve a special mention.

One group, identifiable and much in the news is the "millennials", who have replaced the "Baby Boomers" as an identifiable demographic group. They appear to be willing to embrace the concept of "Medicare for all", which was widely feared as "socialized Medicine" in the days when Medicare was first proposed.

Needs and Wants

The distinction between these two is easily understood:

- Mother to young son, "You need a haircut".
- Young son, "I don't want one. All of the guys are keeping their hair long".

In the case of prescription Drugs, mother has been displaced by the prescriber in defining "needs". Abraham Maslow (546) provided a well-known listing of a sort of hierarchy of human needs. History and research indicate that human activity, including human behavior, is directed toward satisfaction of these basic needs. Maslow's list, with my interpretation, follows. (According to Maslow, an individual normally tries to satisfy the most basic needs first, and having satisfied these, she is then free to devote her attention to the rest of the needs on the list.)

1. The Physiologic Needs – This group includes hunger, thirst, sleep, and so forth. These are the most basic needs, and until they are satisfied, other needs are of no importance.
2. The Safety Needs – In modern society, these needs are more often reflected in the needs for economic and social security rather than in needs for physical safety.
3. The Belongingness and Love Needs – The need for affectionate relations with individuals and a place in society is so important that lack is a common cause of maladjustment.
4. The Esteem Needs – People need self-esteem, a high evaluation of self, and the esteem of others, in our society. Fulfillment of these needs provides a feeling of self-confidence and usefulness to the world; failure to fulfill these needs produces feelings of inferiority and helplessness.
5. The Need for Self-Actualization – This is the desire to achieve to the maximum of one's capabilities, and although it may be present in everyone, its fulfillment depends upon the prior fulfillment of the more basic needs.
6. The Desire to Know and Understand – These needs refer to the process of searching for meaning in the things around us.
7. The Esthetic Needs – These needs may not appear to be present among many individuals because of their failure to satisfy more basic needs, but among some individuals, the need for beauty is an important one.

At first glance, it would seem that pharmaceuticals solve only the physiologic needs. Developments in prescription Drugs, however, give promise of meeting more and more of these needs. Certainly many other products currently offered in pharmacies are designed to meet these specific needs.

Philosophers and theologians have argued about the meaning of life for centuries and I don't want to join that argument. But there's still an important, unanswered question: What do People do when they have enough satisfaction for their physical, safety, belonging, and status needs? What do they pursue then? The answer is self-actualization, the complete fulfillment of all of their human capacities. This means enlarging and enhancing themselves. It means extending their personal identities, their individuality, and their uniqueness.

It's easy to see that most of us are busy trying to fulfill more basic needs than self-fulfillment most of the time. We all spend most of our lives trying to stay alive and healthy, to be secure, to maintain our relationships with our family and friends, and to get some respect and recognition for who we are as People. Most consumers' minds are occupied with their efforts to stay well, get along with People, make a buck, and look good while doing it.

Beliefs or Knowledge?

Josh Billings has wisely noted: "It ain't the things people know that causes all the trouble in the world. It's the things they know that ain't so". Indeed!

> A humorous (?) anecdote, perhaps germane: A man walks into a bar.
> Bartender: "Hi, Joe. I thought you were in Hawaii."
> Joe: "Couldn't go."
> Bartender: "Why not?"
> Joe: "Went to the skin doctor yesterday and he gave me some ointment. The prescription label says "Apply locally."
> Bartender: "Too bad."

(The Reader is encouraged to compose his/her own joke about "Shake well before using".)

> 'Poor devils,' (the physician) said as he sank down in a worn easy chair. "So scared and so stupid – no sense. Had a painful case this evening. Woman who ought to have come to me a year ago. If she'd come then she might have been operated on successfully. Now it's too late, makes me mad. The truth is people are extraordinary mixture of heroism and cowardice. She's been suffering agony and borne it without a word, just because she was too scared to come and find out that what she feared might be true. At the other end of the scale are the people who come and waste my time because they've got a dangerous swelling causing them agony on their little finger which they think may be cancer and which turns out to be a common garden chilblain."

(88)

This incisive observation, a fictional one, was made, not by a physician, or a medical sociologist, but by a very special pharmacist, Agatha Christie. Obviously Dame Christie used her time as a chemist for more than learning about poisons. In this incident, she pointed out clearly the complex and often conflicting fears and wishes of the patient confronted with symptoms. For all the study of these phenomena, we still have little clear knowledge of why a given symptom sends one person quickly to a physician and leaves another nursing her fears at home. Fortunately, there is a conceptual model which helps.

Health Belief Model

The Health Belief Model (HBM) is good Sociology. It explains something we already knew but probably never thought of. (See Figure 7.1.) The HBM is more often used to explain behavior when an individual is "healthy". It can be applied to such current issues as measles vaccinations. In explaining human behavior, the HBM consists of several components:

- The first two are susceptibility and seriousness, or, how likely is the bad thing to happen and how bad will it be if it does.
- Modifying factors include demographic, sociological, and knowledge variables.

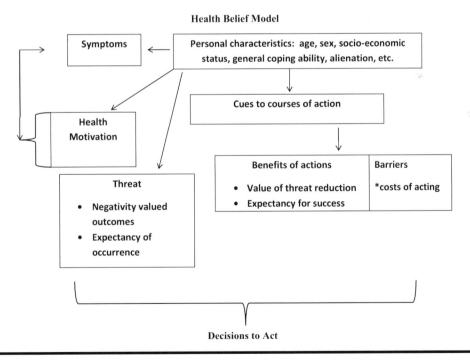

Figure 7.1 Health belief model. (Model derived and constructed from narratives of K. Lewin, *A Dynamic Theory of Personality*, Translated by D. K. Adams and K. E. Zenner, McGraw-Hill, 1935, and Irwin M. Rosenstock, "Historical Origins of the Health Belief Model", *Health Education Monographs*, Vol. 2, Winter, 1974.)

- There are cues to action, family pressure and/or prior illness, experience, press and Public service announcements, etc.
- Perceived benefits and barriers – what's in it for me if I do it? – feeling better; approval of peers; self-satisfaction; or it's too expensive, inconvenient, or has a social stigma, etc.

All of these factors go into what the HBM says is the "Likelihood of Taking Action".

Fortunately, good sociology often turns out to be common sense. Rosenstock, an excellent sociologist, translates this into words we can all understand. He tells us: "that in order for an individual to take action to avoid a disease he would need to believe (1) that he was personally susceptible to it, (2) that the occurrence of the disease would have at least moderate severity on some component of his life, and (3) that taking a particular action would in fact be beneficial by reducing his susceptibility to the condition or, if the disease occurred, by reducing its severity, and that it would not entail overcoming important psychological barriers such as cost, convenience, pain, embarrassment" (90). Now that makes sense!

The HBM applies beautifully to the issue of medication compliance, as does the Sick Role Model, which is explained in the following section. I have used case studies in the classroom to show how the HBM can be applied in Pharmacy practice. Here is an example.

A Case – Health Belief Model

A. Abstract

A patient recently diagnosed with hypertension was discovered to be non-compliant with his medication. The pharmacist determined that the patient's beliefs were the major reasons for this. The case describes the use of the HBM in explaining the relationship between Health beliefs and non-compliance.

B. Dilemma

Patients do not always take their medications as prescribed. Although this problem is well documented, the causes are not well established. However, it is clear that patients' Health beliefs are a major factor affecting compliance behavior. The pharmacist is in an excellent position to assess those beliefs and determine if modifications are necessary to ensure appropriate compliance behavior.

C. Case

Mr. and Mrs. Dobbs came into the Pharmacy to refill Mr. Dobbs' prescriptions. While filling these prescriptions, the pharmacist noticed on the family profile system that Dobbs had received a new prescription for hydrochlorothiazide (HCTZ) 50 mg/d 4 months ago that was never refilled. Since the prescription was supposed to be refilled every 3 months, the pharmacist asked Dobbs why he had not refilled it.

Dobbs stated that he got the prescription when he visited his wife's doctor to get treated for a backache. He was given a few Drug samples and was told to return in a week. He received the prescription for HCTZ at the second visit. Although his blood pressure was taken during both visits and the doctor told him he had high blood pressure, Dobbs thought his medication was for his back. Since it did not relieve his back pain, he stopped taking it. Not only did the Drug not work, but it often made him wake up in the night to go to the bathroom. "Besides," said Dobbs, "I really don't think I have high blood pressure. I have never been sick a day in my life and I am not the nervous type".

The pharmacist excused herself to call Dobbs' physician to confirm the diagnosis. He learned that Dobbs had diastolic blood pressure readings of 103 and 101 mm Hg during his last two visits. The doctor prescribed the HCTZ at the second visit and Dobbs was supposed to return for a recheck in 3 months. The physician was distressed to learn about Dobbs' non-compliance and asked the pharmacist to convince the patient to take the Drug and to return to his office for a recheck in a month.

The pharmacist returned to Dobbs and explained to him the physician's concern that he take the HCTZ. He stated that high blood pressure is a symptomless disease that frequently occurs in men Dobbs' age (he is 55) and that untreated hypertension can lead to heart disease, kidney trouble, or stroke. The pharmacist explained to Dobbs that HCTZ was prescribed because it is very effective in the treatment of hypertension. If Dobbs wished, the pharmacist would take his blood pressure after 1 month of treatment to determine if the Drug was effective.

Dobbs seemed willing to take the Drug regularly but expressed concern about the frequent urination associated with the medication.

The pharmacist recommended taking the Drug in the morning before breakfast to reduce that problem. Dobbs agreed to take the medication in that manner and promised to see the pharmacist in about a month. He did not have his blood pressure taken by the pharmacist.

One month later, Dobbs came in for a refill. He smiled at the pharmacist and said, "I just got back from the doctor's office and he was very pleased. My blood pressure was fine because of the medication, and I don't need to get up in the middle of the night anymore. I really appreciate the information you gave me about high blood pressure because I certainly did not understand it before".

The pharmacist accepted the thanks and offered to teach Dobbs how to take his own blood pressure so he could monitor his own Drug therapy.

D. Overview

Dobbs' reaction to being diagnosed as hypertensive can be explained using the HBM. This model examines how patients' beliefs affect their compliance behavior. The HBM states that compliance behavior depends on four patient facts: (1) motivation toward good Health, (2) perception of susceptibility to the disease, (3) perception of the personal severity of the consequences of the disease, and (4) assessment of the costs of taking the Drug compared to its benefits.

While Dobbs' motivation toward good Health is not established, his denial of his condition is explained by his perception that he was not susceptible to that disease. This perception may have been caused by the serendipitous diagnosis of his condition and by the fact that hypertension is essentially a symptomless disease. The patient's perception of the severity of the disease was low because he did not know the medical consequences. Finally, Dobbs' assessment of the costs of taking the Drug (e.g., increased tendency to urinate) far outweighed any observed benefit of compliance.

With this analysis of Dobbs' beliefs in mind, the pharmacist's approach to educating the patient was very appropriate. The explanation of the disease and its sequelae helped Dobbs understand his susceptibility to hypertension and the possible harm he faced if he failed to treat it. The pharmacist also altered Dobbs' assessment of the costs versus benefits of compliance action by: (1) suggesting a morning dose to minimize the diuretic effect and (2) suggesting self-monitoring of blood pressure to demonstrate the Drug's effectiveness.

Attitudes and Evaluation of Drugs

Attitudes tend to be the result of "social knowledge", the accumulated information, and past experiences that exist uniquely in individuals and collectively in societies. This knowledge consequently influences the perception of experiences and future behaviors. What an individual or group knows about Drugs, from reading information, listening to the media and promotional campaigns, receiving descriptions of others' experiences, and recalling her own previous experiences, will affect the actual use of Drugs. Social knowledge about the effects of a certain Drug additionally will influence the experiences users have with that Drug.

The nature and meaning of Drug use are described, remembered, and transmitted through a society in a symbolic form, as images, concepts, representations, or metaphors. In other words, People's experiences with and uses of Drugs are constructed and motivated as much by the "social" effects as by the physiological effects (315). This helps to explain various types of Drug-taking behaviors that are not based on scientific knowledge or the results of pharmaceutical research but rather on myth and cultural belief.

Famed consumer motivation specialist, Earnest Dichter, postulated, more than 50 years ago, some fascinating ideas about patient attitudes toward Drugs (Table 7.1). He felt we still believe in magic, albeit scientific magic, ["magic bullets" (34)]. A human's basic motivation is directed toward good Health and remains unchanged. The thing that has changed is the remedies, some diseases, and the practitioners and institutions involved.

Feedback serves as a powerful reinforcement of behavior in all areas, and Drug use is no exception. Prior personal experiences with a particular Drug, either by a prescriber or a patient is often a major determinant in future use. Unfortunately, the effects of Drug therapy are extremely difficult to measure and interpret correctly. Thus, feedback often may be judged incorrectly, leading to improper Drug use decisions. Laymen are not trained Drug evaluators and, with the exception of those physicians who are also clinical pharmacologists, neither are many prescribers.

Some of the factors that can confound the evaluation of a Drug's true effects include the following:

1. The difficulty of separating coincidental effects from cause and effect relationships: Many illnesses are self-limiting, but Drugs used coincidentally for treatment may be believed to provide a cure even if they are ineffective pharmacologically. Perhaps this is a factor in the frequent

Table 7.1 Patient Attitudes toward Drugs

Drugs	Nature of Attitude
1. Anesthetics	Justified by Adam's sleep during "rib surgery", but some women feel that (after the Bible) they are destined to bring forth children in pain.
2. Cold remedies	Attitudes tend to be very individualistic – ranging from fatalism (nothing works) to the fighter (no cold can lick him!). Remedies tend to be a source of personal pride.
3. Laxatives	People seldom consult physicians here, so self-medication is frequent. Psychological factors important and may, in fact, cause constipation.
4. Contraceptives	The success of the oral contraceptives reflects social change. Use of "the pill" and other methods depends on varying motivations ranging from the frigid woman to the domineering male.
5. Eye drops and eye washes	The eye is the window of the soul, but resistance to use of eye preparations may be strong because they are vulnerable and sensitive. Users of eye drops are thought to be vain, while eye washes are thought of as part of total, good Health Care.
6. Vitamins	The one influence in his/her well-being for which an individual may exercise considerable control is his/her diet. Thus, we have a preoccupation with vitamins.

Source: L. Dichter, *Handbook of Consumer Motivations*, New York: McGraw-Hill Book Co., 1964, with permission (450).

prescribing of antibiotics for the common cold; usually the cold goes away in a week, and if a prescriber gets into the habit of using antibiotics, she eventually may convince herself that the reason the cold goes away is because an antibiotic was used.

2. The failure to separate pharmacologic effects from placebo effects: Both are important components of Drug therapy, and certainly placebo uses are appropriate and effective in many cases. It is important, however, that the physician and the pharmacist clearly understand the distinction between pharmacologic and placebo effects so that proper Drug use decisions may be made.
3. The lack of patient feedback: A lack of patient contact after treatment may be interpreted by the prescriber as being a result of the success of the Drug therapy used. Obviously, this might not be the case. The patient might have gone to see another physician, decided to bear

up under the problem until it went away by itself, or even have died. Unfortunately, such reasoning is itself reinforced by Advertising, such as that for a prescription sedative stating, "When your patient doesn't call the next day, you'll know she slept".
4. The failure to recognize side effects or relate them to the use of a particular Drug product: This sometimes occurs because it is difficult to monitor patients, especially in an ambulatory situation. Thus, feedback that might have modified a prescriber's future use of Drugs is not easily obtained.

The Sickness Career

It is helpful to begin with the concept of sickness as a "career", as diagrammed in Figure 7.2. We can start with an assumption of wellness, although we have seen repeatedly that "well" and "healthy" are elusive terms. But we have to start somewhere and "normal" seems best.

Trying to define "normal" for society is difficult but is not really necessary for the present discussion. Normal, for our purposes, and for those of the patient, is whatever the patient perceives it to be. For that reason, of course, the characteristics of normality vary from individual to individual. In any case, changes from normal can take several forms. The most typical one is what we usually call "symptoms". For most People, pain is not normal, nor is dizziness, nor is constipation. Thus, these symptoms represent a change from normality. Another kind of change is altered capacity – for instance, the inability to cut the grass without becoming winded. This kind of change may, of course, be attributed to something other than illness, such as aging. (Indeed, some such changes *should* be so attributed, but stereotyping can result in misdiagnosis.)

It should be obvious that some People enter the Health Care system without experiencing any change from normality. Many hypertensive patients, for example, are diagnosed even though they are asymptomatic. Such patients begin their sickness career as a result of routine checkups or screening programs.

Drug manufacturers and Public Health proponents also are concerned with "helping" People decide that a change has occurred. "Cancer's Seven Danger Signals" are described in terms of deviations from normality, while some commercials for nonprescription Drugs describe, or at least imply, physical changes that should (or should not) occur in a normal individual.

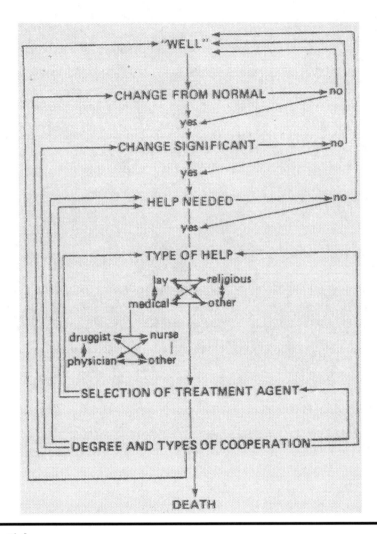

Figure 7.2 Sickness as a career.

The role of tolerance threshold should be obvious. Some People stoically "grin and bear" levels of pain that would send others immediately for help. Some variations are cultural – men are supposed to be "macho" – but ethnic variations in response to pain have also been demonstrated.

Symptoms are likely to be defined as serious in a direct relationship to their unfamiliarity to the patient or to the degree to which they seem threatening. Symptoms that persist or recur tend to be viewed as serious.

Assumptions about cause include a component of ambiguity. The seriousness attached to back pain, for example, may differ depending on whether the patient believes it is due to muscle pain or to a kidney disorder. The same is true for assumptions about prognosis. Symptom seriousness appears to be related directly to the length of time it is expected to last, to the degree of incapacity expected to be associated with it, and to the degree to which death is thought to be a likely outcome.

Interpersonal influence often takes the form of what has been referred to as the "lay referral system" – i.e., the network of friends and relatives who are consulted when a symptom is experienced. It should be apparent that the influence of these significant others is in turn a function of the degree to which they are influenced by their personal perceptions of the factors under discussion.

It is well known that many symptoms are experienced routinely by the population, yet many never do anything to relieve these symptoms. Some studies have shown that social stress from other life crises may be a trigger to action. A person who has lived with intermittent bouts of stomach pain may, when stimulated by a divorce action, suddenly decide to seek care.

Treatability apparently affects perception of seriousness in that conditions perceived as untreatable are likely to take on the identity of handicaps rather than of sickness. Physical manifestations (such as visibility to the patient and to others) are likely to result in attaching greater seriousness to symptoms. The same is true for the way the patient handles her symptoms. Grimaces and groans by the patient, whether voluntary or involuntary, are likely to lead to a greater level of severity being attached to the condition by those around him.

It should be clear from the foregoing that Health decisions are complex, subjective, often emotional, and subject to influence by others.

Significance of the Change

Among the facts that appear to enter into the patient's decisions concerning symptoms are the following:

1. Extent of interference with normal activities or characteristics.
2. The clarity of the symptoms.
3. The tolerance threshold of the symptomatic person.
4. The familiarity and seriousness of the symptoms.
5. Assumptions about cause.
6. Assumptions about prognosis.
7. Interpersonal influence.
8. Other life crises of the symptomatic person.

9. Assumptions about treatability.
10. Physical manifestations.
11. Impression management (452).

This list is not necessarily exhaustive, and the evidence supporting the impact of each factor is sometimes equivocal. Nevertheless, there is some evidence in *each* case that these factors play some (usually unquantified) role in the complex decision-making process of the patient as she pursues her sickness career.

It has also been found that the more a condition inconveniences an individual (or sometimes those with whom she relates), the more likely it is to be viewed as significant.

Need for Help

We have shown that there are a number of often-related factors involved in the decision that a symptom is significant. Even having made that decision, however, it is by no means universally true that the patient will decide to seek aid as opposed to self-treatment or even capitulation to the illness. Examples of the behavior variations involved can be seen in the results of a number of studies.

In one study, Bush and Osterneis (452) used a quantitative technique called path analysis to determine some of the factors involved in the use of prescribed and nonprescribed medicines.

- Perceived morbidity is the principal predictor of medicine use, especially prescribed medicine with physician intervention.
- Anxiety has an effect on the use of prescribed medicine.
- The less convenient and available medical care is perceived to be, the more likely persons are to use nonprescribed medicines.
- Age, sex, and race are factors in both types of medicine use, with males, non-whites, and the young using fewer Drugs.
- Neither Medicare, Medicaid, nor economic class had significant effects on Drug use.

Type of Help Needed

Once the decision to seek help has been made, the patient is still faced with a decision as to type of help. Although the physician is our society's model for primary care, she is by no means the only alternative. There are, for example, dentists, podiatrists, optometrists, chiropractors, clinical psychologists, and many other non-physician Health Care providers. Choice of type will be a function of social, cultural, economic, educational, emotional, geographic, and legal factors.

Appropriateness of a Particular Treatment or Type of Setting

For our purposes, this type of decision will be examined in the form of Pharmacy patronage motives. Consumers are motivated toward purchase in a particular outlet, as well as toward the purchase of a particular item. The same subconscious and overt motives may be factors in patronage of a particular Pharmacy or in the purchase of a product.

Common factors in several studies lead to the following list of significant patronage motives:

- Convenient location: close to home, work, physician, or shopping
- Like the personnel
- Price better than that of other pharmacies
- Parking
- Less waiting time
- Professional and convenient services
- Quality and merchandise assortment

If we assume that the pharmacist is successful in motivating her clients to patronize her Pharmacy, we can assume further that she would have some interest in the motivating factors behind their purchase. The motivation behind their *prescription* purchases is obvious. They have no choice other than the choice of having it filled or not and which pharmacist to fill it. Inherent in this situation is the potential for considerable customer dissatisfaction that the pharmacist would do well to recognize.

It has been shown that patients strongly dislike the bother, delay, and experience of purchasing prescriptions. People actually do not buy prescription Drugs. They do not really taste them, never analyze them, seldom appreciate them, or really test them. What they buy is the right to continue to be healthy. The Pharmacy is like a tax collector to whom People are compelled to pay a periodic toll as a Price for their Health. This makes the Pharmacy a basically unpopular institution. It can never be made popular or pleasant – only less unpopular, less unpleasant. Nobody likes a tax collector, not even a handsome Adonis or a seductive Venus.

The prescription is different from most other purchases. Generally speaking, a product should be more than a means of achieving objective utility. Even the other necessities of life offer more than this. Food can be purchased in ever-changing packages and variations. Clothing and shelter may be stylish and can be changed to suit the whims of the consumer. None of this is true of prescription Drugs. Practically the only way to build in any subjective utility is through the services that the Pharmacy offers. The objective of a Pharmacy's efforts ought to be to offer a cluster of such value satisfactions that People will want to deal with it rather than its competitors. This involves (1) making a careful calculation regarding what it is that the customer really values, (2) supplying services that meet these needs, and (3) communicating to the consumer the fact that one is doing this.

More than 50 years ago, the American Pharmaceutical Association, concerned about Pharmacy's image and planning a Public relations program, commissioned a national study to determine the level of consumer awareness of the nature and value of comprehensive Pharmacy services (453). It is interesting to review the findings, in view of what has changed and has not changed since. A contemporary study is needed but is unlikely to find a sponsor. I have summarized just a few of the findings in the paragraphs that follow.

In this study, slightly different reasons were found to be involved in the choice of a Pharmacy. Patients expect – and indeed want – professional attention and services, since the central issue is the patient's Health, and it is a matter of deep concern.

Patients are the focus of a "push/pull" effect. On the one hand they have been pushed away by increasingly negative feelings toward their community pharmacist. At the same time, they are pulled to the mass merchandiser and discount Houses by the allure of perceived lower Prices for prescription medication. However, the psychological satisfaction which the patient sees as missing in her relationships with the community pharmacist is even more lacking in dealing with the mass merchandiser. Direct personal contact between the community pharmacist and her patient – on a professional level – is indicated. For example, prescription medication should be delivered to the patient by the pharmacist him/herself, so as to create a feeling of personal interest and to answer any questions.

The Public is often unaware of what services the modern community pharmacist actually performs. And equally important, she is unaware of the *value* of these services. Further, today's patient reacts positively to a program of comprehensive pharmaceutical services when informed of its features.

It should be borne in mind that consumers generally will base purchase decisions on more than a Price if they receive equivalent perceived value or satisfaction in return.

Patients feel the pharmacist should share in the physician's responsibility for the appropriateness of the prescription medication and they rely on the pharmacist for the proper directions for medication use. This is considered an essential service.

The ideal practicing pharmacist is one who closely resembles patient's concepts of the "old-fashioned" family pharmacist – one who will provide the kinds of personal services covered by the term "comprehensive pharmaceutical services". Further, the pharmacist, particularly among older patients (who, after all, require more prescription medication), has a "carry-forward" credit in terms of a favorable impression created by "the old corner Drug store".

Since most patients realize it is the physician who prescribes the Drug product and the manufacturer who sets the cost to the pharmacist, both the physician and the manufacturer are to some degree held responsible for high Prices.

How much has changed in "retail" Pharmacy in the years since this study was conducted? How much is disappointingly the same? It is certain that there have been some dramatic differences in the nature of Pharmacy practice, as we noted elsewhere in this text. But what is the Public "face" of the pharmacist today? The very existence of mail order prescriptions strongly suggests that some proportion of patients value Price over the full package of professional services which personal contact with a pharmacist has the potential to deliver.

The Sick Role

The essential companion to the concept of a sickness career is Talcott Parsons' sick role model (261). It is especially important to the issue of patient compliance. But first, let's look at some of the general distinctions.

Three types of behavior are relevant to anyone serving the needs of patients or potential patients. These are, with definitions:

1. Health behavior: "Any activity undertaken by a person who believes himself to be healthy, for the purpose of preventing disease or detecting disease in an asymptomatic stage".

2. Illness behavior: "Any activity undertaken by a person who feels ill, for the purpose of defining the state of his Health and of discovering suitable remedy".
3. Sick role behavior: "Activity undertaken by those who consider themselves ill for the purpose of getting well" (260).

Health Behavior

Hardest of all Health-related behavior to predict is that of the "healthy" individual. Included in such behavior are decisions to obtain preventive care or detection tests as well as activities designed to maintain a state of wellness, such as dental hygiene and good nutrition. The individual has no clear-cut symptoms to prompt such action, yet the time, effort, and money spent on this type of activity are potentially the most productive of those spent on any Health Care activity. The HBM, described earlier, was formulated to explain aspects of Health behavior.

Illness Behavior

Understanding of the behavior of People when they are ill has been enhanced by viewing this behavior as the "sickness career". The sickness career begins with a state of wellness. As already noted, being well or healthy will mean something different to different People. There have been a variety of studies of this phenomenon, and the general criteria by which People view themselves as "well" include:

1. A feeling of well-being.
2. An absence of symptoms.
3. An ability to perform normal personal and work functions.

Although these criteria will not be uniform from person to person, their meaning for any given individual will form a baseline of Health against which to judge changes. When a change from a state of wellness is perceived, there will again be varying reactions. Most People – even those who feel well – are able to identify the presence at any time of some symptoms. Often they will view these symptoms as normal, although the symptoms may trigger a desire for further information.

Ultimately a decision must be made by the patient about the significance of symptoms. A variety of factors can go into a patient's determination of the significance of a symptom. Some examples:

1. Interference with normal activities and functions (e.g., bowel habits, work ability, or leisure activity are affected).
2. Clarity of symptoms (sharp pains or symptoms visible to family or friends are likely to be judged important).
3. Tolerance threshold (some People can tolerate more pain, either because of personal characteristics, cultural factors, or the nature of their work).
4. Familiarity with symptoms (common symptoms that one has experienced previously and recovered from are likely to be viewed as less serious than those that have not been previously experienced).
5. Assumptions about cause (e.g., in the case of chest pain, it may be viewed as anything from a heart attack to indigestion).
6. Assumptions about prognoses (if long-term incapacity or possible death is associated with the symptom, it is likely to be viewed as more serious).
7. Interpersonal influence (this item refers to effects of the lay referral system).
8. Other life crisis (in some cases, a symptom that might have been viewed as normal assumes greater proportions in the face of family or work crisis).

Symptoms are at the heart of pharmaceutical care. Without them, patients often will not seek assistance. They are the basis for self-medication (read the packages of OTC products). But the response to symptoms is by no means uniform or predictable.

People approach chronic and acute Health problems in different ways. For chronic ones, they devise strategies of care (determined partly by their roles, attitudes, and resources) over months and years and apply them during flare-ups. For acute problems, decisions about care are made in the short run and hinge mostly on symptoms. Analysis shows that actions complement or substitute for each other. Self-care actions (nonprescription Drug use and restricted activity) tend to co-occur and so do actions based on medical care (prescription Drug use and medical contact). The two domains substitute in one way (nonprescription Drug use greatly reduces chances of prescription Drug use) and join in another (restricted activity increases chances of medical contact).

Whatever sophisticated technical references there may be for her symptoms, the person who has symptoms will be concerned primarily with whether she hurts, faints, trembles visibly, loses energy suddenly, runs short of breath, has had her mobility or speech impaired, or is evidencing some kind of disfigurement. Aside from what these may signify to her about her disease or her life span, such symptoms can interfere with her life and her social relationships. How much they interfere depends upon whether they are permanent or temporary, frequent or occasional, predictable or unpredictable, and publicly visible or invisible, upon their degree (as of pain), their meaning to bystanders (as in disfigurement), the nature of the regimen called for the control of the symptoms, and upon the kinds of lifestyle and social relations that the sufferer has hitherto sustained.

Even minor, occasional, symptoms may lead to some changing of habits. Thus, someone who begins to suffer from minor back pain is likely to learn to avoid certain kinds of chairs and may even discover, to her dismay, that her favorite sitting position is precisely what she must eliminate from her repertoire. Major symptoms, however, may call for the redesigning or reshaping of important aspects of a lifestyle. A stroke patient writes: "Before you come downstairs, stop and think. Handkerchief, money, keys, Book, and so on-if you come downstairs without these, you will have to climb upstairs, or send someone to get them". People with chronic diarrhea need to reshape their conventional habits like this person did: "I never go to local movies. If I go....I select a large house....where I have a great choice of seats....When I go on a bus....I sit on an end seat or near the door".

Once a symptom is viewed as significant, a decision must be made whether help is needed, and, if so, what kind of help. The enormity of sales of nonprescription Drugs attests to the fact that self-treatment is often the first treatment choice. If consistent with the sick role, the individual chooses to seek professional help. Often a "lay referral system" is used, either for its own value or to encourage or recommend physician contact.

The Sick Role in Acute and Chronic Illness

Understanding the "sick role" or behavior expected of a person defined as sick is made easier by placing it in historical perspective. Treatment, both medical and social, of the sick person has changed with the level of civilization. At the most primitive level, the member who was ill was left to tend for herself or die, with no obligation placed on her neighbors to come to her aid. As civilization advanced, illness was frequently ascribed to evil spirits, and methods of assistance were limited to incantations and sometimes magic potions. The *Old Testament*, while changing the frame of reference somewhat, still placed illness in a religious context and is rife with references to illness as punishment for sins – either the patient's own or those of her family.

The *New Testament* brought about a sharp change in attitudes, even to the point of allocating "grace" to those who associated with or aided the sick. By the eighteenth and nineteenth centuries, secular authorities had become influential in Health Care, and as it became obvious that Health Care contributed to the common good, "contributions to the care of the sick grew larger, finding in the course of time, social security as its most striking expression" (262).

In spite of this progress, vestiges of the old attitudes remain. We still have difficulty adopting a wholesome attitude, for example, toward mental illness, and a subconscious uncomfortable reaction to crippled people is still widespread. All of this background is necessary to an understanding of the behavior pattern that society expects of those who are officially "sick". Sociologist Talcott Parsons has characterized the sick role as consisting of two rights and two duties (261).

>*Rights*: Freedom from blame for illness.
>Exemption from normal rules and tasks.

The rights are bestowed conditionally, however, and are appropriate only if the patient fulfills her duties.

>*Duties*: To do everything possible to recover.
>To seek technically competent help.

Obviously, there are deviations from this model, but when such deviance occurs, society's approval is usually withheld.

The sick role gives the individual a reasonable excuse for making claims on others for care. People with symptoms (i.e., who are "ill") can, with confirmation, adopt this special social role. A person can enter the sick role if a doctor confirms that the person is ill or if the family or friends of the individual are willing to accept the status of "sick". Thus, illness (individually defined) becomes sickness (socially defined), especially if a physician confirms the existence of disease. Indeed, the prescription may be thought of as a "ticket" to occupy the sick role.

Considerable evidence exists to suggest that four factors play an important part in determining whether one is allowed to be "sick":

1. Legitimization by physician: Someone is under a doctor's care. (Prescriptions are important evidence of this.)
2. Symptoms: Pains, discomfort, or other manifestations that indicate a change in Health.
3. Functional incapacity: The inability of persons to perform normal work activities.
4. Prognosis: The expected outcome of the illness, i.e., probably get worse, get better, stabilize, uncertain, etc.

As valuable as the sick role model is for understanding patient behavior, it should be clear that it does not apply to all cases. How, for example, is the *chronically* ill patient to "recover?" Indeed, such people cannot, but they can adopt a chronic illness role. This role is frequently a difficult one and medication may be not only part of the solution but also part of the problem. The benefits of Drug therapy that *works* are most easily understood as the elimination of problems.

Chronic illness is a twentieth-century phenomenon. Prior to this time, illness was generally acute in nature and limited in duration. Advances in sanitation, as well as other advances in medical knowledge and management of illness, resulted in impressive gains over the infectious and parasitic diseases. Regimens for curing or preventing previously irreversible or fatal diseases are currently available that could not have been imagined a century ago. These gains have not been entirely free of negative consequences. The successful treatment of acute life-threatening illnesses has resulted in an increase in the number of individuals with residual limitations and chronic physical or emotional problems. The difficulties attending many chronic conditions continue long after the acute stage of the illness has been successfully managed.

The way ill persons define chronic illness depends on the extent of abnormality of biological structure and function: the nature and severity of symptoms; the competence and skill to manage or control symptoms; and the values, norms, and expectations of others. Except for the anatomical or structural changes caused by the disease process itself, most of the factors that determine the meaning of illness are related in some way to the sociocultural world of the ill person.

The world of the chronically ill is made up of family, friends, and health care professionals, each with a personal perspective on the meaning of the illness and each, therefore, with a framework or rationale for responding to the ill person. Differences in perspectives and expectations between and among these sets of individuals create ambiguities, confusion, tension, and sometimes distress for the individual with chronic illness.

Professionals frequently have treatment goals that are at odds with those of patients. Professionals may define illness only, or primarily, in terms of physiological deviations from normal (elevated blood gases, diminished breath sounds, sugar in the urine, low hemoglobin) and plan treatment to manage these abnormalities with little concern for broader aspects of the patient's life. The individual with a chronic illness may, on the other hand, define the situation primarily in terms of her quality of life and establish goals related primarily to social functioning (eating out, entertaining friends, spending time with children, maintaining some level of gainful employment).

The simultaneous achievement of both sets of goals (professional and personal) may be difficult, and the potential for tension and misunderstanding between patient and caregiver is great. Unless steps are taken to change or modify goals, the final outcome may be discouragement, disappointment, and perhaps "giving up" on the part of both the professional and the patient. What is needed is communication and negotiation to achieve a compromised, but common, goal. Sharing a common goal, professionals and patients can establish reasonable criteria for judging the success of treatment. It may be that the most appropriate and humane criteria for measuring success are related to the clients' ability to function at some acceptable level of social intercourse and not near-normal body chemistries.

Three examples should provide some insight into the measures necessary to assist the patient (and the Reader) in assessing the negative effects of illness and the positive (or negative) effects of therapy. The tenets of the HBM are important here too.

Rheumatoid Arthritis

Arthritics may be put on strict Drug regimens: the Drugs hopefully provide control to help the arthritic normalize. Patients with long histories of frequent flare-ups often undergo sequential trials of potent anti-rheumatic Drugs, all of which have adverse side effects. Some have a difficulty in recalling the sequence of these trials: frequently they were not told what was in their injections and did not ask. For them, the balancing was weighted in favor of relief at any cost: "When you're hurting like that you have to do something".

Ulcerative Colitis

Many of the most important ramifications of this illness are personal and social in character. For much of the time, these latter problems are the foremost concern of persons chronically ill with ulcerative colitis.

Emphysema

Possibly the main problem of People who suffer from emphysema is the management of scarce energy. They may be able to increase their energy through a proper regimen. Primarily, however, they must allocate their energy to those activities which they must do or wish most to do. Hence, two key issues for them are symptom control (energy loss) and the balancing of regimen versus other considerations.

Whether a patient does or does not comply with their prescribed regimen and how they comply is determined in part by how the regimen interferes with her lifestyle and mobility needs. In part, it also depends upon how she comprehends or miscomprehends the uses and effects of therapy.

Sometimes Drugs via aerosol spray may be prescribed to immediately relieve periodic respiratory distress. These Drugs may be ordered at most three/six times a day because of undesirable side effects. When an activity requires extended oxygen expenditure, there is a likelihood of Drug overdose, since these sprays provide extra needed energy to complete an activity.

Also, although bronchodilator Drugs help breathing, these frequently cause untoward side effects such as nervousness and sleeplessness. Sometimes sedatives are required to counteract these side effects, but such Drugs may leave the patient groggy to get around. When Health personnel are not attentive to the patient's Drug balance problems, she may doubt both the usefulness of the therapy and the competence of the physician.

Besides the exemption of the chronically ill from the classic sick role, it is important to note that there is some evidence of unwillingness to grant the exemption from blame to People with certain maladies. Syphilis and gonorrhea are easily understood historic examples, but more recently, there is a certain reluctance to grant full rights to those who suffer from emphysema caused by smoking, hypertension due to obesity, or cirrhosis resulting from alcohol abuse. AIDS is, of course, an extraordinarily complicated situation with stigmatic implications for many of its victims. But even such a blameless condition as epilepsy does not assure freedom from blame for its victims.

Because of changes in the demographic makeup of the population, it is necessary to note that a further problem with chronic illness conditions is that they are not distributed randomly among the populations but are prevalent among those of advanced age. Normative expectations applied to older chronically ill People may be ambiguous because of certain similarities between typical attributes of being ill and being old. Expectations concerning aging may, like being sick, involve impairment of certain types of usual role performance, exemption from obligations, and other forms of permissiveness. Like the occupant of the sick role, the old person is not held responsible for her condition nor can she stop it by act of will. Again, such secondary gains as are associated with aging are mitigated by the lack of regard in which the state is often held. Ambiguities in the case of old, chronically ill People may have unwelcome consequences. There is evidence that older People with chronic illness tend to tolerate functional impairments unnecessarily (in that such impairments could be ameliorated with medical care) because they erroneously associate the symptoms with aging rather than illness. Professionals are not immune to this:

> Physician: The reason you are having trouble with your knee is your age.
> Patient: My other knee is the same age, and I'm not having trouble with *it*.

Compliance with Medication Regimens

Non-compliance with medication regimens, i.e., "Take as directed" flies in the face of the sick role. One is after all expected to "try to get well". "You're not even trying to get well", your mother says as you prepare to leave the House without a cap after missing school because of a cold. There go your "rights"! You are definitely going to be blamed and marched right back to school – wearing your cap.

Non-compliance also flies in the face of common sense. Why would one: take off work, wait for a long time in a doctor's lobby, listen for perhaps ten minutes to a physician (after thirty minutes in an exam room where you thought the doctor would "be right in"), back to your car, drive to the Pharmacy of your choice (or one designated by your "carrier"), pay whatever is your share, drive home to the immediate question from your spouse – "What did the doctor give you"?, and not take the medicine the way you're supposed to? Crazy, huh? (Two notes: that a prescription is a "gift from the doctor", and if somehow you didn't get a prescription, you're probably not really sick. See Latent Functions of the Prescription in Chapter 1.)

Answers to the long, rambling, question I posed can be found in an abundant and growing literature including my friend Jack Fincham's very excellent Book, *Patient Compliance with Medications* (111).

Non-compliance can take several forms (there is no limit to the human imagination). A few are as follows:

- Failure to have the prescription filled.
- Failure to have needed refills.
- Discontinuing use – "saving some" for later.
- Taking more than prescribed dose.
- Taking less than prescribed dose.
- Ignoring warnings – "Shake well", "No alcohol", "Take with food", "No Milk Products", etc.
- Taking with OTC or other Rx Drugs you didn't tell the prescriber about.

The consequences of non-compliance are very real and affect literally every player in the pharmaceutical delivery system.

- The patient, of course, and potentially her family.
- The prescriber and their evaluation of the Drug's effectiveness.
- The entire marketing effort of Big Pharma which was aimed at getting the prescription written in the first place.
- The pharmacist, especially with regard to unfilled or un-refilled prescriptions.
- Third parties because of the side effects.

It is worth noting that in the case of compliance, this is one time when decisions should be left up to the patients, for good or ill. Prior to actually receiving the physical product, others have been deciding what to produce, what to say about it, what to prescribe, what to dispense, and what to pay for. Some non-compliance may simply result from these circumstances.

"I had hardly sat down before the doctor reached for the prescription pad". One hears that all the time. Thus, some kinds of non-compliance have been shown to be intentional.

At the outset, failure to have a prescription filled or refilled may be a function of cost, even in the era of third-party coverage. Many considerations are involved in determining what Drug costs really mean to the patient. They include the following:

1. Cost of the prescription.
2. Cost of Drug per day.
3. Cost for partially versus entirely filling the prescription.
4. Cost of total treatment.
5. Proportion of total treatment cost.
6. Its position in cost sequence.
7. Perceived cost.
8. Expected cost.
9. Past cost experiences.
10. Importance of the cost, based on ability to pay.
11. Opportunity cost – what is given up to purchase the Drug.
12. Inconvenience or convenience of dosage form used in improving compliance.
13. Psychic or symbolic cost.
14. Cost of alternatives, including non-compliance.
15. Cost of competing products, their Generic equivalence or non-equivalence, and their therapeutic effectiveness.

Each of these items warrants the physician's consideration inasmuch as each alone, or in combination with others, may affect whether or not the patient ever receives the Drug or takes it properly. It should be noted that some of the factors that may inhibit the patient from getting the prescription filled initially may actually *promote* compliance once that step is taken.

Besides cost issues, which would seem to be obvious, there is a whole range of other functions which may affect compliance negatively.

The label on the prescription may be a problem "Take one tablet three times a day before meals and at bedtime". How many tablets should one take? One before a couple of meals, and then the third one at bedtime? Or did the doctor really mean, "Take one tablet before each meal and another one at bedtime."? There is the potential of plus or minus 25% difference there.

Sometimes the physician, remembering her Latin will write, "Ut dict", abbreviation for "As Directed", which the pharmacist will probably put on the label. Here is the point where "Comprehensive Pharmacy Service" should come into play. At least a question, "How did the doctor tell you to take this"? which would provide a minimal clue to what the patient heard and remembered. This can be very fuzzy. If the pharmacist suspects the patient is confused, should she call the doctor? What if the patient brought in the prescription after the doctor went home? What is the pharmacist's legal and ethical obligation in such a situation?

There is simply no room here to cover every factor which might contribute to poor compliance, whether intentional or unintentional. Nor is there room to cover every potential remedy, but it is the "clear and present duty" of all involved to explore and initiate every option to assure optimal Drug therapy.

As described above, there are numerous ways to see *cost* as a factor in compliance. Once the initial cost is considered, however, there may be a wide variation in what it costs the patient to use the Drug each day. Although it is unlikely that the patient has considered this in terms of the few cents that are usually spent daily for needed medication, she may have looked into how much "half" of the prescription will cost. Such partial prescription filling is often tried by low-income patients who either cannot pay the full cost or who are unsure whether or not the medicine will "work." The patient should be made aware that she will actually be penalizing herself by filling only part of the prescription if the pharmacist uses the professional fee rather than a markup system.

Another factor relates to the duration of treatment. The physician should be aware that in writing a prescription, authorizing five refills, and expecting the patient to get them all, she is writing an order for $200–$300 of medication or much more. The patient's experience and perceptions also have something to do with the role of cost in compliance. A $50 prescription charge means different things to different People. Income, the nature of the illness, the physician's indications of what charges to expect, and the level of prescription charges paid by the patient in the past, all affect their reaction to the charge for each new prescription.

Non-economic costs include the time the patient spends to get a prescription filled. There may be psychologic costs in admitting that one is ill enough to need a prescription and, indeed, the prescription itself may symbolize that weakness. On the other hand, some patients may feel that receiving and taking medicine is necessary to gain attention or to prove that they are really sick.

What is the Price of alternatives to Drug therapy, including non-compliance? Drug charges may not seem excessive if the alternative is an extra 2 or 3 days away from work. How the patient responds to the cost factors described is almost certainly affected in some way by (1) the proportion of the total treatment cost that goes for medications and (2) at which point the Drug costs actually appear in the "cost-of-illness" sequence. For example, the average patient is unlikely to notice a $50 Drug charge on a $1,200 hospital Bill, but even a prescription fee may become the "last straw" if it follows charges for physician services and x-ray and laboratory studies.

Physicians should be aware that seemingly minor differences in similar Drugs may have major implications for compliance. The ease of administration, comparatively rapid onset of effect, or in some cases the physician's choice has a dual effect on encouraging compliance. For example, certain psychotropic Drugs can be prescribed in large doses twice a day, rather than in smaller doses three or four times a day, with a cost saving to the patient. Both the lower cost and the less frequent dose would favor compliance.

As noted above, a full discussion of the multitude of factors which may affect compliance is BTSB. Using the writings of a number of researchers, the schematic shown in Figure 7.3 was constructed. The Reader will note that the figure contains elements of both HBM and sick role.

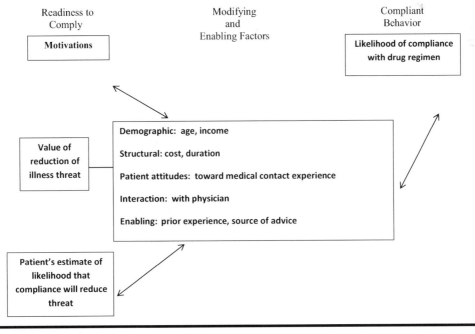

Figure 7.3 Factors affecting compliance.

The potential role of the pharmacist will be obvious as she is the "last chance" to assure that the patient understands not only how to use the medicine but also the importance of compliance. Performance by the prescriber in communicating the necessary information as well as her skill is persuading the patient of the importance is also essential. Another case study which I have used in Pharmacy classes will illustrate how the pharmacist may internalize the tenets of the sick role in compliance.

A Case – Sick Role and Compliance

A. Abstract

   A pharmacist must be more than a Drug dispenser. She must also be a source of confidence, support, information, and advice. The sick role is an awkward one for People who have always been healthy and requires extra sensitivity on the part of the pharmacist. The ramifications of the sick role affect the patient, her family, neighbors, and fellow workers. Armed with this knowledge, the pharmacist must encourage appropriate behavior in patients.

B. Dilemma – How to encourage assumption of the sick role temporarily

   It is crucial for the pharmacist to add to the cautions, advice, recommendations, and warnings given to the patient by the physician. The pharmacist should reinforce the seriousness of the condition enough to encourage the patient to follow the treatment regimen but not cause additional anxieties or a fatalistic orientation. The pharmacist must learn to walk this delicate tightrope by dealing with each patient individually.

C. Case

   Tina Furner was feeling pretty confident. She had just received her Pharmacy license and had no problems during her first week of unsupervised practice. She was thinking about what to make for supper that night and about an appropriate shower present for Cousin Nelly. Just then, Moose Grebowski walked in. Moose was really Erwin Thomas Barkley Grebowski, III, but everyone who knew him called him Moose because of his 220-pound, football player appearance. Moose had just graduated in the same class as Tina from North-South College and was on his way to football practice camp with the Big Apple Acres of the Mid-Mountain Football League, a farm club for professional teams.

   Tina couldn't hide her shock when she read the four prescriptions Moose handed her: propranolol, hydrochlorothiazide, digoxin, and captopril. Moose had some major heart problems. Tina regained her composure and prepared the four items, and then took them out to Moose who was sitting in the corner half way through a one-pound box of potato chips. Moose came to the counter and when Tina began to read the directions, he interrupted to say that he promised his father that he would get the medicine, but that he had no intention of swallowing any of it, or of resting completely for 3 weeks, either.

Tina was stunned and unsure of how to react. Now she wished that she had attended more Pharmacy administration course lectures. She told Moose that there was no shame in being sick and that if he took it easy as directed, he could gain enough strength to lead a normal life. Moose said, "I've never been sick a day in my 22 year, and I'm not going to give in to weakness now". Moose went on to say that his buddies were expecting him for a weekend camping and rock-climbing outing tomorrow and that tonight he had his first and long-awaited date with Peg Galore. He said he hoped to go canoeing with her. Moose asked Tina as he was leaving not to say anything about his conditions, because he wanted no one to know about it. Tina protested one last time as Moose left the store. Tina considered calling Moose's mom or stopping by his House to talk some more with him or even consulting with Moose's physician. Had she some experience in this area, she felt it might have been easier. She spent the next three hours thinking about the alternatives and then got very busy. She went home exhausted and the next day telephoned Moose's House only to be told that he was still sleeping because he got home at 5:00 am after his date. She dropped the pursuit since she didn't know who knew, what she could and should do, or where to turn. Tina heard from one of the neighbors on Monday that Moose had died over the weekend while rock climbing. She was really shaken, and for the next 2 weeks kept asking herself, "What could I have done to prevent this"?

D. Overview

Tina Furner must consider all of the facts and impressions available to her and act as she deems best in the patient's interest. Sometimes this may even involve doing something against the patient's wishes.

What patients and their families read and hear may affect compliance with effects ranging from a general distrust of medicines to a specific Drug reaction in a television newscast. Routine, effective medication use is not news. Medication *misadventures* are news, and a given item may add to any general angst concerning Drugs.

Why all the fuss about compliance? An advertisement that appeared in a medical journal shows a physician observing, "When my patients don't return, I assume the therapy is working." On the facing page, one of those patients says, "I couldn't tell my doctor his migraine therapy didn't work". The text of the ad cites data indicating that nearly half of all migraine sufferers have given up on their physicians either because of failure to improve or because of side effects of the medication prescribed. This example is illustrative of the complexity, subtlety, and importance of the compliance problem. Among the potential consequences of this particular situation with migraines are:

- Physician misjudgment of the effectiveness of the prescribed therapy, in this case probably resulting in repeats of this scenario with the next medication prescribed for this patient.
- Loss of income to the pharmacist.
- Loss of confidence by the patient in the efficacy of medications and perhaps in the skill of the physician.
- Continued migraine attacks with continued erosion of the patient's quality of life.
- Loss of patient productivity. (One estimate, cited in the ad, was that annual lost productivity from migraine attacks fell in the $6–$17 billion range.)
- Cost of other therapies, including OTC medicines, used by the patient to "try to cope" but to no avail.

There are literally hundreds of Reports describing the rates of non-compliance among patients with various medical conditions.

Compliance is often thought of (as it should be) in terms of therapeutic success or failure. If patients can reach a certain level of compliance, an improvement in symptoms may occur, a lessening of disease morbidity might be seen, or there might be a possibility of achieving a total cure. Conversely, if there is non-compliance, predictable continuation of symptoms, worsening of disease, or worse yet death may occur depending upon the condition being considered. Problems with patient compliance are similar across diseases, regimens, and age groups. Compliance is an equal opportunity problem.

Compliance is an equal opportunity problem for Big Pharma as well. Evidence of their concern is exhibited by the extensive coverage of the subject in an expansive 2019 presentation in the leading Drug marketing journal, *PM360* (457). Interviews with some "heavy hitters" in the industry made it clear that they are not sitting idly by awaiting prescriber and pharmacist initiatives. Some of the proposals sound like something out of *Star Trek* but illustrate just how seriously the compliance (they prefer "adherence") problem is taken.

Just one example – an AI-powered companion robot, called Mabu, for use in the home. Mabu is small enough to set on a counter and interact with patients by means of a tablet (not the kind you swallow) using "natural language processing and behavioral psychology" and adapting to patients' preferences over time. Mabu collects daily interactions to be sent to a cloud-based platform for providers to monitor. There's more here than just medication reminders. Mabu can evaluate a patient's emotional state, provide wellness tips, even contact care providers if needed. (Perhaps Mabu should have been named Big Brother.)

There's more. The article finishes with, "using technologies such as pharma-compliant virtual portals, real-time web meeting technology and/or asynchronous but interactive online discussion forms, Pharma can gain insights on how to improve adherence, while reducing the patient burden!! Got that?! Beam me up, Scotty!"

What is the "take away" message on compliance? First, to understand the non-compliant patient is to understand ourselves. Our Drug-taking behaviors, whether compliant or non-compliant, are better viewed as self-regulation behaviors. We tend to act according to our own best self-interests (as we define them). Our actions are understandable and (to a degree) predictable. We act to bring or restore normalcy and homeostasis to our lives. We act to reduce stress posed by fears and threats and disruptions to our daily routine. We formulate our actions based on information provided to us about our disease and the Drugs prescribed and based on cues derived from our own illness and Drug-taking experience. We make decisions with information we have at hand. If our personal database were loaded differently or if our personal Health perceptions were different, we would probably exhibit different actions.

Other Influences on Medication Use

In addition to the obvious role of prescribers and pharmacists, nearly every aspect of society impinges on it. Some of it seems to be cultural with Big Pharma frequently portrayed as the villain. A number of those whom I have labeled (somewhat unfairly) "Medical Muckrakers" are at the forefront.

Strong Medicine (113), by Arthur Hailey, is fiction but with a strong ring of truth. The heroine who begins her work in Big Pharma as a salesperson, in the course of the novel, finds herself in top management. A woman of strong moral character, she comes into contact with a number of others and situations who test her resolve.

Strong Medicine, published in 1979, was on the top 20 best seller list for the year. The novel was the subject of a TV mini-series in 1987 starring, among others, Dick Van Dyke. Hailey was also author of the very successful *Airport* and *Wheels*.

The collective influence of many critiques of the 1960s and 1970s was led by Ivan Illich's *Limits to Medicine – Medical Nemesis* (251), whose impact lasted for years. Illich, an academic, in maintaining that the medical establishment was a threat to Health, captured many Readers with such evocative statements as, "Physicians are those [experts] trained to the highest level of specialized incompetence". Specifically, Illich critiqued the pharmaceutical industry for its role in the worldwide "medicalization of life", a theme that continued to be raised with respect to Medicine as a whole and medicines in particular. His targets ranged from the misuse of the antibiotic chloramphenicol (which was part of a well-known medical "horror story") to overconsumption of medicine that, he admitted, reflected a "socially sanctioned, sentimental hankering for yesterday's progress".

What to Do

There are a variety of ways by which the individual and collective consumer may control Drug use and distribution. Organizations such as Consumers' Union have devoted considerable effort to identifying for their members' methods of reducing Drug costs. Consumer involvement has been encouraged by the publication of a variety of consumer-oriented books and articles aimed at increasing the consumer's awareness of the Pharmacy system.

Organizations representing the interests of the elderly, such as the National Retired Teachers Association and the Gray Panthers, have become increasingly active in the Drug area, stimulated by the fact that persons over the age of 65 use four times the amount of Drugs that younger persons use. Strongest of all is the American Association of Retired Persons (AARP). This organization not only operates the largest private mail-order prescription operation in the United States (for its members) but is also politically active in influencing Drug-related Legislation. The AARP also sponsors community surveys on Pharmacy Prices and services.

How can patients get the information they need? Angell (233) offered some suggestions for use in the doctor office visits. Here is one:

> When your doctor prescribes a new drug, ask him or her, these questions. What is the evidence that this drug is better than an alternative drug or some other approach to treatment? Has the evidence been published in a peer-reviewed medical journal? Or are you relying on information from drug company representatives?

I read this to my personal physician (also a pharmacist and a former student of mine). He simply chuckled.

The elderly People deserve special consideration, consuming, as they do, far more medication than their younger cohorts.

Death or Maybe Not

I will not even attempt to summarize the brilliant and eloquent dissertation on immortality or amortality by Yurul Harari (455) in his Book *Homo Deus*. His description of the role of technology, notably medications, in the possibility of a life expectancy of 150 years or more is both hopeful and frightening. You just have to read it to re-think your vision of the future.

A more somber view, also that of Harari (459): "As far as we can tell, from a purely scientific viewpoint, *human life* (emphasis added) has absolutely no meaning". No thanks! Government, Big Pharma, and the People are far too diligent laboring to sustain life and to give it meaning. But, for a thoughtful discussion of terminal illnesses, the Reader is referred to Murphy's, *It's Okay to Die* (535).

Conclusion

Evans (53) summed up the substance of this chapter as well as I could hope to:

> We must teach the public (People) the proper way to use these chemicals (drugs) so that as little harm results, as is possible. Drugs are not "abused", but uninformed people are abused by misusing

drugs. No drug is harmful if properly used. No drug is safe if used without knowledge and caution. So far, we have failed in our task of teaching the correct use of drugs. We have been too distracted by the "Drug Problem" to study the "Health Problem". If this situation continues, the world in the year 2000 may be a nightmare.

Or as Dubos has written:

Solving the problems of disease is not the same thing as creating health and happiness. This task requires the kind of wisdom and vision which transcends and which apprehends in all their complexities and subtleties the relation between living things and their total environment.

(226)

Chapter 8

Response of Big Pharma

Introduction

From the material in Chapter 3, it should be clear that Big Pharma has faced a number of charges of misconduct. A partial list:

- Too high prices
- Too high profits
- Unethical practices
- Too much promotion
- Misleading or even false advertising
- Co-optation of prescribers
- Molecular manipulation – "Me Too" Drugs

It should be obvious that it is the marketing practices of the industry that are the source of a major part of the criticism. The industry has been attacked by the Commissioner of the Food and Drug Administration for its Advertising practices, by United States legislators for its pricing practices, and by Health professionals for its distribution practices. All of these are part of the marketing function. Yet little of the industry's defense has centered on explaining or justifying the functions of pharmaceutical marketing.

It seems apparent that the marketing functions of the pharmaceutical industry are poorly understood by its critics. No honest discussion of the cost of Drugs could speak of 7,000% markups based on the cost of ingredients, as did the Kefauver Committee, unless they were misinformed concerning the nature and role of marketing costs in the total cost of goods and in the determination of profits.

Pharmaceutical marketing, then, needs defense. What defenses are available? Manischewitz and Stuart (329) have offered several alternatives, all of which have some utility for the pharmaceutical industry. They are:

1. A plea of not guilty – "I didn't do it. I'm really a good guy".
2. A counterattack – "My accuser is a liar, and here's my proof".
3. A plea of guilty as charged, with an appeal for mercy.
4. Admission of guilt, with a promise to do better.

Before examining each of these alternatives in their turn, it is necessary to point out that the response must vary according to the particular accusation to which the industry is responding. Some of the most widespread criticisms of marketing in general have been the following:

1. Marketing creates unnecessary wants.
2. Marketing manipulates People against their wishes.
3. Products are too numerous and unsatisfactory.
4. There is too much Advertising, and too much of it is undesirable.
5. There are too many retail outlets.
6. There are too few retail outlets.
7. Prices are too high – primarily because marketing costs too much.

In the face of so much unwanted, but not unwonted, criticism, what can Big Pharma do? Taking considerable license here is what I think the rather well-known Bard of Avon might say. Confronted by the "slings and arrows of outrageous" (insert Congress and Consumer Advocates), Big Pharma would prefer to "take arms against a sea of troubles, and by opposing end them". Certainly, Big Pharma would not allow them to "quietus make," never "fardels bear", and never, never with a "bare bodkin" (45).

So how, and how well, did Big Pharma cover its collective bodkins? Big Pharma has responded by organization, retort, and political action. In this section, we provide some detail on the organizations which represent Big Pharma. Some examples of the retort are offered from excerpts of the Proceedings of Investigations (see Chapter 4). Any *detailed* political actions of Big Pharma, especially lobbying, and campaign contributions are BTSB.

Response to Government

Review of the material presented in Chapter 4 should establish that Big Pharma *did* respond to the various Investigations. Sometimes the spokesperson was the representative of an individual company. Often it was offered by the Pharmaceutical Manufacturers Association (PMA) (now Pharmaceutical Research and Manufacturers Association).

PMA was founded, late in 1958, presumably in anticipation of what lay ahead. PMA leaders, especially Joseph "Joe" Stetler and Gerald Mossinghoff, were the target of detailed questioning and each invariably offered lengthy prepared statements "for the record". On more than one occasion individual companies declined an invitation to appear and their absence was carefully noted by the respective Committee chairs.

PMA was a comparatively late arrival on the scene as the industry was already represented by a number of organizations. Here are a few:

- Drug Chemical and Associated Technology Association, founded in 1890 as the Drug Chemical and Allied Trade Association. Large, 500+ members.
- National Pharmaceutical Council, founded in 1953 primarily to resist Generics.
- Food and Drug Law Institute, founded in 1949.
- Drug Information Association (DIA), founded in 1964 primarily as a result of the thalidomide tragedy. Global membership – "Science, Health Care, and Regulation".
- Health Marketing and Communications Council, formerly Pharmaceutical Advertising Council. Members are advertising and public relations (PRs) firms serving the Drug industry.
- Consumer Health Care Products Association (1991) had two name changes; Proprietary Association (1881) and Nonprescription Drug Manufacturers Association (1989). Represents the OTC Drug makers.
- Association for Accessible Medicines, formerly the Generic Pharmaceutical Association, new emphasis on biosimilars.
- Partnership for Prescription Assistance, part of PhRMA and partner with American Academy of Family Practice.

Each of these organizations, and there are others, has its own mission and constituency and there is some overlap in membership.

Now let us return to the four defenses suggested above by Manischewitz and Stuart (329).

Not Guilty

Manischewitz and Stuart qualify the not guilty plea by modifying it to a general character reference for marketing (or in this case for the pharmaceutical industry). To a degree this is the position which has been adopted by the pharmaceutical industry.

A good deal of any formal defense offered is composed of reference to the technical advances in the industry and to the Code of ethics of various segments of the industry. While this does have some merit in establishing the industry as an honest citizen, it does little to answer specific claims.

It would seem, however, that a "not guilty" plea could be substantiated in reference to certain charges; specifically, that marketing creates unnecessary wants, or that marketing manipulates People against their will. There seems scant possibility that marketers of prescription Drugs create a market for unnecessary Drug therapy. To accept this as a valid charge would require acceptance of a total disavowal by the medical profession of its ability to make objective decisions regarding Drug therapy. The same would be required to accept a charge of manipulating the physician's will.

Counterattack

A properly conducted counterattack would be composed of formal, thorough, and objective research aimed at refuting, point-by-point charges of the critics. An honest appraisal of past performance of the industry indicates that it has performed rather well in some areas but poorly in others. Considerable data have been provided, for example, to show that concentration (with the concomitant temptation toward Price fixing) in the industry is not as serious a problem as some critics indicate.

Some outside evidence is now available that charges of "too many" and "ineffective" which have been leveled, particularly at Drugs which preceded the 1962 Drug Amendments, may also have been exaggerated. The findings also lend weight to the theory that medical intelligence will not allow for long the survival of ineffective Drugs, regardless of the effectiveness of the marketing activities.

A great deal remains to be done, however. Suggested as some fertile research are the following:

1. What has been the contribution of the market research department in the development of products better suited to the needs of the market?
2. What is the real contribution of the content of Promotion in terms of its value as a source of information about Drug products for the physician?
3. What has been the effect of the high degree of Regulation on the industry in terms of product changes, new product development, and marketing practices?
4. What are the social and economic values of the distribution system which prepares the Drug product in such a way as to provide place, time, and form utility?
5. What is the present and future role of community-level pharmacists as marketing institutions, and is this role compatible with the growing move toward professionalism of pharmacists?

The above are but a few of the scores of research studies needed to determine the real value of pharmaceutical marketing. Unfortunately, the number of such studies presently under way seems to be rather limited. The research staffs of the individual firms are either too busy with needed corporate research or disinclined to engage in research of this type. Support of outside firms (university and private research organizations) had been slow to develop.

Another means of counterattack is legal reform. If the laws and Regulations appear to be unjust, unduly restrictive, or too broad, this is a logical course of action to pursue. Far superior to engaging in costly and lengthy court battles, however, would seem to be the process described above of research on the nature of the problem and then informing influential critics, lawmakers, and administrators of the true nature of the problem.

Guilty

Two "guilty" pleas are available – one with a plea for mercy, the other with a promise to do better. Some "guilty" pleas have already been entered. Executives of at least one major pharmaceutical firm, for example, have expressed concern over the inability of the industry to justify pricing policies, particularly disparities between pharmacist–institutional–Government Prices (65).

There are other areas in which the industry would find it difficult to develop any strong defense. One such related charge is that there is too much advertising, which in turn causes high prices for Drugs. It seems fairly certain that most marketing practitioners in the industry would agree that the volume of advertising is too great. It seems obvious, however, that this condition obtains, not because of any industry-wide conspiracy to glut the mails and drive Prices upward but rather due to an inability of the industry, to date, to find a workable alternative.

What is needed, then, is more efficiency in the marketing process. There seems little incentive, for example, for the advertising agency to work full force toward reducing the volume of advertising when the agency fee is a function of this volume. However, there are new arrangements available between the advertisers and the agency which remove these blocks. Also, many companies are working toward building efficiency into their promotion by editing mailing lists, revamping detailing procedures, and reviewing journal advertising.

A summary defense of pharmaceutical marketing would have to admit that the system is imperfect and inefficient at best, but that it is also the best system known to the world today. Certainly, we must encourage efforts to make pharmaceutical marketing more efficient. Those shortcomings, which can be corrected only through Legislation or Regulation, must be so treated. There is an ever-present danger, however, of "throwing the baby out with the bath water," if legislators and administrators in their zeal impose restrictions on the industry which are inhibitory to a reasonable rate of progress. One means of preventing this is a concerted effort toward assuring a complete understanding of the functions of marketing by these individuals.

Big Pharma Speaks

Speaking at a major conference on Drugs and Society in 1963 (69), John T. Connor, later to be Secretary of Commerce under LBJ, voiced a common theme:

> Despite the recent public attention to the price of drugs, I believe the criterion to which our society gives the highest priority in judging the performance of the pharmaceutical industry is the significance of its contributions to the rate of medical progress. The inherent risks in medical progress have been well described by other participants at this conference. Nevertheless, the public is

in a hurry to see remedies developed for serious diseases that still take so many lives.

In his lengthy presentation Connor, then a Merck Executive, gave only this to support Drug Prices and that would seem unlikely to silence critics:

> Since 1940 our sales have risen 607%, our profits 632%, and our expenditures for research and development 2,052%. Nearly 10 years ago we started putting more dollars into research and development than we paid out to the stockholders in dividends, and we are still doing this. The rest of us in the company are now working for the scientists, and the stockholders seem to be content that this is so.

As part of its prepared statement during the Kennedy Hearings in 1973, after the Senator had been critical of Drug pricing practices, the PMA responded as follows:

> The firm considers all the features of its product in determining its price – information, availability, warranty, dependability, service, complexity, market, quality, risk productivity, and sophistication. It considers medical, governmental, and public policy issues, and the impact on and value to the consumer. It weighs competition. It assesses the demand for the product in terms of real value in relation to the value of competitive therapy. It takes a long view of such demand. It assesses its function as a factor in medical research and development and weights its obligations and, or opportunities in funding increased research through the revenues generated by its sales.
>
> The price it sets is not simplistic. It varies by the differing dosage and quantity sizes, by distribution policies, return goods policies, and other factors. The very diversity of marketing character, timetables, investments, and methods leads to diverse pricing structures, competing in many ways with other products, therapies, or consumer preferences. Price and cost comparisons between products, therapies, companies, and countries are difficult inasmuch as each producer brings unique qualities and requirements to the market.
>
> (151, pt. 3)

While more from the Hearings is contained in Chapter 3, another excerpt illustrates the approach taken by a member of Big Pharma to explain pricing:

> Schering prices are established at a level which covers our successes and our failures, the cost of materials, and of efficient manufacture at reasonably attainable volumes, the cost of quality control under the highest standards, the cost of efficient marketing, including that of communicating product facts and benefits, the administrative cost of operating the company, and the taxes payable to national, regional or local governments. The cost of the active substance is a small portion of total costs. Our pricing should also provide an average, long-run corporate-wide, after-tax return on stockholders' equity at a rate at least equal to that of the pharmaceutical industry as a whole, since we require earnings to support continued corporate growth and to compensate corporate investors for the use of their capital. All of this is evaluated against a background of the high risk involved in bringing a new pharmaceutical to market. We consider the expected response, based on an analysis of the value of product to the user, as compared with the value and price of alternatives he may have. We attempt to forecast the attainable sales volume for the product life cycle. We give thought to the significance of the product with respect to our entire product line and its effects, if any, on the prices, sales, and profit margin of our other products. And, finally, we consider the magnitude of the investment required and the degree of risk we undertake.
>
> *(151, pt. 2)*

An Alternative View

On December 14, 1967, George Squibb was a guest of Senator Gaylord Nelson and his Committee. His appearance, vocal and written testimony, is notable not only because of the eponymous company for which he once served as President but also because it was generally received as being negative toward the industry, in which the family name had been recognized since the company's founding was by his great grandfather.

People in Big Pharma were quick to point out that George Squibb was retired from the industry and certainly didn't represent their views. My own view is that his paper was well reasoned and not particularly negative. Squibb did point to deficiencies in the industry's grasp of the big picture and some flaws in their strategy. For my part, after re-reading it several times, his choice of the title, "Drug Prices the Achilles Heel of the Pharmaceutical Industry", was right. Again, in my view, Squibb was simply cautioning that the industry, while very strong, still had vulnerability.

Squibb's testimony is lengthy, and can't be provided verbatim, but I have chosen a few excerpts which I hope capture some of the essence of his message. (The full text from the Proceedings can be found in Ref. 37.)

> Drug prices have been under attack from many directions ever since the Kefauver investigations. Particularly sharp have been the criticisms by politicians and economists and there is no sign of abatement. Indeed there is renewed vigor in the attacks from political sources as the government turns its attention more and more to enacting and implementing new social legislation providing all kinds of medical benefits to the aged and needy. The potential effect of the attacks on the pharmaceutical industry in the light of current trends toward government-supported medicine indicates the urgent need for a careful re-examination and reconsideration of all aspects of pharmaceutical company operations, short and long-term, as well as the more specific question of pricing philosophy. There is no doubt that there are developing new forces and new pressures that must be carefully studied and understood if the industry is to continue—progressive and productive—making major contributions to the medical knowledge of our times.
>
> There are those in the pharmaceutical industry who draw confidence from the fact that prices and profits have held firm in spite of the various attacks and highly unfavorable public attention absorbed by the industry, and who feel therefore that these latest blasts need not cause major concern, particularly because they are based essentially on the same data and the same product and company examples which Kefauver used originally 6 or 7 years ago. It would seem that this opinion may lead into serious difficulties if it is followed by the majority of pharmaceutical houses because it fails to take into consideration a whole set of new circumstances which have only come into existence the last 18 months or so. The basic new fact is, of course, that now the government itself under its Medicare programs must pay a large drug bill. It now has

a direct interest in the prices charged for drugs, and any proper economies that can be made are suitable matters for attention.

***

The pharmaceutical industry marketing brand name products cannot lay all of its higher prices to research expense. The figures for research as a percentage of sales dollars, or on profits before taxes, or by any other measure do not justify a claim that the price differential between branded and non-branded products is due to research on the former.

The industry cannot cite its risk from the uncertainty of research results or from product obsolescence as the reason for the price differential. For some of it, no doubt, but not much, because year after year the profits of the industry are far above the average for other major industries and currently appear to be improving rather than worsening.

The industry cannot use nearly as forcefully as it once could the argument that the price differential is due to better manufacturing procedures, quality control, and generally more careful and therefore more expensive production all the way from the conception of its formulas to their final distribution.

At the present time, there seem to be three definite and separate methods to get at the "high" prices of patented or licensed drug products. First, to attack the patent system itself; second, to charge illegal acts under the antitrust laws to the industry; and third, direct attack on intra-industry procedures which can be claimed to contribute to "high" prices.

Some of these debunking efforts have been, to say the least, inaccurate, unfair, and on occasion quite misleading, but on the other hand there have been a number of clear-cut failures within the industry upon which can properly be based criticism. It does appear, however, that a few mistakes, a few shortcomings have been exaggerated beyond reasonable levels to smear an industry whose performance generally has been excellent.

Probably this scrutiny is the most detailed and at the same time far-reaching that has given to any industrial group by such a wide variety of examiners from the press, academic life, and from the government.

The publicity given to industry procedures, profits, promotion costs, and comparative financial data of all kinds exposes no illegal or improper activities *per se*. The charges of too much advertising – too much sales pressure – too much profit – all seem to beg the real question – "should there be some limitation imposed from without to the operations of the pharmaceutical business?" Anyone can run his shoe business or his farm machinery business any way he wants to in terms of new product activities, production procedures, or sales costs, but can this be permitted in the pharmaceutical business when products are involved upon which depend the nation's health? Anyone can make all the profit he is able to in the furniture business, the food business, the automobile business, but can this be permitted in the pharmaceutical business when that profit comes from prices on products used to treat illness? More than that, these products are required for illness, which can afflict everyone no matter of what economic status, but which more often than not is the particular burden of the poor and undernourished and aged segments of the population.

It is squarely on this point that the industry today must do its most serious thinking. Is there some kind of special responsibility inherent in the nature of the product and service it supplies that requires the limitation of price and profit by some artificial standard? And if so, by what standard, and who sets it? Would the industry be under attack today if its profits were on the average of all major industries or if its expenses for selling and distribution were more in common proportion to those found generally in other consumer goods industries? The answer is probably "Yes" – although in a different way, and with emphasis more clearly given to the social responsibility concept rather than to the out-of-the-ordinary procedures and results of pharmaceutical companies.

Squibb's was one of the best "sermons" the industry could have heard – for the time. Subsequently many things changed. Waxman–Hatch dealt with the Generic quality issue. The Medicare Drug coverage exploded. Some Drugs now have Prices Squibb couldn't have dreamed of. George Squibb died in 1993.

Response of Big Pharma to the People

Much of the effort by Big Pharma to inform and justify itself to the People can be categorized as PRs. The money spent on PR was the subject of brief scrutiny in at least two of the Hearings.

Big Pharma's current activities in the area of PR seem, at least to me, to be minimal. There is the more or less standard TV ad extolling the efforts and accomplishments of "America's Pharmaceutical and Biological Research". No individual company PR effort is visible. (Although Bayer was reported, in 2019, to be launching a major TV campaign called, "Why We Science", to highlight the value of their products in consumer lives.) One seldom (never?) sees a company President in an ad or on a talk show, but Bill Gates and Zuckerberg are known in every household. Has the Reader even heard of Leo Sternbach? Assuming the answer is "no", he is the chemist who synthesized both Librium and Valium. Big Pharma needs some heroes! Roche could still take the credit for having hired him and supported his research.

Some Ideas for Big Pharma

Big Pharma has a story to tell, which I believe they have yet to do well enough. In this section, I will lay out some of the elements that I believe to be worth explaining to Big Pharma's Public.

Public Perceptions of Pharmaceutical Marketing

Few industries have been criticized more often, more inaccurately, and more unfairly for their marketing activities than the pharmaceutical industry. The term "marketing" is often used imprecisely and in a disparaging sense.

Critics believe that marketing adds little value to pharmaceutical products.

These opinions, which are often strongly held, indicate a great need for clarification of the role of marketing in the pharmaceutical industry and for a description of the substantial value it adds to products.

What Pharmaceutical Marketing Is and Does

There is obvious added value in having medicines available in convenient dosage forms, palatable flavors, and efficient packaging. Marketing, however, adds many other more profound values to pharmaceutical products, but most of these values are less obvious and are generally not understood.

The fundamental role of pharmaceutical marketing is technology transfer. A medication has value only if it is available when and where it is needed. The essence of pharmaceutical R&D is assembling information about how chemical compounds work in the body. The essence of pharmaceutical marketing is communicating this information to providers and consumers. Thus, research, development, and marketing are elements of an information continuum, whereby research concepts are transformed into practical therapeutic tools and information is progressively layered and made more useful to the Health Care system. Transmitting information to end users through marketing is a crucial element of pharmaceutical innovation. Unless physicians are informed about the treatment opportunities offered by new medicines, there is effectively no innovation.

The thread of marketing is woven throughout the fabric of the pharmaceutical industry. It binds together the many aspects of this complex industry and underlies the business operations of all successful pharmaceutical companies. At a time of strict governmental Regulation of Health Care, policymakers and the Public must recognize that marketing by the pharmaceutical and other Health Care industries is, and must be, an integral part of any system that evolves. A more complete understanding of pharmaceutical marketing is required to recognize that, not only is marketing a necessary business function, it is also vital to the nation's Health.

What Drives Product Development?

Companies are increasingly organized to reflect the fact that R & D and customer needs must be closely linked for commercial success. The involvement of marketing personnel on product development teams provides the perspectives of the patient, physician, and payer.

Product development is a cycle that starts with the patient, is guided by the patient, and ends with the patient. Marketing transmits information at each stage of the process. Marketing sequentially:

1. Guides the creation of medicines, based on an assessment of patient medical needs.
2. Communicates to prescribers the availability and attributes of medicines.
3. Encourages patients in their proper use.

Marketing moves us from a general condition of unmet patient needs to a stage at which many of those needs are fulfilled by new therapies. The cycle begins again as marketing reveals product shortcomings.

In addition to its primary job of determining and satisfying the needs of patients, marketing now has the added challenge of demonstrating the economic value of products to payers. Governments, managed care organizations, employers, and other purchases of Health Care are now scrutinizing the Price and value of all components, including pharmaceuticals.

Additional developments in pharmacoeconomics have continued, and the research literature now abounds with comparisons of alternate Drug therapies, Drug therapy with other treatments, and assessments of a medication's value, as opposed to its Price.

These initiatives have become a driving force in the marketplace. The number of published Health economic evaluations of pharmaceuticals has exploded in recent years. Studies have expanded into such areas as quality-of-life assessment, outcomes measurement, and decision analysis. Companies are paying particular attention to making pharmacoeconomic studies an informative and scientifically valid component of product marketing strategies. The techniques they pioneered are now used as serious tools for decision-making by formulary Committees, third-party administrators, and Government policymakers.

Marketing Exerts Downward Pressure on the Price of Medicines

A unique problem for the pharmaceutical industry is the Public's often negative perception of its products. Everyone wants quick symptom relief or effective cures, but few can fully appreciate the value of products that accomplish these apparently simple objectives. Patients having diseases without symptoms often resent an expense that shows no immediate or visible benefit and would prefer instead to purchase something with clear value – new clothes, a movie ticket, or dinner at a restaurant. The purchase of medications by a sicker or chronically ill patient is complicated by the emotions secondary to illness. Finally, medications are often paid in part by up-front and out of pocket, whereas other, often more expensive Health Care components have the financial cushion of primary insurance coverage. These factors combine to make medicines unpopular – and their Prices even more unpopular. There is no right Price – only a "too high" Price.

Marketing does help, however, in controlling the Price of pharmaceuticals, as companies compete for market share. The entire Generic pharmaceutical industry is based on competition focused on pricing, but Price competition is also ongoing among different branded products in the same therapeutic class. Although different products are rarely therapeutically equivalent, a rough substitute can often be found. Thus, an over-priced product, resulting from poor market analysis, will find few buyers.

Communicating with Prescribers Linking Products to Patient Needs

Pharmaceutical companies would prefer not to spend money on Promotion; they would rather use the money for operations or pass it along to shareholders. Unfortunately, however, although marketing may succeed in providing the right product, at the right Price, the product will fail in the marketplace without a strong communication link with prescribers and dispensers. Promotion is the vehicle for such communication.

Certainly, one objective of Promotion is to drive sales. The marketing communications activities of the industry, however, are primarily informational and serve to educate the medical profession regarding how to use a medicine, when to use it, and when not to use it. These are among the most important activities of the industry. At its core, this research-intensive, high-technology industry is also an information service industry.

The American Medical Association believes that industry support of medical education is "a critically important part of the health care system", and then FDA Commissioner Kessler stated that "the FDA has long realized that industry-sponsored presentations by physician researchers can play an important part in informing and educating health care professionals" (546).

If a ban were suddenly placed on all Promotion of medicines, the effect on the knowledge levels of prescribers, barring the introduction of some new information source, would be immediate and negative. Accordingly, responsible critics of this essential source of information must offer an alternative. Any alternative information system must be measured against the present one in terms of scope, objectivity, timeliness of information, effectiveness of communication, and cost.

Marketing communications by pharmaceutical companies are a key channel through which physicians obtain information about medicines. In contrast with the training and formal continuing education programs available to most doctors, marketing communications from pharmaceutical companies present information about their products that is timely and dynamic.

Successful pharmaceutical Promotion relies on physician understanding of the condition being treated and the mechanism of action of the medication being offered. For example, one of the tasks of those companies introducing the first beta-blocker, the first oral anti-diabetic agent, was to review the physiologic principles underlying the Drug's action. Considerable educational value accrues from this activity.

Educational activities directed at prescribing must sometimes be preceded by efforts to assist in the diagnosis. An example is the condition of ulcerative colitis. Research in the early 1960s showed that primary care physicians were slow to reach the diagnosis of this condition. This often resulted in delays in selecting effective therapy, sometimes with tragic results. Educational efforts by the manufacturer of the leading medication were targeted at improved diagnosis. These efforts certainly helped sales but also resulted in more prompt patient care.

Competition exposes physicians to multiple biases and multiple facets of the story, as each company promotes the advantages of its own product and compares it to the alternatives. This exposure to different perspectives enables physicians to make a more informed choice of the best medicine for the individual patient.

Cost Savings through Marketing Directly to Patients

Despite the failures mentioned previously, the extensive marketing effort directed at physicians does reflect the industries' understanding of the need to communicate effectively with prescribers. One great omission in pharmaceutical marketing, however, has been the absence of a major effort in the last, crucial, step in the information continuum – communication with the ultimate end user, the patient. Increased spending on marketing to consumers would have beneficial economic and clinical effects. Medications could be used more appropriately and consistently by patients, and as a result, overall Health Care costs would most likely decrease.

Leading pharmaceutical firms have become sensitized to this failure of information "throughput" to the ultimate consumer and are beginning to mount serious patient- and provider-directed compliance education programs. Research confirms that these marketing efforts aimed at improving compliance with medication regimens can be effective in lowering overall treatment costs.

The major responsibility for the proper use of pharmaceutical products resides with the firms that manufacture them. Those firms which have committed marketing resources to improved compliance with medications have "taken the bull by the horns". They realize that although prescribers and dispensers have a role in compliance education, they cannot be expected to assume the point position. It is the companies themselves who must spearhead efforts to educate consumers about medicines and to educate providers in effective techniques for talking to patients about medicines. The companies must shoulder the additional marketing costs associated with these activities.

Pharmaceutical marketers have begun to focus some marketing effort directly on consumers. Although controversial, these programs have probably resulted in greater Public awareness of disease risks; in earlier treatment of hypertension, ulcers, smoking, menopause, and depression; and in improved management of contraception.

Paul Rubin, a former senior economist with the Federal Trade Commission, noted that "[a]dvertising and promotion of prescription drugs is beneficial to consumers because of the information provided. Deception in this market – of physicians or consumers – is particularly improbable".

Pharmaceutical Marketing Stimulates Demand – Good for the Health Care System

Stimulating demand for pharmaceuticals through marketing contributes to a sound market, and attempts to manage demand, by controlling the flow of information through restrictions on marketing, will create an inefficient market.

The free flow of information is essential to our market-directed economy, the basic purpose of which is to satisfy consumer needs. In the Health Care arena, patients, providers, and payers have somewhat different needs and make choices of goods and services based on their own objectives, economic situations, and values. To make informed choices, each of these players requires good information regarding the availability, cost, and quality of competing products and services.

In an efficient Health Care market, the supply–demand relationship is continuously tuned through the flow of information – and that information flow is facilitated by vigorous marketing. This is the classic role of marketing in an economic system. There is some concern, however, that marketing, by stimulating demand for products and services, drives up Health Care costs by forcing upon the system goods that are unnecessary or overused. These value judgments, however, are best made by the consumers, who know their individual needs and can make a good cost–benefit decision – if they have relevant, high-quality information.

The system is not perfect. Medicines sometimes are overused, but their *underuse* through poor compliance and under-prescribing is more common and represents a greater cost to society. Compared with other forms of treatment, medicines are usually the cheapest route to an effective outcome, and their underuse results in increased treatment costs and represents a burden to the economy.

Although information about medicines is needed for the operation of a sound market, it is also important that marketing practices be appropriate and that the information be accurate. Examples of inappropriate pharmaceutical marketing practices include misinformation, unsubstantiated claims, or bribery – subtle or overt. Thus, the *quality* of information should be controlled but not the *quantity*.

Tell the People

A number of years ago we conducted a content analysis of high school textbooks to determine how much credit redounded to the Drug industry for advances in Drug discovery. The answer: very little. NIH and other Government Agencies recorded most of the credit, with a historical vignette or two, such as penicillin. I suggested to a couple of People in the industry an informational packet be prepared for distribution to the authors of such textbooks and perhaps even teachers. If such an effort was ever undertaken, I am not aware of it.

Another option might be a documentary series, call it "The Story of Medicines". The History and/or A & E channels would seem to be logical targets for such a venture.

In 1986, Glaxco funded a symposium, *The Inside Story of Medicines*, developed in conjunction with the American Institute of the History of Pharmacy (26). Then Surgeon General, C. Everett Koop provided the keynote address. The symposium was developed into a traveling exhibit as well. The symposium was well received and offered a very positive and unbiased view of the origins of medicines and the benefits they have conveyed. But that was more than 30 years ago. What is needed, today, I believe, is a greater effort to explain to the Public how the industry works, especially regarding its marketing practices.

PMA Monographs

Two monographs published by the, then, PMA warrant attention. The first titled, *The Pharmaceutical Industry Prices, Profits, Patents and Promotion* (109), is notable for addressing the criticism of Big Pharma head on. The format consisted of a series of questions and statements.

They were:

- "Medicines cost too much...."
- "How have pharmaceutical prices changed in comparison with other prices"?
- "How does research affect prices"?
- "Duplication of R&D is costly and wasteful..."
- "A few pharmaceutical companies control the market and this leads to higher prices..."
- "Prices vary from one country to another...."
- "Why not buy from the manufacturer with the lowest prices"?
- "Profits are too high...."
- "Pharmaceutical firms are guaranteed high profits with little risk..."
- "Would government manufactures eliminate profits"?
- "Patients create monopolies...."
- "What do developing nations gain by respecting patents"?
- "Would abrogation of patent protection lead to cheaper medicines"?
- "Trademarks establish monopolies."
- "What benefit does the consumer receive from promotion"?
- "What value does medical promotion have for developing nations"?

PMA, of course, provided answers to each item from their perspective. It is not known how and to whom this monograph was distributed, nor what impact it might have had, but it was remarkable for having no "preaching" either at the beginning or the end – just issues and PMA's answers. Nevertheless, this was in *1980* – 40 years ago!

Another notable PMA effort was a series of advertisements under the heading, "New Medicines for Older Americans". The contents were reports of medicines in development to treat debilitating diseases affecting older Americans. Cooperation on the project was gained from a number of organizations: Alliance for Aging, American Cancer Society, American Diabetes Association, Arthritis Foundation, College of Cardiology, and National Council on Aging. Again, the results of this project were in 1989, and are not known, but it could hardly have done any harm.

Statesmanship

More than 50 years ago, a PR specialist told the PMA that the industry needed to engage in "Statesmanship" [Dictionary definition: actively engaged in conducting the business of a Government or *in shaping its policies* (emphasis added)]. I agree wholeheartedly, but to this date, I have seen little obvious evidence of a willingness to assume that role. Big Pharma has a respect problem.

In his remarks, the Speaker told his audience that the:

> ...interpretation of the industry's ordeal at the bar of public opinion is that it was part of a much larger set of dynamics; that scrutiny of drugs as a component of health, and of the drug industry as a component of the health team, will continue; that we had the key issues highlighted and telegraphed to us; and that we were given added time to try to deal with them ourselves. If one places this interpretation on the sweep of events, he is a proponent of improved performance and improved relationships, for he realizes that the industry will never again be left alone. And he may be grateful because he has been granted an opportunity to assure that changes shall be evolutionary rather than revolutionary processes.

He pointed out that in the Public eye "we are drug companies, drug distributors, drug stores, dangerous drugs, illicit drug traffic, drug quacks and drug failures". Big Pharma is not just the member of PhRMA but the hundreds of manufacturers who are not members.

Years ago, the comedian, Rodney Dangerfield, succeeded in getting his complaint – "I don't get no respect" into common use. Certainly there have been biased reporting, half-truths, and unsubstantiated headlines which are, in part, responsible for any lack of Big Pharma respect. Politics play an important role, with Big Pharma a too-easy target. Nevertheless, as the Speaker noted, "respect is attainable, desirable and highly relevant".

In any free-world society, it is the People who govern and recognize that they must, among other things, be informed about the institutions and business enterprises around them so that they can collectively exercise reasoned judgment instead of permitting ill-advised and unwise actions based on misinformation, confusion, or short-sightedness. Obviously, this means the use of mass media and the variety and scope of those media has never been greater.

The Speaker, referred to above, closed his remarks with the following (To the Reader: remember this was a half century ago):

Part of the price of public respect, then, is to examine with ruthless objectivity what we do that brings us all this harassment, and to make a straightforward attempt with better than deliberate speed to correct these deficiencies, whether real or apparent.

The other part of the price of public respect is better communications. The U.S. Prescription drug industry and our individual companies must seek the kind of public understanding that has to precede public support.

***

The willingness to examine ourselves in terms of our total performance and to change those things that need change—and the willingness to engage in truly two-way communication with public audiences—these, I hold, are the price of public respect.

Statesmanship, as defined, will be necessary to accomplish this.

Maybe We Can Help

A number of companies include in their direct-to-customer (DTC) ads a phrase such as "Maybe we can help" – if the viewer cannot afford the advertised medicine. The notice tends to be in quite small print and shown very briefly. Nevertheless, it is possible for the alert viewer to respond. I accessed a few of those and found them to be reasonably informative but confusing. (That is not necessarily a criticism – the issue is itself confusing.) All that I accessed made it clear that their program did not apply to patients covered by insurance or Government prescription coverage. Some included or referred the viewer information about such things as side effects, dosage directions, and the like. Here is one example.

Humira, marketed by AbbVie, has several uses. Indications for use include rheumatoid arthritis, plaque psoriasis, and Crohn's disease. A sub-cutaneous kit lists at $5.811 for two kits. Price support is available for each paying customer only and not for insurance plans. The viewer is referred to drugs.com discount card. According to the site, offers may include a printable coupon, a trial offer, or free samples. Applicants may have to complete a questionnaire. An 800 number is provided for more information. There is Generic competition.

Other DTC Drug ads also offer a path to financial assistance, but the viewer must be quick. The notice is typically shown in very small type and only very briefly. Certainly it must be possible to navigate one's way to apply for relief. The computers which answer the 800 calls can be confusing and some plans allow the viewer the print out discount cards. I have no printer and can only wonder how many others seeking help are similarly underprivileged.

This is one effort by Drug companies to blunt the ever-present charge of "Greedy". To date, I have seen no studies of the number who successfully use this kind of service. For the manufacturer, such programs must certainly be an expense to administer. Certainly that is the reason for referring patients to drugs.com discount card.

Conclusion

In a long and detailed front-page article in the *Wall Street Journal* (20 February, 2020), Brody and Armour described surprising bipartisan efforts to overhaul Drug-pricing Regulation. They noted a number of legislative proposals with both Democratic and Republican sponsors. (At the time of this writing, none had been enacted.) The writers noted the President's very vocal concern about the issue which promises to be very much a part of the Presidential campaign by both parties.

Especially interesting was the note that PhRMA has 47 lobbying firms on retainer with 183 registered lobbyists. In spite of what seems extraordinary activities, and more than $100 million in Advertising, the benefits of their products' Public perception of the industry, according to Gallup, are at the very bottom.

It would seem clear that something isn't working for Big Pharma.

In considering how Big Pharma might approach communication with the People, perhaps the art of poetry can help clarify. Essentially, the poet has four resources with which to work: words, rhyme, meter, and imagery. Of these four aspects of poetry, the first three are quantitative – they can be measured accurately and the poet can, consequently, control them with reasonable certainty. But the fourth aspect, imagery, is qualitative; it cannot be pre-measured because its value (or weight, or impact) depends on how the Reader subsequently perceives it and reacts to it. The poet, therefore, cannot control the effect of imagery directly but can influence how it will be perceived by carefully selecting imagery that is universal and profound – and in this manner exercises indirect control.

In communicating Big Pharma's message to the People, it is the imagery that is most important.

Chapter 9

Little Pharma and Friends

Introduction

When planning this Book, it was my intention to use this chapter to focus on the Generic portion of the Drug manufacturing industry, with the brand name producers loosely constituting Big Pharma. History, however, makes it clear that not only is the Generic segment Big, but the lines between the two segments have become increasing blurred. Further, as "Pharma" allows of no formal definition, it is obvious to me at least, that "pharma" consists of many parts and certainly not only those who make medicines – brand or Generic.

Generic Pharma – Not So Little

The Generic Drug industry has an interesting history in the same sense as the purported Chinese curse, "May you live an interesting life". Generic Drugs were bound up in a number of controversies over many years. Early on, there were genuine and often substantiated claims that Generic Drugs were of substandard quality. This concern plus physician insistence that their prescriptions for brand named products not be "substituted" by Generics was important. State laws and Regulations were passed forbidding pharmacists from substituting a Generic product for a brand-named one without approval by the prescriber.

It got very messy. Some pharmacists were found guilty of illegal substitution. The reason for such behavior was simple economics. With the use of the professional prescription fee, the net profit realized from a Generic prescription was almost always greater than that for a brand name.

Ultimately, economics and quality assurance largely won at some expense to the prescribers' right to specify a brand name. Early on, there were temporary measures. Prescriptions were printed with a place to check "Dispense as written". There were options depending on whether the prescriber signed the prescription on the left or right side. But, third-party payers used their muscles.

Once the quality issue was nominally resolved, it was obviously time for the payers (third party) to get involved and their course of action was equally obvious. Whenever possible, pay at the Generic rate.

For the patient, there is actually one option. Accept the Generic or pay for it yourself. With the Public having recovered from the days of Generic beer and cigarettes, and with plenty of experience with Generic over-the-counter (OTC) Drugs, the "issue" seems to be no longer much of an issue. With time (and Waxman–Hatch), prescribers and pharmacists have long since "moved on".

According to the Association for Accessible Medicines (AAM), nine out of ten prescriptions today are dispensed as Generics. (Note that AAM was formerly the Generic Pharmaceutical Association – yet another organizational name change to reflect changing times.) AAM has also expanded its sphere of activities to add "biosimilar". (See below.)

The Generic Drug Fee Amendment Act, as extended in 2017, was designed to provide extra money for the FDA in order to speed up the approval process. So far, the rate of approval has not shown remarkable improvement. It is estimated that some 500 branded products still do not have a Generic equivalent. That is not necessarily due to slow approval rates, however. Many of these products have sales too low to make the FDA approval process cost-effective.

Appearance and Labeling of Generics

In the days before the legal and regulatory reforms, it was not unusual for Generic manufacturers to supply products identical in appearance to their brand name counterparts. Thus, the patient was unaware that the pharmacist had engaged in illegal/unethical substitution. Big Pharma responded by invoking "trade dress" regulations as well as dosage forms that could not be duplicated. The hollow "v" in the Valium tablet and the Spansules introduced by, then, SKF are examples. A new problem then emerged as

Generics were often made in the simplest form available. Patients taking multiple medications were then faced with two, three, or more "little white pills" which were virtually indistinguishable. A further problem emerges today when the pharmacist switches Generic suppliers and the patient's next refill is different in appearance from the previous prescription. The pharmacist can, and should, attach an auxiliary label alerting the patient to the change. In some States, it is also a requirement to include on the label something like – "Diazepam (name of manufacturer) substituted for Valium". There is evidence that there remains some degree of patient confusion.

Big Bio

"Big Bio" is certainly an appropriate companion name to "Big Pharma" although it is not in wide use – so far. One can already see the term, "biologicals", used more and more to distinguish this area of research and development from the traditional focus on chemical molecules.

Biologics are materials grown in complex living systems, not synthesized in a laboratory. Many biologics have a Generic name ending in the suffix, "mab". Officially, that stems from mAB, which scientists know means monoclonal antibody. Explaining what that means is certainly BTSB. But if you see it, such as in Humira's adalimumab, you can be sure it's one of those.

Biologics have already shown that they will be a major factor in the future treatment of medical problems. More than one of them, Humira, for example, has been approved to treat two or more seemingly unrelated conditions. In the case of Humira, it is approved for certain rheumatic/arthritic conditions, as well as Crohn's disease and ulcerative colitis. The common factor is immune suppression. It occurs to the Author that this could create confusion in the mind of the casual direct-to-consumer (DTC) television viewer who is being treated for arthritis with Humira and sees an advertisement promoting its use with ulcerative colitis. Some sort of note by the advertiser would seem to be in order.

Ads for biologics are frequent in DTC commercials with Humira, Enbrel, Otezla, and others broadcast regularly. Biologics tend to be very expensive. And for that reason alone, one would expect interest in a Generic version. And, of course, there is. For biologics, the term dujour is "biosimilar". And, biosimilars have already been the target of the same sort of controversy that Generics experienced.

A biosimilar is a biologic medical product that is "almost" an identical copy of an original product offered by another company. The original product is, however, still protected by Patent. Thus, you can't market a product that is still protected by Patent but you can, with FDA approval, market one that's "almost" the same. The FDA has come up with something called the 351a Pathway – an abbreviated licensure pathway for biological products shown to be biosimilar to or interchangeable with a reference product. This Regulation was made possible Legislation, the Biologics Competition and Innovation Act, signed by the President in 2010. Think of it as a sort of Waxman–Hatch for biologics.

What Is Special about "Specialty Drugs"?

There is now a relatively new sub-industry on the scene. Several things make these new products special. They are different concerning all of the "Four P's" in Chapter 2. The Products are not chemical molecules. They are derived from human cells and termed "biologics". The Price has not been seen before, often as much as $1,000 per month. Place has been constrained almost for the first time in the industry (methadone being an exception). And, surprisingly, at least one, Kyleena, is being promoted as DTC on Google.

Specialty Drugs are used in a variety of conditions – alcohol/opiod dependence, cancers, anemia, and even as a contraceptive intrauterine device (Kyleena, above). In 2018, Bristol-Myers Squibb boasted the top two sellers in dollar volume, followed by a Pfizer product, and then one by Johnson and Johnson. Such sales are in the billions. These biologics are often given by infusion or injection, thus requiring quick distribution and special skills in handling at the delivery site. The FDA, recognizing the special characteristics of this class of biologicals, has issued "Risk Evaluation and Mitigation Strategies" (REMS) to help insure that the benefits of use outweigh the risks. [**Author's Note:** Only a Government Agency could come up with such an obfuscating title. With this as a model, I have now named the little lean-to where I keep my lawnmower: The Carport Storage Facility (CSF)].

The FDA is authorized under REMS to select pharmacies based on unique capabilities in managing patient regiments and often extremely complex administrations. The FDA also may require sale of the biologic to a named patient and prohibit sale in "regular" pharmacies.

Little Boutiques

To use a baseball analogy, a few words about the development of a kind of Big Pharma "farm club". A number of firms are operating in a very narrow, focused area of research in which they have developed advanced expertise. This is particularly true in the area of biologics.

Firms with concentrated expertise may not have the capital to move forward with the development process and most do not include marketing. One of several things can be opportunities for such a boutique. Depending on various business factors, a Big Pharma member may simply acquire the smaller company with all of its technology. In other cases, a promising compound may be purchased individually with the proceeds of the sale funding more promising research.

Finkelstein and Temin (218) write of "outsourcing" various components of the Drug research and development process, sometimes for a specific scientific expertise, sometimes for clinical trials. They also note that outsourcing in, say, India can result in considerable savings. Outsourcing of *marketing* functions includes the historical use of advertising agencies rather than preparing in-house advertising campaigns. "Detailer for hire" has been tried, but there are serious difficulties with training and supervision.

Back to the Future – Compounding Pharmacists

The image of "Doc", in the corner drugstore trying to decipher the physician's prescription, with multiple ingredients and deciding how best to prepare the mixture seems to be having a kind of rebirth; of course without the ancient trappings.

Compounding pharmacists are growing in numbers. The International Academy of Compounding Pharmacists (IACP) claims to have 4,000 members including non-pharmacist technicians. The IACP sponsors an advocacy group, the Partnership for Personalized Prescriptions.

Typically, there are standards. There is a Pharmacy Compounding Accreditation Board (PCAB), a part of the Accrediting Commission for Health Care. Accreditation involves facilities, credentials, continuing education, and the like. In the United States, the pharmacists are identified as members of the Professional Compounding Centers of America (PCCA).

Unaccountably, telephone requests for more information to all of the entities mentioned above were not returned, but I have interviewed members of PCCA and have determined that PCCA is a combination of customer/manufacturer/distributor. PCCA will prepare custom formulations for an individual pharmacist and ship them with that pharmacist's name/logo on the labels. This is not to imply that PCCA pharmacists never prepare a prescription "from scratch". They do; but far more frequently, use mixtures they order and buy from PCCA.

Friends

Both Big and Little Pharma occasionally need help. The more formal kinds of help are found in the form of advertising agencies and market/marketing research companies.

Advertising Agencies

A beautifully illustrated and concise history of medical advertising to the end of the twentieth century can be found in *Medicine Avenue*, published by the Medical Advertising Hall of Fame (165). In the Book, the authors note that, early on, many Drug companies handled their own Advertising internally, citing CIBA, Geigy, Abbott and Upjohn as examples. Indeed many of the independent agencies were founded by former Drug company advertising executives.

The explosion in DTC Advertising of legend Drugs has resulted in former consumer advertising agencies acquiring or merging with former medical advertising agencies and vice versa. There is a mutual need for the respective talents and experiences of each.

Advertising agencies, on behalf of their clients, must deal with many issues. Considerations include the selection from a large number of potential media and the optimal expenditure of their clients' moneys. This entails knowledge of such things as circulation, readership, and editorial content for journals. Selection of the most efficient mail targets is essential for direct mail, but this is aided by mailing list specialists who can tailor the list to the product. They are aided in their efforts by the work of companies doing market and marketing research.

Market/Marketing Research

Market research, crudely defined, consists of determining what potential exists for the sale of one's product. Marketing Research involves determining the positive and negative effects of one's marketing activities.

Many Drug manufacturers conduct both kinds of research internally, but there are available entities, like advertising agencies, that operate on behalf of the Drug makers. Often research is conducted for an individual product as an isolated project. Such efforts can range in size and complexity from small focus groups to national studies.

There is available market intelligence from firms who collect information independently and make it available, for substantial fees, to any customer. There are many such firms, but we will focus on two.

Raymond A. Gosselin founded the eponymous Gosselin Survey, purportedly based on his master's thesis in the middle of the twentieth century. The methods were simple. A national sample of pharmacies was selected to which were sent a field of "agents", usually Pharmacy students, to gather data. In each of the sample pharmacies the agent recorded, for a predetermined number of prescriptions and over a pre-selected time period, the Drug prescribed, the quantity and the physician specialty, patient and physician identity were, of course, not gathered.

This somewhat crude measure in fact provided the manufacturers with important data on time trends, regional differences, and specialty of prescribers. The manufacturers had their own internal sales data which, combined with those of the Gosselin Survey, provided valuable market intelligence, even though somewhat rudimentary.

A much more sophisticated market gathering system was developed in the National Disease and Therapeutic Index (NDTI). The NDTI was started in 1958 and was also national in scope. It involved a representative sample of more than 3,000 physicians. Every quarter for 2 days, these physicians record for each prescription issued: Drug name, amount, dose, duration of therapy, indication or intended use, desired action, patient gender and age, where the prescription was issued (office, hospital, etc.), other Drugs the patient is taking, and concomitant diagnosis.

The marketing value of this information should be obvious, but there are some subtle dividends as well. The physician uses her own words to record "desired action", words that may find their way into advertising copy. Diagnosis, if off-label and appearing frequently, may suggest a new indication for which to seek FDA approval. The physician is, of course, compensated for her time and the Drug maker subscriber pays handsomely.

There are many market and marketing research services offered to the industry. Indeed, an entire Book could be devoted to a listing and discussion of all these services. Some are done by auditing or surveying, while others involve individual in-depth personal interviewing or the use of the "focus group" technique. Focus groups basically represent bringing together a small number of subjects to interact with one another regarding a specific question. The following represents only a sample of such services: Advertising copy testing, readership studies, promotional effectiveness analyses, attitudinal studies, concept testing, awareness and use studies, test market analysis, high prescriber identification, acquisition and licensing studies, forecasting, and strategic planning studies.

Because of the abundance of market and marketing research services offered to the pharmaceutical industry, one may be left with the impression that these offerings satisfy all the needs of companies, and that the function of the market research department within the company is simply to analyze the data provided in these services. This is not the case; many research studies are initiated, carried out, and analyzed by in-house personnel. In some cases, this is due to requirements of confidentiality. In others, company personnel may have more knowledge of a particular subject area. Also, there may be a need for correlation of the market research study with other areas of the company such as research and development or sales, and this is often more easily accomplished by in-house staff. Finally, a company may view the use of its own staff as being less costly than contracting out a project. Analyses of internal company data such as factory sales, promotional spending, and detailing call reports, also generally fall within the market research department's area of responsibility.

The services provided by independent research companies are generally classified into two major categories – syndicated or custom. A syndicated service is defined here as one in which all subscribers receive identical information. These services are generally supported by a large number of subscribers. The custom service, on the other hand, is supported by only one client to whose specific needs the service or project is tailored. Only the contracting client receives the information in a custom project. Another categorization of those services is based on their periodicity or continuity. They may be periodic, continuing (and periodic), or ad hoc in nature.

There are segments of the broadly defined development process that benefit from the use of marketing data. Diverse conditions such as osteoarthritis and hypertension are often found to co-exist in a patient. If an anti-arthritic compound has a blood pressure-elevating property, this compound would not be used to treat arthritis patients who are also hypertensive. Data from physician panels on medical practice can quantify how frequently these conditions can exist together, and thus suggest the minimization of usage potential that would be caused by this property of the compound. Questions on the need for specific dosage forms required for a product may be answered by reviewing marketing data. Diagnosis data, for instance, would indicate that otitis media is mainly a disorder of pediatric patients. If an anti-infective with efficacy in otitis media cannot be formulated in liquid form, it must be used infrequently.

The task of market and marketing research is to keep those who need to be kept informed supplied with all the facts possible to amass. The extraordinarily dynamic nature of the pharmaceutical industry, coupled with the ever-increasing ability to collect facts, suggests the need for and ability of the market research function to contribute even more significantly in the future. It is also important to note that market research can result not only in a profitable product but also in better Drug therapy. Indeed Government might "profitably" engage in similar research efforts.

Conclusion

By now, I hope to have established that "Pharma" is much more than what is implied by the use of the term as it is commonly used. The agencies, corporations, universities, and, yes, even the Government are all involved. They discover, develop, sell, distribute, price, and control the substances that cure, relieve, enhance, and, sometimes, diminish the medical and economic quality of People's lives throughout the world. By any measure, Big Pharma is immense! And it is incredibly complex, fraught with social, psychological, economic, philosophical, even theological issues. Dealing with all of these issues in humane, moral, and economic ways is a challenge to, literally, everyone. Add to this, the emergence of biotechnology.

Biotechnology has emerged as a major force in Health Care and it is associated with major sociopolitical issues. For example, social and ethical issues abound with regard to genetically engineered drugs, patents on live organisms, and the ethical issues involved with these developments. What potential effects will the products have on the environment? How does science deal with emergent life forms? Do we have the right or obligation as a society to regulate this branch of science? When we consider gene therapy, are we entering into areas the consequences of which we do not fully understand? These are just a few of the questions with which we must deal as the scientific community and the pharmaceutical industry continue to work and market in the biotechnology field. There are also legal and political issues involved with genetically engineered Drugs.

Chapter 10
Greedy Big Pharma

Introduction

"Greedy" and "Big Pharma". The terms just seem to fit together so naturally! Rather like "spawn" and "tornadoes", or, back to the subject, "obscene" and "profits". In this chapter, we examine some of the evidence and some of the rhetoric.

My handy Webster defines greed as "inordinate or reprehensible acquisitiveness". Inordinate simply means your Prices/profits are too high judged against some standard of "ordinateness". Reprehensible is easy. You are taking money from sick people.

The Government in its actions, especially of the Congressional Hearings, described in Chapter 3, has been harshly critical of both Big Pharma's Prices and profits. Further, the People must buy products they don't want in order to thrive, feel better, or even survive. That's reprehensible isn't it??? The image from my comic book days of Scrooge McDuck, reveling in his wealth, "burrowing through it like a gopher" comes to mind.

Two Parts of Greedy

To reprise the two components of Webster's definition of greedy (although most critics probably have not availed themselves of it), we find two operative words – "inordinate" and "reprehensible".

Turning to Webster again, we find two synonyms for inordinate – "unregulated and disorderly" as well as "exceeding reasonable limits".

Webster finds "reasonable" to mean, "not extreme or excessive". (As often happens with Webster, we now find "exceeding the ordinary" – a bit redundant.) Why bother with all of this? Because calling someone or some entity loudly and frequently in print, "Greedy", is, I believe, very serious.

I'll get back to reprehensible later but "inordinate" is the usual, and reasonably objective, means on the basis of which the charge, Greedy, is made. In a nutshell, Drug Prices are too high and Big Pharma profits are also! Both are inordinate!!!

The profit issue is usually based on some kinds of interindustry comparisons used by various critics, writers, and members of Congress. Nearly always such comparisons clearly show Big Pharma to be at the top of any list of profitable industries. "Being at the top of such a list is seen to be *prima facia* proof of inordinate profits". And the industry can hardly be considered to be "unregulated", a term of which cannot be applied, unless it is meant as *self*-regulated.

Another evidence in the "inordinate" rubric, is the Consumer Price Index (CPI). The CPI is widely used for all kinds of things. The concept is simple. Take the combined Prices of a "market basket" of goods for the current year and compare them with the Prices of the same goods in prior years, and voila! You can measure whether the Price of goods is increasing or decreasing. The CPI is tied to any number of things such as pension plans.

There are some technical problems with regard to (and this is important) its value as an indicator of consumer welfare. In a highly technical, loaded with esoteric formulas paper, Cleeton and colleagues proved (to their and my satisfaction) that the CPI just doesn't work for that purpose (499). They list four reasons:

1. It disregards new drugs at the time of introduction.
2. The rapid rate of introduction of new drugs.
3. The relation between drugs and other health entity inputs.
4. The decreasing portion of prescription drugs that are purchased in retail pharmacies.

Based on this research and the common sense understanding that the prescription drug "market basket" must change frequently, it would seem dangerous to rely too heavily on the CPI as a measure of success or failure in Price controls.

So how is the CPI doing as regards to Big Pharma? The 2019 Administration claimed that the CPI for Drugs annualized had declined for six of the last 7 years. One of the 20 or so Democratic candidates for President said, in rebuttal, that the CPI is "flawed". Actually, the *Washington Post*, in an article dated August 15, 2019, maintained that the Drug CPI in 2018 fell for the first time in 40 years.

The two most important "flaws" in the Drug CPI are: which Drugs to include and which Price to assign to them. The Bureau of Labor Statistics (BLS) has developed a myriad of formulas to deal with those and other problems. We won't go into them here and I don't understand them anyway.

Now to "reprehensible": The charge here is that Big Pharma is taking money from "sick people". That is, of course, true. It is the core of the pharmaceutical business. Added to that is the fact that the People really don't want Big Pharma's products, at least not in the sense that they want a new Tesla or an ice cream sundae. (There are a few exceptions, Viagra, for example.) In these circumstances and under this definition, Drug Prices and profits will always be reprehensible, not unlike the reprehensible ransom paid to kidnappers.

"Reprehensible" is a subjective judgment in contrast to "inordinate" which (even though experts disagree) can be buttressed by facts and figures.

AARP and Greedy Big Pharma

Calling someone or some entity "Greedy" is at least unpleasant and at worst downright nasty. The American Association of Retired Persons (AARP) has been among the most vocal of those applying that appellation to Big Pharma.

In the March, 2019, issue of the *AARP Bulletin*, the organization announced a national campaign, "Stop RX Greed". This would be a "national campaign to persuade federal and State lawmakers to take action to lower prescription prices". AARP noted that the United States, in contrast to some other countries, has no system in place to negotiate Prices and discounts with the Drug industry. AARP also criticized Drug-sponsored patient financial help programs such as discount coupons and income-based programs of patient cost reductions as actually fueling sales for brands versus Generics.

Among actions suggested by AARP to their members were the use of hashtag #StopRXGreed to show support for the campaign and it seemed to be working. In a Gallup poll conducted in September, 2019, Big Pharma scored a negative −31. (Government was second last.) It was the lowest marking for Big Pharma in 18 years. In that period, only four had ever, even for 1 year, ranked lower – Government, oil and gas, real estate, and auto.

AARP argued in their Report that several options were available to limit or reduce Drug Prices. First was to increase Generic competition. Given that estimates show about 90% of prescriptions are now dispensed as Generics, the additional savings available would seem to be relatively small. They proposed limiting out-of-pocket costs to Medicare Part D enrollees, but the rest would have to come from someone's pocket. Value-based pricing was also proposed, meaning that some evidence of increased effectiveness and/or safety should be assessed for each new product. Then, however, they admit that measurement of differential values is difficult. (Some of these problems are discussed in Chapter 14.)

AARP's "bottom line" in their discussion is a quote from a Public Policy expert at Boston University. "Real people should not have to beg, borrow or steal to control their disease". One can hardly disagree with that sentiment, but solving such a problem is not easy in our Capitalistic System unless, of course, Big Pharma really is "Greedy" or even "Evil". Use of such terms as "staggering" or "sensationally high" (21), which characterize many published analyses, can only add to the negative image.

Congress and Greedy Big Pharma

Much has already been said about the attention given by Congress to Drug Prices in Chapter 3. And the issues, not much changed since the middle of the twentieth century, are being re-examined today. A 30-year-old retrospective look at how Congress saw things then is provided in the Majority Staff Report of the U.S. Senate Special Committee on Aging (172). The title, *Skyrocketing Prescription Drug Prices*, provides some idea of what to expect.

The Committee on Aging was chaired by Senator David Pryor (Ark.). The Committee met only twice, in July and November of 1989. Remarkably, the majority Staff Report was issued in January 1990 just 2 months later. The two sessions resulted in nine findings which are reproduced here.

> **Finding 1:** Skyrocketing prescription drug cost have collided with funding limitations in Medicaid, the taxpayer funded health care program for the poorest Americans, resulting in cutbacks that impede access to prescription drugs and other essential health care items and services.

Finding 2: There is evidence that prescription drug manufacturers price their products as high "as the market will bear," rather than setting prices based on the amount of revenue needed to recoup the cost of their investment in research and development.

Finding 3: Physicians and pharmacists in over 90% of the nation's hospitals and at least 42% of U.S. health maintenance organizations (HMO's) have independently concluded that many prescription drugs are therapeutically interchangeable when used to treat patients suffering from the same ailment.

Finding 4: Based on the knowledge that many different drug products are often used to treat the same medical condition, hundreds of hospitals and HMO's have forced drug manufacturers to compete and offer reduced prices in order to be listed as a preferred product on the hospital or HMO formulary.

Finding 5: With the growing success of negotiated drug prices by HMO's and hospitals, manufacturers have increasingly devoted their sales forces to lobby, curry favor with, and even intimidate formulary managers into purchasing their products.

Finding 6: Prescription drug manufacturers have waged an all-out national campaign to undermine and frustrate State efforts to negotiate lower prices for therapeutically duplicating drugs.

Finding 7: Medicaid programs typically do not use their formulary process to negotiate drug prices with manufacturers, they are much more open to manufacturer influence, and pay much higher prices than hospitals and HMO's for the same drug products.

Finding 8: Medicaid prescription drug programs can save millions of dollars by creating therapeutic formularies, if the formulary is based upon clinically well-founded comparisons of safety, efficacy, and cost, and is used in price negotiations with manufacturers.

Finding 9: Taking into account the impact of high prices and high prescription drug consumption in the United States, Americans not only spend more for prescription drugs than the citizens of any nation in the European Economic Community (EEC), but are also less well protected by health insurance, contributing to the competitive disadvantage of U.S. employers in the international company.

(172)

Examples and evidence of each were provided. The Report then presented three options for Legislation "to mitigate the impact of rising drug prices".

The three options included: (1) a voluntary approach designed to assist States in arriving at scientifically and clinically valid assessments of Drug equivalency, (2) a "flexible mandate" that encourages immediate State action in anticipation of an eventual Federal mandate, and (3) a centralized, mandated Federal program. A mandate would be enforced through approval of State Medicaid plans by the Secretary of Health and Human Services (HHS).

In a Foreword to the Report, Senator Pryor intended "to introduce legislation early this year (1990) to help states control spiraling drug costs by negotiation prices with manufacturers". I have not been able to identify such specific Legislation, but some elements based on the Findings have been implemented. Some have not, and this material is presented as evidence of the long-standing struggle.

Risk versus Reward

Should the financial reward reflect the amount of risk involved in the Drug research and development process? Finkelstein and Temin (218) devote an entire chapter in their Book, *Reasonable RX*, to answering the question, "Are Drug Companies Risky"? They note that the standard response by Drug companies to charges of high Prices is a "payback for the risk that firms takes for these wonderful, innovative drugs". After stipulating that the process of discovering and developing new Drugs is "fraught with risk", the authors ask whether the Drug risk translates into company risk? After some quite impressive stock market calculations, the authors conclude "Investing at the drug company level is a good, solid, and basically riskless proposition".

Finkelstein and Temin attribute a comparably risk-free future to several factors. One is the emergence, through mergers, and acquisitions of members of a new Drug discovery industry. In essence, this is "outsourcing" Drug discovery. By means of this technique, Big Pharma can afford to wait for someone else's discovery, buy it or buy the whole, usually much smaller, company. Outsourcing clinical trials to Contract Research Organizations (CRO) is also a trend.

Lest the Reader judge the forgoing to be a defense of Big Pharma, be assured that it is not.

Greedy Big Tech

My term, as used here, is considerably younger than Big Pharma but shares a number of characteristics. Most importantly, all of the People are affected by it, as is the case with Big Pharma. One way in which the two differ is that the People give every evidence of *wanting* the products of Big Tech. That would seem to relieve Big Tech of the "reprehensible" charge. Before the Reader blandly accepts that premise, I suggest she read Yuval Harari's *Sapiens* (459).

There are several things that Big Pharma and Big Tech have in common. They are both big. They, generally speaking, are profitable. They share some hazards. The World Health Organization has officially labeled some of their products "addictive". There can be side effects – hand, neck, and vision problems. Adverse reactions are possible – little things like the smart phone catching fire while the user is airborne. The single most important mutual characteristic with Big Pharma is that everyone is affected by the industry and its products.

The industries also *differ* in a number of significant ways. While Big Tech, like the modern pharmaceutical industry, is relatively young, it differs in not being represented by a full-blown trade organization such as PhRMA. When Congress holds Hearings, as they are doing, it is persons with names like Gates and Zuckerberg who are called to testify. Although Big Pharma executives are also occasionally called, their names rarely make headlines. Can the Reader name the CEO of Pfizer or Merck? The image of Big Tech is thus more personal.

The *issues* differ as well. Let's look at Prices. Complaints about the Prices of high-tech products and services are rare. Well, Google, Facebook, etc. are free, aren't they? Not according to Christopher Mims writing in the *Wall Street Journal* on June 8, 2019. Mims charges that the consumer pays in an indirect way. In his words: they "suck up our personal data and prioritize user growth over the *health* (emphasis added) and privacy of individuals and society, so that they can sell more ads". A sort of third-party payment plan?

Remember "molecule manipulation" and Big Pharma? Again, in the *Wall Street Journal* on August 19, 2019, Congressman Josh Hawley wrote, "What passes for innovation by Big Tech today isn't fundamentally new products or new services, but even more sophisticated exploitation of people". "There was a time" Hawley continued, "when innovation meant something grand and technology meant something hopeful, when we dreamed of curing diseases and creating new ways to make things." Hawley, too, speaks of "addiction", but in terms of intentional interface designs to keep users online as much as possible.

Reminiscent of the days of Kefauver and Nelson, there is serious talk of antitrust and monopoly. The ever-brilliant Peggy Noonan wrote in her weekly column in the *Wall Street Journal*, June 8, 2019, describing Big Tech as "too powerful and abusive". Noonan wrote "It's all too human and of course, *greedy*" (emphasis added). Urging action to break up the giants of Silicon Valley, Noonan says: "It all depends on Congress, which has been too stupid to move in the past and is too stupid to move competently now".

But this is beginning to sound like a rant. My Book isn't about Big Tech. Nevertheless, I believed some of the parallels were worth examining. And I could have provided more. If I have the Reader's attention, I'll add just a bit.

Let's begin with a bit of Full Disclosure by the Author.

There is not a 3-year old in my beautiful hometown of Oxford, Mississippi, who doesn't know more about computers than I. I relish a condition someone has described as "voluntary ignorance". I still know practically nothing about computers, and I don't want to know more; hence, "voluntary". I am told by my incredulous daughter that I do, in fact, *have* a computer. Further, I vaguely know that it is the device "from which all blessings flow" and which I do, in fact, use.

I use email, sparingly, and find it useful, sometimes. As I have no printer, there is a limit to its usefulness to any correspondent who wishes to send me, for example, a manuscript. The Web, and good old Google, I found indispensable in preparing this Book and a great deal of fun to research travel destinations and to find addresses and phone numbers. No one, of course, is in the telephone directory, even businesses! In the past, I found AT&T's 411 service helpful, but their computer often responds to the name I give her (it) with something bizarre!

My only exposure to Twitter is via TV where POTUS, members of Congress, and who-knows-who share their thoughts, opinions, and anger throughout the day. I don't tweet.

I did enroll on Facebook for less than a month. Facebook reminds me of the famous Hyde Park Corner in London. I suppose my contemporaries have two or three hours a day to devote to this recreation, I don't! There are too many *books* (not Kindle)!

Perhaps Big Pharma is hard at work researching a breakthrough Drug for my condition (see Evans and Kline, Ref. 53), but I won't take it.

Biologist/philosopher Rene Dubos wrote, 60 years ago, "There is a demon in technology. It was put there by man and man will have to exorcise it before technological civilization can achieve the eighteenth century ideal of civilized life" (226).

Conclusion

In his very excellent and comprehensive Book, *Pharmaceutical Economics and Public Policy* (15), Vogel after a somewhat tortuous, for the average layman, analysis concluded that, "the pharmaceutical industry is barely earning its cost of capital, and, therefore, its profits cannot be considered excessive". Any number of references could be cited with a different view, although without the detailed analysis provided by Vogel.

Profit is the central operative word. For some it is a synonym for greed. Much depends on what is done with the profit. Is research on a cure for Ebola in the third world with no hope of profit a sign of *lack* of greed or just public relations? Profits find their way into the pockets of stockholders. Are the stockholders, then, greedy? And there is the standard, but true, position that profits are essential to continue the flow of new therapies and improvement of the old ones.

Recommended reading in the context of this Chapter is *Code Blue* (543), by Mike Magee, M.D. Dr. Magee is a medical historian and journalist who served for years as head of global medicine for Pfizer and thus brings an insider's perspective to the workings of Big Pharma and especially Pfizer. Indeed, he includes an appendix listing 45 of Pfizer's "penalties and transgressions" between 1950 and 2016. His description of America's "Medical Industrial Complex", with Pfizer as a center piece, is thought-provoking, personal, and sometimes frightening.

For the Reader who likes a good mystery novel, I heartily recommend *Diamond Solitaire* by Peter Lovesey. The Book offers suicides, arson, fraud, and plenty of murders. There is also greed aplenty, all within an international pharmaceutical company. Lovesey's narrative is filled with quite accurate descriptions of the consequences of Big Pharma gone rogue.

It is highly unlikely that the term "Greedy," for Big Pharma will go away, regardless of any qualifications or explanations. Indeed, the charges seem to grow. Carolanne Wright in *Capitalism, Economics, Health*, June 3, 2019, makes a disturbing comparison between Big Pharma and Organized Crime, comparing side effects, killings, and deaths attributed to both.

Chapter 11
Whence the Drugs?

Introduction

There is not enough space even to scan the complete origins of Drugs, even some we have used for centuries. Very excellent and more entertaining than I can provide are available accounts from many sources. One of the most detailed is Sonnedecker's *History of Pharmacy* (20). Also, recommended are Dowling's *Medicines for Man* (393) and Hager's *Ten Drugs* (35). The latter is recent and provides some interesting social insights.

Origins of Drugs

Where do Drugs come from? Or, whence Drugs?

The simplest division of the origins of Drugs would be natural and synthetic. The first known Drugs were, of course, of natural origin. Indeed, some of the Drugs in wide use today were well known in their cruder forms, centuries ago. More than 1,500 years before the birth of Christ, such Drugs as opium, castor oil, and colchicum were listed in the famed *Ebers Papyrus*.

Many of today's Drugs still have their origins in natural sources – animal, vegetable, and mineral. It is expected that many more valuable medicines remain to be discovered from natural sources, particularly plants. Table 11.1 contains a list of some well-known Drugs of natural origin. Of course, many

Table 11.1 Some Drugs of Natural Origin

Adrenocorticosteroid	Ipecac
Bacitracin	Kaolin
Belladonna	Lactose
Cafergot	Marijuana
Castor oil	Opium
Dextran	Papain enzymes
Digitalis	Quinine
Erythromycin	Reserpine

of the more recent Drug developments have been synthetic in nature. Some of the remarkably effective synthetic compounds were the result of direct attempts to develop medications. Others, however, have been accidental by-products of the search for other chemical wonders.

Search for New Drugs in Medical Folklore

Our present medicinal armamentarium is largely founded upon medicinal folklore of the past. Most of our pharmaceutical substances are either directly derived from natural sources used at one time as folk remedies or synthetic derivatives elicited from attempts to improve upon products of nature.

The knowledge of availability and absorbability of Drugs from various dosage forms by certain "superstitious savages" tends to put to shame some of our present day pharmacologists. The Indians of Mexico have long been aware of the advantages of an ointment base "approximating natural skin oils" and have used butter as a carrier for topical application of various "Daturas". From the standpoint of absorption, this is quite superior to our belladonna plaster.

The most distressing fact in regard to our neglect of medical folklore is that it is disappearing at an increasing rate. The advance of civilization and education will soon overtake the remaining primitive areas. Modern education which belittles this folklore will soon eliminate it. A concerted effort should be made to collect and catalog this potentially valuable medical folklore before it disappears.

Advances in Allied Sciences

Among the allied sciences which have contributed to recent advances in Drug therapy are organic chemistry and physiology. Organic chemistry has been and continues to be a source of many new chemical structures with exciting therapeutic possibilities. The physiologists have been responsible for conceptualizing the physiologically active principles in certain organs. Examples of contributions of this type of study are insulin, cortisone, and estrogen therapy.

Biochemistry

This approach to Drug therapy is a more rational one involving the application of biochemical principles to Drug design. So far, this approach has been more successful in explaining Drug action than in developing new Drugs.

Enzyme Inhibition

The enzymes, which modify the activities of the body's catalytic agents, offer a number of approaches to new types of therapy. Many studies of methods of inhibiting different enzyme systems are now underway. Successes are already being seen. Monoamine oxidase inhibitors have been shown to be effective in depression, while inhibitors of dopa-decarboxylase are being used against hypertension.

Clinical Medicine

One of the unique "bonuses" of Drug development and use is the frequency with which new uses are found for existing Drugs. The constant vigilance of researchers and practicing physicians has made possible the use of scores of products in conditions for which they had not even been considered.

Serendipity

Chance has played a considerable role in Drug discovery. A French pharmacist discovered the value of the anthelmintic piperazine while using it in the treatment of gout. Chlorothiazide, a valuable diuretic, was the product of an unforeseen chemical conversion. Needless to say, such accidental discoveries are made only if the scientific mind is open and clever enough to grasp their significance.

Exploration of Natural Products

Mention has already been made of the role of natural materials in folk medicine. Often overlooked is the fact that most of today's antibiotic therapy is a result of the systematic exploration of the anti-infective properties of various living organisms. The ability to synthesize certain antibiotics by no means lessens the potential contribution of natural materials. Many expect "Drugs from the sea" to be the next major frontier for natural product Drug development. (The television ad tells us many times daily of the memory enhancer found in jelly fish!)

Modification of Existing Drugs

The greater knowledge of Drugs and their actions, as well as the greater number of Drugs available, has created many opportunities for structural modification. The most commonplace example of this process and its results was the conversion of salicylic acid into aspirin, a much better tolerated substance. Recently, improvements in tranquilizers, steroids, and diuretics have resulted in Drugs which have been made safer and/or more effective through modification of their basic structures. (It should be noted here that some Drug industry critics have charged that many of these changes have little real value but were rather "molecule manipulations" prepared for the sole purpose of introducing a new product to the market.)

Planned Programs of Chemical and Biologic Research

Both private enterprise and the Government have engaged in special programs aimed at developing types of Drugs or combatting specific illnesses. A national program of cancer research, the coordinated marijuana research of the National Institute of Mental Health, and various special research foundations of pharmaceutical manufacturers have made important contributions to the knowledge of special types of Drugs.

Random Screening

The rationale for this process might be summed up in the phrase "anything's worth a chance". This method involves submitting chemical substances to varying tests on the off chance that they might exhibit biologic activity.

The federal Government maintains a program of random screening against a range of experimental tumors. No major successes have been reported from this process, but the severity of the cancer problem would seem to justify what Slack and Nineham refer to as a "blunderbuss approach" (228).

The "blunderbuss" approach in the commercial setting would seem to be wildly impractical. Kirsch and Ogas (364) referred to calculations done by a subsidiary of Novartis who concluded that the total number of possible Drug compounds in the universe is 3×10^{62}. In real-world terms, it would mean that if one were able to test 1,000 compounds every second to see if they might be a remedy for even a single condition, one wouldn't have made a dent in the number by the time the sun goes down. Even the Government doesn't have that much time!

The preceding paragraphs contain descriptions of the many procedures used in attempts to discover new therapeutic agents and new uses or safer modifications of older Drugs. The mere discovery of biologic activity in a new compound, however, is only the beginning of the complex process necessary to convert what is usually a raw laboratory product into a safe and effective Drug product. The process by which this is accomplished is known as product development.

Drug Product Development

Drug product development involves three major parallel interactive types of activity: biologic development, marketing development, and something we have called physico-chemical-pharmaceutical development.

The last named, physico-chemical-pharmaceutical development, is probably the least known to the layman. The cumbersome name applied to this part of the process is symptomatic of the complexity of the process. Within this chain of events, we find occurring the first recognition that the given substance or combination is somehow inherently unique. The researchers then set about to prepare more of it (to supply to the biologic researches), to prepare it more efficiently (because they know that the marketers will wish to have a product prepared with a minimum of wasted cost), and to prepare other substances which differ structurally only slightly but which, as experience has shown, may display markedly different effects on the body. From information obtained in the biologic testing, decisions are made concerning the dosage form(s) most preferred. The considerations which must go into development of the proper form for final use seem endless. If the product is to be turned out in the form of tablets or capsules, the other materials in the product, even the binders and diluents, must be compatible. If it is likely to be used in pediatrics, taste is a factor. Even esthetics must be considered, as the physical appearance may be significant in the overall therapy. Since the area under study is by its nature innovative, what have been called "fundamental surprises" is inevitable. Good research must often result in the unexpected or the process is not research. Consequently, each new product may be expected to offer its own special physico-chemical-pharmaceutical challenges.

The biologic development program is to many the most exciting. This phase has its real beginning in the first evidence that the Drug substance causes something to happen, some sequence of events to be altered, and some shift in behavioral pattern in a living organism. The ultimate goal of the sequence of events which follows will be to determine whether it is possible to administer the substance to humans in quantities sufficient to bring about a desired biologic effect (usually, but not always, connected with disease prevention or treatment) yet small enough to be relatively safe. (This relativity factor is an important one philosophically and medically speaking. Since no Drug is absolutely and totally "safe" to use, each Drug product on the market represents some calculated assessment of the ratio of benefits in terms of effectiveness to costs in terms of dangers.)

This process will involve a variety of tests in a number of different kinds of animals before the first dose is ever made available for human use, even in a test. Studies will be made to determine the effective and fatal dose ranges, the effects on different animal species, the effects on reproduction, the side effects, the mode of metabolism, and the length of time it is active in the body. When all of these tests and the experience gained in previous studies have been evaluated, clinical pharmacology will begin. (The animal testing uses quaint terms such as LD_{50} – the dose at which half the rats die. The "happy" measure is the ED_{50}, the dose at which the desired effectiveness, "E", is achieved in half the rats.)

In addition to the central purpose of testing the safety and effectiveness of the new Drug in humans, the clinical trials are also used to evaluate the work of the specialists in pharmaceutical development in producing an effective and compatible product.

The marketing development activities begin very early in the total process. Indeed many Drug products have their origins in the market research department, where specialists identify medical needs and communicate them to product development personnel for exploration. Once a Drug with some medical potential has been identified, efforts will begin to determine if it has any market potential, i.e., the ability to return to the manufacturer a profit on investment.

If the market potential does seem significant, the remaining time will be devoted to ascertaining the results of the testing of the new product, as well as changes occurring in the marketplace, and to preparing the marketing resources of the firm (e.g., Advertising, sales force, distribution network) for the introduction of the product.

Marketing in the Last Century

Although this chapter is focused on the origins of Drugs, let's take a look at the "Four P's" one more time. Toward the end of the twentieth century, I had the opportunity to nominate the five most important developments in each of the "Four P's" in the preceding century. The Drugs themselves – Products – were included, but so were the other components of the Marketing Mix (Chapter 2). Here is what I came up with. The limit to five items in each category was arbitrary, and it will surprise me if the Reader would not substitute her own list.

Product

When considering this category, the immediate temptation is to list individual medications, for example, penicillin. But here, in Table 11.2, is my list beginning with the transfer of the compounding function from pharmacists

Table 11.2 Major Developments in Pharmaceutical Products

Transfer of compounding to Drug manufacturers
"The Pill"
Psychotropic medications
Dosage form developments
Generic pharmaceuticals
Other possibilities
• Antibiotics
• Vaccines
• AIDS medications
• Services as "Products" at retail

to pharmaceutical manufacturers. From today's perspective, this is a natural evolution, but from a historical perspective, it was a revolution. An entire profession built upon a special knowledge of product preparation was relieved of that function and faced with the challenge of discovering and justifying new reasons to be. It is only recently that the challenge appears to have been met.

I have chosen "the Pill" for my next product candidate. There are, of course, many "pills", but the oral contraceptive as a social concept required much more than pharmacology and chemistry to reach the marketplace and to stay there. Carl Djerassi, in his very personal survey of the state of contraception published nearly 20 years ago, quoted Aldous Huxley from more than 20 years earlier: "Most of us choose birth control – and immediately find ourselves confronted by a problem that is simultaneously a puzzle in physiology, pharmacology, sociology, psychology and even theology" (467).

The next class of product is the result of two individual Drugs, one a clear medical breakthrough and the other a (probably) fortuitous case of mistaken identity. The first of these, chlorpromazine, changed both the length and character of hospitalization for mental illness. The second, meprobamate, was responsible for the Public awareness of the possibility of legal use of mind-altering substances. New terminology was necessary with the ultimate term, "tranquilizer".

The fourth class of product developments I have grouped under "dosage forms" but could as well have called delivery systems and saved for the discussion of the future. In any case, sustained release of oral medications, patches, implants, and the like have totally and forever changed Drug administration and set the stage for even more dramatic developments in the future.

Generic pharmaceuticals, the fifth on the list, belong in the pricing discussion as well. As a *product* issue, they represent a trend toward commodity status for both prescription and nonprescription medications. Without the possibility of "substitution," brand names were the backbone of the industry for many years. The existence of Generic divisions in dozens of what were once brand name manufacturers attests to this total change in the Generic market.

Other possibilities (and the Reader will certainly be eager to add more) include the entire field of antibiotics, vaccines which have measurably improved life expectancy in this century, AIDS medications which may do so, and the redefinition of the product of retail pharmacy to include services and outcomes.

Price

As Table 11.3 indicates, the first development considered under Price is that of a pharmacists' professional fee. That fee is at the heart of negotiations with third-party payers today, but this was not always the case by any means. As long ago as 1962, McEvilla (66) and others were advocating adoption of the professional fee concept in the pages of the *Journal of the American Pharmaceutical Association*. Over time, the fee concept was adopted and now serves, along with a confused jungle of product reimbursement procedures, as the basis for most pharmacist payment systems.

Fair Trade is listed next because the issue occupied the time and attention of pharmacy (especially NARD) for so long and eventually failed. Fair Trade or "Resale Price Control" had its legislative beginning in 1931 in California with a Fair Trade Act that required wholesalers and retailers to observe Prices set by the manufacturer. Subsequently, nearly every state enacted such laws. Although the market rationale for such Legislation is complex, Fair Trade clearly protected the independent pharmacists from Price competition. Support for enforcement of these laws ultimately failed.

The pricing pattern change listed in Table 11.3 refers to a shift in prescription Drug pricing. For years, beginning in 1960, Professor John Firestone of the City College of New York calculated and published a Price index for prescription Drugs. Supported, or at least encouraged, by the (then) Pharmaceutical Manufacturers Association, the index uniformly showed little increase and sometimes a decline in Prices. Without exploring the technicalities of Firestone's calculations, the results did reflect a pattern called "skimming" in the marketing literature. This means that new products were initially offered at what would be their highest Price with Price *decreases* following in response to competition and other factors. Inflation and other alterations in market strategy have resulted in a reversal of this practice such that many products, some of them rather old, have experienced a pattern

Table 11.3 Major Developments in Pharmaceutical Pricing

Professional fee
Fair trade
Rx pricing
Development of oligopoly
Focus on economic outcomes/Price versus value

of continuing Price *increases*. This pattern may be altered, however, by the development which will be described next.

For most of this century, a comparatively few Drug companies developed, patented, manufactured, and sold pharmaceutical products to retailers, at Prices of their own determination. Pharmacists could, in effect, "take it or leave it." Inasmuch as the demand for the product was already developed, they tended to "take it", McEvilla described this oligopoly in terms of a "kinky" demand curve (66). Today, and increasingly in the future, because the patients' Drug costs are paid by comparatively few buyers, the power has greatly shifted. A company representing perhaps 20 million patients and 100 million prescriptions annually can now often tell the *manufacturers* "take it or leave it".

In response to the foregoing, and because of some innovative economic research, the focus has shifted to an appreciable degree from the Price of a Drug, to the costs of treatment, and often to the ratio between that cost and its benefit. Quality of life issues, cost-effectiveness, and cost-utility analyses have made simple Price comparisons a thing of the past.

Place

Among the many effects of World War II was a shortage of person-power in the work force. With (mostly) men in the service and women filling jobs heretofore unthinkable, some things had to change. One of these was the tradition of personal service in retail stores, including Drug stores. Once people became accustomed to making their own selections, there was no turning back and this was closely tied to the next two developments (Table 11.4).

In a 25-year review of the development of Drug chains, Godfrey Lebhar, Editor-in-Chief of *Chain Store Age*, described the genesis in these words:

Table 11.4 Major Developments in Pharmaceutical Distribution

> Self-service
> Rise of chains and decline of the corner Drug store
> Shift of nonprescription medications out of pharmacies
> Impact of hospital Pharmacy practices
> Clozaril/methadone incidents
> **Other possibilities**
> • Mail-order prescriptions
> • Wholesale versus direct
> • Drive-in pharmacies

The fact is that when the chains first came into the picture the competition of the established corner druggist was hardly of the aggressive type. The retail druggist of those days was essentially a professional man, interested primarily in compounding prescriptions accurately and selling proprietary and other medicines and medical supplies. He expanded into other lines not by choice or any particular desire to become a merchant but by force of economic circumstances.

The result was that although the druggist of those days performed an essential service and did a satisfactory job on the professional side, he left himself wide open for the kind of competition which the chains introduced.

(469)

The dominance of the chains in pharmacy today has changed the profession into one of employees from what was largely entrepreneurial in the first half of the twentieth century.

Paralleling the growth of the chains and in part due to natural interests by large retail corporations was the incursion of food stores into the nonprescription Drug marketplace. To a generation today who expect at least one aisle in any major food store to be devoted to health and beauty aids, it would seem impossible that at one time many Drug manufacturers had a strict Drug store-only distribution Policy. Pharmacists' objections when such products as Contac and Sucaryl began to be sold in food stores were understandable given the *history* but unrealistic given the *times*.

Hospital pharmacy has changed dramatically in the past 40 years at least, moving out of its traditional basement location often to the patient's bedside. From a marketing point of view, the hospital pharmacy administration has moved into a position of prominence and power among Drug company customers. The American Society of Health-System Pharmacists' Clinical Midyear Meeting has become one of the most successful Drug marketing events in all of pharmacy.

The final point on this list is less a development than a possibility. In the case of Methadone, the Government, and in the case of Clozaril, a manufacturer, have attempted to limit the distribution of a specific medication to certain pharmacies. Traditionally, a pharmacy license assured free access to all legal medications. While neither of these efforts to restrict distribution was successful, some believe that there is merit in the idea and feel that more will follow. Specialty pharmacies, described in Chapter 10, are similar.

Promotion

The basic marketing literature suggests that Promotion be the last of the "P's" to consider as the function of Promotion is to inform the customer about the other "P's". Promotion, in the form of Advertising, has a rich history in the field of pharmaceutical marketing. It has also, along with pricing, received a great deal of criticism.

First on our list of developments are the media. While Drugs had long been advertised, it remained for radio to make truly national Promotion possible, and Drug Promotion helped make the expansion of radio possible. When television followed it, pharmaceuticals could be visually portrayed in a dramatic, if sometimes tasteless, way as a necessary part of life.

The second item on the list may be a bit of a surprise – it surprised me when I really thought of it – *The Physician's Desk Reference*, a remarkable Book. This quasi-official reference text has proved to be indispensable to hundreds of thousands of health professionals most of whom are unaware that the Drug companies pay to have their information included. Of course, "smart" phones have made the now enormous print version impractical.

Describing Promotion as medical education is meant in two ways here. In one sense it is meant the long-standing practice of Drug company financial sponsorship of educational programs for physicians and other Health professionals. Certainly the subject matter is virtually always related in some way to a company product, but the audience (possible bias not withstanding) is afforded an educational experience.

Advertising, in journals especially, contributes in two ways to the educational process. First there is whatever information of value is gained from the advertisement itself. Second is the real but unofficial subsidy of the non-promotion editorial material which the Readers might not otherwise receive. Criticism aside (although there is plenty of it), if it were not for pharmaceutical advertising a new system of education about medications would have to be invented (see Table 11.5).

The direct-to-consumer (DTC) Promotions of prescription Drugs is the next item. By some accounts, the phenomenon was first noticed when, in

Table 11.5 Major Developments in Pharmaceutical Promotion

> Media development
> Physician's desk reference
> Promotion as medical education
> Direct-to-consumer Promotion of legend Drugs
> Changing appeals
> **Other possibilities**
> - Changing targets
> - Sampling changes
> - Supreme court decision

October 1981, Merck, Sharp, and Dohme promoted their pneumonia vaccine, Pneumovax, directly to consumers in several publications including *Modern Maturity* and *Reader's Digest*. The advertisement, which was addressed primarily to the elderly, alerted Readers to the availability of the product, noted the product's benefits, indicated that Medicare would reimburse the cost of the product, and suggested that readers mention the product to their physicians.

The appeals/messages used in Drug Advertising, especially to physicians, have changed considerably over the past 50 years, partly due to Regulation and partly to market forces. In either case, the messages still contain needed information on safety, effectiveness, and use, but now to a greater extent they tend to focus on economics, quality of life, and other "non-clinical" issues. This change suggests a greater concern with the socioeconomic aspects of selling Drugs than with the clinical concerns of the prescriber. It also suggests a much greater interest in influencing different targets, i.e., Pharmacy Benefit Managers (see Chapter 6).

Sampling, long a favorite and presumably effective, promotional technique has undergone serious Regulation and no longer is treated in the sometimes cavalier fashion that was the case in the past. Also a consideration under Promotion, but probably under Environment as well, was the U.S. Supreme Court decision in the 1970s that prohibition of Advertising of professional services under professional Codes of ethics was a violation of First Amendment rights. That prohibition has since been overturned.

In addition to the exposition of some major developments in the "Four P's", I have added a few Environmental factors that, directly or indirectly, affected them.

Environmental Developments

In the section to be discussed with the items in Table 11.6, the temptation to list a hundred or so items was almost overwhelming. However, a few examples should suffice to show that pharmaceutical marketing is, and will be, a victim and a product of the environment. The evolution of the Food and Drug Administration under the various amendments to the Food, Drug and Cosmetic Act is well known. For marketing students, two of these deserve special attention. The Durham–Humphrey Amendment created a retail-prescriber monopoly, something not often seen in a free market and it gave to a Federal regulatory Agency the power to determine which products were to be so regulated. It created a *prescription* Drug industry. The so-called 1962 Amendments gave the FDA even more power including greater strength in regulating Promotion.

The Congressional Investigations item covers a multitude of events with the first, famous series of Hearings being those conducted by Senator Kefauver. Ostensibly to investigate pricing, but fueled by the Thalidomide tragedy, the Hearings not only resulted in the 1962 Amendments but also forever raised America's consciousness about an industry that was just about to realize its importance in the Health history of this country.

In part because of the Investigations just mentioned, and also because of professional critics, the environment includes much more interest and awareness by the general Public of workings of the pharmaceutical industry. When the first effective antibiotics (led by tetracycline) appeared, they were referred to as "wonder drugs". The members of the Public were excited by the prospects of future research. Today, there seems to be both hope and skepticism when the industry is discussed.

The Waxman–Hatch Patent Extension Act is included for two reasons. First, it is the only example of a commodity for which a Patent extension is

Table 11.6 Major Environmental Developments in the Pharmaceutical Marketplace

Durham–Humphrey amendments – 1962 amendments
Congressional Investigations
Public interest and knowledge
Waxman–Hatch Patent extension
Third-party payment programs
Rx-to-OTC shift
Evolution of Pharmacy education – practice

even a legal possibility. Second, it is a classic example of political action in which both interested parties got something they wanted. The Generic manufacturers had easier access through the FDA and the research companies had at least the possibility of longer market life for their patented products.

Third-party payment prescription programs are essential phenomena of the second half of the twentieth century. The prescription Drug marketplace was already an anomaly. One must see one professional (prescriber) to go to another professional (pharmacist) to obtain needed goods. Insurance, Government, and employee benefit programs have added yet another layer of complexity, so that this particular market bears little resemblance to any other.

The prescription to nonprescription shift is a comparatively recent development with enormous potential impact. Drugs for which a prescription were once required are now available in increasing numbers, without a prescription. Once two or three of these switches were effected, the product planning strategies in the Drug companies had to include such possibilities in the future. Further, those third-party payers, considering their own budgets, also now think in terms of how shifted Drugs may be deleted from their benefits package.

Finally, a word about the efforts of pharmacy education and practice to construct a future. Many people do not know that the 6-year Doctor of Pharmacy degree was proposed in 1950! (Today, a 7-year Doctor of Pharmacy Degree is the norm.) A half century later, this was realized. During that interim, the profession has undergone many changes that have not been uniformly positive throughout all segments of practice. Nevertheless, Pharmacy is, and pharmacists are, different from the perspective of marketing.

Invention, Discovery, and Development

The terms are not mutually exclusive, nor are they clearly defined. Chemists, especially, invent new molecules. They can literally create a substance that never has been seen before. A radical shifted here or there and one has invented something completely new at least as far as one knows.

Discovery may mean finding a substance that no one has reported finding before. There is no assurance that it hasn't been around for a long time. Big Pharma is busy trying to discover potential new Drugs throughout the animal and plant kingdoms and in the Earth's geological makeup. (And soon from outer space?)

For Big Pharma, the challenge is to select from literally billions of possible substances to develop. For Big Pharma, wedding all three of these processes is their *raison d'etra*.

As this is a "history" Book, I decided to examine the state of the Drug development efforts. Using several references contemporary at the middle of the twentieth century (19, 348, 465, 466), I essayed to construct a series of product considerations which might have been employed at the time. Here is my list based, loosely, on these references:

1. What is the prevalence of the disease?
2. What is the frequency of use?
3. Is there a definite need for the product?
4. Will the product contribute something entirely new?
5. Are we making a contribution to therapy by adding this product?
6. What income class of population is affected – low, medium, high?
7. Are sales governed by geographical limitations?
8. Are the advantages of the product so great that a limited number of people can be expected to purchase it even at a high Price – thus making it possible to manufacture it in the pilot plant until large-scale and low-cost manufacture can be instituted? (This sale at a high Price to a relatively small group will be a means to absorb some of the research expenses.)
9. What age groups are affected?
10. Will our firm play a leading role in developing the product?
11. Does the preparation fit and round out the general line of our products?
12. Are we offering an improved product?
13. Will the expected improvement make the product more useful than its competitors?
14. How quickly can the product be copied by others?
15. Will an extensive educational campaign be necessary?
16. Will sales fluctuate with the seasons?
17. What are the competitive products and Prices, and how firmly are these preparations entrenched?
18. Who makes these products and what relative position does the manufacturer hold in the industry?
19. Are there any hazards in the manufacture of the product, such as combustion, objectionable odors, and poisonous type of Drugs?
20. Will it fill idle time of plant and equipment?
21. Can present plant equipment be used?

22. Can the product be sold without prescription?
23. Can it be nationally introduced and what is the cost of physicians' samples?
24. Is there an export market?

Many items on the list are relevant today with the addition of considerable detail. A contemporary list would probably fill a small Book. Of course, various departments – marketing, legal, financial, Policy, personnel, etc. – would have their own special lists.

Curiosities and Surprises

As it is impossible to predict the outcome of a new Drug development during clinical trials and especially after marketing, some surprises are inevitable. Side and adverse effects are troubling and sometimes tragic (e.g., Thalidomide).

It is now axiomatic in medical circles that in the normal course of marketing a new Drug "the favorable reports will always appear before the unfavorable". The history of the so-called "wonder drugs" bears this out. The reason is not only that the pharmacist, investigator, and physician are always optimistically hopeful of new cures, but also that, given the complex and diverse nature of patients, all the possible effects of a new Drug are slow to appear.

The only way this situation can be improved is by a better fundamental understanding of the mechanisms of the human body and disease, and of the biologic actions of Drugs on both, so that nasty jolts can be foreseen and forestalled. There are still large gaps in knowledge of Drug action and of the body's complex reactions and interactions. Even if all reactions were fully known and coded into a giant computer, it would still be impossible to predict every chance effect or disaster, for the human is a highly mixed breed, genetically. No two individuals ever respond in exactly the same way to a Drug. In truth, the giving of a Drug, old or new, is always an experiment. In this immensely complex situation, more knowledge, rather than more politics or Regulation, is urgently needed. Sometimes the surprises are good things. (One Drug used to treat congestive heart diseases was found to be useful for glaucoma.)

Adverse effects, not discovered in the routine clinical trials, are not unusual. One broad spectrum antibiotic especially effective in some infections was found to cause unusual susceptibility to sunburn. MER29 was already being used by thousands of people for atherosclerosis when it was suspected to cause eye cataracts and other adverse effects. (See *The Therapeutic Nightmare* (21) for an especially lurid account.)

Sometimes side effects can have positive results. Diphenhydramine (Benadryl) can cause drowsiness. That's the reason so many other antihistamines can label themselves "non-drowsy". This one was easy. Who *wants* to be drowsy? People who have trouble sleeping! Check the ingredients on your OTC sleep remedy. You'll find it listed.

Recommended Reading

For an in-depth, inside account of the Drug development process, I strongly recommend Werth's two Books, *The Billion Dollar Molecule* and *Antidote* (115,116). Werth was allowed inside a real company, Vertex, for periods 20 years apart and provides a unique account not seen elsewhere.

Additional insights into Drug research and development can be found in *Ten Drugs* (35), *Drug Hunters* (364), and *Small Comfort* (5).

Conclusion

The language of Drug development sometimes takes on a military tone. There is "Blockbuster", a term which originated in World War II during the London Blitz but now used to indicate a Drug with extraordinary monetary and therapeutic potential. "Bombshell", again a military term, is often used for really bad news. Finally, there is "Breakthrough". Remember the Battle of the Bulge?

Several times in this Book, the Reader has been exposed to the terms, "molecular modification" and "drug lag". They both deserve a short comment in the context of this chapter.

The molecule of a blockbuster new drug just begs to be modified, either by the originator to make it better or by a competitor to get a share of the market. The story of Big Pharma is replete with examples. The term "molecular modification" is often used in the pejorative. Its synonym is "me too". Partly true, but in a free competitive market shouldn't competing products, maybe better or with a lower Price, be welcome? Clever chemists take the basic molecule, add or subtract a radical or two, and, with luck, you have a "radical" (pun intended) new drug. Let the marketing department begin! The history of Big Pharma is replete with examples.

As to "drug lag", that too is often used in the pejorative. The blame has usually been laid at the feet of the FDA, whom many fault. In fact, some consideration should also be given to a lag in discovery. The FDA can't approve what it hasn't seen. At least a nod in the direction of the Big Pharma labs would seem to be in order.

Chapter 12

Drugs of the Future

Introduction

Not too long ago (and even more so today), the prevailing wisdom was that optimists were learning to speak Russian and pessimists, Chinese. A similar divide exists with regard to Drugs. Optimists see a kind of nirvana with longer, disease-free lives. Pessimists predict chaos – a society with potential it has not yet learned to use wisely. (Cultural lag)

On a happier note, let's join Dorothy on the Yellow Brick Road. She and her companions are on their way to Oz. In the *future*, the trip will not be necessary for the Tin Man and the Scarecrow because it's just a matter of dropping by the nearest "human parts store" – a sort of NAPA for Homo Sapiens. They have hearts – used ones – that can be transplanted from another "vehicle" which, for a variety of reasons, no longer needs it. The shop can even provide an *artificial* heart along with a maintenance kit filled with Drugs to keep it functioning.

The Scarecrow finds that a brain is a different matter (no, not gray). While there is progress, successful brain transplantation is a little way in the future. "Could I show you something in a liver? It belonged to a little old lady who barely even sipped sacramental wine".

"Courage" is really no problem anymore because right on the corner of the Yellow Brick Road and Bluebird of Happiness Lane is the latest "Brain" store (subsidiary of Microsoft). While the folks cannot offer you a human brain transplant, they have a range of products that are even better. The new "cyber brain" is literally filled to over flowing with artificial intelligence.

"What about a *mind* to go with my new brain? We're still working on that", says the salesman.

I see your friend the Lion (May I call you Leo?) is with you. The People are still working on the brain-mind interface, trying to get a few bugs out. Wouldn't want to have a brain without a mind would we?

Heh, heh!!!

Now here we are in the emotions department. When you get your new heart or brain, you'll want to shop here. We've already made a lot of progress with such unwanted emotions as anxiety, depression, and such. Mostly we've been involved with *suppressing* unwanted emotions. Progress has been a little slower in *enhancing* emotions. We're working on two new products to produce elation and glee. There's always some resistance to products such as that. Remember the silly old slogan of pharmacological Calvinism, "If it feels good, it must be bad".

But Seriously

"What if....?" Those two words have endless possible completions. We love to fantasize and hypothesize. Sadly, someone is always around with the parade-ruining comment, "Be careful what you wish for..."

The future is open to endless speculation and subject to a great deal of prediction. There is a difference between predictions and possibilities, of course. As Starr (254) has written, "A trend isn't necessarily fate", or Dubos, "Trend is not destiny" (226). The movies give us a range of possibilities, from "Armageddon" to "It's a Wonderful Life".

In this chapter, we will look at two areas in the future of Drug use – Drugs and aging and Drugs and lifestyle. Special attention to Drugs for the aged seemed an obvious choice given the continuing rise in the proportion of "old people" in the population and given their disproportional use of medications. Lifestyle Drugs were selected for attention because they can be quite interesting in their nonmedical implications.

Drugs in an Aging Society

In the early 1980s, the aptly-named Institute for Alternative Futures held a conference, "Pharmaceuticals in the Year 2000", the Proceedings of which were later published (375). Trends in aging with implications for the Drug industry that were noted at the conference were: possible increase in self-medication, high concentrations of institutionalization, and, especially, deficits in memory and cognition. In that regard, immune therapy was postulated as a fertile area for research under the theory that older people lose some of their immune mechanisms. So far, there have been no breakthroughs there.

What sorts of Drugs could/should scientists be working on for the future, as regards to the elderly? Some of the most interesting prospects are offered by Evans and Kline (53), as a result of a Conference sponsored by the American College of Neuropsychopharmacology more than 50 years ago in 1967. The Proceedings are an exceedingly rich source of possibilities, predictions, and societal analysis. They were published under the title, *Psychotropic Drugs in the Year 2,000 Used by Normal Humans.* We will re-visit this source in the Lifestyle Section which follows, but they have a great deal to say about Drugs and aging.

Future Drugs for the Aged

Heinz Lehman (53) reviewed three theories of aging which only concern us as they might affect the development of Drugs. (He also provided a succinct definition of aging – "the increased probability of death".) Skipping the scientific details, note that Lehman suggests the use of antioxidants and "free radical scavengers" to prevent aging. Presumably, such agents will fall in the purview of Big Pharma.

On a more pedestrian level, Vitamin E and Vitamin C are recommended as a protection against radiation. Radiation – cosmic rays – is theorized to cause age-related changes in the body's molecules resulting, according to the theory, in problems with skin, bones, and blood vessels. That's where the antioxidants come in, and they're cheaper than wearing body armor against radiation.

Gleaning from Lehman's analysis of some of the psychosocial needs of the aged, one can imagine a number of ways in which Drugs might be employed:

- Drugs to provide an artificial sense of achievement to meet the need for love/respect.
- Substances, Drugs, to be routinely added to the older person's food to compensate for the diminishing of the sense of taste, flavor enjoyment being a need.
- A Drug to generate a sense of "newness" to meet the need of novelty in life. Get rid of "been there done that" as a mantra.

- Improve, or at least stabilize, memory. This is, of course, the Holy Grail of Alzheimer's research.
- Provide emotional stability without sedation. Surely no one "in their right mind" would want to cause the disruption Aunt Maude did at the supper last night.
- Reduce depression and the chronic ruminations that render the condition chronic.
- Reduce irrational anxiety. The ideal anxiolytic would result in a greater appreciation of the positive things in life while reducing the feeling of constant threats. Also there should be reduced or eliminated addiction potential.
- Assure not just the right *quantity* of sleep but also the *quality*, old people being shown to be deficient in deep (Stage Four) sleep. Also related to sleep is dreams. Given the current state of knowledge on dream mechanisms, I don't expect much any time soon for the elderly or anybody for that matter. Would it not be possible someday to steer the brain pharmacologically to favor dream mechanisms that are acceptable and euphoric rather than horrible and nightmarish? Or am I just dreaming?
- Aches and pains – when I begin listing my own aches and pains, a friend of mine describes it as an "organ recital". Of course, there are an ample number of mild analgesics, and low-dose aspirin has been shown to reduce the danger of heart attacks.
- Extended sleep – Lehman (53) suggests having the old person sleep 3–5 days a week, with occasional necessary food for intake. That, in my opinion, is going way too far!

I also recommend to the Reader a recently published Book, *Immortality, Inc.*, by Chip Walter (549). The author describes how the private sector is investing billions to find ways to increase the human life span and limit the effects of aging. The social consequences of any success are thought-provoking, and at times, troubling.

Lifestyle Drugs

There are a number of informal definitions of Lifestyle Drugs. Here are a few:

- Drugs that are not medically necessary.
- Drugs that confer no Health benefit, are not indicated for any medical condition, and have no medical indication.

- Drugs that if not taken, do not result in additional Health risk.
- Treatments that increase patient satisfaction but without which they could live.
- Drugs used to treat indications that are personal choice rather than physician-diagnosed illness or to treat problems that affect Health and wellness only marginally.
- Products that improve perceived quality of life, without improving medical outcomes, or reducing overall Health Care costs.

Evans and Kline (53) and their colleagues at the 1967 Conference offered a number of "possibilities" for lifestyle and life-altering Drugs. A few are presented here with my comments:

- Reduce the need for sleep. Not just artificially keep you awake but by bioelectric-biochemical activity reduction sleep may become unnecessary or at least the need reduced.
- Safe short-acting intoxicants. Given the current knowledge base, but absent the almost certain opprobrium, it shouldn't take long to develop one. There may be some already on the laboratory shelf.
- Regulate sexual responses. No, not just treat erectile dysfunction. Already did that! Kline called this "banking the fires or stoking them to match more closely the appropriate environmental circumstances".
- Increase or decrease alertness or relaxation. Both of these conditions would benefit from enhancement depending on circumstances. Some such Drugs now exist.
- Mediate nutrition, metabolism and physical growth. As of this writing, society is right in the middle of this area along with the controversial science which makes it possible. Harari (455) in Homo Deus gives the issues a thorough airing.
- Prolong or shorten memory. There is more to this than seeking a treatment for Alzheimer's. What if we could be made truly to forget something unbearable or remember in detail our first birthday cake?
- Inducing or preventing learning, "Smart" pills? The *prevent* aspect is a bit difficult to exemplify.
- Provoke or relieve guilt. Guilt, if undeserved or unwarranted, has the capacity to ruin a life. Apparently, technology (474) is available by which a Drug can be placed in a tiny, semi-permeable capsule to "leak" out over time or for a lifetime. Such a technique could also perhaps reduce recidivism among repeat criminal offenders.

- Shorten or extend experience time. If one could, without sacrificing learning, make the time of a professor's boring lecture "fly by" or make it seem that a beautiful concert "went on forever".
- Create conditions of J'amais Vu (novelty) or DejaVu (familiarity). Certainly it would seem attractive to the assembly line worker if every bolt attached was a new experience. Similarly, one's "stage fright" on opening night might be conquered.
- Deepen awareness of beauty or sense of awe. Perhaps these Drugs could be found. Kline (53) in his comment on this wrote, "to experience a fresh the awe of human existence we can perhaps better discover both emotionally and intellectually the nature of the human venture". (See Chapter 14 for more on Lifestyle Drugs.)

It should be obvious that Big Pharma would be vitally interested in future drug prospects. And they are. An example is provided in Table 12.1 wherein an industry consultant projected market opportunities for "unmet needs in the marketplace". Her projections were made in 1989 forward to 2007. In but a single market, neuro-pharmaceuticals, there was an estimated potential of $15 billion additional market. We can assume that more current projections for this and other markets not only exist in company databases and that they play an important role in driving R&D decisions.

Table 12.1   Market Opportunities Based on Unmet Needs

Market Potential	
A = Annual market potential of more than $500 million	
B = Annual market potential of $250–$500 million	
C = Annual market potential of $100–$250 million	
D = Annual market potential of less than $100 million	
Conditions	
Alzheimer's Disease	
Drug that halts underlying disease progression	A
Symptomatic treatment for cognitive decline	A
Symptomatic treatment for anxiety	C
Symptomatic treatment for depression	C

(*Continued*)

Table 12.1 (Continued)   Market Opportunities Based on Unmet Needs

Anxiety Disorders	
Therapy for generalized anxiety disorder	B
Therapy for obsessive-compulsive disorder	A
Eating Disorders	
Improved treatment for:	
Obesity	B
Overweight	C
Mixed overweight/obese	A
Bulimia	D
Anorexia	C
Epilepsy	
Once-a-day formulation of current product	A
Improved Drug for patients refractory to available therapies	D
Mood Disorders	
Therapy for depression with faster onset or reduced side effects	A
Therapy for bipolar disorder/mania	C
Multiple Sclerosis	
Drug that halts underlying disease progression	A
Symptomatic therapy for chronic fatigue	B
Parkinson's Disease	
Drug that halts underlying disease progression	A
"Next generation" of L-Dopa	C
Schizophrenia	
Incremental improvement on current therapies (reduced side effects and compliance problems)	A
Agents for treating negative symptoms	A
Improved therapy for tardive dyskinesia	C

(Continued)

Table 12.1 (*Continued*)   Market Opportunities Based on Unmet Needs

Sleep Disorders	
Non-addicting therapy for chronic insomnia	A
Stroke	
Agents for acute management of stroke	A
Neuro-protectants for management/prevention of neuronal death	B
Stroke-preventive agents	D

Source: The Wilkerson Group, Inc., "The Challenge of Neuroscience: Clinical Perspectives and Commercial Prospects", *Pharmaceutical Executive*, October 1989. With permission, MJH Publications.

Conclusion

There are many, many predictions about the future of Drug therapy. Some are fantasy – far-fetched "what ifs". Some would have seemed to be fantasy not many years ago. Clearly, already, "biologics" have taken the place of "pharmaceutics" in the vocabulary. "Biosimilars" are the new Generics. Genomics is the new economics.

It is clear that Big Pharma takes the new sciences seriously. In a *Wall Street Journal* article on July 24, 2019, 14 major Drug companies were listed as having formed partnerships with genetic databases to assist in Drug discovery. One of the biggest investors in the field is GlaxoSmithKline, which has a $300 million stake in the *23andMe* genetic database according to the *WSJ* article. The partnership has produced six potential Drug candidates with one due to start clinical trials in a year. Privacy concerns have been raised as most *23andMe* customers complete a general Health questionnaire, plus the genetic information also helps identify candidates for clinical trials who are often only a small part of the general population.

It should be obvious from the foregoing, and discussions elsewhere in this Book, that it is possible that we risk "letting the genie out of the bottle". There is a developing potential for nearly a total control of human emotional status, mental functioning, and will to act. These human phenomena can be started, stopped, or eliminated by the use of various types of chemical substances. What we can produce with our science now will affect the entire society. In a sense, we are in the same ethical and moral dilemma as the physicists in the days prior to the Manhattan Project. Our tradition and allegiance to the ethos of science and technology makes us feel the responsibility to explore every lead which may produce new chemicals which can help, or control, man. On the other hand, we obviously see the possibilities for social stagnation or repression when such agents are perfected. Along with the geneticists, with their near ability to modify human genetic potential, we are participating in the development of what can be called a "biological atom bomb".

Chapter 13

The Non-Prescription Products – Market-Profits and Public Health in Conflict

W. Steven Pray, PhD

Introduction

Before a discussion of nonprescription products and devices can commence, it is necessary to define them. At the simplest, they are products available to the U.S. population without first consulting a learned prescriber, such as a physician. They are freely available for purchase from thousands of venues, including, but not limited to, "e-commerce" (e.g., Amazon), pharmacies, department stores, grocery stores, airport kiosks, hotel lobbies, beauty shops, gas stations, vending machines, and "health food stores". Nonprescription products are also referred to as "over-the-counter" or "OTC" medications, as opposed to those available only by prescription (Rx) (554–557). For the sake of brevity, this chapter will sometimes use the "OTC" acronym.

This is the era of evidence-based medicine, wherein the scientific method provides pharmaceutical companies with the methods to prove their nonprescription medications are both safe and effective. The Food and Drug Administration (FDA) is the federal Agency formed to protect the Health of the American Public, and FDA has judged a large number of OTC ingredients to be safe and effective in curing, treating, diagnosing, or preventing a medical condition, if the consumer reads and heeds all of the instructions on the package (554,555). This group of products will be referred to in this chapter as "proven" or "legitimate" OTCs.

Despite the FDA, OTC manufacturers have a long and sordid history of selling OTC products not proven safe or effective, many of which have caused death and illness. These unproven products include: (1) patent medicines, (2) "dietary supplements" (other than vitamins and minerals proven to prevent or treat deficiency diseases), (3) homeopathic remedies, (4) herbs, (5) essential oils, and numerous others. These unproven nonprescription products may be advertised for vague and unproven claims, such as to "provide support" for a specific organ or body system (heart or vision). Many unproven nonprescription products make blatantly fraudulent claims. All of these unproven products meet the legal definition of "fraudulent" (558). They are known in popular lingo as "quackery". Products intended solely for cosmetic use are not included in this chapter.

The number of OTCs available as of this writing (2019) may be as high as 500,000. The majority of OTCs are pharmacological in nature, containing medically active ingredients. OTC product labels and their associated advertisements claim to treat numerous medical conditions, from minor (e.g., dandruff, the common cold, itching), to potentially deadly (cancer, liver disease).

Manufacturers also market numerous medical devices that do not contain pharmacologically active ingredients, but they also claim Health benefits. Laws are in place to control these products. Some medical devices are safe (dental floss), but others carry known dangerous devices (ear candles).

How did the United States arrive in a situation where products proven safe and effective are sold side by side with fraudulent products? Why are fraudulent OTC products sold without oversight? Why doesn't some Government Agency force manufacturers to prove their claims? The answers to these questions are complicated; this chapter will examine the interplay among OTC manufacturers, the regulatory Agencies (FDA, the Federal Trade Commission [FTC]), the profession of Pharmacy and those associated with it (i.e., Pharmacy associations, Pharmacy publications). To do so, it is vital to explore the history of OTC products. This chapter will address numerous controversies, both historical and current. The Reader will notice one underlying theme: Whenever there is a conflict between Public Health and profits, OTC manufacturers may act in their own self-interest, regardless of potential dangers to people who purchase their OTC products.

Patent Medicines: Once Popular Nonprescription Products

America has been inundated with unproven products, even before the Revolutionary War created the country. In 1630, for instance, a Massachusetts man was fined for selling a worthless cure for scurvy (555). During the period prior to 1906, the United States was in the midst of the "patent medicine" craze (555). The traveling medicine salesman and his patent medicines has long been a staple character in Western movies and television shows. Traveling by horse and buggy from town to town, he promised to cure any medical condition with his secret formula. Each bottle of the magic elixir typically cost "one thin dime, one tenth of a dollar". With extravagant promises, he bilked the unwary, gullible, and scientifically illiterate victims. The purchasers eventually discovered that the bottle's contents were worthless and/or dangerous, but it was too troublesome to track down the seller and demand the dime back. Those patent medicines were also widely hawked in newspapers and advertising circulars; ads for them were even painted on the side of barns.

The widespread sales of patent medicines are an indelible stain on the history of American medicine. They were indirectly hazardous to purchasers by giving them false hope allowing them to neglect legitimate medical care. Many were also directly hazardous, containing deadly and addictive substances.

Characteristics of Patent Medicines

The term "patent" is often misinterpreted to mean that manufacturers applied for, and were granted, a federal patent for their secret formulas. However, a formal registration with the U.S. Patent Office would have required the sellers to reveal the ingredients in their secret concoctions, which they would never voluntarily do. The only thing patented was the trade name done so no competitor could use it. Of course, the unwary consumer assumed that the formula itself was patented and approved by the prestigious federal patent office. The manufacturers never clarified this misconception, and the false respectability it implied made them rich.

Patent medicines shared several common features (555):

- Labels of these predatory products promised fantastic cures.
- Labels did not disclose ingredients.

- They were advertised with overblown claims void of scientific proof. Products might contain alcohol, heroin, cocaine, morphine, opium, cocaine, or any other addictive substance without a hint of their presence.
- Labels promised to cure many conditions with radically different etiologies, such as infectious, autoimmune, and carcinogenic diseases.
- Labels often promised to cure serious conditions such as consumption (tuberculosis), cancer, insanity, epilepsy, diabetes, blood poisoning, and asthma.
- Labels virtually never listed contraindications, precautions, or adverse effects.

Patent Medicine Manufacturers: The Proprietary Association

At the height of the patent medicine scandal, millions of American citizens purchased worthless and dangerous remedies every day. How did this come about? The predatory manufacturers bear the primary responsibility, but much of the blame lies with the Proprietary Association (PA). This group was formed in November of 1881, its first mission being to fight for repeal of a 4% patent medicine tax that was enacted during the Civil War. The PA was successful in repealing the tax through an entreaty to Congress (559). Other early activities demonstrate an overriding focus on maximizing profits and protecting the secrecy of the industry's patent medicines. For instance, the PA:

- Attempted to stabilize the Prices of Patent medicines by representing Drug manufacturers at meetings of Drug wholesalers and retailers.
- "Vented its wrath" when Pharmacy journals printed the secret and closely guarded formulas of PA members' patent medicines.
- Tried to restrict trademark infringement and label counterfeiting.
- Lobbied against a tax on grain alcohol, a vital ingredient in patent medicine manufacture.
- Fought to keep an emergency tax enacted during the Spanish-American War at a minimal level.
- "Took quick and decisive action whenever there was any hint of a measure restricting patent medicines in State legislatures or the national Congress" (558).
- Supported a resolution at its Eighteenth Annual Meeting in New York City in 1900 to refuse to sell patent medicines to retail druggists who cut Prices (560).

In his landmark 1905 series for Collier's national magazine exposing patent medicines, *The Great American Fraud*, Samuel Hopkins Adams exposed a particularly pernicious PA activity (561). He revealed that U.S. newspapers were at the "beck and call" of patent medicine interests. At a PA meeting, F.J. Cheney, marketer of Hall's Catarrh Cure, explained to his fellow patent medicine marketers how he forced newspapers to actively resist patent medicine Legislation. The scheme was wonderfully simple: Whenever Cheney sent advertising contracts to newspapers, he inserted a clause in red letters reading, "It is mutually agreed that this Contract is void, if any law is enacted by your State restricting or prohibiting the manufacture or sale of proprietary medicines". The clause was also used to combat Legislation that would force manufacturers to publish their formulas or disclose on the labels the presence of dangerous or addictive Drugs. Cheney boasted to other PA members that this clause was "pretty near a sure thing" (559). As a result, newspapers of the 1890s were filled with patent medicine advertisements which were not controlled in any way, and those newspapers were virtually void of any editorial balancing the ads with warnings to Readers as to their lack of safety and efficacy (559). Cheney was also the PA President at the time. Adams reported that the appeal of his scheme was so great that "many of the large firms took up the plan and now the 'red clause' is a familiar device in the trade". Adams also noted that the PA's largest expense was legislative work.

In 1906, federal Agencies began a push to force patent medicine labels to announce the presence and percentages of alcohol and narcotics (562). The proposal would have forced manufacturers to use capital letters to label alcohol content. George L. Douglass of the PA argued against this move, stating, "Would you make a scarecrow out of the label"? He asserted that alcohol is actually beneficial, and that advising customers of its presence would frighten customers away. The PA experienced massive pressure to reform their practices during the fight for the 1906 Pure Food and Drug Act (see below) and sought to head off more restrictive laws by holding a special secret meeting at which it urged members to stop making patent medicines containing narcotics and excess alcohol (559). The PA also urged its Legislation Committee to engage in activities that would exercise restraint in these areas.

In 1989, the PA changed its name to the Nonprescription Drug Manufacturers Association (NDMA) (563,563). The new name "...better suited the modern definition of the OTC drug industry at that time". The organization voted in 1999 to change the name yet again to the Consumer

Healthcare Products Association (CHPA), reporting that the new name "reflects the Association's expanded role on dietary supplement issues..." (565–568). At the time of the final name change, the organization boasted a membership of 75 manufacturers, 20–25 of whom also manufactured dietary supplements. CHPA's senior Vice-President proudly declared that it would become the "lead voice in the area of dietary supplements" (566). CHPA intended to confer legitimacy on these unproven products by representing the manufacturers before the FDA, the FTC, Congress, State legislatures, State regulatory bodies, and international commissions. By this move, CHPA became as closely allied with OTC products lacking safety and efficacy as it was during the patent medicine days.

According to CHPA, its current mission is "Empower self-care by preserving and expanding choice and availability of consumer healthcare products" (564,569). CHPA has stated, "As throughout its history, CHPA is dedicated to safe, effective and responsible self-medication" (564,569). However, a close scrutiny of some of its actions, to be described below, demonstrates a focus on profits at the expense of their purported dedication to safety, efficacy, and responsibility.

The Fight against Patent Medicines

Eventually, the excesses of the patent medicine manufacturers caused responsible investigators to speak out. It must have seemed an impossible task to those early heroes. They faced the daunting prospect of a host of well-heeled manufacturers who would stop at nothing to silence anyone who opposed them. Newspapers could not be counted on to publish any article that would endanger their advertising revenue. The answer was popular magazines. The first was *Ladies' Home Journal* (556). In 1892, Editor Edward Bok made the decision to cleanse its pages of all patent medicine ads. He next began a crusade against patent medicines, publishing a series of damning exposés from 1905 to 1907. He detailed a long litany of lies, greed, and willful intent to fleece the American Public through a variety of pernicious practices.

Other journals joined the crusade. In 1905, *Collier's* published a series of articles written by Samuel Hopkins Adams, entitled, *The Great American Fraud* (see above) (561). Other articles appeared in 1912 and 1913. They extended Bok's work, exploring many of the most jealously guarded secret marketing tactics of the industry. Dr. Harvey Washington Wiley continued the attack with a series of articles in *Good Housekeeping* in 1912–1916.

Their work, aided by a 1906 law (discussed below), gradually spurred the downfall of patent medicines, although medical fraud never entirely disappeared.

Laws That Regulated Nonprescription Products

The history of the laws that now regulate nonprescription products is tangled and lengthy. Throughout the deliberations over these laws, the PA fought constantly to prevent any type of governmental control over their businesses and profits, often working against the welfare of the American Public.

The 1906 Pure Food and Drugs Act

During the early 1900s, it became apparent that the American Public needed protection from adulterated and misbranded foods and Drugs. As a result, concerned lawmakers proposed a new law to ensure the purity of foods and Drugs and also to stop the sales of patent medicines. During the long deliberations, the PA actively battled the law. For instance, PA attempted once again to remove a provision that would require patent medicine labels to disclose the presence of narcotics. The PA was mostly unsuccessful and the Act was ultimately signed into law by President Theodore Roosevelt in 1906 (555). The editor of the *Journal of the American Medical Association*, arguably the most prestigious U.S. medical journal, wrote with enthusiasm: "Certainly the powerful Proprietary Association of America has not proved to be so powerful after all" (559). After the law took effect, the federal Government hauled many patent medicine manufacturers into court for untruths on the labels. Unfortunately, many fines were so low (1 cent to $50) that they were a joke. The PA again demonstrated an eye on the bottom line when its spokesmen pointed out that it was cheaper to plead guilty and pay the tiny fine than to stand on their convictions about the safety of their products and defend them in open court (559). Thus, latent medicines continued to be sold under the new law, albeit with a new set of Regulations.

Despite its innovative protection for the American consumer, the 1906 Pure Food and Drugs Law had a number of shortcomings. Several efforts were made to remedy these, but the PA helped ensure that no new Legislation would be forthcoming (559). In order to help in these efforts, the PA began a journal known as *Standard Remedies* in 1915. It vigorously and bitterly attacked any critic of patent medicines.

PA also continued to battle against any further Government control of Advertising (559). In 1915, PA urged its members to police itself by adopting a voluntary code (559). However, later that same year, PA reported that manufacturers no longer needed to worry about their ads. Apparently, World War I had pushed newspaper publishing costs so high that even the most misleading ads were being accepted without question.

The 1914 Harrison Narcotic Act

One of the most startling deficiencies of the 1906 Pure Food and Drugs Act was its failure to prohibit the presence of addictive narcotics such as opium, morphine, and cocaine in patent medicines (555). Sales of these narcotics were a primary source of revenue for Drug stores, and druggists protested when New York attempted to stop their sales (555).

Addicts loved widespread availability of their favorite addictive substances which could be purchased without the need for a physician. In their never-ending greed, patent medicine manufacturers also found a way to increase sales by focusing on parents and their babies (555). They were aware that many babies experience colic. Infant colic has a medical definition, and its causes include intestinal gas and a need for parental attention (554). The infant's crying can be full-force and may last for hours, days, or weeks. Parents are at their wit's end from lack of sleep and inability to soothe the baby. In desperation, parents turned to a widely promoted group of patent medicines known generically as "soothing syrups." The products promised to soothe the baby sufficiently so it would sleep, and the haggard parents could also have a restful night. The deadly secret was that they contained powerful narcotics that drugged the baby into sleep. An unknown number of babies never woke up due to morphine, opium, and/or paregoric poisoning. Parents shared accounts of their profound grief in the popular press as warnings to others. It is heart-wrenching to read the harrowing accounts of the parents' pain and anguish when discovered their babies dead the next morning. Despite the hue and outcry, patent medicine manufacturers continued full steam ahead, marketing narcotics to babies. One article asserted that druggists would never refuse to sell these deadly products as long as there was a profit to be made from them (555).

In 1913, U.S. Representative Burton Harrison offered a bill to control nonprescription narcotic sales (555). Predictably, it was opposed by the patent medicine manufacturers. While it was not perfect, the law, as it was passed in 1914, did a great deal to stop the epidemic of baby deaths due to the deadly soothing syrups. Further, addicts all over the United States went into withdrawal from inability to obtain their favorite narcotic patent medicines.

The 1938 Food, Drug, and Cosmetic Act

In the late 1920s, there were several unsuccessful attempts to increase federal oversight of the remaining patent medicines (567). The PA responded by attempting to create a new Advertising Code. This self-protective move was provoked by heavy criticism about their Advertising (555).

In 1930, Ervin F. Kemp, PA's General Representative since 1905 (also the editor of *Standard Remedies*), approached J.J. Durrett, the man in charge of governmental enforcement (555). Kemp complained that patent medicines were more strictly regulated than prescription medications. Durrett replied that patent medicines were receiving by far the most lenient treatment of any group of products and that he (Durrett) might even work to make sure that patent medicines were more tightly controlled than before. Clearly, there was a shifting attitude toward these predatory products.

President Franklin Roosevelt recognized that a revision of the 1906 law was needed to address patent medicines and other issues (555). He asked his trusted advisor, Rexford Tugwell, to lead the charge in 1933. Tugwell submitted a draft of a bill to both Houses of Congress. His first draft would penalize false advertising of foods, Drugs, or cosmetics by prosecution in federal courts (570).

During the prolonged struggle that led up to the 1938 Food, Drug, and Cosmetic (FDC) Act, the PA vigorously attempted to protect the interests of the manufacturers rather than those of the consumer. (In 1933, the PA membership included 80% of the producers of "packaged medicines" in the United States.) At their 1933 meeting, the PA "strongly assailed" the original Tugwell Bill. One of the PA members stated that there was already ample basis for prosecution of false Advertising, and that the Government should not be able to form an opinion that an advertisement would be deceptive (571). Hearings on the bill were conducted in December 1933 by Senator Royal Copeland. Opposition from the PA reached such a fevered pitch that one journal pointed out that proprietary manufacturers were "the first group of industrialists to openly declare war on the Roosevelt administration (559). H. B. Thompson, general counsel of the PA, asserted that the bill would give "unlimited powers to the Secretary of Agriculture", and that it was a "chamber of horrors" (572). He stated "I have never in my life read a bill or heard of a bill so grotesque in its terms, evil in its purpose, and vicious in its possible consequences" (559).

In an effort to deflect PA's concerns over the Tugwell Bill, Copeland introduced a modified version of the Tugwell Bill in the Senate in January 1934. (Thereafter, Tugwell's name would no longer be applied to the bill, and it would be known as the Copeland Bill.) Copeland's bill attempted to mollify Drug manufacturers by omitting a provision that would have required full formula disclosure on proprietary products, a measure the manufacturers continually fought. Simultaneously, a Representative Black introduced a measure in the House that was prepared by the National Drug Trade conference (573). Predictably, Drug interests supported the less restrictive Black Bill that they had, in fact, prepared (574).

In December 1934, the FDA blamed the proprietary medicine industry for defeat of regulatory Legislation, charging that the industry had put forth a "vast amount of misinformation that the Copeland Bill would result in destruction of legitimate industries, interfere with the right of self-medication and deny manufacturers their constitutional rights" (575). Also in December of 1934, Frank A. Blair, PA President, justified the organization's refusal to support the older Tugwell Bill. He asserted that the bill would "encroach upon the rights of the manufacturer and consumer alike" (576). Blair nonetheless stated that he hoped to create a spirit of friendly cooperation between the nonprescription medicine industry and the FDA, stressing that the correct route to reform should be a revision of the badly outdated 1906 Pure Food and Drug Act, rather than creating a new law. James F. Hoge, attorney for the PA, asserted that the Tugwell Bill would have given the federal administration sweeping and inadequately supervised legislative executive and judicial powers. In January of 1935, the PA sponsored a bill in the House that contained 28 points, which Blair and Hoge asserted would adequately revise the 1906 law (577). This was known as the Mead Bill (578). It was favored by the PA because it did not authorize seizures and criminal prosecutions for misbranding, as did the Copeland Bill. (Throughout the 1920s, the PA had objected repeatedly to multiple seizures (559)). In April of 1935, W.Y. Preyer, the Chairman of the Advisory Committee on Advertising of the PA (also first Vice-President of the Vick Chemical Company), spoke out against the Copeland Bill (579). He stated that the bill would seriously curtail advertising, weaken the value of trademarks, and work grave hardships upon legitimate business. He also bemoaned the possibility that companies would be required to disclose their formulas. Eventually, the PA succeeded in having amendments from their PA-sponsored bill transferred to the Copeland Bill. They denied seizure control to the federal Government, and thereby weakened it badly (559). As a result, the PA supported this virtually toothless 1935 Copeland Bill. During the summer of 1935, Hearings continued on the Copeland Bill. One witness providing comments was an attorney for the Lydia Pinkham Company, a leading source of unproven products. The company had disseminated a pink slip suggesting that women might not be able to buy Lydia Pinkham's products if a new law were passed. It stated that the company was trying to stop passage of the new law and urged Readers to write letters to Congress immediately. Despite the hopes of reformers, no bill was enacted by the 1935 Congress.

The Copeland Bill was picked up for consideration by the 1936 and 1937 Congresses but not passed. In January of 1937, the executive Committee of the PA announced that the Copeland Bill was not satisfactory in every detail to the members of the packaged medicines organization (a synonym for the PA) (580). PA recommended changes that would further weaken the bill. For instance, they suggested deletion of any requirement for disclosure of active ingredients and removal of a provision that would require medical warnings to purchasers.

Despite several years and incredible effort, the PA and others had prevented passage of an updated law. The situation changed radically in 1938 with the "Elixir of Sulfanilamide Tragedy" (555). A nonprescription product made by S.E. Massengill Company with a toxic solvent killed more than 100 people (555). Despite its deadly composition, its sale was perfectly legal under the inadequate 1906 law. The PA and others who had long opposed a new law ducked and ran for cover and Congress overrode industry to enact the law in 1938.

The tortuous history of the 1938 law was summed up in *Business Week* in June, 1938 as:

> Industry lawyers who ably influenced the course of the legislation—such as James R. Hoge of the Proprietary Association… content themselves with knowledge that in five years of unrelenting warfare with rampant idealism they have succeeded in effecting a compromise measure which will not seriously interfere with the marketing of the great bulk of goods…
>
> (581)

The Durham–Humphrey Amendment (See Also Chapter 5)

Until the early 1950s, there was widespread confusion about which medications could be sold without a prescriber's order. The FDC Act of 1938 stated that a medication would be misbranded if it failed to carry adequate directions for use and/or failed warn purchasers of situations in which certain uses would be unsafe (555). Certain hypnotic and narcotic medications were also required to carry this precaution: "Warning—May be habit forming". The FDA attempted to clarify this confusion with a 1938 Regulation that allowed the manufacturer to omit the adequate directions for safe self-use if it also warned pharmacists and the Public with this label: "Caution: To be used only by or on the prescription of a physician, dentist, or veterinarian".

Other than these points, the FDA intentionally refrained from listing medications that would require a prescription. There were three reasons for this seemingly irresponsible stance (555). First, FDA foresaw that a fixed list would constantly require updating as new information was submitted to the Agency. Second, FDA did not feel capable of deciding which medications would be justifiably labeled as "dangerous". Finally, and most critical to this chapter's underlying theme, FDA trusted manufacturers to use patient safety as the primary criteria in deciding which medications would be safe for self-use.

The results of the FDA's inaction were predictable. Manufacturers disregarded Regulations and made decisions based on profit, among other criteria. One manufacturer would omit self-care directions for a specific ingredient, restricting it to prescription status. Another manufacturer would sell that identical ingredient directly to consumers by placing directions for self-care on the label. Widespread confusion reigned.

Greedy pharmacists stepped into this regulatory void. During the 1940s, pharmacists created a severe national scandal by indiscriminately selling numerous dangerous medications without a prescription (555). They included:

- Barbiturates and other sleeping medications for insomnia. (In one landmark case that made national headlines, a Kansas City resident was mailed as many as 93 barbiturate refills, from a Los Angeles Pharmacy. She was not able to walk during her last days, as evidenced by blood smears along her walls. When she was discovered dead in her home, there was evidence of rats having partially consumed her body.)

- Dexedrine and Benzedrine to combat fatigue
- Thyroid for weight reduction
- Male and female sex hormones for glandular disturbances
- Sulfas and antibiotics for venereal disease. An Investigation in New York revealed that 25% of pharmacists were actively diagnosing and treating venereal diseases (555).

Pharmacists also refilled prescriptions endlessly. It seemed that many viewed a prescription as a license to give that patient the specified medication for years and years, without any further consultation with the prescriber.

By 1951, it was clear that these issues would require the Government to clearly specify which medications were prescription only. Representative Carl Durham and Senator Hubert Humphrey authored an amendment to the FDC Act that would require prescription Drugs to carry a clear note known as a "legend". Legend Drugs would be noted by this container label: "Caution: Federal law prohibits dispensing without a prescription". The question of whether a medication was legend (Rx only) or OTC would be easily solvable by looking at the label. Confusion would be resolved. FDA would be empowered to decide which medications would be Rx only.

Vested interests mounted vigorous opposition to the Durham–Humphrey Amendment (555). At the opening of the PA's Sixty-Ninth Annual Conference on May 14, 1951, James F. Hoge (PA general counsel) called the measure "the most dangerous threat to freedom of medical care in America since the famous Tugwell bill of 1933...it jeopardizes the traditional right of self-medication and choice of remedies". He further characterized it as "a handmaid of socialized medicine" (582).

The American Pharmaceutical Association (APhA) also worked to stop the amendment (555). It stated that the bill would restrict the relationship between pharmacists and physicians. APhA also passed a resolution to give as little power as possible to the FDA in deciding which medications would be Rx only. APhA editorialized that the bill was an attempt by FDA to encroach upon the practice of medicine.

Despite strong opposition from the PA and APhA, the Durham–Humphrey Amendment was signed into law by President Truman in 1951. It can now be viewed as the most important piece of Legislation in regard to nonprescription products. It was the first time there was a clear demarcation between self-care products and those that require diagnosis and monitoring by a learned intermediary/prescriber.

The 1962 Kefauver–Harris Amendments

In 1962, Senator Estes Kefauver led a fight in Congress to control Prices of prescription medications. As debate swirled through Congress, the thalidomide tragedy intervened. Eventually, Kefauver's Legislation became an amendment to the FDC Act requiring manufacturers to prove safety and efficacy of all prescription products marketed between 1938 and 1962. It also required premarketing approval for any medications proposed for prescription marketing after 1962 (555). After the amendment's passage, FDA quickly initiated a procedure known as the Drug Efficacy Study Implementation (DESI) review. The United States Vitamin (USV) company decided to fight. USV had peddled bioflavonoids for bleeding, hypertension, ulcerative colitis, and a wide variety of other pathologically unrelated conditions. Fearing the outcome of any review of its unproven claims, USV challenged FDA's authority to require proof of efficacy. The lawsuit went all the way to the Supreme Court; USV lost because they were forced to admit that had no proof at all that bioflavonoids had any activity for any condition, and the products were eventually forced from the market (555). The full ramifications for OTC manufacturers resulting from Kefauver–Harris are described below.

FDA's Review of OTC Products

Genesis of the FDA OTC Review

The Kefauver–Harris Amendment was described above as the genesis of a review of prescription products. The nonprescription industry foresaw an extension of the review to nonprescription products, one of the most dangerous threats they had ever faced. Up to this time, OTC manufacturers blithely marketed many thousands of products, with no Government Agency legally empowered to review and approve their ingredients for safety or efficacy. Advertisements were never reviewed for truthfulness. There was no guarantee that all ingredients were listed on labels. If the FDA were to require proof of safety and efficacy, and also truth in Advertising, the OTC industry's free ride would halt. Profits would drop as dollars would be diverted to research. Highly profitable products might be forced from the market.

Thus, during deliberation on Kefauver–Harris, the OTC industry spoke out forcefully. On August 21, 1962, PA's James F. Hoge urged a "thoroughgoing, analytical revision" of the proposed law. He pointed out that requiring proof of efficacy for nonprescription products could pose serious trouble for manufacturers. He also objected to a proposal requiring complete formula and content information on the labels (583). Hoge's objections were identical to those of the old patent medicine days. Manufacturers still refused to prove their medications effective and also refused to reveal their formulas.

The PA's fears were well-founded. In 1972, FDA announced that it would extend the safety and efficacy review to nonprescription products (555). The proposed review would evaluate safety and efficacy of all OTC products marketed in the United States before May 11, 1972. Products marketed under New Drug Applications (NDAs) or covered by "safety" NDAs before the Kefauver–Harris Amendments were adopted would be exempt since they had already been thoroughly examined.

Organizing the Review

FDA personnel soon realized that the task they were undertaking seemed impossible. The process used for evaluating prescription medication involved examining one product at a time. However, this process could not be duplicated with OTCs in light of existing resources, since the number of OTC products was estimated to be as high as 500,000. Therefore, the FDA OTC Drug Evaluation Division adopted a different strategy. The impossibly large number of trade-named OTC products contained only 722 different ingredients. If the Agency assessed each ingredient, the work would be streamlined and manageable. FDA began to organize the work by dividing the 722 ingredients into 26 separate therapeutic categories. Each category would be subjected to a three-phase review.

Phase 1

The first phase of the review was evaluations of ingredients by expert Panels who were not FDA staff. Using unbiased expert reviewers was perhaps intended to stop OTC manufacturers from claiming that any negative reviews were due to previous adverse experiences with FDA staff.

Each advisory Panel consisted of seven members to prevent a tie vote. Panels were made up of physicians and specialists from the medical area under consideration, a toxicologist, and a pharmacist. Some members were clinicians and some were academicians. The antacid panel included gastroenterologists with distinguished careers. The antimicrobial first-aid panel included dermatologists and microbiologists. Each panel's experts were similarly chosen, and their opinions were virtually unimpeachable. Manufacturers were represented by an industry liaison who had no voting power.

Panel assignments covered almost all OTC products. Examples of Panel assignments are antidiarrheals, laxatives, eye products, internal analgesics, external analgesics, ear products, and gastric products. Manufacturers were fully aware that the process was in motion. FDA informed them that if they wished their products' ingredients to be evaluated, they should submit samples of each to the Agency by a specified deadline. They were also asked to submit any data on safety and efficacy.

After the deadline expired, Panel deliberations began. Panels looked at the manufacturer-submitted data and gathered all available information from the published literature. Panels carried out an exhaustive examination of the available data to determine whether existing research was carried out in a proper manner, for example, appropriate sample sizes, correct statistical tests. Each ingredient was assigned to one of three categories:

- Category I – Sufficient evidence exists that the ingredient is safe and effective. The legal term for these ingredients is GRASE (generally recognized as safe and effective).
- Category II – Sufficient evidence exists that the ingredient is unsafe or ineffective, or both.
- Category III – There is insufficient evidence to judge the safety and/or efficacy of the ingredient.

Panels also assessed the safety and efficacy of combination products, and the truthfulness and accuracy of the product labels. For each ingredient placed in Category I, Panels recommended labeling for the consumer. Each Panel's evaluations were published in the *Federal Register*. The Phase 1 monographs were titled "Advance Notice of Proposed Rulemaking". With the publication of this document, Phase 1 ended for that specific product category and that Panel was disbanded. During the review, the Panels examined 20,000 volumes of data regarding 1,454 advertised or potential uses of 722 ingredients, during the 508 meetings (554).

Phase 2

Phase 2 marked the beginning of FDA personnel becoming involved. It was designed to give manufacturers a time period in which to react to the

Phase 1 document, if they desired to take concrete action. Some OTC manufacturers were not badly affected while others had to make some important decisions. If a specific product contained only Category I ingredients, there was no need to make changes to the formula at that time, assuming they eventually conformed to all labeling requirements. For ingredients in Category II, however, there was already incontrovertible evidence that they were unsafe and/or ineffective. Manufacturers had to decide whether to avoid further FDA action and discontinue the offending products or reformulate them with Category I ingredients. They might also stall as long as possible before the FDA finally forced them to reformulate under threat of federal action. This option was legally risky, since patients injured by the product could now point to the *Federal Register* publication as ammunition against the manufacturer.

If a manufacturer's product contained Category III ingredients, there were interesting options. Reformulation to include Category I was also an option here. There was also the option to stall, hoping some other company would conduct expensive and time-consuming research to prove the ingredient's safety and efficacy. Any manufacturer could then take advantage of others' hard work. The third option would be to carry out the research. For multinational companies with large research budgets and one or more products with tens of millions in yearly sales, conducting groundbreaking research might be attractive. On the other hand, regional companies with small budgets would see little immediate benefit in expending millions on products whose annual sales averaged several hundred thousand dollars.

Phase 2 took as long as 15 years for some categories. Eventually, FDA decided to announce a date beyond which no more submissions would be accepted. After that date, the Agency carefully evaluated all submitted evidence. Some manufacturers submitted research designed to prove safety and efficacy, but their studies did not meet the standards of quality research and were rejected. Other studies were accepted. The result was that some ingredients assigned to Category III by the Panel were moved to Category I by the FDA. Ingredients might also move from Category I to Category II or Category III because of new safety or efficacy concerns. FDA also addressed all comments about the ingredients or proposed labeling. FDA issued its decisions and explained the justifications for them in a Phase 2 document published in the *Federal Register*. This document was known as the "Tentative Final Monograph" or "Proposed Rule."

Phase 3

After publication of the Phase 2 document, Phase 3 began. Phase 3 was another period of time for manufacturers to submit data, hoping to prove safety and efficacy of Category III ingredients. FDA announced a deadline after which no new data would be accepted. FDA then conducted a final evaluation of all newly submitted data and made its final decisions. Ingredients were placed in one of only two categories. Those with sufficient evidence of safety and efficacy (i.e., GRASE) were said to "meet monograph conditions". Those not meeting monograph conditions became known as "non-monograph". The results were published in the *Federal Register* as a "Final Monograph" or "Final Rule" (554,555). FDA gave manufacturers a period of time to comply with the final monograph, usually 6 months. This allowed time for (1) reformulating or discontinuing products with non-monograph ingredients, (2) ensuring labeling conformed to the Final Monograph's requirements and (3) discontinuing combination products not allowed by the Final Monograph. Offending products still being marketed after expiration of the grace period could be seized by the FDA, as adulterated and/or misbranded. The Final Monographs were given force of law through publication in the *Code of Federal Regulations* (see Chapter 5).

Benefits of the FDA OTC Review

Eventually, the majority of nonprescription product ingredients will be thoroughly examined. Pharmacists and the public can be assured that products contain only safe and effective ingredients (with exceptions noted below). As far as manufacturers are concerned, the review is a mixed blessing. The bad news is that they can no longer continue to market ingredients of unknown safety and efficacy (again there are glaring exceptions noted below). The good news is that a manufacturer wishing to establish a line of nonprescription products need only look at the Final Monograph or *Code of Federal Regulations* to see which ingredients can be marketed as GRASE and the appropriate labeling required to sell them without further FDA oversight.

The OTC Label

It would be misleading to suggest that the only benefit of the FDA OTC Review was requiring proof of safety and efficacy for nonprescription ingredients. Even the safest and most effective nonprescription ingredient might become unsafe of ineffective if misused. FDA needed to go further to ensure that patients could use these safe and effective ingredients without the need for consultation with a pharmacist or other medical professional. The solution was forcing manufacturers to use comprehensive labels.

In approaching the issue of proper labeling for self-care products, FDA had to evaluate the difference in Rx and OTC products. Consumers are not considered medically sophisticated enough to treat some medical conditions (e.g., hypertension, gout, epilepsy) and they cannot safely self-treat with prescription medications (554). Only a licensed prescriber has the training and experience to treat those conditions. Prescribers are known legally as "learned intermediaries".

By contrast, FDA does not require a learned intermediary in the sales of OTCs. There are no laws in the United States outlining who can sell OTCs; they are sold in pharmacies, beauty shops, gas stations, hotel lobbies, airport shops, and vending machines. (There are just a few exceptions to be discussed below as the "third class of drugs".)

How did FDA attempt to ensure that purchasers use OTCs correctly? An equally important benefit of the FDA OTC Review was requiring manufacturers to use labeling approved by the FDA. Approved labels would ensure safe self-use by including:

- Ingredients (both active and inactive)
- Ages below which the product is not safe
- Duration of use before seeing a physician
- Dosing
- Directions for use (with illustrations when required)
- Who should not use the product
- When to stop use of the product and see a medical professional
- Precautions, warnings, and contraindications
- Instructions for pregnant and breast-feeding women
- Drug interactions
- Any other matter considered critical by the FDA

Of course, this entire process assumes that the purchaser will "read and heed" the label. In an ideal world, the purchaser of an OTC would read the entire label before purchase and re-read the entire label before the first and subsequent uses. The customer would heed all precautions, warning, and directions on the label. This ideal cannot be reached for several reasons. First, research has proven that consumers ignore most of the label, including the directions; they may not even know the active ingredient(s) of the product. Second, labels are created with font sizes so small that reading is difficult if not impossible. Further, a large number of people are illiterate and, therefore, unable to read or heed the label. Finally, America has numerous immigrants for whom English is not their native language, making the nonprescription label unintelligible. These problems underscore the vital role of the pharmacists in OTC sales.

Criticism of the FDA OTC Review

The FDA review was (and still is) a lengthy and cumbersome process, having begun in 1972. While most categories are finalized, others (e.g., internal analgesics) remain in process at the time of this writing (2019).

A critical point must be made. To fully protect the Public, the FDA should have forced an immediate halt to sales of all OTC products not yet proven safe and effective. FDA should have only allowed products to be sold after all of their ingredients were proven safe and effective and also after the labeling was judged to be accurate and truthful. This process would not have been possible. OTC manufacturers and all of those selling them would have brought enormous political pressure that would have forced the FDA to reconsider such a move. Patients would have clamored for their favorite OTCs. In light of the political realities, FDA decided to allow companies to continue to market OTC products during the entire length of the OTC Review. This meant that the American consumer was exposed to products of unknown safety and efficacy for several decades, directly against the interest of Public Health. Despite this startling and dangerous situation, at least there was a hope that in the far future all OTC products would be safe and effective.

Nonprescription Products Not Reviewed

Some nonprescription products were granted "grandfather" status by the 1938 FDC Act, meaning that they did not have to comply with the law as long as the label remained the same. This was the reason that companies were allowed to continue to sell nonprescription phenazopyridine for urinary tract pain without a label precaution urging the patient to consult a physician. An FDA officer confirmed to the Author that the Agency would eventually pursue these old products despite their status.

Homeopathic products were not reviewed. Through a loophole inserted in the 1938 FDC Act, Senator Royal Copeland, the major sponsor of the law, inserted an exemption that allowed some homeopathic products to be marketed without proving efficacy (555). Dr. Copeland was also a homeopathic physician (555). This move to protect his unproven therapies could be viewed as an abuse of Senatorial privilege.

A 1994 law known as the Dietary Supplement Health and Education Act (DSHEA) allowed marketing of a large group of unproven products known legally as "dietary supplements", even though they are not known to be necessary for any dietary purpose. The term does not apply to vitamins and minerals of known value to human Health). Rather, it includes herbs, minerals, amino acids, plant pollen, and thousands of potentially dangerous and worthless remedies. The FDA cannot require manufacturers to provide evidence of their value. As will be discussed later, the retrogressive DSHEA took American medicine back to the days of patent medicines. This group of products will also be discussed in greater detail below.

Each of these unproven nonprescription products presents unknown dangers to consumers. They fit the legal definition of "fraud" and are popularly referred to as "quackery", discussed in detail below.

OTC Manufacturers and the Review

The true extent to which OTC manufacturers attempted to influence the FDA OTC Review is unknown, since the *Federal Register* did not identify the authors of comments. However, some clues to their input are available. By 1992, the PA had assumed its intermediate name, the Nonprescription Drug Manufacturers Association (NDMA). In that year, NDMA President James D. Cope boasted at PA's annual meeting that 17 NDMA task groups had

> ...interacted with FDA on 27 ingredient or category issues, including analgesics/sleep aids, benzoyl peroxide, dextromethorphan, and oral health care. And we have had more than 140 task group meetings in response to FDA's questions as to the safety or effectiveness of these ingredients.
>
> *(584)*

Cope mentioned at NDMA's 1994 annual meeting that NDMA had held 150 task group meetings on safety/efficacy issues (585). He also stated "Assuring the public that OTC products are safe and effective is the fastest-growing area of the association's programs..." By 1998, the PA underwent its final name change to the Consumer Healthcare Products Association (CHPA). CHPA reported in 1998 that the NDMA/Cosmetic, Toiletry and Fragrance Association Joint Oral Care Task Group had submitted extensive comments to the Plaque Subcommittee of the FDA OTC Review (586). In 2000, CHPA commented on a proposed FDA Regulation to tighten up the criteria for selecting medications to be included in the OTC Review. CHPA worried that the proposed rule could inhibit introductions of new nonprescription ingredients (587).

Manufacturers were also active in areas other than the Drug review. In 1990, NDMA issued a news release asking FDA to establish a separate office of OTC Drugs (588). NDMA also urged FDA to establish a permanent OTC advisory group; it succeeded when FDA decided in 1992 to create a Nonprescription Drugs Advisory Committee (NDAC) (589).

The Prescription-to-OTC Switch

The process by which prescription medications are given nonprescription status is known as the prescription-to-OTC switch. It is also called the "Rx-to-OTC switch movement". This process has ensured that a steady stream of safe and effective new OTC products steadily become available to the American Public (554,554).

Methods by Which Switches Occur

The first method by which OTC medications switched to OTC status was through the FDA OTC Drug Review. FDA asked the Phase 1 advisory Panels to judge whether Rx ingredients might be sufficiently safe for self-use. The Panels identified 27 Rx ingredients that could possibly be labeled for 31 different medical conditions (554,554). FDA disagreed with nine, but the remaining 18 were granted interim OTC status. They included hydrocortisone, diphenhydramine, oxymetazoline, and fluoride dental rinses. This method of switching is no longer available as the Panels' work was completed years ago.

The second method is known as the "Switch Regulation". It would be logical to assume that the manufacturer of the prescription product would be the one to seek OTC status. However, the Switch Regulation is a little-known rule dating to 1956. It allows any interested party to petition the FDA to switch any Rx ingredient to OTC status. This method was last used in 1971 for the successful switches of dextromethorphan and tolnaftate. An interesting 2001 situation involved this Regulation (555). Managed care companies petitioned FDA to switch Rx antihistamines to OTC status. The products involved were Claritin, Zyrtec, and Allegra. The switch would have saved one company $45 million, since its insurance policies denied reimbursement for OTC products. Thus, costs would be shifted to the consumer. CHPA voiced its opposition to the insurance company's move, asserting that only the manufacturer of the Rx product should initiate a switch petition. CHPA stressed that only the manufacturer would have the complete set of data concerning safe and effective use.

The third method of switching is the one most commonly used today. This method is related to the NDA. After discovering a new medication, a company must file for a patent, which gives it a 20-year period during which no other company can market it. The company must also conduct research on its safety and efficacy and eventually file an NDA with the FDA. The NDA might be composed of hundreds of thousands of pages of supporting research.

If the company later wishes to market a different Rx dosage, or formulation of that medication, a full new NDA is required. Conversely, a proposed change might be deemed by FDA to be relatively minor (e.g., a change in an inactive ingredient). In this case, the FDA might require only a supplemental NDA, addressing that limited issue. After a medication is approved for Rx sales, the parent company's patent will eventually expire. This allows any other company to market the same medication under a different trade name or as a Generic after successfully submitting an Abbreviated NDA (ANDA).

If a company wishes to switch an Rx medication to OTC status via the NDA, there are several avenues to do so:

- Submit a full NDA to support OTC status. This would be needed if the OTC version under consideration is to be a new dosage or formulation. For example, the proposed dosage might be one-half of the Rx dose. An NDA would be required to prove that the lower OTC dose would still be effective. If the company wished to sell an OTC liquid form of an Rx tablet, a full NDA would be required to prove that the OTC liquid was also safe and effective. In these cases, the manufacturer's new studies give it 3 years of marketing exclusivity against competing ANDAs during which other companies cannot market the ingredient.
- If the company wishing to conduct the switch is the holder of the original NDA or if it holds an ANDA for a closely related ingredient, it may choose to submit a supplemental NDA for the OTC version.

- If a company wishes to market an OTC version of an ingredient that is in all respects identical to an existing Rx product, it may choose to submit an ANDA.

Factors Considered in Approving an Rx-to-OTC Switch

As discussed above, the 1951 Durham–Humphrey Amendment to the 1938 FDC Act clearly demarcated Rx and OTC medications for the first time. Prescription status was mandatory for any medication with a potential for harm (e.g., unreasonable toxicity), or which would unduly challenge a patient's ability to understand the method of use or collateral measures for use, or which would be subject to patient misuse. In 1985, FDA clarified that it would examine four factors in deciding whether to approve an Rx-to-OTC switch: safety, efficacy, labeling, and other issues.

Safety is the most intricate of the four criteria. This is understandable. As discussed above, a switch would move a medication from prescriber/Pharmacy-controlled sales requiring a learned intermediary to open sale by anyone in any location, including vending machines. The medication proposed for a switch must have a high level of safety and low toxicity. This would disqualify medications requiring careful dosage adjustments, such as digitalis, phenytoin, and warfarin. The medication must also have an acceptable benefit-to-risk ratio, meaning that it must cause a low incidence of adverse reactions when used as directed. It should also possess little risk of masking a serious underlying disorder. The medication should have a low potential for abuse, misuse, or addiction. Its use should not require medical examinations or lab work. The method of use and collateral measures necessary for use must be appropriate. In other words, the condition the product is to treat must be amenable to self-treatment, the patient must be able to self-diagnose that condition, and patients must be able to recognize the condition's symptoms. When all of these criteria are applied, it is evident that many prescription medications would never be approved for OTC use. The criteria also ensure that nonprescription medications approved by the FDA are only labeled for minor medical conditions, most of which would improve whether the patient used self-therapy or not. The rules also help FDA determine the appropriate labeling of a switched product, such as ages of use, time limits on use, dosing, directions for use, when to stop use and see a physician, warnings and precautions, and Drug interactions.

Efficacy of a switch candidate is also examined by the FDA. To meet the efficacy standard, a significant number of patients should experience the benefit described on the product's label. It would seem evident that any prescription product under consideration had already been exhaustively examined for efficacy, since that would be part of the basis for its approval as an Rx product. However, in some cases, the manufacturer might attempt to market a smaller dose than the Rx strength, or a dosage form different from the Rx version, and it must prove that these novel formulations meet the efficacy standards.

A third area to be examined before the switch is approved is the proposed labeling. A label must be adequate for proper use without the help of a learned intermediary (see this concept above), and all wording must be sufficiently clear for an ordinary person to fully understand it. The FDA occasionally applies a miscellaneous standard that is not one of the first three. For instance, the Agency once considered switching birth control medications to OTC status but did not pursue the switch for unknown reasons,

Types of Switches

There are two types of switches, complete and partial. When a complete switch occurs, the ingredient becomes OTC in all dosages and versions. It is no longer marketed in any Rx-only version. Examples include topical minoxidil for androgenetic alopecia, pyrantel pamoate for pinworm, and nicotine gum and patches for smoking cessation. In a partial switch, a lower dose becomes available for OTC sales, but one or more higher doses remain available only by prescription. Examples include naproxen, ibuprofen, and H-2 blockers (e.g., cimetidine, famotidine). The indications may vary for the Rx and OTC products. For instance, Rx cimetidine is labeled for treatment of ulcer, but ulceration and gastric bleeding must be monitored by a physician, so OTC cimetidine products cannot carry this indication.

Examples of Rx-to-OTC Switches

Switches remain an ongoing process as of this writing (2019). In chronological order, switched ingredients include doxylamine (1978), hydrocortisone (1979), fluoride dental rises (1980), diphenhydramine for cough (1981), miconazole and dyclonine (1982), ibuprofen (1984), loperamide (1988), permethrin (1990), naproxen (1994), famotidine and cimetidine (1995), minoxidil and nicotine (1996), cromolyn nasal and ketoconazole shampoo (1997), loratadine (2002), omeprazole (2003), ketotifen ophthalmic (2006), orlistat and cetirizine (2007), lansoprazole (2009), fexofenadine (2011), oxybutynin transdermal (2013), triamcinolone nasal and esomeprazole (2014), budesonide nasal and adapalene (2016), levocetirizine (2017), and brimonidine ophthalmic (2018).

A Third Class of Drugs – Opposition from OTC Manufacturers

The United States has only two classes of medications, prescription and nonprescription. This has led to a seeming anomaly. Suppose a medication is slated to become a nonprescription item at midnight on the first day of June. Until the closing hours of May 31, consumers must make physician appointments to have the medication prescribed for them. They obtain it at a Pharmacy where they are counseled on its use. Suddenly, at 12:01 am on the first day of June, all controls on its sale are removed. The product can immediately be sold in any gas station, laundromat, vending machine, hotel lobby, airport snack bar, or quick stop. There is no requirement that any person advise them on its sale. The grocers, hairdressers, and gas station attendants who sell it have no legal, moral, or ethical responsibility to monitor the customer's purchases in any way.

Pharmacist counseling before sale of nonprescription products may prevent situations such as the death of Krissy Taylor, who was initially thought to have been misusing Primatene Mist (590). Pharmacist counseling might also have prevented such problems as a 76-year-old psychologist from Maryland who had to be hospitalized for ulcers from taking aspirin nightly for 2 years (591). She acknowledged "I did not read the labeling, and I did not ask my doctor's advice". A 21-year-old marketing major from Florida died after taking Benadryl and Unisom together and exceeding labeled doses of each (592). Health officials said it was doubtful that the student was made aware of the deadly scenario that could result when the medications were combined. A pharmacist could have advised her not to combine them. In 1997, the FDA received almost 131,000 post-marketing Reports of adverse Drug reactions, many of them involving nonprescription products (e.g., Aleve, Humulin, and Rogaine) (593). In regard to nonprescription products, the unique knowledge of the pharmacist could have been brought to bear at the point of sale and may have prevented a large portion of these problems.

In an effort to address these issues, the United States might look to other countries. Virtually every other country has a third class of Drugs for potentially dangerous nonprescription medications. Third class products cannot be sold until a pharmacist questions the patient and approves the sale. This added layer of safety is designed to protect the consumer from misuse. However, the PA/NDMA/CHPA has vigorously opposed any move to require pharmacist consultation prior to sale. The reason for this stance is entirely self-serving. OTC manufacturers hope that their advertisements, however misleading, will be the major force driving consumers to request a specific OTC product. An informed pharmacist could upset this equation by suggesting that the patient see a physician or use another product. The safety of the Public is not their major concern in this long fight.

PA's opposition to pharmacist-only sales dates back to the early 1950s. In 1952, the PA was an unincorporated group of 150 manufacturers representing 90% of patent and proprietary products. PA took note of an attempt by New Jersey to restrict sales of patent and proprietary medicines to Drug stores (594). The State apparently wished to ensure that a pharmacist would be present to advise consumers on the safe use of all nonprescription products. PA was the principal plaintiff in a lawsuit challenging the proposed requirement. In the words of one author, whenever a state sought to restrict sales of pharmaceuticals to pharmacist-only status, "The Proprietary Association, aided by drug wholesalers, grocery associations, and some pharmaceutical manufacturers, fought to defeat such laws and, where laws existed, to have them interpreted in the courts to their advantage" (594).

By 1973, the FDA OTC Review discussed above was underway. FDA received the Phase I expert Panel Report of the antacid expert Panel. The Report suggested that a label be placed on antacids referring the patient to the pharmacist for professional advice (595). Pharmacist groups backed this proposal, but OTC manufacturers, sensing a challenge to open sales, predictably opposed it. The FDA caved in to industry interests, and pharmacists were not allowed on antacid labels at that time. However, the issue would arise again in the context of pharmacist-only sales.

The concept of a pharmacist-only class of Drugs waxed and waned throughout the latter two decades of the twentieth century. It heated up in 1984 when the FDA switched ibuprofen to nonprescription status. Many thought it too unsafe for OTC sales, sparking the call for a third class. Charles Pergola, the PA Chairman, quickly addressed the issue (596). He stated that PA supported switching Drugs from prescription status to nonprescription status, by speaking of the Rx-to-OTC switch of hydrocortisone several years before: "...in the year before it went OTC, the measured prescription sales for topical 0.5% hydrocortisone were $12 million...In 1982, after the switch, OTC hydrocortisone sales totaled $56 million..." The PA's overwhelming interest in profits was seldom so starkly evident. But Pergola also spoke forcefully against the establishment of a third class using an argument that would become the basis for the PA party line. He stated,

> A product is either safe enough and labeled properly to be sold OTC, or it isn't...If there is any question whatsoever about the consumer's ability to get sufficient information to take that product safely, then we say it should remain prescription.
>
> *(596)*

Pergola's argument against a third class of Drugs failed to address two major issues:

- With OTC medications such as phenylpropanolamine (no longer marketed), for which alarming dangers emerge, there would be no third class to which they could be switched until the issues are settled.
- The PA was always a steadfast supporter of moving medications from Rx to OTC status, since it would increase profits. The onerous burden on the FDA with any proposed switch is to discover every danger to consumers before approving the switch. A third class of Drugs would serve as a time to gather information about dangers to the Public of more widespread use prior to unrestricted OTC sales.

Later in 1984, a group of Illinois pharmacists grew sufficiently alarmed about OTC dangers to voluntarily move OTC ibuprofen behind the counter, creating their own third class (597). On a CBS program covering the event, Jack Walden of the PA said that the Illinois pharmacists were "the same type of people who, for 100 years, have been trying to make people buy all their drugs in drugstores". The reporter characterized the PA in this manner, "The most vocal of the concept's detractors, the Proprietary Association...has always dismissed the move for a third class of drugs as a profit-motivated play for a druggist's monopoly".

FDA Commissioner Jere Goyan stated at a 1984 meeting of the National Association of Retail Druggists that he thoroughly supported the concept of a third class of Drugs (598,598). He also revealed that PA opposed his appointment as FDA Commissioner. This is understandable when one realizes that Goyan was a pharmacist.

In 1989, new Rx-to-OTC switches caused the concept of a third class of Drugs to resurface. The PA (changed to NDMA as of 1990) came out swinging. In an interview, Vic Clough, NDMA's Public relations spokesman, stated, "...a third class would deny the merchant the right to sell and the customer the right to buy safe, well-known proprietary medicines at convenient locations or at competitive prices" (600). Speaking of the switch process, he added, "It is an advantage any time a good product can be made available to more people".

In a 1990 editorial, pharmacist-author Richard Harkness speculated as to the PA/NDMA's real motive for denying the need for a third class, "...(their) profits will suffer" (601). He also pointed out the PA/NDMA's habit of intentionally downgrading the pharmacist by using the outdated term "druggist" in many of its official statements.

The PA/NDMA decided in 1988 to write a Position Paper on the third class of Drugs, which they revised and released in 1990 (602). This paper unfavorably viewed the third class system used in virtually all of the rest of the world, pointing out the "...advantages" of the U.S. system". The paper listed consumer benefits to denying a third class: convenient availability of products, comparative shopping for Prices, and purchases in a wide variety of retail stores. It purposely overlooks any mention of adverse reactions resulting from lack of pharmacist counseling (e.g., not catching contraindications, Drug interactions, precautions).

The FDA bought into the NDMA line. In a 1991 article on Rx-to-OTC switches, as the Agency explained in its consumer publication,

> In 1974, in connection with an FDA monograph on OTC antacids, some pharmacy organizations commented that such a third class of drugs should be created. Others, including the Department of Justice, objected to a third class of drugs, stating that it would restrain competition, inconvenience the consumer, depart from U.S. economic policy, and cause price increases for the consumer with no attending benefit.

(603)

FDA concluded that

> ...no controlled studies or other adequate research data have been supplied to support the position that any class of OTC drugs must be dispensed only by pharmacists in order to ensure their safe use....There is at this time no public health concern that would justify the creation of a third class of drugs to be dispensed only by a pharmacist or in a pharmacy.

The NDMA thought so highly of this FDA article that they reprinted it and disseminated it to their members (604).

In 1991, John Weidenbruch, NDMA's general attorney and State Legislative Counsel, spoke out about the third class. He stated, "Restriction of products to pharmacy sale would deny consumers the right to buy safe products at convenient locations of their own choice and at a competitive price. It would deny general merchants the right to sell these safe products" (605). His comments were primarily a call to allow unrestrained availability of OTC products, and he wrongly conveyed the impression that all OTC products are safe (twice in one quote).

In 1991, California Assemblyman Bruce Bronzan moved to create a third class by banning sales of phenylpropanolamine (PPA) to any person younger than 18 in that state because of such dangers as anorexia, renal damage, hypertension, and mood swings (606). The California Pharmacists Association pushed for an amendment that would create a pharmacist-only category for phenylpropanolamine and other dangerous medications. An aide to Bronzan predicted that they would have a long fight with PPA makers.

In 1991, NDMA voiced concern about the slow pace with which Rx medications were moving to OTC status. In a response letter, Arnold Vasa from Pharmacists Planning Service (PPSI) pointed out that the relative speed in other countries is balanced by the third class with its safety advantages (607). John T. Walden, NDMA's Senior Vice-President and Director of Public Affairs, attempted to rebut Vasa's argument by pointing out the situation in other countries (608). While such issues as competition, open trade, monopoly, profit, distribution, control of Prices, and discounts feature prominently in his letter, the word "safety" was never raised. Pharmacist Richard Lauring responded to Walden's letter with the following,

> Our system (the United States system) is the most expensive in the whole world. The reason, as everyone seems to agree, is that it is demand-driven. Who knows this better than (Walden's) own association? Through advertising and promotion, NDMA members have a constant battle over "market share" for their products. Nowhere is the cost to the consumer actually considered. In all other countries, restraint in all areas of medicine is of great concern.
>
> *(609)*

On September 4, 1991, the National Consumers League held a symposium on Drug distribution in Washington, with an emphasis on a third class of

Drugs (610). The symposium was targeted to Congressional staff and was supported by the Public Citizen Health Research Group, National Council of Senior Citizens, APhA, American Society of Hospital Pharmacists, California Pharmacists Association, and National Association of Retail Druggists (NARD). NDMA President James D. Cope was a panelist, and noted

> Since 1915, there have been 514 bills or regulations introduced in the states and two in Congress (applying to the District of Columbia) to create some version of a pharmacist-only class of drugs. All were rejected. Whatever it is called, the issue is the same—a restriction on consumer access and choice. Third-class is pharmacy monopoly...

He also pointed out that OTC Drugs are available in more than a million retail outlets, while a third class would only be available in 65,000 pharmacies. (It is not clear whether his figure of one million outlets includes vending machines in hotel lobbies, gas stations, and beauty shops.) At the September 4 meeting, Cope also distributed briefing kits presenting NDMA's arguments against a third class in detail, providing quotes against a third class, and giving highlights in the fight against a third class in the form of a chronology (611). An aide to Rep. Ron Wyden stated that his interest in the third class issue began because of safety issues centering around phenylpropanolamine (612). A Report of the meeting attempted to counter NDMA's argument that a third class would create a pharmacist monopoly (613) It mentioned that prescriptions are monopolies, as are Drug Patents, yet the NDMA does not complain about either of those problems. In some instances, monopolies help protect the Public Health and welfare.

In 1992, NDMA distributed to selected members of Congress a seven-minute video ("Less For More: a Third Class Idea") attacking a third class legislative proposal sponsored by NARD. According to NARD, the video "... uses incongruous analogies, makes inaccurate statements, and draws faulty conclusions to mislead viewers with respect to the purpose and benefits of a pharmacist legend category of drugs" (614).

In August of 1992, the FDA again refused to create a third class of Drugs, acting against a proposal from PPSI (615). NDMA spokesman Frank Rathbun said the American system is not broken, so should not be fixed. The leader of the PPSI effort mentioned dangers of OTCs, such as phenylpropanolamine, ibuprofen, and ephedrine.

NDMA's role up until 1992 had been so pervasive that one Pharmacy author stated "NDMA...has led the opposition to creating an additional class of medications" (616). When the Clinton administration took office, NDMA wasted no time creating a briefing book entitled *Self-Medication's Role in U.S. Health Care*, which was disseminated to 700–800 members of the Senate Labor and Human Resources Committee and the House Energy and Commerce Committee (617). NDMA also sent it to trade associations and Health Policy groups in the public and private sectors.

In 1992, the General Accounting Office (GAO) of the U.S. Government was charged with carrying out a study of a third class. The study (*Nonprescription Drugs: Value of a Pharmacist-Controlled Class Has Yet to Be Demonstrated*), completed in 1995, stated that there would be no value in a third class. NDMA deputy director Frank Rathbun was pleased, stating that the Report's title "says it all" (618). NDMA reported the issue to their members and added an intriguing note: "In preparing the Report, GAO conducted literature searches, field interviews in six of the 10 countries studied, and interviews with U.S. and State Government officials, pharmacy associations, academicians, consumer groups, manufacturers and NDMA" (619). Thus, NDMA provided its own views to the federally-mandated GAO, undoubtedly biasing the GAO against the concept. This is a perfect illustration of the old chestnut about asking the fox to guard a chicken coop. In 1996, NDMA held its annual meeting. During one session, Daniel O'Keefe Jr. (NDMA senior Vice-President and general counsel) joined forces with James D. Cope (NDMA President) to gloat that NDMA efforts had killed the third class of Drugs (620).

In 1997, the PPSI President, attempted to raise the issue of a third class again via an interview in a Pharmacy journal (621). PPSI was persisting in their drive to move phenylpropanolamine and other dangerous OTCs to a third class. However, the author pointed out that NDMA had successfully fought the issue for years, had blocked a move toward a third class in Georgia's legislature, and was working to prevent similar Legislation in other States.

What is the real reason behind the PA/NDMA/CHPA's leadership in defeating the proposals for a third class of Drugs? Their charge that druggists would have a monopoly is undoubtedly part of it, but there may be far-deeper objections that they will not voice aloud. The PA members have spent untold billions advertising their products directly to consumers. The Advertising has one easily stated message to the Public, "Go out immediately and buy *our* products. No other product should be considered". When OTCs are available in any location, there is no university-educated pharmacist to tell patients that a specific product is not the best medical choice. Under a third class of Drugs, patients would be forced to approach a pharmacist for advice, and the pharmacist might invalidate this message and change the consumer's mind. Any of the following could occur:

- The pharmacist might triage the patient to a physician, dentist, or other Health professional for further diagnostic work.
- The pharmacist might advise the patient that no product is needed.
- The pharmacist might advise the consumer to buy a competitor's product.

All of these pharmacist-directed possibilities would negate the billion-dollar Advertising goals. Could this be the reason that the PA/NDMA/CHPA never wanted pharmacists to have a mandated role in sales of nonprescription products?

Quackery – Nonprescription Products and Devices Lacking Proof of Safety and Efficacy

What Is Quackery?

Patent medicine salesmen were originally referred to as "quacks", because their repetitive and baseless sales pitches reminded listeners of the empty quacking of a duck. What is "quackery"? In an authoritative review of the term "quackery", a medical bioethicist attempted valiantly to define the surprisingly elusive term (622). He observed that there is universal agreement that quackery is bad, even though there is no agreement on the meaning of the term. Despite this opinion, several authoritative definitions can easily be located, as the word was well known and commonly used by pharmacists and the Public (622). Articles in journals for medicine, dentistry, dietetics, and Pharmacy inveighed against quackery with venom and anger (623–632). Codes of Ethics (e.g., APhA) strongly exhorted practitioners to refrain from engaging in quackery.

Perhaps the simplest definition of quackery was published in a 1990 brochure entitled, "Quackery…The Billion Dollar Miracle Business" (640). FDA, FTC, the Postal Service, the Department of Health and Human Services, and the Pharmaceutical Advertising Council jointly defined quackery as "…the promotion of a medical remedy that doesn't work or hasn't been proven to work".

The APhA was greatly vexed by quackery prior to the 1990s. In September 1963, the *Journal of the American Pharmaceutical Association* carried a cover with the stark words, "MEDICAL QUACKERY" (641). Cover artwork depicted a wolf with the mask of a sheep hovering in front of its face. Inside this issue, APhA published the following description of quackery for its Readers:

> When an untrue or misleading health claim is deliberately, fraudulently, or pretentiously made for a food, drug, device, or cosmetic, this is quackery. When the maker of the claim has reason to know that it has no foundation, he is practicing quackery. It matters not whether the quackery is practiced by the witch doctor or the licensed medical practitioner; the Indian medicine man or the pharmacist; the proprietary drug manufacturer or the prescription drug manufacturer; the health food manufacturer or the clerk in the health food store; the health lecturer, the self-styled nutritionist, the doorstep diagnostician, the fly-by-night operator of some of our most respected food, drug, device and cosmetic manufacturers—it is still quackery.
>
> *(641)*

This issue also featured such articles as "Enforcement of Anti-quackery Laws", "Broadcasting Code against Quackery", "Campaign against Quackery", and "Investigation of Medical Quackery".

The leading U.S. Pharmacy organization stood firmly against quackery as late as the 1960s. The nation's regulatory Agencies warned consumers about the dangers of unproven medications. Sadly, the supporters of quackery were poised to drown the American Public in unproven products, despite the best efforts of those who opposed quackery.

The Conspiracy to Legitimize Quackery

The United States is mired in a vast conspiracy to make quackery acceptable to all Americans, to community pharmacists, and through them, to their patients. The conspiracy is far-reaching; it involves pharmaceutical manufacturers, the "dietary supplement" industry, Congress, major Pharmacy publications, and nationally respected Pharmacy organizations. (In this context, "dietary supplements" refer to unproven quack products such as herbs. It does not include vitamins and minerals whose safety and efficacy are scientifically established in the treatment and prevention of specific deficiency diseases.)

Several factors came together to drive the rehabilitation of quackery. First is the "new age" and hippie movements of the late 1960s that aimed to demolish or replace traditional institutions, such as the Government, religion, and organized medicine. This "New Age" ushered in renewed interest in beliefs characterized by one writer as "lunacies", such as astrology, fairies, ghosts, psychics, vampires, channeling, séances, witchcraft, UFOs, crop circles and abductions by extra-terrestrials, reincarnation, numerology, and pyramid power (642,643). This growing tendency to believe in the unverifiable was accompanied by a waning confidence of the Public in traditional or mainstream medicine. The Public turned in large numbers to practitioners such as naturopathic doctors, Ayurveda healers, herbalists, homeopaths, aroma therapists, and uncountable others whose practices were formerly condemned as quackery (644–647). As these practitioners and their unproven methods gained a new cachet of respectability, the term "quackery" gradually began to seem quaint and unfashionable.

Second, quackery provides jobs for hundreds of thousands of Americans; and it is possible to become wealthy by founding an empire by hawking unproven products and therapies. The opportunities for quacks can be compellingly demonstrated by touring the main streets of America's cities. There are thousands of so-called "health food stores". These strange businesses provide bogus medical advice and recommend their expensive quack products. Ironically, they virtually always owned and staffed by people with no education in any branch of medicine, and they are legally free to advise customers on any critical Health Care condition, such as cancer. Most cities also harbor such quacks as reflexologists, herbalists, iridologists, acupuncturists, chiropractors, and innumerable other avenues to obtain unproven products and therapies. Victims don't even have to leave their houses. The Internet is a poorly policed and medically irresponsible compendium of unproven therapies readily available to anyone with online access and a search engine (648–650). The sheer number of websites exclusively devoted to pushing unproven products to a gullible, unsuspecting, and/or uncaring American Public is elegant testimony to the acceptance of quackery in all its pernicious forms. Anyone willing to stand against this onslaught of unproven therapies and cry "foul" is trying to stem a tide of Biblical proportions. Cries of "quackery" are completely drowned out.

Finally, there exists in American Pharmacy an unwillingness to address the issue of unproven products. Those who are positions of responsibility (e.g., publishers, editors, association leaders) have abrogated their responsibility to American Pharmacy and the Public by refusing to recognize and forcibly condemn quackery in its various guises. In a move reminiscent of the traveling medicine shows, certain Pharmacy journals have long pandered to the monied interests by allowing them to unashamedly tout the unproven virtues of their products without any counterbalancing editorial comment or disclaimer. It is understandable but regrettable that these same journals would be unwilling to publish critical analyses of the very products that provide advertising revenue. Thus, fear of alienating advertisers has tied their hands when it comes to exposing the web of deceit that quackery has morphed into since 1994. All one needs to do is examine Pharmacy journals for ads and articles that give credibility to any unproven therapy (e.g., homeopathy, herbals), while simultaneously looking in vain at the same journals for any article rendering a critical analysis of those same unproven therapies.

The Nutrition Labeling and Education Act of 1990

In 1990, the Nutrition Labeling and Education Act became law (555,651). It amended the FDC Act to require that all dietary supplements bear nutrition labeling. FDA issued a set of proposed rules that would have required vitamins, minerals, and herbs to be held to the same standards as other medications. Any claims made would be forced to withstand scientific scrutiny. Health food stores reacted with predictable frenzy. A leaflet obtained at one of these establishments during this time bore the message that every consumer's freedom to buy supplements such as legitimate vitamins and minerals was in imminent danger unless they wrote their Congressman immediately. The hoax was successful in convincing the Public that FDA intended to take vitamins and minerals off of the market, and the subsequent flood of letters was effective. Senator Orrin Hatch of Utah succeeded in ensuring passage of a 1992 law to exempt dietary supplements from NLEA rules and imposing a 1-year moratorium on FDA with respect to dietary supplements not in food form (555).

Establishment of the National Center for Complementary and Alternative Medicine (NCCAM)

Orrin Hatch's triumphant defense of unproven dietary supplements in 1990 was just the beginning of a groundswell of quackery. In 1991, the efforts of several people led to the establishment of an Office of Alternative Medicine, within the National Institutes of Health (555). Its mission was to investigate unproven therapies. The prime movers behind this were Senator Tom Harkin of Iowa, who believed bee pollen had helped his allergies, and a constituent, Berkley Bedell, a believer in the ability of colostrum from the milk of a Minnesota cow to cure Lyme disease (652). The office eventually morphed into the National Center for Complementary and Alternative Medicine (NCCAM) (653,654). In 2015, this Agency was renamed the National Center for Complementary and Integrative Health. Critics have charged that the Agency, whatever the name, is little more than a Government boondoggle from the New Agers, designed to divert money from legitimate medical research to quacks (655–657).

L-Tryptophan – the 1993 FDA Report

For many years, the FDA acted against unproven products on a case-by-case basis. With inadequate funding and manpower, it was not possible to be everywhere at once. A good example of FDA using its power wisely came in the wake of a deadly tragedy (555). In 1989, FDA warned consumers not to take L-tryptophan sold as a sleep aid, although evidence of safety and efficacy were lacking. Unfortunately, it was found to be the proximate cause of at least 1,500 cases of eosinophilia-myalgia syndrome, with 31 or more deaths (555). FDA imposed a detention on the imported supplement and recalled it to prevent further deaths.

FDA Accelerates Its Anti-Quackery Activity

The L-tryptophan tragedy galvanized FDA into action. In 1993, the Agency released a study of unproven products, referring to them as "dietary supplements". This Report was entitled *Unsubstantiated Claims and Documented Health Hazards in the Dietary Supplement Marketplace* (555). The 104-page Report revealed that 20% of the industry consisted of products presenting safety concerns or making unsubstantiated claims. (The other 80% was merely vitamins and minerals marketed at reasonable potencies that made no unsubstantiated claims.) Some of the supplements of concern had already caused serious and life-threatening health hazards. The Report examined amino acids, glandular products, herbs and herbal combinations making claims in the areas of immune systems, arthritis, cardiovascular systems, diabetes, hormones, cancer, herpes, strep throat, gout, multiple sclerosis, varicose veins, cataracts, gallstones, and appendicitis. None of the claims had been substantiated by the FDA prior to marketing. The Report also included an FDA study in which personnel visited Health food stores to ask whether they sold anything for high blood pressure, the immune system, or cancer. Of the 129 requests made by FDA personnel in Health food stores, 120 resulted in recommendations for one or more specific supplements. Cancer remedies recommended by the nonmedical staff at health food stores included shark cartilage, saw palmetto berries, honeysuckle, pancreatic enzymes, colonic rinses, germanium, Siberian ginseng, red clover, Venus flytrap, antioxidant vitamins, bee pollen, herbal teas, lion teeth, and aloe vera. The Report was attacked by the President of the National Nutritional Foods Association.

The 1994 Dietary Supplement Health and Education Act (DSHEA)

The 1993 FDA Report sent a chill through the quack products market, then still in its infancy. Backers recalled the success against the FDA in its attempt to control dietary supplements. There were also fears that the FDA might act against unproven supplements as they acted against L-tryptophan. It became apparent to dietary supplement backers that the FDA would have to be muzzled. In 1993, Senator Orrin Hatch served as the standard bearer for the supplement industry when he sponsored the DSHEA, with support from the supplement industry (555,658). The number of letters written to Congress in support of the law's passage exceeded those written in protest over the Vietnam War (658). When it was passed into law in 1994, DSHEA defined dietary supplements as any product other than tobacco intended to supplement the diet, including one or more of the following dietary ingredients: a vitamin, mineral, herb, or other botanical, amino acid, dietary substance for human use to supplement the diet by increasing the total daily intake, or a concentrate, metabolite, constituent, extract, or combinations of these ingredients (604). The FDA explained the constraints that had been placed upon it by the law. Manufacturers were given freedom to market a wide range of products in a free manner as compared to legitimate FDA-regulated products (583). Consumers and manufacturers would carry full responsibility for checking safety of supplements and determining whether their claims were truthful. The FDA would not authorize nor would it test dietary supplements (606). Manufacturers would not be required to provide information to FDA before marketing a product. There would be no premarketing review or approval of supplement ingredients (607). Once a dietary supplement was marketed, the FDA would bear the burden for demonstrating that the product was unsafe prior to taking any action to restrict its use (608,609). The only concession to evidence-based medicine was the requirement that supplements bear a disclaimer: "This statement has not been evaluated by the Food and Drug Administration. This product is not intended to diagnose, treat, cure, or prevent any disease". While the statement is legally required on the container's label, it is virtually always missing when unproven statements are made in product reviews and is often miniscule or entirely absent from advertisements. In effect, the DHSEA was retrogressive, granting legal immunity for proving safety and efficacy to a dizzying array of strange products marketed as "dietary supplements".

In the ensuing years, sales of unproven supplements reached fever pitch, so much so that reports of serious injury (e.g., severe hepatic injury with kava) and well-controlled studies that demonstrate lack of efficacy (e.g., St., John's wort for depression) were ignored and soon forgotten (659,660). In testimony before the Senate, a physician referring to the post-DSHEA pro-quackery climate said ruefully, "Under current law I could literally pack capsules full of grass clippings from my lawn and market them as just about anything I liked" (655). The DSHEA can be viewed as retrogressive. A great deal of the Public Health protections made since 1906 (e.g., pre-marketing approval) were invalidated. By promoting sales of quackery, DSHEA took America back to the days of patent medicines.

FDA and Quackery Post-DSHEA – Defining Fraud

In a consumer-oriented document entitled "How to Spot Health Fraud", FDA educated the Public to avoid Health fraud (661). FDA defined Health fraud as "articles of unproven effectiveness that are promoted to improve health, well- being or appearance". This includes Drugs, devices, foods, or cosmetics, whether intended for use in or on human or animals (558,661,662). The FDA and the FTC can both pursue Health fraud violations (663). FTC prosecutes fraudulent Advertising. FDA prosecutes manufacturer that commit Health fraud in the areas of safety, manufacturing, and product labeling. Labeling includes the actual product label, as well as package inserts and literature that accompany the product.

The boom in quackery has overwhelmed the FDA. The Agency admitted that its resources are limited, forcing personnel to follow a priority system (661). Products that pose a direct risk to consumers due to their potential to cause injury or adverse reactions receive the Agency's top priority for Health fraud Investigation. Products that are not directly harmful, but could cause the patient to delay or completely forego legitimate medical help, are indirect risks and are a lower priority for Investigation. When FDA explained this system, it also admitted the following fact, "While FDA remains vigilant against health fraud, many fraudulent products may escape regulatory scrutiny, maintaining their hold in the marketplace for some time to lure increasing numbers of consumers into their web of deceit" (661).

Pharmacy Codes of Ethics Change to Embrace Quackery

Various Pharmacy Codes of Ethics display an interest in appealing to the consciences of pharmacists who engage in quackery. In 1848, the Philadelphia College of Pharmacy stated in its principles for conduct,

> Whilst the College does not at present feel authorized to require its members to abandon the sale of secret or quack medicines, they earnestly recommend the propriety of discouraging their employment, when called upon for an opinion as to their merits.
>
> *(664)*

The 1852 Code of Ethics of the APhA states that its members have agreed to "discountenance quackery and dishonorable competition in their business" (664). It also urged the "discontinuance of secret formulae and the practices arising from a quackish spirit". The 1922 Code stated that members should "discourage the use of objectionable nostrums". It also stated that

> The Pharmacist should hold the health and safety of his patrons to be of first consideration; he should make no attempt to prescribe or treat diseases or strive to sell drugs or remedies of any kind simply for the sake of profit...He should not accept agencies for objectionable nostrums nor allow his name to be used in connection with advertisements or correspondence for furthering their sale.
>
> *(664)*

The 1952 Code included the clause about Health, safety, and profit; however, in lieu of the second clause, it substituted, "The pharmacist does not lend his support or name to the promotion of objectionable or unworthy products" (664). The 1969 and 1981 Codes each contained a virtually identical clause,

A pharmacist should never knowingly condone the dispensing, promoting or distributing of drugs or medical devices, or assist therein, which are not of good quality, which do not meet standards required by law or which lack therapeutic value for the patient.

(664)

The APhA Code was updated in 1994, and it lacked any reference to quackery, nostrums, unworthy medications, medication quality, or medications lacking therapeutic value for the patient, including only a vague reference to telling the truth and acting with conviction of conscience (665).

The self-stated objective of APhA is improving medication use and advancing patient care (666). The organization adopted the value statement, "Integrity. We act in an honest, ethical, and transparent manner, and accept responsibility for our actions" (666). Despite this statement, the evolving Codes of Ethics betray a gradual weakening of the organization's initial repugnance of quackery and call into question its definition of "honesty". APhA has virtually embraced quackery through its acceptance of Advertising dollars from quacks for its publications and accepting quack booths at APhA conventions, such as a booth by Boiron, a leading manufacturer of homeopathic products, at the 1995 Annual Meeting (667). Speakers at various APhA-sponsored meetings also present programs that cast quackery in a flattering light, failing to critically examine its shortcomings, such as a talk of herbals and homeopathy sponsored by Boiron, also at the 1995 APhA Annual Meeting (667). Thus, a close look at evolving Pharmacy Codes of Ethics and the practices of a major national Pharmacy association leaves the pharmacist with a definite feeling that quackery has become accepted.

Pharmacy Textbooks Endorse Quackery

Pharmacy students have limited opportunity to learn about the existence and extent of quackery in America. Since the products and devices are available without prescription, one logical place to discuss it is within a nonprescription course. The leading text is APhA's *Handbook of Nonprescription Drugs* (HND). It failed to include any chapter on quackery (e.g., herbals, homeopathy, and dietary supplements) in any edition through the tenth (1993). In the eleventh edition (1996), HND finally included a chapter on Herbs and Phytomedicinal Products, co-authored by a leading pharmacognocist, including only 73 references. The twelfth edition of HND (2000) included two relevant chapters, one on homeopathy and one on herbal remedies, in a section titled, "Alternative Therapies". The homeopathic chapter unfortunately reflected a strongly positive bias toward this unproven pseudoscience. The thirteenth edition of HND (2002) included homeopathy and herbal chapters in a section titled, "Complementary Therapies". The homeopathy chapter was co-authored by a nurse/homeopath, and it lacked a critical view. The fourteenth edition of HND (2004) contained a section titled "Complementary and Alternative Medicine", with the herbal and homeopathy chapters, and a new chapter on non-botanical natural medicines. It retained the authors and their biases for the homeopathy chapter (one was now a professor at a naturopathic college; the other was director of a school of homeopathy). Thus, one of the leading nonprescription products textbooks chose a homeopath and a professor of naturopathy to inform students about homeopathy. Further, it waffled about whether these unproven therapies are to be called alternative or complementary, finally calling them both. It becomes clear that the growing acceptance of alternative remedies by pharmacists may be due in no small part to the nonprescription textbook faculty choose for their use as Pharmacy students. Textbooks with a positive bias toward quackery risk imparting this bias to the students who are required to purchase and study them. They foster a fertile environment for the proliferation of quackery in Pharmacy.

Pharmacy Journals Endorse Quackery

Pharmacy journals rapidly embraced quackery in the 1980s, and the number of papers skyrocketed in the years after DSHEA. The reason was advertising profits. Quackery-selling companies such as Boiron (a homeopathic company) began to spend unprecedented dollars on ads. The resulting profits rapidly turned the editorial bias from critical to favorable, a trend that should be no surprise to those who have followed the rise in popularity of quackery.

The APhA (now known as the American Pharmacists Association) has several publications which reveal the organization's attitude toward quackery. As previously stated, the organization's attitude against quackery in 1963 was sufficiently negative to result in an anti-quackery-themed issue of the *Journal of the American Pharmaceutical Association*. In 1975, an editorial in the same journal bemoaned the *New York Times'* acceptance of laetrile for cancer (668). The newspaper apparently stated that laetrile may be ineffective, but at least it would be harmless. The editorial forcibly disagreed with the sale of ineffective remedies, even though they might be harmless.

APhA soon changed radically in its publications. Various issues of APhA's *Pharmacy Today* featured ads touting homeopathic products such as zinc lozenges for colds. They allowed a naturopath to write a column known as "Alternative Medicine" (669). In the August 2005 issue, the "Product Showcase" featured a homeopathic product dubbed "Complete Flu Care 4 Kids" (670). In promoting this supplement for children with influenza, APhA endorsed the efficacy of its unproven ingredients, which include herbs, potassium iodide, and duck heart/liver (671). None of the ingredients is proven to ameliorate the symptoms of influenza in any way, but especially not when highly diluted according to homeopathic pseudoscience. Further, APhA failed to require the manufacturer to include this list of ingredients in its ad to allow the discriminating pharmacist to discover their unproven status. In the September 2005 issue, APhA promoted black cohosh for menopause symptoms and published a naturopath-authored article on green tea's purported benefits in slowing the growth of bladder, breast, and rectal tumors (672,672).

American Druggist (AD) featured a column dubbed "On Nutrition" in 1985–1988. The author, William H. Lee, was described as a master herbalist. The poorly referenced columns presented credulous discussions on such topics as valerian for stress, feverfew for migraine, ginkgo for the side effects of aging, and algae for infections. In 1996, AD favorably profiled a pharmacist who developed a partnership with an acupuncturist, an alliance that helped his bottom line (674). A 1997 column described the efforts of Rite-Aid Pharmacies to become the "premier source for vitamins, minerals, and herbs..." by providing reference binders on each topic to its 15,000 pharmacists (675). In 1998, AD offered an article entitled, "Integrating Herbal Therapy into Practice" (676). Clearly, before it ceased to exist, this journal had expressly endorsed quackery.

Pharmacy Times was once a bastion of professionalism. A 1983 article was titled, "Why Many 'Health Foods' are Not Safe and Effective" (677). It explored the ethical dilemma pharmacists faced in recommending products lacking in scientific evidence of safety, such as herbs. However, in 1995, the magazine made a turnabout as it inaugurated a column known as "Pharmacists & Natural Medicine", written by Constance Grauds, described as President of the Association of Natural Medicine Pharmacists. The columns often featured the address and website of the organization to facilitate Readers' joining. Her columns appeared as late as 2000. The unreferenced or spottily referenced articles were uncritical of quackery, endorsing such unproven therapies as feverfew for arthritis, milk thistle as a "potential lifesaver", selenium for prostate cancer, and aromatherapy (e.g., lavender) for burns, sores, and ulcers (678–681). In 1997, an article touted natural medicines as a "rare opportunity for pharmacists" (682). A 1998 article asked, "Modern and Traditional Medicines: Can They Coexist" (683)? Not surprisingly, the answer from this journal was affirmative. Adversarial letters from Readers in 1997 and 1999 equated the use of unproven herbs to playing chemical Russian roulette and also bemoaned the fact that the trust of pharmacists was being sacrificed to the sales of unproven snake oils (684,685). The latter author asked the magazine's Readers rhetorically, "Do you really have your customer's best interests at heart"? The August 2005 issue offered coverage of a potpourri of unproven therapies: an article featuring homeopathic antisnoring tablets and sprays, "news" about a $64.99 product for hair loss containing squash seed oil and other unproven ingredients, an ad for an unproven supplement containing biotin alleged to help grow healthy nails, and an informative article about quackery in diabetes (686–689).

U.S. Pharmacist published an article critical of quackery in 1991 (690). It also published a series of articles on alternative medicines from 1998 to 2003. The series had no regular author, although several wrote more than one monograph. The articles presented a more critically balanced examination of herbs (e.g., evening primrose, kava-kava, hawthorn) than that seen in other journals. However, two articles published in 2002 and 2003 presented an uncritical view of traditional Chinese medicine, authored by a "Practitioner of Oriental Medicine" (691,692).

Drug Store News once claimed to reach 70,000 chain Drug pharmacists (693). Its articles frequently extolled quackery, including one by a homeopath touting unproven supplements such as borage oil and flax oil for menstrual cramping and menopausal complaints (694). Another commended such "OTC giants" as Warner-Lambert, SmithKline, and American Home Products for jumping on the herbal bandwagon with such products as herbal teas and supplements (695). A 1998 ad hawked "Blood Tonic Syrup", a Chinese herbal supplement (sic) liquid composed of nine herbs and honey that promised to promote production of all three types of blood cells, naturally relieving anemia without side effects (696).

Drug Topics coverage of unproven therapies increased radically in the mid-1990s. A 1996 article aimed to prepare pharmacists for "CAM" counseling by providing guidance to C.E. courses and websites and advised pharmacists about obtaining credentials for homeopathy, acupuncture, and naturopathy (697). A 1997 C.E. article exhorted pharmacists to "get their heads out of the sand and learn more about these alternative treatments" (698). The same year, an article favorably highlighted unproven homeopathic lozenges for colds that were said to be "taking the nation by storm" (699). In 1998, the dam seemed to burst for this journal's acceptance of unproven medicines. A 12-page supplement to the magazine explored the role of glucosamine and chondroitin for arthritis, sponsored by a "nutraceutical company" (700). In a 1998 cover story, the magazine asked, "Alternative Medicine? How Bountiful is the Harvest? Where does it Fit in the Pharmacy" (701)? In the conclusion, the author asked whether pharmacists should "cash in on this very ancient, yet very new, dimension of medicine"? She answered her own question with an unequivocal, "You bet." She cited data confirming that 84% of survey respondents already agreed that the business should not be lost to other outlets. The appeal was mainly that, "It's a highly profitable arena that may cover financial deficits seen in the prescription department." The magazine had finally stated clearly the appeal of quackery to scientifically trained pharmacists – when the Pharmacy is in financial trouble, it makes sense to turn to quackery, stealing patients from such outlets as Health food stores and supermarkets. The journal confirmed that outlook in a 1998 profile of a pharmacist with "stunning success" in promoting alternative medicine who stated, "I make more money off the acidophilus than I do off of managed care third-party payments" (702). In response to a cogent editorial disapproving of alternative medicine in the prestigious *New England Journal of Medicine* (NEJM), *Drug Topics* gave ample space to the Vice-President of the America Herbal Product Association to allow him to push the alternative medicine party line in a clear refutation of the NEJM physician authors' viewpoints (703,704). In 1998, *Drug Topics* also featured an article devoted to the ramblings of a pharmacist laden with such quack "degrees" as D.H.M., D.H.Ph., and N.M.D. (705). Among other unsupported musings, he asserted that "....the medical community is starting to look at supplements as a 'first line of defense'...The challenge becomes being able to increase sales by educating the consumer..." Three 1999 articles revealed the growing trend to embrace unproven products. One raised awareness of continuing education featuring unproven products and favorably discussing several organizations devoted to them (e.g., American Botanical Council, American Association of Homeopathic Pharmacists) (706). In a cover story, the journal also urged pharmacists, "Don't Miss This Boat", the boat of interest being the marketing opportunity presented by unproven therapies (707). This article quoted a faculty member who described the revamping of a university course in order to "...(bridge) the gap between mainstream Western medicine and some of the products currently being recommended and used by people in the herbal product area". In other words, the college's avowed purpose was to help students see unproven products and devices in the same light as proven therapies. A third 1999 article profiled a pharmacist/Pharmacy owner whose recommendations of complementary products for such serious conditions as Epstein-Barr virus and chronic fatigue syndrome had moved from skeptical to confident, reporting that his profits had doubled since he introduced unproven therapies (708). He hired a massage therapist who practiced the unproven therapies known as therapeutic touch and reflexology and promoted his Pharmacy as "The Bridge between Traditional and Holistic Remedies". In a fourth 1999 article, *Drug Topics* revealed that Rite-Aid Corp. had formed a partnership with General Nutrition Companies Inc. that would result in the chain opening full-line GNC Health food stores inside of 1,500 Rite Aid stores (709). By now, *Drug Topics* had become a leading proponent of quackery and had thereby moved firmly into the forefront of the quackery craze. Finally, one C.E. article critical of quackery appeared in 2001 (710). However, the journal quickly reversed course by publishing letters critical of the offering. One disgruntled Reader (who did not reveal his dual roles as a coeditor of the *Journal of the American Nutraceutical Association* and also as a homeopathic medicine manufacturer) complained that it was "biased", but the author answered that he relied on current scientific data (706,711,712). Another Reader (who described herself as a Pharm.D. with a post-doctoral degree in traditional Chinese medicine [TCM]) offered a long-winded, self-serving explanation of that unproven medical system (713).

The National Association of Retail Druggists also included quackery in its publications. In 1989, it accepted Advertising revenue from Boericke and Tafel, Inc. for "Alpha CF", an unproven homeopathic remedy that promised to aid in cold and flu by stimulating "the body's own natural defense system – the immune system – to help ward off the attack" (714).

The authors of the ground-breaking 1998 editorial in *The New England Journal of Medicine* offered this succinct and guilt-inducing charge: "It is time for the scientific community to stop giving alternative medicine a free ride" (704). By extension, the authors could well have included the Pharmacy community and its long-standing willingness to give unproven products the same "free ride". The nation's leading Pharmacy journals have a duty to their readership to present a balanced and critical look at the subjects of their articles. However, when the duty to its Readers and the duty to its sponsors are in conflict, it is apparent that advertisement-supported journals may default on their professional duty and opt to tow the party line of quackery.

Quackery – New Names Confer False Respectability

The 1994 DSHEA effectively ended use of the term "quackery", as it granted unprecedented legitimacy to unproven products in one fell swoop. After that time, unproven products were increasingly referred to as "unconventional", or as components of "alternative care" or "complementary care", or by the abbreviation "CAM" (Complementary and Alternative Medicine) (587,590,610–612). These terms were coined to permanently and irreversibly blur the line between legitimate medications and unproven medications by suggesting that there is a legitimate alternative to proven therapies. It also suggested that quackery is a safe and effective "complement" to proven therapies (613,614). Unfortunately, neither assertion is true. Medical therapies and products are either proven to be safe and effective or not proven to be safe and effective (583,615). There is no middle ground where patients can feel protected by resorting to alternative or complementary medications or products that lack proof of safety and/or efficacy. To imply otherwise is a cruel and misleading manipulation of a medically unsophisticated Public. Unfortunately, those who push such remedies on the Public resist the suggestion that their products should undergo the same testing as those used in legitimate medicine (583,587).

When national organizations sell booth space to exhibitors whose product line includes unproven medications, attendees should register their disappointment with a letter to the national office, stressing that future transgressions will result in a loss of membership. Similar letters can be tendered to textbook authors and their publishers, and to accrediting and licensing bodies, asking that they not give unwarranted legitimacy to unproven medications.

Pharmacists throughout the United States engage in quackery. Some practice unproven therapies such as iridology to boost their monthly income, but far more sell unproven products. Concerned academicians can report these offending pharmacists to the state board or other governing Agency, asking that the Pharmacy be issued an order to cease Promotion of unproven therapies. Should the pharmacist engage in "diagnosing" medical conditions through unproven therapies, such as iridology or reflexology, the State medical board or State Health department might also be able to intervene.

Conclusion

In the period before the 1900s, nonprescription medications were sold without any federal Regulation. However, during the 1900s, the nation enacted numerous laws to protect the American Public from unsafe and ineffective nonprescription products. Some of the laws were driven by deadly tragedies. Eventually, the FDA developed a comprehensive review process to ensure that nonprescription ingredients sold to the Public would be both safe and effective. The review was utilized the best precepts of evidence-based medicine. If the review had encompassed all nonprescription products, the benefits to the Public would have been immeasurable.

Unfortunately, the FDA never reached the lofty goal of creating a safe and effective nonprescription marketplace. Unbridled greed from vested interests worked against the FDA to create a favorable climate for quackery in several ways. First is a medically illiterate and gullible Public that believes the myth that "natural is safe" causing millions to put their trust in herbs and other quackery. Second is the successful machinations of Orrin Hatch, who created a legal climate that sanitized quackery and legitimized fraud. Third is the proliferation of a group of companies known as Pharmacy Benefit Managers; they ensure that community pharmacies can no longer expect decent profits from prescription sales. As a result of these forces, Pharmacy organizations and textbooks endorse and embrace quackery in large numbers. The impact of widespread use of unproven nonprescription product on the Health of the American Public is unknown and potentially deadly. All for the sake of profit.

Chapter 14

Issues and Studies in Pharmacoeconomics

Introduction

Pharmacoeconomics is a fairly new term, but as an area of study and research, it has been around for a long time. There is no accepted definition, but the field can be divided into two areas. The first is the application of economic principles to problems involving the People, costs, funding, and projections of needs. The second application is to the workings of the pharmaceutical industry – Prices, profits, R&D costs, and the like.

Chapter 15 will provide details specific to the economics of Big Pharma. There will be some overlap between that and the present chapter, with Chapter 15 providing insights into pricing strategies and tactics, rarely covered in published writing.

The driving force behind the application of economic analyses of pharmaceuticals is to respond to a changing, more cost-conscious market by providing persuasive, comparative information to decision makers about the costs and outcomes of therapeutic alternatives. The intended effect is to influence positively the utilization of an individual company's prescription Drug product(s). As a consequence of this effect, most pharmaceutical manufacturers currently regard the application of economic research, as a competitive marketing strategy, albeit tactical in nature, since it is product-specific in scope and supports the immediate business objectives of the firm.

One of the functions of economic studies appears at the interface with Policy. Does research affect Policy, or does Policy affect research? One school of thought would argue that Health Services Research (of which Health Economics is a subset) does not directly influence Policy since policymakers do not share the empirical basis for rational decision-making that researchers value. Rather, they are influenced by intuition, political reality, and a desire to do what is "right". Research findings are often considered only post hoc if the findings support the policymakers' set of beliefs and values.

The other side, of course, would argue that if research outcomes are presented in a format that is acceptable and understandable, then Policy initiatives can be influenced by Health Services Research. The value of Health Services Research per se is of importance when it focuses attention on the magnitude of a problem of societal concern.

Perhaps the most immediate Policy issue to which Health Economics is being applied is worldwide pricing. Kolassa (498) has estimated that within 10 years, the worldwide industry pricing environment for pharmaceuticals will show: (1) a continual decline of Price growth; (2) harmonization of Price Regulation systems and program evaluation methods; (3) mandatory cost–benefit analyses to gain approval or use; and (4) a need to "sell price" as a positive component of the Drug product or to justify the Price charged.

The Emergence of Socioeconomic Research

Luce and Elixhauser (537) provided, 30 years ago, a preview of what they referred to as Socioeconomic Evaluations at the advent of the emergence of this vital field of research. Some excerpts of their far-seeing views are presented, verbatim, here.

Definition of Socioeconomic Evaluations

> Socioeconomic evaluations are research methods based on the social sciences, primarily economics and psychology. They are methods that enumerate the costs and consequences of medical products and services. Costs are the monetary valuations of resource inputs required to produce a health outcome. Consequences are the monetary and nonmonetary results of

applying a particular intervention. It is vital to recognize that socioeconomic evaluations are grounded in the clinical efficacy of the interventions they evaluate; the clinical effects of a medication must be clearly understood before the relevant socioeconomic hypotheses can be generated.

It is helpful to visualize two streams of events pertaining to each medical intervention. The first is the medical stream. In this stream, a patient arrives at a physician's office, receives treatment, and is cured or not cured. Paralleling this stream is the socioeconomic stream of events. Each activity in the medical stream is associated with a particular socioeconomic result—medical services and other resources are used; the patient's level of social, personal, or employment functioning is altered, etc. The task of a socioeconomic evaluation is to delineate this latter stream of events.

Through socioeconomic evaluations, it is possible to make more informed decisions regarding the use, distribution, and financing of healthcare services and technologies. Although socioeconomic evaluations are not a panacea for rising health care costs, they provide information that health care decision makers can use to optimize their resource allocation decisions.

Types of Socioeconomic Evaluations

There are a number of evaluations that can estimate the socioeconomic effects of medical technologies. They are distinguished primarily by whether, and how, costs and consequences are measured. Three types of studies assess both the costs and the consequences of medical interventions: Cost-benefit, cost-effectiveness, and cost-utility analyses.

In cost-benefit analysis (CBA), the costs and the consequences of a technology are expressed in monetary terms. This often means placing a dollar value on health outcomes.

***

Cost-effectiveness analysis (CEA) was developed to address limitations of CBA, and it has been used extensively in medical care. In CEA, input costs are measured in monetary units, but health outcomes or consequences are measured in their natural units, such as number of lives saved, years of life saved, cases diagnosed, or cases prevented. The strength of CEA lies in the fact that no dollar value is placed on human life or health outcomes.

***

Cost-utility analysis (CUA) addresses this limitation of CEA by measuring the utility or value of years of life rather than just enumerating them. Outcomes are measured in terms of their quality or states of consumer preference.

***

Another type of socioeconomic evaluation that can be helpful in assessing health care technologies is the cost-of-illness (COI) study. Cost-of-illness studies are the precursors of other socioeconomic evaluations. Rather than looking at the impact of treatments, studies focus on the economic consequences of the medical conditions themselves.

***

The choice of which socioeconomic evaluation to perform is guided by the interventions, the clinical problem, the data available, and how outcomes can be valued (monetarily, in natural units, or in terms of patient preferences). These socioeconomic evaluations attempt to measure the social and economic effects of diseases or their treatments. They step beyond an assessment of the clinical efficacy of a treatment or intervention and attempt to reveal the effects of medical technologies in a much broader sense. One type of socioeconomic evaluation is not inherently better or worse than another; however, in any particular case, one method is likely to be more appropriate than another based on the types of questions asked and the types of data available.

***

In assessing a research report, it is important to evaluate whether significant changes might be anticipated if other costs and consequences had been incorporated and if other alternatives had been compared. The perspective of the analysis also determines, to a large extent, the outcome of a study. Studies conducted from the perspective of society take into account costs and consequences regardless of those to whom the costs and consequences accrue. Therefore, these studies are least likely to result in a shifting of costs from one segment of society to another. Socioeconomic evaluations are important tools for decision makers in the health care field. These decision makers face increasingly difficult choices between competing alternatives, such as choices between medications with apparently equivalent efficacy. If these choices are based simply on a comparison of the monetary costs per dose of the drugs, other important costs and consequences may be disregarded, including costs such as those associated with the utilization of medical resources to treat significant adverse reactions and consequences such as differences in quality of life. Socioeconomic evaluations can provide balanced and impartial appraisals of the relative costs and efficacy of interventions and are becoming essential tools for decision making.

Source: Bryan R. Luce and Anne Elixhauser, "Socioeconomic Evaluation and the Health Care Industry", Journal of Research in Pharmaceutical Economics, *Vol. 2, (4), 1990, and reprinted in* Studies in Pharmaceutical Economics *(Ref. 4). Quoted with permission.*

The Cost of Illness

When terms such as cost–benefit are used, the "cost" refers to the Drug costs. There are estimates of the cost of Health Care at the national level and the "costs" of various conditions such as hypertension. These tend to be gross measures and are often just estimates.

The best early work on cost of individual illnesses was done by Dorothy Rice and Anne Scitovski who focused on indirect costs such as loss of productivity, morbidity, mortality, and other costs. Rice, an eminent biostatistician, served as Director of the National Center for Health Statistics (1976–1982) and has been cited as a major factor in the passage of Medicare. Scitovski, a Health economist, collaborated with Rice in a number of reports (449, 477–480), notably, but not limited to the costs associated with AIDS. She has also analyzed the very difficult question of the amount of resources that should be spent on care of the dying patient in the face of scarcity of resources (487).

The indirect costs are difficult to measure and are often not economic in nature. Nevertheless, they are very real and important to the patient, family, Government, and as we shall see, Big Pharma. Direct costs are important in estimating cost–benefit and cost-effectiveness (see Chapter 15) but indirect costs are no less real, even if intangible. It is the struggle to measure the intangibles that have led to research in the area of Quality of Life (QOL).

Quality of Life Assessment (QOL)

Before providing an overview of QOL Assessment, I cite a study, which has been widely quoted, by Jachuck and co-workers (481). In their study, *physicians* reported improvement in 100% of the patients, while only 45% of the *patients* indicated that they felt better. To confound the results further, when patients' relatives were interviewed, they reported *worsening* in 10% of the cases.

Admittedly, it's only one study but intuition suggests that the physicians using their recognized, objective measures of patient progress may reach a different conclusion regarding progress than does the patient.

In another example of doctor–patient discordance, Pearlman and Uhlmann (483) interviewed elderly patients with five chronic diseases (arthritis, ischemic heart disease, chronic pulmonary disease, diabetes mellitus, and cancer) and their physicians. Patients generally perceived their QOL to be slightly worse than "good, no major complaints" in each chronic disease. Physicians' ratings were generally worse than and only weakly associated with the patients' ratings. Significant independent correlates of patients' ratings of QOL included the patients' perceptions of their Health, interpersonal relationships, and finances. These results suggest that QOL in elderly outpatients with chronic disease is a multidimensional construct involving Health, as well as social and other factors and that physicians may misunderstand patients' perceptions of their QOL. Among other implications of QOL is the observation by Diamond (482) that a discrepancy between the regimen prescribed by the doctor and that followed by the patient is a good measure of the differing views of the relative merits of the medication. (Of course, there are many reasons for non-compliance.)

The utility of QOL analysis and some of the economic implications are demonstrated by the case study of auranofin (Trade Name, Ridauran) conducted by the then, SmithKline Beecham, (SKB). The Drug had many of the characteristics to make it a good candidate from QOL study – troubling side effects, high dollar costs, delayed benefits, skeptical prescribers, and effective competing remedies. SKB planned and conducted one of the most thorough and commercial cost-effectiveness QOL trials to that time. Especially important was the resulting publication in quite respectable media (489–491).

This was a very detailed study done using trained interviewers over a period of months with 19 different instruments. Added to these were data on economic parameters, unusual at the time. The data were obtained by yet another questionnaire administered to the patient and from Health institutions and providers. Measures used were:

- Outpatient expenses
- Visits, radiographs, lab tests, medications, aids and devices, treatments, surgery, other
- Hospitalizations
- Nursing home care
- Non-medical expenses
- Paid help, unpaid help, own earned income

Changes between baseline and 6 months on economic outcomes and on the QOL measures described above were calculated. The Investigations favor the Quality of Well-Being (QWB) and Health Assessment Questionnaire (HAQ) as best capturing "what patients and society decision makers seek to achieve thorough arthritis therapies". Much of their analyses, therefore, focused on the interaction between QWB/HAQ results and the economic data. (Remember, this was 25 years ago!)

By the authors' calculations, the overall economic effects of auranofin on the experimental patients were:

$1,160.00	Additional Medical
9.50	Travel
23.80	Work lost by family and friends
13.10	Paid help
263.50	Unpaid help

From this, is subtracted, realized extra earnings of $615, leaving a net annual cost of $855. (This does not include the cost of the auranofin, which was calculated at $405.50).

Auranofin cost more than did placebo therapy (not surprisingly), but patients receiving the medications showed statistically significant improvements on the QWB and HAQ scale scores compared with the placebo controls.

The authors made a brief comparison with the cost of total joint replacements, while noting limits to the comparability. This was, then, the only cost-effectiveness comparison with another therapy.

An unusual component of the study was Willingness to Pay (WTP). What percent of their family's total monthly income they would be willing to pay on a regular basis for a complete cure of arthritis? These subjects would, on average, pay 22% of their household income or would accept a mortal risk of 27% to cure their arthritis!

It will be obvious to the Reader that this was a complex and expensive study. SKB showed considerable courage in undertaking such an effort. They used the results of the published reports in their Promotion with mixed results due in part to the nature of the arthritis market and the competition.

The FDA is likely to begin considering QOL data in its overall Drug approval process. While it is unlikely that the Agency will ever *require* QOL studies, if a manufacturer is able to identify a distinct segment of the patient population which may experience QOL benefits from a Drug, this information may assist in (or accelerate) securing approval to market the Drug. For some types of Drugs, FDA is considering the possibility of granting a QOL indication in situations where the clinical data are compelling. The most likely candidates for a QOL indication are cancer chemotherapeutic agents.

Returning to the theme of this chapter one might logically ask, "What are the economic implications of QOL"? Intuitively some are very real, losing one's job, for example. The totality of the economic issues is diffuse, difficult, and often expensive to measure. And there is not total agreement on what factors are at work in the individual's assessment of what constitutes her life quality. Perhaps those who construct the questionnaires and interview schedules get it wrong?!

Ciba Geigy executive C.R.B. Joyce provided an incisive look at QOL studies in clinical assessment and notes that Health goals may differ depending upon who is setting them.

> Health goals, then, may be set by the individual, his peers, or society at large. The distance covered in the direction of the goal may also be estimated by the individual, the peer group or an "assessor designated by authority". Peers, including relatives, may also have to both set goals and assess progress for such difficult groups of patients as children, schizophrenics and those who

suffer from 'old-timers' disease. Peer goal-setting and evaluation may be unavoidable in such conditions, but it represents what may be called pseudo-quality of life method if applied in those where it is not obligatory; the disparity between patients', relatives' and doctors' opinions of progress under treatment has been well documented.

(492)

True QOL measurements according to Joyce are obtainable only from individuals who measure progress toward goals set by themselves. The authoritative setting of goals and assessment of progress toward them represents the realm of the economists and politicians. Nevertheless, it is possible to identify benefits which accrue to various parties interested in QOL improvements. The patient is the most important of these parties.

The Economics of Non-Compliance

As compliance issues have been discussed at several points in the Book, we limit coverage here to economic considerations. Fincham (111) has produced the definitive, to date, elucidation of the dimensions of the problems of non-compliance, some of the remedies, and an excellent literature review. He cites studies that are disease specific, including some of the economic consequences resulting from the medical results of non-compliance. Examples:

- Asthma – wherein the "high price of medications" was found to be a factor (439).
- Infectious disease – with evidence of over-prescribing, resulting not only in non-compliance, but also bacterial resistance with subsequent resistance and resultant additional costs (493).
- Cardiovascular diseases – caused in part by a cap on the number of prescriptions in a State Medicaid program (494).
- Diabetes – hospitalizations and re-admissions were more common in the non-compliant group (495).

There are more such examples, but the economic links in non-compliance should be obvious. We have noted in Chapter 7 that the Drug industry takes seriously the problems of two kinds of non-compliance: failure to have an original prescription filled at all, and failure to receive the authorized refills.

McCaffrey and others (201,399) studied unclaimed prescriptions citing estimates of 140 million unfilled prescriptions annually (this was in 1994) with a loss to pharmacies of $2.8 billion. Obviously there is a similar but indeterminate loss to Big Pharma. The researchers after a review of past studies conducted their own study using a national stratified random sample of 1,742 retail pharmacies. Cost was cited by 6.3% of the respondents as a reason patients failed to claim their prescriptions. Anti-infectives were the therapeutic category most often listed. The authors note that an unclaimed original prescription also means a loss of authorized refills, perhaps as many as a dozen if a year's supply was authorized.

For the Drug industry, filled and unfilled prescriptions represent the greatest economic concern. We have already seen the concern expressed in their trade journals. The number of prescriptions dispensed annually in the United States exceed 2 billion, although that number would be much higher but for the phenomenon of unfilled/unclaimed prescriptions. Some statistics suggest that sales consist of about an equal number of new and refill prescriptions, although these proportions vary significantly by therapeutic class. As the population continues to age and chronic diseases become even more prevalent, refills will predominate. Thus, failure to refill will become an increasingly more important Health and business problem.

An example of the importance of refills is presented in Table 14.1. In this example, a hypothetical new product for a chronic condition is tracked for its first 12 months on the market. In the first month, 20,000 new prescriptions are generated. New prescriptions increase by 10,000 per month until the ninth month, where they stabilize at 100,000 per month. As the data show, assuming complete compliance with refill directions, refills constitute nearly 90% of sales by the end of the first year. Generating new

Table 14.1 Hypothetical Prescription Pattern for First 12 Months of a Chronic Medication

	Month											
	1	2	3	4	5	6	7	8	9	10	11	12
# New Rx[a]	20	30	40	50	60	70	80	90	100	100	100	100
# Refill Rx[a]	0	20	50	90	140	200	270	350	440	540	640	740
% New Rx	100	60	45	36	30	26	23	20	18	15	13	11
% Refill Rx	0	4	55	64	70	74	77	80	82	85	87	89

[a] In thousands.

prescriptions gets the motor started, but assuring compliance keeps it running and helps it gain speed. In this simplified example, promotional efforts generated 840,000 *new* prescriptions, but there were 3,570,000 *refills*.

Way back in its March 25, 1992 issue, the *Wall Street Journal* reported on the efforts of two pharmaceutical manufacturers (ICI Pharmaceuticals and Searle) to improve the compliance rates of patients taking some of the companies' leading prescription products. Those efforts, which included such tactics as regular telephone calls to remind patients about refills, newsletters to users, and a toll-free number for patients' inquiries, are costly, but the investment has an enormous potential for return to the manufacturer, as well as possible reductions in hospitalization cost as shown before. Improvement in medication compliance is definitely beneficial to everyone involved.

Economic Epidemiology

Henry Sigerist has stated: "Illness creates poverty, which in time creates more illness". There in all of its succinctness, is a definition of Economic Epidemiology. The late James Visconti, 50 years ago, incorporated the concept and formalized it in his doctoral dissertation (with minimal assistance from his doctoral advisor, your Author). In spite of its obvious utility, it seems to have been widely ignored. I did find some interest in the concept during a consultancy with World Health Organization but nothing formal seems to have come of it except for WHO's continued interest in adverse Drug reactions to which Visconti had applied his work (76). It deserved attention here because of the implications for Policy by the Government and marketing strategies by Big Pharma.

There is a variety of definitions for epidemiology, but most are quite similar. A good one is provided by Morton and Huhn: "Epidemiology is the study of the distribution of a disease or condition in a population and of factors that affect or are associated with the occurrence of cases" (484). Economic epidemiology might, technically speaking, be considered part of social epidemiology, insofar as economics is considered a social science. In any case, they defined economic epidemiology as "the study of factors and conditions that determine the occurrence and distribution of economic consequences of disease with the purpose of interrupting the natural history of these events".

What is the ultimate objective in studying the economics of a disease? In the broadest terms, the answer to this question is the same as the answer to a similar question concerning the pathology of a disease: to increase our understanding of the disease so that it can be prevented or treated more effectively. In stricter terms, we study the economic impact of disease to place the disease within a cost framework of all diseases so that we may determine priorities (i.e., which diseases are most costly in terms of direct and indirect expenditures) and, once priorities on particular disease states to be attacked are determined, to investigate the natural history of the disease with the hope of interjecting preventive barriers that are both logical and practical from a medical as well as an economic standpoint. We may think of this latter objective as a strategic decision about when and where action will be most effective. Economic epidemiology must go beyond incomplete evidence to fill gaps in knowledge for more effective recourse allocation, prevention measures, and solutions to disease problems. Economic epidemiology is based upon existing bodies of knowledge that lead to a definition of the nature, extent, and significance of the problems and to the framing of questions for which answers are to be sought. The formulation of hypotheses follows a critical appraisal of existing disease information to disclose gaps in knowledge.

Insofar as the techniques of economic epidemiology are closely related to those of cost–benefit and cost-effectiveness analyses, the need for use of these techniques parallels its use in the latter types of applications. These techniques have been used for a variety of purposes, including the identification of the cost of illness for purposes of forecasting the economic responsibilities of the person contracting the disease; determining optimal allocations of biomedical research expenditures; selecting the most appropriate program for controlling diseases; and choosing from among research, education, and treatment as means of dealing with medical problems.

Health Care has traditionally concerned itself with either prevention or therapy, whereas epidemiology has focused on the prevention activities, and economic epidemiology should be no exception. Prevention involves studying the succession of events that cause the exposure of certain types of individuals to specific types of environment leading to or aggravating bodily changes in those individuals. These environments will have economic elements, and bodily changes may be accompanied by changes in the economic status of the individual and the society of which she is a part.

An epidemic has been defined as "the occurrence in a community....of a group of illnesses of similar nature, clearly in excess of normal expectation" (486). Under this definition, one is tempted to describe the current rate of increases in most Health Care costs, particularly hospital costs, as a form of "economic epidemic". Carrying the simile further, we might point out that costs are also communicable. For example, an economically debilitating illness may make a family a medical ward of the community. Thus, the costs are transmissible. It is also worth noting that both chronic and acute costs exist and that they parallel the medical characteristics of disease in both the nature of their severity and the effective term.

It is in the area of prevention that the economic epidemiologist may make the greatest contribution. Indeed, the most challenging purpose of economic epidemiology is that of identifying those economic components of causal (or contributory) mechanisms that enable the formulation of effective preventive measures with the ultimate goal of either reducing costs or increasing the effectiveness of Health Care investments.

Economic epidemiology should provide a strategy for action. Just as in clinical medicine, where physical, social, psychological, and laboratory information is gathered to establish certain facts for treatment and prevention, in economic epidemiology data are collected to establish facts for preventing economic problems.

Major aims and purposes of economic epidemiology include:

1. Analyzing the interactions of agent, host, and environmental factors in the natural history of disease in order to discover gaps in knowledge and to contribute to preventing economic consequences of disease.
2. Describing and analyzing disease economics (costs) and their distribution according to such variables as age, race, sex, occupation, economic status, and payment mechanism.
3. Filling gaps in knowledge about the costs of disease processes by observing illness and its economic consequences in populations.
4. Studying immediate and special problems in the field of Health economics, including the cost of new diseases (e.g., Drug-induced disease) and administrative problems (e.g., cost–benefit and cost-effective analysis of preventive Health programs, cost and benefits of monitoring Drug use and Drug reactions).
5. Stimulating and using an orderly approach to scientific research in the costs of illness.

From the standpoint of economic epidemiology and preventive medicine, it is not enough to be aware of the definite association between disease and economic consequences. The manner in which disease factors influence departure from Health and contribute to economic disability also deserves attention. Equally important is the identification of points of intervention to reduce or to prevent economic disability from disease. These concepts provide the basic framework for economic epidemiology. By applying these economic principles, researchers can make progress in preventive medicine and reduce the cost of disease.

Conclusion

A *Wall Street Journal* article (May 25, 2019) described the approval of the "Priciest Medicine, Zolgensma, with a 'sticker price' of $2,125 million". That's well over the Price of its competitor, Spinraza, a bargain at $750,000 for the first year and only $375,000 for following years.

In one of the more recent entries into the library of Books about Drug Prices, Schoonveld (497) posed the question: "How will stricter controls over pricing and patient access to drugs evolve as a new generation of expensive biotech drugs threatens to bankrupt pharmaceutical budgets"? The answer to that question remains to be found.

In another question Schoonveld asks: "How did the drug industry, with its life saving innovations, manage to earn a Public image that is much worse than industries with products that kill, such as the gun and tobacco industries"? Without necessarily accepting the premise, I suggest that there are multiple answers – most of which have been provided in this Book.

Chapter 15

On Drug Prices

Dr. E. M. "Mick" Kolassa

(**Author's note**: Because of the continuing interest in the issue of drug prices, I have allotted a full chapter to that "P". Much more detail can be found in Dr. Kolassa's two books, *Elements of Pharmaceutical Pricing* and *The Strategic Pricing of Pharmaceuticals*, my references 10 and 11 respectively.)

Introduction

In the early 1980s, the standard approach to pharmaceutical pricing was to set the Price of a new product higher than the market leader and enjoy the revenue. The few exceptions to this rule found no benefit to their lower Prices and eventually raised them. These Price increases were soon copied by other firms, who found the lack of Price sensitivity provided an opportunity to spur sales growth with little effort – most firms quickly fell into a pattern of one or two large Price increases annually.

Some major changes to the pricing environment sent a shock into the system. The Waxman–Hatch Bill transformed Generic Drugs from a mere annoyance to a major market threat, and the emergence of managed care and hospital buying groups gave rise to new concerns about Price sensitivity. Research and development departments in many firms focused much of their attention on creating agents that were similar in mechanism and structure to already marketed products, giving rise to the "me-too" era of new Drugs.

The pharmaceutical industry reacted to these and other trends by following a new rule: Price new products at or below the Prices of competitors, hoping to eliminate Price as an obstacle to product adoption (715). National account groups then set to work discounting from these already lower Prices. The federal Government further complicated the working environment by granting itself access to the best Prices the pharmaceutical companies made available, effectively penalizing Drug firms and their customers. These new laws also deprived the pharmaceutical firms of their most potent sales growth tool, Price increases. The penalties for increases above the rate of inflation were enough to convince most firms to rein in their increases.

Seeking order in this increasingly chaotic environment, many firms turned to mechanistic approaches to pricing. Hundreds of millions of dollars have been spent on pricing research studies to determine the perfect Price point, and companies have relied on fairly simple, often misleading, survey research findings to build strategic plans. Rigid internal pricing protocols have been established (and often ignored) by many firms. This, together with the research just mentioned, provides many firms with an illusion of some control (716).

The net result has been continually lower launch Prices that soon decay in an environment of Price negotiations and the unfortunate situation that many within the pharmaceutical industry do not have faith that their products are Priced appropriately (717). Failure to understand the role of Prices in decision-making has caused many firms to forego a significant amount of profit in the quest to remain competitive with other firms whose actions they often have not taken the time to explore and understand. Rather than taking place in an environment of collusion and Price fixing, as alleged in the retail Pharmacy class action suits, the pricing actions of most pharmaceutical firms in recent years have been reactive, haphazard, and driven by short-term considerations. Those actions have resulted in leaving a significant amount of money "on the table". Short-term thinking leads to uninformed, emotional decisions, which, I believe, describes the majority of pharmaceutical pricing decisions made in the past several years.

Pricing – The Forgotten "P"

Raymond Corey once wrote "...pricing is the moment of truth – all marketing comes to focus on the pricing decision" (718).

Most people involved in the field of pharmaceutical marketing are aware of the "Four P's" of marketing, also called the marketing mix: product, Promotion, place, and Price. But most marketing efforts, with rare exceptions, are focused on the product and Promotion, with virtually no thought given to distribution issues (place) and very little serious attention given to pricing. Nagle and Holden observed that the first three elements of the marketing mix – product, Promotion, and distribution – represent the firm's attempt to create value in the marketplace, while pricing is used to capture some of that value in the form of profits (719). Failure to develop and execute an appropriate pricing strategy usually results in the failure of the firm to capture an appropriate share of the value of the product, which translates into lower profits.

Working with several firms over the years, I made the same observation again and again: very few people in the pharmaceutical industry (or any industry, for that matter) pay close attention to their Prices. To be certain, account managers, contract managers, and others spend a great deal of time bringing Prices down, but very few people are charged with assuring that the Prices charged are appropriate and profitable.

The field of pharmaceutical pricing is complex, convoluted, and often ambiguous, but it is not unfathomable. The failure to manage pricing within the industry is a symptom of a much larger problem, one that is shared by other industries: the rampant lack of knowledge about the market and the competition. It is astonishing how little product managers, marketing researchers, and their superiors know about the markets in which they compete. Failure to understand one's customers and one's competitors is certain to lead to poor pricing decisions. For many, failure to understand is compounded by the failure to learn and apply basic pricing principles in pharmaceutical markets.

The New Product Dilemma

New products are often greeted with enthusiasm in consumer markets, but new products in pharmaceutical markets are often seen as problematic. Despite the clinical value of the product, systems must be changed to accommodate the use of the new medication. Unfortunately, few companies work with their customers to ease the problem of new product inclusion, instead taking actions to force the adoption of the product into the system. This often results in a reaction by affected parties, who delay new product evaluation or take some other steps to forestall product uptake. Understanding the world in which the customer operates and taking steps to bring your new product into that world with the customer's workload in mind can enhance the adoption of new Drugs.

Market Segments

Vital to appropriate pricing is an understanding of the various segments in which the company competes, especially the degree of Price sensitivity within each segment. Legislation and litigation have forced companies to reconsider the segments they had previously identified, but few have done more than simply reclassify groups into new segments and establish arbitrary guidelines for discounting within each segment. There is also a considerable amount of confusion between the classification of segments and channel members, intermediaries that are vital for distribution or financing but do not play the role of customers in any traditional sense.

The tools and techniques discussed here have applications in each segment of the pharmaceutical marketplace. Many will find that too much attention has been paid to intermediaries in the distributive process that have wrongly been classified as market segments. Wholesalers and most retailers fall into this category and, except in the most rare of circumstances, these groups should not receive special Price consideration.

The lack of market and competitive knowledge and the use of general assumptions have seduced many in the industry to assign higher levels of importance and Price sensitivity to several segments. Additionally, the typical approach to pharmaceutical marketing itself has fed this problem because those involved in the marketing of pharmaceuticals tend to focus on their products and to view every aspect of the market through the filter of their own impression of the products. This is the reason many promotional campaigns focus on the mechanism of action of a Drug rather than its end benefit. These forces (product focus, lack of awareness of market and competitive issues, and a general lack of familiarity with pricing concepts) combine to bring about two "disorders" that must be corrected. These pharmaceutical pricing diseases are: Fear of Pricing and Managed Care Myopia.

Fear of Pricing

This malady is manifested in two ways. First, because of recent Legislation and litigation, many corporate attorneys (whose primary purpose appears to be sales prevention) have decided that the word "Price" will not be uttered within the confines of the corporate campus and that any sources of pricing information may constitute an attempt to collude, thus forcing the firm to Price in a vacuum of no information. This problem is compounded by the deeply held belief of many in the industry that the Price of the product has taken on newfound importance and that any product, no matter how beneficial from a clinical perspective, will fail miserably unless it is priced at a discount. Thus deprived of market information on which to base pricing decisions, the company instead often assumes that every new product must be priced low relative to the competition. A small case will illustrate. (There are many others.)

TAP's proton pump inhibitor, Prevacid, was launched at a 10% discount to Prilosec, Astra Merck's pioneer product which was on its way to becoming the biggest pharmaceutical brand in history. Many believed that a significant discount for Prevacid would be disastrous to the Astra Merck product. TAP, however, seems to have understood the costly mistake of deep discount pricing. It chose to Price only slightly below Prilosec, allowing its representatives to claim that it is little less costly, but not attempting to devalue the therapeutic class (and leave a lot of money on the table while doing so).

Because we are not privy to the reasoning behind the pricing in this case, it is difficult to evaluate the success of the approach. From this sample, however, we see more high-priced successes than low-priced successes and no high-priced failures. The role of Price in the success of a pharmaceutical product may be more closely related to the firm's confidence in the product and its ability to market the product than to a physician's decision to prescribe it.

This problem has been aggravated by the fear of pricing, but many firms have long suffered from it. Inverted focus causes firms to Price their products according to the firms' own biased assessment of the value of the products – or worse, according to costs. Additionally, because of their failure to understand their customers, these firms often introduce new products into the marketplace that are met with hostility as opposed to the open arms anticipated by the marketing team. This problem results in disappointing market performance and often is followed by rampant discounting in an attempt to "get the product moving".

As previously discussed, firms that understand their customers have a much better chance of competing successfully. Those who choose instead to focus their efforts internally, not taking the time or expending the effort to truly understand their markets, will continue to make costly and avoidable mistakes, as the next discussion outlines.

Managed Care Myopia

In the late 1980s, many firms established account management groups to market (or, rather, sell to) managed care and other buyers perceived to be large and influential. These account managers then set out to define and describe managed care and its growing influence. Because selling to managed care was their job, they made sure the company took this emerging market very seriously, and they overstated the importance of managed care in product selection.

Convinced that managed care is only concerned about Price, some firms found it virtually impossible to resist discounting to this segment, and account managers continually provided horror stories of closed formularies and "NDC lockouts" that required huge discounts to assure product use. Most firms in the United States have responded to these threats by offering generous discounts in exchange for favorable treatment and generally have not realized the gains they had expected.

Although it is true that managed care now accounts for more than 50% of the outpatient prescription market in the United States, data from IMS indicate that few of the managed care plans have actually restricted the use of branded pharmaceuticals. In fact, there are no indications that the growth of managed care is responsible for a significant proportion of the growth of sales for branded pharmaceutical products over the past few years and that the discounts provided to these payers have had little, if any, effect on product use.

Some managed care organizations, specifically the staff models such as Kaiser and Group Health, do have the ability to affect sales because they take possession of the products and dispense the prescriptions that are written by employee physicians.

Most firms have been eager to contract with managed care organizations based on the threat of their ability to control use. Pharmaceutical marketers have bemoaned the shrinking of the unrestricted cash market, where patients pay for their own prescriptions, believing that this market offers greater opportunities for pricing flexibility and a higher rate of profit.

Two facts must be understood. First, when the patient must pay for the prescription, he or she must be sensitive to the cost, as the ability to pay will determine the likelihood of the purchase. The bulk of the cash segment prior to Medicare coverage was senior citizens on fixed incomes, and seniors tend to use more prescription Drugs than younger patients. They request products with Generic alternatives and lower cost agents. A patient covered by a prescription plan, like patients in most European nations, cares nothing about the cost of the medications. Physicians may ask patients whether they have prescription coverage, knowing that a prescription card means the patient will have the prescription filled, regardless of the cost.

Competition among managed care plans has grown intense, and the appearance of restrictiveness on the part of a plan, manifested by refusing to pay for prescriptions ordered by its doctor, results in dissatisfied members who will look for a less restrictive plan. Member satisfaction has become a key performance measure among managed care plans, and losing members while trying to restrict pharmaceuticals, which only account for approximately 10% of Managed Care Organizations (MCO) spending, makes little sense.

The Need to Price on Purpose

The failure to take pricing seriously results in lower profit margins. It is that simple. Many firms appear to have surrendered pricing authority to their competitors or to their customers, neither of whom is at all concerned about the financial success of the firm. They may, in fact, benefit from the firm's demise. Companies must make serious commitments to invest in pricing skills and to use Prices to capture the value of their products, not to lower their value. Profitable pricing requires constant attention and continual learning, and it requires an understanding within the firm that the role of Price is to secure the financial well-being of the firm and *not* to move more unit volume.

The Growing Importance of Pharmaceutical Pricing

While Public officials in the United States often note the growth of Health Care spending, especially for pharmaceuticals, and point to this growth as an indication of the need for tighter controls on Health Care costs, few have acknowledged the inevitability of cost increases in a system that provides goods and services at little or no cost (720). It has been said that there is almost no limit to the amount of free medical care an individual is capable of using.

Even though many Health Care insurance plans are comprehensive packages of Health Care goods and services meant to provide an overall benefit, the components of the benefit are often budgeted and managed as separate entities, resulting in conflicts between budgetary authorities (721). Thus, it has become common that the greater good of the total system is often subordinate to individual budget performance.

Costly new pharmaceuticals could not have come at a less opportune time for most Health Care systems. Prior to the early 1980s, the majority of medical procedures and services were reimbursed on the basis of cost (722). Providers were compensated based on the cost of providing the service, plus a fee or markup. Under such a system, there was little, if any, incentive to control expenditures. In fact, the opposite occurred, as providers could increase their incomes by simply providing more services. Beginning in the late 1970s, however, programs were developed and Regulations were drafted and implemented to hold down Health Care costs, and the concept of managed care began to take hold.

In 1982, the enactment of the Tax Equity and Fiscal Responsibility Act (TEFRA) changed the basis of hospital reimbursement for procedures and services provided to Medicare patients from a cost-based program in which hospitals and other providers of Health Care billed the Medicare system on the basis of the costs incurred in delivering care, plus a markup, to one in which a per-case payment limit was imposed, establishing a fixed amount of reimbursement for each covered procedure (723). This change in reimbursement basis, called "prospective payment," imposed a condition on hospitals that the institution must provide a service at or below the fixed rate reimbursement – without regard to the individual institution's costs or cost structure – or suffer an economic loss. Many managed care providers also implemented such systems of reimbursement.

At approximately the same time as the imposition of the prospective payment system, the manufacturers of pharmaceuticals began to increase the Prices of their existing products, in addition to bringing new medications to market at higher-than-traditional Prices for pharmaceutical products (724,725). These concurrent phenomena of rising Drug Prices and restrictions on a provider's or insurer's ability to recover costs resulted in the implementation of several approaches to control Drug expenditures, the most widely used of which are the restrictive formulary and formal Drug utilization review (DUR) programs.

Pharmaceutical companies are placing a great deal of faith in the ability of pharmacoeconomic studies to overcome Price resistance. As Horn's recent experience demonstrates, even unbiased and well-balanced studies that conflict with the views (and self-interest) of those in charge of budgets cannot single-handedly overcome this mentality, and firms that believe their own studies will be more influential than academic studies will be sorely disappointed (728). As long as individuals within the system are charged with controlling Drug expenditures, this silo approach to budgeting will continue. The way to overcome this myopic approach to the control of pharmaceutical costs is to establish and promote the value of pharmaceuticals in relation of other Health Care resources. In this endeavor, many related obstacles must be overcome, including the lack of appreciation for the value of pharmaceuticals. Although patients think little of spending several hundred dollars for physician office visits and diagnostic procedures, they (and others) recoil at the thought of a Drug costing as much. This is due, in part, to the failure of the industry to promote the value of pharmaceuticals and to sell the end result (lack of disease) instead of the chemical itself.

As long as this and other obstacles exist, there will be misguided efforts to control the use of pharmaceuticals, and these efforts will reduce the profitability of pharmaceutical research. Those charged with recommending or setting the Prices and pricing strategies of pharmaceutical products must understand and manage this environment or risk significant declines in profitability.

Prices, Politics, and Problems

The Prices charged for pharmaceuticals have been the subject of Public Policy scrutiny for decades. Politicians wishing to demonstrate their concern for the welfare of citizens have periodically determined that the Prices charged for medications provide a relatively risk-free platform to show that concern. The pharmaceutical industry, in turn, goes into a defensive posture and pleads the need for research as its only defense for Prices. The net result, inevitably, is that the industry loses ground, either through a damaged Public image or through the loss of some pricing freedom.

Although research is the heart of the branded pharmaceutical industry, the Public has not shown willingness to accept that as an argument for "high Prices". The problem lies in the failure of the industry to establish – and hence the Public's failure to understand – the value of pharmaceuticals relative to other Health Care goods and services. Until that relationship is established and communicated in a credible and understandable manner, pharmaceutical firms will have continuous problems with their Prices and Public Policy.

What can companies do to at least moderate the criticism? As already mentioned, pleading the need to generate research funding is not the answer. Perhaps, as with the case of gasoline and other "negative goods", the answer lies in communicating some positive aspects of the products while acknowledging that a sizable proportion of the market will never admit to the value of the products. Premium-grade gasolines are positioned to enhance the performance of a car and to protect an investment, and pharmaceuticals can be positioned similarly.

A Pharmaceutical Pricing Philosophy

The unique nature of pharmaceuticals, being the product of profit-seeking corporations but considered by many to be a "Public good", has resulted in major differences between pharmaceutical markets and the so-called free markets. The fact that most pharmaceutical purchases are directed purchases and the fact that few patients can correctly be considered well-informed consumers are just two of the reasons pharmaceutical markets are unlikely to be truly free markets.

This is not to say that the development and marketing of pharmaceuticals will not continue to be a profitable – and noble – endeavor; it simply means that many of the tools and techniques for pricing and market analysis developed for free consumer markets will not have direct applicability in the market for medications. There are two important issues.

Willingness to Pay

Pharmaceutical companies should rightly expect to be rewarded for providing value to the Health Care marketplace. Even most critics will agree with this statement. The problem arises when the industry's rewards and the value provided appear to be out of balance. This is more a problem of poor communication of value than of overpricing, but the latter is the impression held by many.

Economists specializing in Public Policy have developed tests to determine the value of a program. These tests are based on the amount taxpayers or consumers state they would be willing to pay for a particular benefit from the program.

These tests have been transferred into the realm of Health Care and are widely used in pharmacoeconomic studies in Europe. They have also been used in the United States, both for pharmacoeconomics and for pharmaceutical pricing research. Although the concept of willingness to pay is compelling, we must admit that, because of the distortions in our Health Care system due to differences in payment sources for Health Care and the lack of direct decision-making authority for patients, such measures may not only be impractical but also be misleading.

Take, for example, the case of a treatment for Alzheimer's disease. The individual caring for the patient (the caregiver) could be asked, "What would you be willing to pay for this medication that stops the progress of the disease"? A typical response may be, "I would pay anything to help my wife (husband, mother, or father)". When pressed for a dollar amount, the respondent may give unrealistic figures because he cannot make a fully informed assessment of the value of the medication and may simply be grasping at straws in desperation. Such desperate measures are not uncommon in terminal, debilitating diseases and, the results of such lines of questioning provide little information of value in setting an appropriate Price.

Pricing on Purpose

Many of the problems encountered in the domain of pharmaceutical pricing have occurred because those involved in the decision were not proficient in the field of pharmaceutical pricing and because erroneous, but often logical, assumptions were made concerning the role and effects of Price in the market. Pricing mistakes emerge from failure to consider all the potential consequences of pricing actions – failing to "Price on purpose".

Pricing on purpose means that each Price considered has been evaluated for its effect on the Health Care system and members of that system and balanced with a realistic assessment of the willingness and ability of those members to take action. As the cost of pricing mistakes increases, the need to Price on purpose grows.

Pricing Terminology

This discussion introduces the various terms and buzzwords of pharmaceutical pricing and addresses the different pharmaceutical Prices that exist in the market. Although the term pharmaceutical market has often been used, there are, in fact, several pharmaceutical markets, each with its own set of Prices and pricing methods. There are retail, hospital, and managed care markets; branded and Generic markets; and chronic and acute markets. Each is approached somewhat differently.

It is important to define some common terms used in pharmaceutical pricing before we examine these various markets.

Important Terms in Pharmaceutical Pricing

As with all specialized areas, pharmaceutical pricing has its own vocabulary, complete with acronyms. Here is a list of common pharmaceutical pricing terms and their definitions.

Actual Acquisition Cost (AAC). Retail Pharmacy reimbursement arrangements are often based on the AWP (see below) plus a fee. Knowing that retailers no longer pay the published AWP for prescription Drugs, many payers attempted to reduce the reimbursement by discounting the AWP by 5% to as much as 20%. Because this system penalizes the pharmacies that are unable to secure significant discounts from wholesalers, some payers have instituted a payment schedule on the basis of AAC plus a fee. Billing complexities and schemes, however, make it difficult to ascertain the AAC.

Average Wholesale Price (AWP). Neither an average Price nor a Price charged by wholesalers, this figure is a vestige of earlier times. Few, if any, wholesalers even consider AWP today when pricing their prescription products. It is, however, commonly used by retailers and others who dispense medications as the basis for many pricing decisions. Due to its availability from many sources, the AWP is often used as a surrogate for actual Prices when studying prescription Price trends.

Direct Price. The Price paid by retailers, before discounts, for products from those manufacturers who sell directly to non-wholesale accounts such as retailers, hospitals, private practice physicians, and Public Health clinics is called the direct Price.

MAC. MAC is the maximum allowable cost which is the federally set reimbursement rate for Generic Drugs used in Medicare and Medicaid. Many other players use MAC systems as well.

OBRA 90. The Omnibus Budget Reconciliation Act of 1990, a law drafted by the Senate Committee on Aging, required manufacturers to pay rebates to state and federal Governments for products used by Medicaid recipients.

Rebate. A rebate is a retroactive discount that is paid to a customer after that customer has purchased the product from a wholesaler or retailer. The rebate allows the manufacturer to offer a lower Price to some customers without taking on the burden of special distribution.

What Is a Pharmaceutical Price?

Although it might appear otherwise, given the number of sources of Drug pricing information, comparing or computing the Prices of Drugs is not straightforward. Differences in the manner in which various Prices are set and used render many comparisons virtually meaningless.

Different Prices are charged to and by different members of the distribution channels used for pharmaceuticals. Some Prices are set using traditional methods, while others are set according to competitive conditions. Even within the same Pharmacy, several different pricing methods will be used, depending on a number of factors. Figure 15.1 outlines typical approaches to pricing both branded and Generic products in a retail Pharmacy. These and other retail pricing tactics are discussed below. In the hospital setting, different rules and methods are used. The flow of Prices within hospitals is presented in Figure 15.2.

As Figures 15.1 and 15.2 demonstrate, the Price of a pharmaceutical product depends on a number of factors. Prices and costs of drugs vary on many levels and depend upon factors such as the location of drug administration, the relative commercial success of the agent, and the type of manufacturer supplying the drug, to name just a few.

AWP

The AWP is the most common figure used for Drug Price comparisons. This figure is a vestige of a drug distribution system that disappeared in the early 1980s. Until the early 1980s, there were several hundred small, independent Drug wholesalers, each operating regionally. Due to the inefficiencies of such a fragmented system, the operating costs were quite high. The average markup above cost by wholesalers to their retail customers (primarily pharmacies) was 20% to 25%, depending on the manufacturer.

While most pharmaceutical manufacturers used a wholesaler-only method of distribution to the retail class of trade, a significant number of large firms, including Upjohn, Merck, and Squibb, had invested in their own distribution networks and preferred direct sales over the use of wholesalers. By convention, wholesalers added 20% to the Price of products from companies following a wholesaler-only Policy while adding 25% to the Prices of products from those companies who chose to "compete" with the wholesalers.

Wholesalers have two different methods of pricing to the retailers: AWP minus and cost plus. As the names imply, one method begins with the published AWP while the other ignores this figure. In recent years, cost-plus pricing has become the norm for most wholesalers.

Figure 15.1

Ex-Factory Price (Wholesaler Cost) → Wholesaler Price (Retailer Cost) → Retail Price (Patient/Payer Cost)

Branded Pharmaceutical

Ex-Factory Price (Wholesaler Cost) → Wholesaler Price (Retailer Cost) → Retail Price (Patient/Payer Cost)

$10 less cash discount (2%) → "Cost" ($10) + 2% to 5% → "Cost" (AWP, $12) + fee = $17

Generic Pharmaceutical

Ex-Factory Price (Wholesaler Cost) → Wholesaler Price (Retailer Cost) → Retail Price (Patient/Payer Cost)

$1 less cash discount (2%) → "Cost" ($1) + 2% to 5% → "Cost" (AWP, $3) + fee = $8

Or

$1 less cash discount (2%) → "Cost" ($1) + 2% to 5% → Brand Price less 30% = $11.90

Figure 15.1 Flow of Price for a retail-dispensed outpatient Drug.

Figure 15.2

Ex-Factory Price (Wholesaler Cost) → Discount ("Chargeback") (Hospital Cost) → Hospital Price (Patient/Payer Cost)

Branded Pharmaceutical

Ex-Factory Price (Wholesaler Cost) → "Chargeback" (Hospital Cost) → Hospital Price (Patient/Payer Cost)

$10/100 doses, less cash discount (2%) "Cost" → ($10)-$2 "Chargeback" → Fixed Charge per dose $2.25 x 100 = $225

Generic Pharmaceutical

Ex-Factory Price (Wholesaler Cost) → Wholesaler Price (Hospital Cost) → Hospital Price (Patient/Payer Cost)

$10/100 doses, less cash discount (2%) → "Cost" ($10) → Fixed Charge per dose $2.25 x 100 = $225

Figure 15.2 Examples of the flow of Price for a hospital-dispensed Drug.

Price reporting services, however, still rely upon the AWP because, until recently, many companies published only that figure (often called the "suggested price to pharmacy"). The AWP, while not the cost paid by retailers, still provides the basis for much retail pricing, with retailers euphemistically referring to the difference between their actual cost and the AWP as "earned discount".

This situation is more pronounced with Generic Drugs. Many Generic companies have taken advantage of this use of AWP by substantially inflating their published AWPs. This system allows a retailer to acquire a Drug

Table 15.1 The Difference between Costs and AWP for Packages of 100 Tablets

Product	Ex-Factory Price	AWP	Percentage Difference (%)
Tylenol	25.93	31.13	20
Mutual acetaminophen w/codeine 300-30	3.94	10.00	174
Tagamet 300 mg	77.36	96.70	20
URL Cimetidine 300 mg	29.93	76.40	155
Xanax 0.5 mg	61.86	77.66	25
URL Alprazolam 0.5 mg	4.81	61.12	1,168

Source of data: Medispan Price-Check Data Base, February 1996.

at a low cost ($2.50 per 100 tablets, for example) while relying on a published AWP ($20.00 or more) for its own pricing. It is not uncommon that the $25.00 retail Price for a Generic Drug renders a gross profit well above $20.00 for the retailer. It is also common for the AWP of a Generic product to remain stable while the actual selling Price declines.

Table 15.1 shows the wide disparity between actual selling Prices and published AWP's for several pharmaceutical products. It is obvious that AWP is not an accurate measure of the Prices manufacturers charge.

Price Decision-Making

Pricing decisions are reached in a number of ways, using a varied range of considerations, types of information, and internal processes. Each pricing decision is unique, depending on the company, the medication, and the external factors that affect both. In this section, the factors that should be considered when making pricing decisions are discussed. There is no one "best" or "right" manner in which to set Prices, but there are a group of considerations and processes that appear to offer a company the best chance of making informed pricing decisions.

Key Factors in the Pricing Decision

The pharmaceutical pricing question most frequently asked by those observing (or criticizing) the pharmaceutical industry is: How are Drug Prices set?

Many self-proclaimed experts have offered answers to this question, usually armed with summaries of financial statements that document the way in which pharmaceutical companies spend their revenues. This financial information is not, in fact, related to the pricing of a new medication. Attempts to reduce the pricing process to a simple formula not only are misleading but also reflect an absolute lack of knowledge about the pricing of medicines.

It is unlikely that any two pharmaceutical companies set Prices using the same thought processes – or even consider the same issues when establishing a Price. Moreover, it is unlikely that a single company would Price any two different products in the same way, given differences in markets, timing, market entry dynamics, and other environmental factors. This lack of singularity, which critics may question, is actually quite appropriate. No two companies have exactly the same needs, philosophies, or resources, and no two separate products will be marketed using precisely the same strategy, even if sold by the same company. These basic differences demand different pricing criteria and different Prices.

The pricing of pharmaceutical products, as with the pricing of any product or service, should be market based. Contrary to the widely held notion that pricing is simply a matter of adding up costs and establish a markup, pricing experts agree that costs help establish a Price floor but the market provides most of the information for the pricing decision. As competition within pharmaceutical markets, especially Price-related competition, heats up, the need for market-based pricing will continue to grow.

There are some general rules, or considerations, that should be included in every pharmaceutical pricing decision. These factors, presented in Table 15.2, must be addressed, either formally through adherence to a company Policy or informally by a product manager or other individual charged with developing

Table 15.2 General Factors to Consider When Setting a Pharmaceutical Price

1. The Prices, product features, and past actions of the competition
2. Specific patient characteristics
3. The economic and social value of the therapy itself
4. The decision-making criteria of prescribers and those who influence that decision
5. Characteristics of the disease treated by the medication
6. Company needs, in terms of market position, revenue, and other issues
7. Company abilities, including available budgets and willingness to support the product
8. The current and anticipated environment for insurance reimbursement
9. The Public Policy environment

a pricing recommendation. The failure to address these factors can contribute to many pricing missteps in pharmaceutical markets.

Competition

The importance of competitive analysis in pricing cannot be overstated. It has been suggested by many researchers that the pricing and presence of competitors, together with the uniqueness or therapeutic value of the new product, are the major determinants of launch Prices. Reekie, in his manuscript "Pricing New Pharmaceutical Products", found that the Price levels of current competitors and the anticipation of future competitors were the driving factors in setting Prices for pharmaceuticals (729). New entrants that offered significant benefits over current competitors were consistently priced above the prevailing Prices in the therapeutic class. Those products offering little or no therapeutic advantage tended to be priced at or below prevailing levels.

An interesting finding of Reekie's study, however, was that, even for unique products offering improvements, those that had close or superior competitors entering the market within 2 years of their launch tended to be priced lower than those that anticipated little or no competition from new products in the near future. The general rule can be seen graphically in Figure 15.3. The rule portrayed in Figure 15:4 is a simple application of the three basic pricing strategies:

These strategies also depend on other factors, such as the needs and abilities of the company, the sensitivity of the specific market segment to Price levels, and the therapeutic value of the product itself. Thus, the considerations presented here are not discrete entities to be considered separately, but a complex system that must be evaluated as a whole.

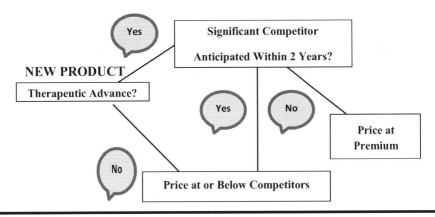

Figure 15.3 Competitive considerations in pricing.

Skimming. The product, anticipating little direct completion, is priced above prevailing levels to maximize profits.

Parity. The product is viewed internally as being little or no different from current competitors and is priced equivalent to the prevailing levels.

Penetration. A product is viewed as equal to or slightly inferior to current or anticipated offerings and is priced below prevailing levels in hopes of gaining market share with its low price or of erecting a barrier to entry for anticipated future competitors.

Figure 15.4 Reekie's three basic pricing strategies.

Patient Characteristics

Although in many markets the patient bears no direct financial burden, this is not the case in all markets. In markets without universal coverage for pharmaceuticals, the patients who will be the final users of a new agent must be considered in the pricing decision. This is especially important for the elderly on fixed incomes.

Such considerations are not simply altruism, although there is room for compassion in every strategy. The fact is, patients who are unable to afford a medication will often not take it. Compliance, both with the daily dosing and the length of therapy, is a growing concern and a source of significant unrealized revenue. It is not uncommon for 50% of patients prescribed a medication for a chronic disorder that is relatively asymptomatic to drop out in the first year. How much of this is due to failure to understand the importance of compliance versus inability to afford the medication is not yet known, but if a significant proportion of this can be eliminated with a lower Price, the product may earn more with a lower Price than a higher one.

Some patient groups, such as AARP, are highly organized and able to exert political and economic pressure on a company. The areas of mental Health, Parkinson's disease, HIV, and cancer all have active support groups that are playing a growing role in therapy selection. The degree of patient involvement in therapy decisions appears to be growing across most major therapeutic categories, and the market power of these groups must play an ever-growing role in pricing decisions.

Given the focus on and need for Health Care reform and cost containment, an agent that can deliver documented cost savings should (in ideal circumstances) be well received. But one must look to other issues as well to assure the acceptance of this argument. The reimbursement and Public Policy environments will both affect this.

The Decision-Making Process

The specific decision maker for the use of the agent plays a large role in the effectiveness of any pricing approach. Products that will be used primarily on an in-patient basis will be subjected to significant Price scrutiny, as the institutional market is, perhaps, the most Price sensitive single pharmaceutical market. Because of the influence of multiple decision makers, including Pharmacy directors and hospital administrators, the cost of any new agent will be considered carefully before the agent is adopted. Several studies have shown that clinical pharmacists, through various outreach and educational efforts, can bring about a significant change in physician prescribing behavior. That pharmacists can – and do – intervene in and influence the prescribing decision, then, is well established. Their potential role in the use of a new product must be seriously considered.

Primary care physicians are often more risk averse than their specialized colleagues and are unlikely to adopt a new medication as rapidly as a neurologist or a cardiologist (730). New agents whose use will be limited to specialists are unlikely to come under any Price scrutiny by the prescriber, since specialists tend to be less concerned with (or aware of) the costs of the treatments they order. It stands to reason that they would be likely to receive feedback on Drug costs from patients than primary care physicians, who see patients more regularly and are more likely to operate under systems that force them to bear (or share) the costs of their decisions.

Disease Characteristics

The characteristics of the disease itself can provide some of the most valuable guidance in establishing a pricing strategy. Experience shows that disorders of an acute nature, such as minor infectious diseases and pain due to injury, tend not to be accompanied by Price sensitivity. Patients receiving a prescription for an antibiotic or analgesic usually receive no refills and often do not follow-up with the physician. This appears to hold true even in situations where the patient pays the full cost of the prescription.

Research indicates that there could be an additional dimension in this – that of the symptoms of the disease. Physicians appear to overestimate the cost of medications that treat chronic, asymptomatic diseases, such as hypertension, and to underestimate the cost of medications that treat more symptomatic disorders such as arthritis and acute infections. It has been postulated that this is due to the type of patient feedback the physician receives. Thus, it is likely that the prescriber will overestimate the cost of your product if it treats a relatively asymptomatic chronic disorder and generates a large amount of negative feedback (731).

Company Needs

While the cost of goods and company-established minimum selling margins play a role in the establishment of a Price floor, other company-specific issues must also be addressed. New research investment or activities that are expected to require significant amounts of funding might well necessitate the charging of a higher Price for agents about to be launched, providing the higher Price would not negatively affect the sales of the product.

Conversely, a new agent may be seen as simply providing the company with experience in a therapeutic category prior to the introduction of an agent that is felt to be superior some years later. In this case, a low-price strategy on an agent without significant advantages could allow the company to develop this experience and important relationships with prescribers and key thought leaders in this market.

Company Abilities

The ability and willingness of the company to support the pricing strategy must always be considered. A high Price in a sensitive market requires significant resources by way of economic studies and, often, senior management time to alleviate much of the Price resistance. Similarly, a low-priced strategy in an outpatient market is likely to cost more in promotional expenses than parity pricing if the strategy is to be successful. This is because physicians, as previously mentioned, tend not to respond to low-priced appeals. A successful low-priced approach requires significant promotional expenditures to saturate the market with the message that the product is less costly and to induce physicians to consider cost.

Prescribing physicians do not actively seek out price information and often do not respond to low prices even when they are aware of them. A penetration strategy requires greater promotional coverage and more creative selling messages to instill a sense of economic responsibility (or guilt) in prescribers than the approach of simply charging whatever the competition charges.

Whether the company chooses a price that is significantly above or below the prevailing Prices in the market, top management must be willing to spend the time and the money necessary to support the pricing strategy.

Public Policy Considerations

Last, but certainly not least, is the Public Policy environment. In the foreseeable future, a company must consider the responses and actions of Government officials and patient advocates when setting a Price. Criticism by one of these individuals, no matter how unfounded, can result in severe limits on the potential success of a new Drug. Once a working Price has been developed for a new agent, if there is potential for it to be brought to the attention of a highly placed critic by a constituent or other individual, the company must investigate ways to avoid the problem or be prepared to address the issue directly with the critic.

These factors and issues will affect every new pricing decision made. Figure 15.5 provides a summary of these issues in schematic form, with the final Price at the center of the chart. Note that the Public Policy environment surrounds the other considerations. It must be a major consideration in every pharmaceutical pricing decision (732).

The Value of Pharmaceuticals

The main impediment to the appropriate and equitable pricing of pharmaceuticals lies in society's lack of acknowledgment of the value of pharmaceuticals, both in the macro sense – the financial savings gained through the use

PUBLIC POLICY		
Competiton	Disease Characteristics	Value of Therapy
Prescriber Decision Making	PRICE	Patient Characteristics
Company Needs	Reimbursement Environment	Company Abilities
PUBLIC POLICY		

Figure 15.5   **Pricing considerations for new pharmaceuticals.**

of pharmaceutical products as a whole – and from a micro perspective – the financial and patient-specific benefits from the appropriate use of many, if not most, new Drugs. Part of the problem lies in the failure of society to take a system-wide view when evaluating Health Care, part in the long-term demonization of the pharmaceutical industry by critics, and a great deal in the industry itself.

The first two issues are self-explanatory; the third, and by far the most damaging, issue requires some discussion. Most pharmaceutical companies have actively worked in ways that devalue pharmaceutical products. The companies' own conduct has reduced the value of medications in the eyes of customers and society at large. For the past several years, Prices in pharmaceutical markets have gone in two directions: increasing or holding firm in outpatient, cash-based markets and charging lower Prices in hospital, and managed care markets. Although these lower Prices are in response to perceived market demands and are often accompanied by well-reasoned strategies for the discounts, Public knowledge of these multi-tiered Prices has brought many to question the appropriateness and equity of the non-discounted Prices. Regardless of the legality of multiple Price levels, which has been upheld time and again, two observations must be made:

1. There is little evidence that the deep discounting associated with managed care contracts has substantially affected the use of pharmaceutical products. In most therapeutic areas, the market share for individual products is the same in managed care markets as in cash markets.
2. The act of discounting, especially at some of the levels reported, signals (rightly and wrongly) that the company is willing to accept less for its product than it charges those who do not benefit from discounts. This is interpreted as over-charging.

Pharmaceutical firms must consider the financial and political consequences of pricing decisions and recognize that the granting of discounts is a pricing decision that cannot be made without careful consideration of the effect of those discounts on all aspects of the business. Firms must work to rationalize and manage all pricing activities while simultaneously working with Public officials to recognize the value of pharmaceuticals as a cost control tool. I am afraid, however, that this value will not be acknowledged as long as perceptions of unfair pricing, brought on by wide Price ranges (and Public criticism – Author's note), continue to exist.

> (**Author's note:** *It is not possible to include in the space available all of the concepts and techniques which Kolassa offers in his two books cited at the outset. His chapter on the role of Price in Decision Making by Prescribers, Patients and Third Parties is particularly compelling as is his chapter relating Price to Value. In the remainder of Chapter 17, Kolassa provides some cogent views on the future of drug pricing.*)

The Future of Pharmaceutical Pricing

> The [pharmaceutical] industry has not been successful in halting the attacks, but on the other hand the attacks to date have not had much effect on the industry in terms of lessened prices or profits, or changes in operational procedures. Whether this stand-off can continue under current conditions and for how long is of course the dominant issue at hand.
>
> – *George Squibb*

There is an old Arabic saying: "He who tells the future, even when correct, lies". Therein dwells the danger of prognostication. A reading of George Squibb's 1969 Book chapter (733), quoted above, would have led many to believe that the end was near for the pharmaceutical industry. Fortunately, for all of us, it is still here. But when, if ever, will the doomsayers' predictions come true? Twenty years ago, there were predictions that, in the very near future, MCOs would dictate virtually 100% of pharmaceutical product use, and they would use only the cheapest product. So what's happened? The principal result of managed care's entry into the US Health Care system was the dramatic increase in the use (and sales) of prescription medicines. According to J.D. Kleinke, noted Health economist and entrepreneur, "One of the hallmarks of managed care in the United States has been the deliberately liberalized use of pharmaceuticals" (734). A funny thing happened on the way to the future.

Still, change is inevitable. Some changes in the pricing environment have taken place, and more will certainly occur. The advent of the Medicare Part

D benefit has resulted in deep discounts to secure formulary placement, widening further the gap between list Prices and actual selling Prices. As I write this, the gap between list Prices and selling Prices is the subject of litigation at both the State and federal levels. The most certain result will be the end of the AWP ... and good riddance! Outside the United States, we see that Germany has implemented reference pricing for several classes of Drugs, Canada has used pharmacoeconomic arguments to deny reimbursement of many new agents, and the French and Japanese pricing authorities have forced Price cuts and rebates for most Drugs. In the United States, we see that the cost of some new cancer agents has shot past $100,000 for a course of therapy. These are all major changes, coming from several different directions.

The pharmaceutical industry has done little of consequence in response to these and other changes. Prices are still often set based on the results of faulty assumptions and flawed marketing research. They are managed with little regard for the long-term future of the company, and they are defended with the same arguments that haven't worked for years. Fortunately for the industry, thus far, the changes and challenges have been minor, and rich research pipelines are still rewarded. But what new issues might change that?

Ten years ago, when the first edition of my Book was published, the prognostications I made were minor and almost inevitable. I predicted further consolidation of buyers, a narrowing of international Price ranges, greater use of low Price as a selling point, and continued demands for discounts. The one prediction that was only partially realized was the broadened use of pharmacoeconomics. In the mid-1990s, the industry was abuzz over the prospect that pharmacoeconomics might help us identify, and justify, the right Price for our products. For the most part, that has not occurred, despite the industry's substantial investment in pharmacoeconomics.

The response of participants in the U.S market to pharmacoeconomics hasn't changed much since then. Pharmacoeconomics is still not trusted or relied upon, especially if the companies themselves perform or sponsor the studies. Some foreign pricing authorities use pharmacoeconomics to justify their decisions not to cover new agents, and some costly products have been able to support their Prices with economic data. Still, pharmacoeconomics has not proved to be the panacea many had predicted, unlocking the door to more profitable and value-oriented pricing. In fact, it is often used to slam the profit door shut by internal decision makers who believe they can sell product only with lower Prices.

Part of the problem is the rigidity that has emerged among marketers, especially their insistence on the almost exclusive use of cost–utility analysis which, despite its inconsistencies and acknowledged flaws, has become the industry standard. This rigidity may make pharmacoeconomics easier, but it violates the very economic principles upon which the field was founded. The result is a lot of studies that have little practical use in the marketplace. As a noted economist recently said to me, "Pharmacoeconomics is like teenage sex. Everybody is doing it but nobody is doing it very well". This does not mean that pharmacoeconomics isn't useful or even necessary, but that, in its current form, has failed to address the very issues it was designed to resolve.

The $100,000 Prisoner's Dilemma

Perhaps the biggest question about pharmaceutical Prices now and in the foreseeable future is "How much higher can they go"? With new cancer therapies offering a few months of additional survival at a six-figure cost, many believe that it is only a matter of time before the Government somehow intervenes and forces those Prices lower. No one in the industry wants to see this happen, although many of its critics would be thrilled. The problem seems to be intractable because of game theory's classical Prisoner's Dilemma. In the Prisoner's Dilemma, two "prisoners" must decide whether to "betray" the other and escape punishment or "trust" the other's loyalty, refuse to talk, and be equally punished. You win only if you betray and the other player trusts. If the other player betrays too, you're both worse off. The best outcome is actually for each to "trust" the other; you both get punished but not as much. The dilemma is this: how do you know what the other player will do? Will he trust and pursue the greater "common good"? Or will he betray and tend to his own needs? Will individual pharmaceutical companies, in the face of potential Government Regulation, forego a large amount of individual potential profit so that all can continue to enjoy moderate profit? Or will one company "betray" the rest, opting for the big profits and thereby triggering a payer reaction? There is every reason for the industry to show restraint in pricing, because the consequences of Government intervention would be devastating. At the same time, an individual firm that chooses to forego the revenue and profits that can be earned through Prices of this magnitude may arguably be failing in its obligations to stockholders. It will certainly be depriving its own research pipeline, which is the future of every firm.

And would the Government intervene? There will probably be a lot of jawboning at high levels that are the equivalent of firing a shot across the bow of Pharma, but, in the end, the response in the United States will probably be through market mechanisms, rather than regulatory action. As we have seen in several non-U.S. markets, the best way to rein in Prices of this magnitude is to refuse to reimburse. When individual payers in the United States believe the Price is not reasonable, they can and will react by refusing to reimburse.

Payers are currently attempting to develop control mechanisms for high-cost products. The most common approach now is through patient cost sharing. A very high proportion of the Medicare Part D Prescription Drug Plan (PDP) formularies relegate high-cost biologicals and other categories to their fourth tier of coverage, requiring patient co-insurance of 20%–40%. It is through this mechanism, in all likelihood, that those Prices will eventually be brought down. These same methods will continue to be used for traditional pharmaceuticals as well.

This means that companies must pay much more attention to the management of their Prices in the long term. They must stop pricing products in isolation (both from other products and from the rest of the market). They must see past what happens at launch. Currently, most firms have a "strategic pricing department" that recommends list Prices and an account management or "managed markets" department that handles day-to-day pricing. There is often little in the way of continuity from "strategic pricing" to "strategic contracting," and the result tends to be wide Price variation or a single-minded "no discounts" approach to pricing. Although each of these is a legitimate choice in some cases, no firm is served well by holding to only a single approach.

Pricing is a process, not an event, and firms that fail to provide the attention and resources to pricing are costing themselves dearly. Pricing departments that report somewhere in the marketing services area of the firm tend to have no authority and only limited credibility and, thus are not very effective. Those firms with pricing departments that report through their managed markets operations do not fare much better, because these operations are usually advocates for the customer and not the corporation. This is not a criticism of the personnel within managed market operations, but a candid reflection on their orientation and the job they are expected to do – which is not the job of pricing. The pricing function must serve a different role, which it cannot accomplish if the compensation and evaluation of pricing personnel is determined by managers whose job it is to keep customers happy.

Someday most firms will realize that, while pricing strategies are really hard to develop, they're also really important. Managing Prices is at least as important as managing volume, cost, and the myriad other business aspects to which firms dedicate untold resources. The basic equation of PRICE – COST X VOLUME=PROFIT holds true, and price is the most powerful profit lever a firm can manage. Unfortunately, most firms have chosen to focus their attention on other aspects of the business and accept Prices or pricing situations that are imposed by the market.

The future of pharmaceutical pricing is in the hands of the industry, as it always has been. If firms elect to continue their current practices, it is highly likely that Prices will continue to be controversial and will be driven ever lower. If firms choose to manage their Prices, the results will be different. Therefore, I have one prediction: The future of pharmaceutical pricing will be whatever the pharmaceutical industry allows it to be, through the actions and inactions of individual firms.

Chapter 16

Summary, Ruminations, and Apologia

Introduction

At the outset, I warned you, the Reader, that this is a *history*. It is the nature of Book publishing that there will have been changes even in the few months between submission of the manuscript and actual publication. This is especially true for the subject matter at hand. During that period, there will have been a Presidential election. New members of Congress will begin their tenure. Mergers and acquisitions will have continued to change the players in Big Pharma. There may even be yet another new FDA Commissioner. And, finally, the People will include thousands of immigrants struggling to assimilate themselves into a Health Care system which is "foreign" to them.

I attempt in this chapter to describe the present as regards to the subjects covered in the preceding chapters. Certainly the Dynamic Tension (Dis – Ease) will continue. And there are a few trends and "what ifs" which I believe are worth noting.

About the "Four P's". They continue to serve as a convenient framework for examining Big Pharma. Unquestionably, new products continue to be discovered and developed. Perhaps we are in the threshold of real progress in areas such as Alzheimer's disease and cancer.

The pressure on Drug Prices continues apace. A variety of solutions have been proposed, but any kind of consensus is still elusive. A Lower Drug Costs Now Act proposed in Congress in late 2019 would expose 250 of the costliest Drugs to actual Price controls. (*Wall Street Journal*, December 12, 2019) The ever-present concern about "Drug Lag" continues to be a theme in almost Jesuitical confrontations.

Place, as we have seen, has been subject to some modification. Mail-order prescriptions continue to grow as a factor and "Specialty" Drugs tend not to be a good fit in traditional distribution channels.

There continues to be pressure on the Promotion efforts of Big Pharma. There is evidence that "detailing" faces special difficulties as electronic media has had a major impact on information flows. This is true of the print media as well. While DTC Promotion of legend Drugs continues, both Big Pharma and FDA also continue to struggle to find common ground.

There are "More P's". The expansion of the number and types of Prescribers has continued. Prescribing is no longer the sole province of physicians. The nature of Pharmacy practice in a variety of settings continues to evolve. There may be pressure of some kind on patents, perhaps a change in effective patent life. No one has loudly espoused an excess Profits tax, but the interplay among Prices, profits, and taxes continues to make anything liable to consideration.

Most of the notable Investigators of the past are no longer with us, but the Investigations continue. At present, they do not achieve the notoriety they once did, but the Nation is struggling with other, different issues which tend to overwhelm the news.

Legislation continues to be proposed but so far nothing of the scope and impact of Durham–Humphrey, Waxman–Hatch, or Kefauver. To date, no member of Congress has emerged as a legislative leader in the Drug field.

The FDA prevails in its role of consumer protector. New challenges appear daily as a result of changes in technology and the explosion of "biotechnology". The FDA will have to continue to adapt to all of these Regulatory needs.

Non-Government Influencers can best be described as a growth industry. Third-party payers, unions, and especially pharmaceutical benefits managers (PBMS) have now enormous power over which prescription medicines their constituents receive or at least those for which they will pay. Their negotiating power will almost certainly increase. They are a major factor in the growth of mail-order prescriptions and exert a great deal of influence on Legislation and Regulation.

The People. Newton Minow, then FCC Chairman, in 1961, famously described television in the early days as a "vast wasteland". Certainly that wasteland has become even vaster. My own, very rudimentary cable service offers me more than 150 channels including such intellectually stimulating as one given entirely to practical jokes, a variety of "courtroom dramas", as well as a plethora of "re-runs", the latter providing evidence of desire for not just nostalgia but also, for many, a welcome change from the violence and questionable taste of contemporary programming.

A new "wasteland" has been provided by electronic media, especially social media. OMG – there is no limit to the power of these channels of instant communication. One can learn just how many "likes" there are for a given message. The magnitude of the influence of these media on opinion and behaviors has yet to be a plumbed – and probably cannot be.

The potential for good of the electronic media in encouraging rational Drug therapy is enormous. There is, of course, Public Broadcasting, C-Span, and the news channels. The value of these and other (one hopes) unbiased sources of valuable information depends, of course, on the choice of the viewer/user when a re-run of MASH is simultaneously available.

Big Pharma's response to the toxic environment in which they find themselves doesn't seem to have evolved much. Commercials that emphasize the dedication and success of "America's Biotechnology Companies" still emphasize the dedication to better Health and the real and potential "breakthroughs". Little or nothing is offered to explain the "high prices". Why does it cost so much to develop and market one of these "breakthroughs"? What is the meaning of a QUALY (which the *Wall Street Journal* described in November, 2019, as an "Obscure Model") to the patient? This is a powerful explanatory tool, easily understood, if properly explained, to an intelligent lay person.

The origins (Whence) of existing Drugs and the exciting future potential using genetics, genome technology, and a variety of new forms of Drug delivery in the body all make for fascinating and hopeful stories. Certainly immortality is too large a story to contemplate, but limiting the process of aging resonates with millions of the elderly or about-to-be elderly.

Finally, there are the Pharmacoeconomic studies necessary to resolve or at least ameliorate the Drug Price problem. After all "Drug Prices are too damn too high". Or are they?

The bad news is that the Dis-Ease in the Book title is almost certainly incurable. The question then becomes, just as in the case of incurable "diseases", what is available to offer remission (even temporary) or palliation? Can social, political, and economic equivalents of analgesics, anti-anxiety agents, and such, ease the Dis-Ease or at least retard its progression? Certainly many remedies have been tried. A few even qualify as "breakthroughs". The hope is, of course, that the Dynamic Tension – Dis-Ease will result in what the redoubtable Charles Atlas promised – all of the muscles get stronger.

Ruminations

This final chapter is an obvious place for the Author and (he hopes) the Reader to ruminate. There is a variety of sources to assist in the process.

- From Physics – "For every action there is an equal and opposite reaction".
- Or the more pedestrian – "Pull the blanket over your head and your feet stick out".
- More hopeful, surprisingly from Oscar Wilde, "We are all of us in the gutter, but some of us are looking at stars".
- From the cynics – "Seeing a code of ethics on the wall is like using a condom. It gives you a feeling of security while you're getting screwed".

In an effort to provide the Reader some rumination material, I offer a few Trends and What Ifs.

Trends

As Paul Starr wrote, "A trend is not necessarily fate". So don't read these as *predictions*:

- Pressure on Drug Prices, just will not go away.
- Continued development of non-drug therapies, such as biologicals.
- Continued international involvement on Prices in Drug R&D.
- Changes in nature and impact of various forms of Promotion, especially detailing which shows a decline in prescriber acceptance.
- Various evolutionary changes in the nature and kinds of Pharmacy practice.
- Vigorous activity in the area of mergers and acquisitions resulting in further blurring of identity of Big Pharma and decline in the cohesiveness of the industry. *Fierce Pharma,* (December 10, 2019), says some M & A deals (BayerMonsanto, Teva/Allegan) were "bad deals".

- Drug shortages as companies drop unprofitable products. Mylan, for example, dropped 350 products from their line citing "no business rationale" for keeping them but predicting no effect on profits. The November 1, 2019 edition of the *Wall Street Journal* reports more than 250 Drugs were in short supply.
- New legislative proposals in Drug Prices era. POTUS offered and ultimately withdrew two. Speaker Pelosi proposed a "fine" for failing to negotiate on Medicare Drug Prices. Presidential candidate Warren's "End Taxpayer Subsidies for Drug Ads Act" would eliminate tax deductions for Drug marketing expenses. PhRMA resists.
- DTC advertisers continue to find loopholes in Fair Balance requirements, referring viewers to websites or "our ad in SCUBA Digest".
- Some companies "giving up", for example, Pfizer "stopped searching for drugs to treat Alzheimer's disease and Parkinson's disease, areas that have challenged the industry", (*Wall Street Journal,* October 30, 2019).
- Various Regulations have unintended consequences as complicated and "patch-work" pricing policies actually hurt small clinics and hospitals which they were intended to help. An article by David Henderson and Charles Hooper in the *Wall Street Journal* on January 1, 2019, says "Companies that cannot effectively Price and promote their products sometimes decide not to make them in the first place". They note that such shortages resulted in the Federal Aeronautics Association (FAA) exempting airlines from having to carry five key Drugs. They quote one airline safety expert: "To think you could fly without epinephrine is crazy".
- Changes in Medical School curricula. According to Goldfarb in the *Wall Street Journal* on August 18, 2018, medical schools are increasingly focused on social justice rather than treating illness. He opines that, "If this country needs more gun control and climate change advocates, medical schools are not the right place to produce them".
- The number of "fast track" Drugs is increasing as stated by Peter Loftus in the *Wall Street Journal* on July 8, 2019. This is especially true for conditions in which the seriously ill patient has "run out of options". Loftus cites several examples of Drug approvals with less than usual proof of efficacy.
- Companies, often as a result of mergers/acquisitions, change their names: Abbvie (Abbott/Life), (Mylan/Viatris).
- Drug Prices continue to rise. According to *MMM Digest*, January 3, 2020, more than 300 Drug Prices were increased at the beginning of 2020. Most of the increases were in the 4%–6% range.

- Declining influence of detailers. *Fierce Pharma* (October 4, 2019) reports that nearly 50% of doctors get most of their Drug information online and nearly 40% don't see detailers at all.
- Biologic Drugs have been described by Scott Gottlieb, a former FDA Commissioner, as "one of the centuries' greatest medical triumphs", (*Wall Street Journal*, August 26, 2019). He saw increasing familiarity with these products among prescribers and easier development of "biosimilars" (read Generics).
- There will continue to be "blockbusters". Angus Liu (*Fierce Pharma*, February 11, 2020) identified 11 Drugs in the pipeline, which he predicted to have sales of $1 billion by 2024. They included two Drugs for Type 2 diabetes and two for multiple sclerosis.
- Some grocers seem to be disenchanted with in-store pharmacies (*Wall Street Journal*, January 27, 2020). Kroger is the exception, citing more grocery spending by Pharmacy patrons.
- Some companies are using electronic medical records ("data mining") in lieu of, or in addition to, clinical trials to speed up FDA approval. FDA has approved new uses for some cancer Drugs based on such data.

Immortality

In the recent incredible Book, *After Shock*, Dr. Sanjiv Chopra wrote: "Every statement about the future ought, by rights, be accompanied by a string of qualifiers – ifs, ands, buts, and on the other hands". The Book will fill you with either hope or dread.

I strongly recommend two Books by Yuval Harari: *Sapiens* (488) and *Homo Deus* (492), which are best read in sequence. Combined, they present both a history of, and future, for mankind. Notable in the context of this Book are his explorations of a life expectancy of 150 years and the potential social consequences. The dramatic extension of life, he predicts, will not be Drug related but the result of other technologies. Drugs, he predicts, will be used far less as medicines than as kinds of life enhancement during those extended years, and he describes the ethical dilemmas which they will present. Also recommended is Chip Walter's *Immortality, Inc.* (549).

Slow or Stop the Aging Process

Johnathan Swift observed that, "every man deserves to live long, but no man would be old". A *Wall Street Journal* article dated October 26, 2019, cites the emerging field of epigenetics as the possible solution to aging, which they call, "the mother of all diseases".

What if a truly safe and effective treatment of memory loss is discovered for treatment in Alzheimer's disease? It takes little imagination to see a temptation for "normal" people to want to use it. With what consequences? (The Author tried a bottle of the widely advertised memory enhancer, Prevagen, described as being found in jelly fish. The only memories it evoked were a variety of sea life. Whew! Sharks!)

A Council on Drug Policy

What if, and this may fall into the category of the White Queen's comment to the wondering Alice, "Sometimes I've believed as many as six impossible things before breakfast". Is it a Wonderland idea to imagine the creation of – let's call it a Council on Drug Policy? Such a Council could serve as a sort of arbitration body to resolve areas of Dynamic Tension – Dis-Ease between Big Pharma and the Government to the ultimate benefit of the People.

My Council would be knowledgeable, disinterested but not uninterested, impartial, practical, and clever. They would not be political appointees, politicians, or Drug industry executives, although such people could serve as resources. The ultimate advocacy group! The Council deliberations would be similar to those described in Chapter 3 but without the political biases in testimony, witness selection, and Press manipulation which so often characterizes Congressional Hearings.

The Council would seek positive and practical solutions, not simply more Regulations.

Other What Ifs

What if Pharmacogenetics realizes its current promise? The potential for pharmacogenetics to revolutionize personalized medicine seems undeniable. Pharmacogenetics is a great opportunity to gain a different perspective on how our bodies affect the medications we take. Pharmacists can play a key role in translating research into clinical practice, and medical schools will need to incorporate it into curricula already woefully short on pharmacology and genetics. And the costs will be substantial. There will be few bargains in genetic therapy.

What if China stops producing or contaminates the pharmaceutical ingredients they now produce for the U.S. market? An article in the *New York*

Times in 1990 (!) stated that the worldwide pharmaceutical industry would collapse. In early 2020, this concern seemed well placed, in view of the Coronavirus Pandemic.

Here's another idea I had before breakfast (see the White Queen, above). Durham–Humphrey took care of the safe and effective provision for Drugs. What if the FDA imposed the same requirements on Drug *Promotion*? Especially for DTC. They have done the "safe" part rather well. But what about "effective", not just for increased sales, but rather for such things as better prescribing with resulting better therapy? Probably impossible, yes, but such efforts would support Big Pharma's claim that their Promotion is educational.

Money Back Guarantee? While Congress and POTUS seem to dither, Drug makers are experimenting with new ways to get paid for their most expensive medicines. A few examples:

- Alnylam Pharmaceuticals will now charge full value for a nearly $600,000 new rare disease Drug only if a patient gets a benefit near what was seen in clinical testing.
- Novartis sells a gene therapy at $2.1 million but gives third parties the opportunity to pay over 5 years.
- Sanofi has a $99 month plan for its insulin products for uninsured patients (*Wall Street Journal*, January 14, 2020).

The current term for such practices is Value-Based Drug Pricing.

Advances in medical records technology are credited with making assessment of treatment results easier. All of this occurs as annual expenditures for prescription Drugs rose from $75 to $335 billion between 1998 and 2018 (CMS Data). And now, a final "what if".

What if Big Pharma, preferably as PhRMA, sponsored the production of a documentary TV series explaining the Drug development process in layperson terms, addressing head-on the Price issue, by highlighting the processes that result in determining the costs. Such an effort could certainly be made entertaining in the hands of competent producers: stories of old Drug discoveries, new breakthroughs, personal stories from patients and physicians, and even profiles of some of the scientists individually responsible for specific discoveries in the laboratory. The Discovery Channel would be an obvious choice for a series such as this, and it would be much more effective than the one-minute commercials now used to extol the importance of the industry. Such an effort could and should include educational efforts to engage the People in rational Drug therapy including themes related to compliance with medication regimens. There is ample material – much of it dramatic to draw an audience.

Apologia

If someone were to paint the pharmaceutical events of the past century, the canvas would have to look like something by Hieronymus Bosch with overtones of Norman Rockwell.

"There's no time like the present", so goes the phrase. It seems, however, that the present, in the case of the Dynamic Tension portrayed in these pages, is very redolent of the *past*. Many of the same arguments and controversies described herein continue today. There have been some notable successes over time, but many still await discovery.

Perhaps a paraphrase of the ever-eloquent Charles Dickens, as provided in the Preface, is now appropriate. "It was a time of breathtaking breakthroughs in Drug therapy. It was a time of appalling tragedies from medications". "It was a time of handsome profits by Big Pharma". It was a time of strident criticism of "Greedy Big Pharma". "It was a time of needed regulation. It was a time of onerous regulation." "It was a time of promise. It was a time of dread."

The questions posed by Evans (53) 50 years ago are as relevant today as they were then:

- What drugs should be invented and when?
- Who should control drug production and use? What control means should be used?
- How free should people be allowed to be in regard to drug use?
- How can effective education about drug use be implemented?
- What limits must be placed on governmental use of drugs to control individuals.
- Where does freedom of research end and public responsibility begin?

I would add, how much are we prepared to pay?

My friend, frequent collaborator, and prolific author, Dr. Albert Wertheimer in our Book, *Social and Behavioral Aspects of Pharmaceutical Care*, authored an Epilogue both prescient and hopeful. It is far too long to reprint here, but it is strongly recommended to the Reader.

Wertheimer wrote: "Fighting disease is like building objects in the sand at the edge of the water. Our interventions, like sand castles, cannot survive in any permanent status".

In the process of constructing this Book, my own "take away" is that the pharmaceutical industry, Big Pharma, and its interaction with the Government and with the People is one of the great stories of the workings of free enterprise in the best democracy the world has yet devised. Each of the entities named in the title has its own desires, internal conflicts, "solutions", failures, and triumphs. Because they are often at odds, Dynamic Tension was, and is, inevitable.

Author's Notes

To those who have read, and preferably bought, this book – Thank you! Even though I have lived, boy and man, for a good part of the period covered, I have discovered that many of the "truths" that I believed to be "self-evident" were not. Some were even outright lies.

I have tried to suppress my occasional biases and admitted some were obvious. Will I appreciate hearing from the Reader about omissions and/or errors? Probably not! Will I welcome even a hint of praise? Certainly, I will acknowledge it as Gospel and well deserved.

But seriously, there has been considerable frustration in the certain knowledge that changes are occurring even as you read this. All of the players are busy trying to augment these changes. I believe the facts to be accurate, but with the considerable efforts of revisionists to change history, who knows?

Someone will eventually ask, "How long did it take for you to write this? (Someone usually does.) The answer is an easy one – about 50 years. It is an amalgam of observations, experiences, opportunities, and, most of all, the attempts to absorb the insights of the hundreds of scholars, politicians, even fiction writers, in their published works, referenced herein. The People are, I believe, well served by the voluminous literature which they produced.

Reading the Proceedings of Congressional Hearings has been a lesson in itself. I was even surprised to be reminded that I had submitted a 20-page written statement on the influence of advertising on prescribing which appears in the Hearings Poly Drug Abuse (153).

Construction of this Book has been for me a constant source of education, re-education, and reminiscence. I know I have sometimes been guilty of repetition but my third grade teacher, Sister Mary Piece O'Chalk (fictitious name), reminded us beleaguered students constantly of its value. I certainly learned the value of repetition by writing, "I will not talk in class" 100 times, when I should have been outside at recess playing baseball.

In a very few cases, publishers have failed to respond to the Author's request to reprint verbatim from materials in their publications. In such cases, I was forced to summarize or paraphrase, thus depriving the Reader of the sometimes more eloquent words in the original work. To these authors, I offer my own apology on behalf of those publishers whose motives I can only ascribe to either *greed* or poor administration.

Someone has written: "Sometimes one is inclined to commit a rant to paper. It is almost always a mistake". I have diligently tried to heed that sage advice.

If I used "BTSB" too often, it was usually simply true. Perhaps the Reader would substitute "BTSA", Beyond the Scope of the Author. Fair Enough!

Samuel Johnson wrote: "Read over your compositions, and where you meet with a passage which you think is particularly fine, strike it out". I didn't do that.

As I near the finish, I hope the Reader will permit me of a couple of literary allusions. At times, I have felt like the Ancient Mariner with that damnable albatross. Other times it was Sisiphus, with that equally damnable boulder. Someone (almost certainly a writer) put it this way, "A book is never finished. It is only abandoned". Indeed! That has certainly been my experience with more than 20 books. I am buoyed, however, by the words of Benjamin Franklin, "If you would not be forgotten when you are dead and rotten, either write things worth reading or *do* things worth the reading".

Post Script

As this manuscript was being finalized, the United States and the world were just beginning their struggle with a medical and financial crisis, as a result of the Coronavirus Pandemic. It is interesting to note that the Government is turning to Big Pharma for solutions. The People watch and wait for both of them to find answers to their Dis-Ease, as well as the disease. One can only hope that all the parties succeed. It is notable that one of the members of "Greedy" Big Pharma – Bayer – donated three million chloroquine tablets, (*Wall Street Journal*, March 20, 2020). It's a start.

Appendix A – Annotated References and Cross Index

Introduction

> The danger of reading too much is that we shall have only the thoughts of others. The danger of reading too little, or none at all, is that we shall have none but our own.
>
> *Lord Acton*

Not every one of these references is cited in this Book, but each was used in some way in its preparation. Some are incomplete by academic standards, but all supply sufficient information to find them for the serious researcher.

The reader will probably note that a significant number of these references were authored by me, former graduate students, and colleagues. Their frequency simply reflects more than 50 years of study, research, and writing, with the collaboration of the many who have made my work possible. I have been privileged to work with each of them.

Excellent and extensive lists of references may be found in Vogel (15), Basara (31), Gibson (27), Fulda (56), Fincham (111), Crellin (70), Pray (55), Evans (53), Kolassa (10,11), Smith (117), Agrawal (71), Temen (49), Finkelstein (218), Becker (270), and Smith (300) among others.

References

1. Mickey Smith, *Principles of Pharmaceutical Marketing*, Third Edition, Lea & Febiger, 1969. Intended as a textbook for Pharmacy students, the book eventually received wider use. Translated into: Russian, Chinese, Spanish, and Korean. Chapters by Dr. Max Ferm, Dr. Joseph McEvilla, and Raymond Gosselin. Second Edition, 1975, Third Edition, 1983, with 20 distinguished contributors. Totally new from the First Edition.
2. Mickey Smith, *Pharmaceutical Marketing: Strategy and Cases*, Haworth Press, 1998, Twenty outstanding contributors. Based on the "Four "P's" of Marketing – Product, Price, Place, and Promotion.
3. Mickey Smith, Ed., *Pharmaceutical Marketing: Principles, Environment, and Practices*, Pharmaceutical Products Press, 2002.
4. Mickey Smith, *Studies in Pharmaceutical Economics*. Pharmaceutical Products Press, 1996, A Classic with 58 contributors. This should be read by the staff of any congressman framing or voting for legislation affecting Big Pharma.
5. Mickey Smith, *Small Comfort*, 1985, Praeger Publishing, reissued as *A Social History of the Minor Tranquilizers*, Haworth Press, 1990. Written after Valium had become a household name and how that happened.
6. Mickey Smith, *Pharmaceutical Marketing in the 21st Century*, Pharmaceutical Products Press, 1996. Translated and published in Japan. Twenty-eight contributors prognosticated on the future. Prescient!
7. Mickey Smith, Ed., *Prescription Drugs Under Medicare, The Legacy of the Task Force on Prescription Drugs*, Pharmaceutical Products Press, 2001, a history of this monumental effort to support legislation. Includes an "Insider's Perspective" by the late T. Donald Rucker and contributions by Dr. Phillip Lee, Joseph Follman, John Inglehart, Thomas Fulda, and Bonnie Wilford. A treasure chest of information and analysis!
8. Mickey Smith and Bernard G. Keller, *Pharmaceutical Marketing: An Anthology and Bibliography*, 1969, an extensive presentation of the published literature, up to 50 years ago. Reprints of incisive works including *The Saga of Vitamin B-13*. Fifty-eight seminal articles by such notables as George Squibb, Estes Kefauver, and Gaylord Nelson. Includes a list of relevant theses and dissertations.
9. Mickey Smith, "The Medical Muckrakers", *Pharmaceutical Marketing and Media*. They're still here! As near as your cable channel. Inspired by *The Therapeutic Nightmare*, (see 21).
10. E. M. "Mick" Kolassa, *Elements of Pharmaceutical Pricing*, Pharmaceutical Products Press, 1997. This was written by a former Pharma executive. This is an eloquent "primer". The only book of its kind by the "guru" of drug pricing.
11. E. M. "Mick" Kolassa, Ed., *The Strategic Pricing of Pharmaceuticals*, Pondhouse Press, 2009. An outstanding companion to his other book. Kolassa is joined by six contributors. In his forward to the book, Kent Monroe writes: "(The book is) one that must be read by anyone involved in the pharmaceutical industry". I would add, "By anyone who contemplates regulating drug pricing".

12. Albert Wertheimer and Mickey Smith, *International Drug Regulatory Mechanisms*, Pharmaceutical Products Press, 2004. A smorgasbord with contributions from forty-two writers from twenty different countries worldwide. From Iceland to Slovenia. The entries from Germany and the U.K., are especially meaningful. A must read.
13. Brent Rollins, and Matthew Perri, *Pharmaceutical Marketing*, Jones and Bartlett Learning, 2014. With permission. Along with nine contributors, the authors provide an insightful and contemporary exposition. Especially valuable for the student are a number of small case studies.
14. Kuniichi Saga, *Pharmaceutical Marketing in Practice*, 1999, written by my late friend Saga San. I know it is good even though it is written in Japanese.
15. Ronald J. Vogel, *Pharmaceutical Economics and Public Policy*, 2007, with permission, Pharmaceutical Products Press. This is a factual, valuable, and objective exposition of the nature of the economics of the drug industry. Timely and an essential guide to understanding the issues. Written at the graduate level with some theoretical economics but very readable.
16. Bert Spilker, *Multinational Pharmaceutical Companies*, Raven Press, Second Edition, 1994. Encyclopedic exposition by a noted industry scholar, physician, and scientist. Sections on corporate issues and external interactions are especially valuable.
17. Bernard Conley, *Social and Economic Aspects of Drug Utilization Research*, Drug Intelligence Publications, 1976. Provides an overview of federally funded drug research from 1960–1975. Includes a section on pharmaceutical economics research as well as drug purchasing and expenditures. Excellent review of the literature of the time.
18. Saurab Sewak, *The Social Value of Pharmaceutical Marketing*, Monograph/Center for Pharmaceutical Marketing and Management, University of Mississippi, 1999.
19. Austin Smith and Arthur Herrick, *Drug Research and Development*, Revere Publishing Company, 1948. Interesting historical view of "another time", especially as regard to patents, trademarks, and copyrights. Smith later headed the Pharmaceutical Manufacturers Association.
20. Glenn Sonnedecker, Ed., *Kremers and Urdang's History of Pharmacy*, Fourth Edition, J. B. Lippincott, 1976. The definitive work. Good section on legislative standards and on compulsory health insurance.
21. Morton Mintz, *The Therapeutic Nightmare*, Houghton Mifflin Co., 1965. Regarded by some as the ultimate "muckraker" book. May have done for drugs what Rachel Carson did for pesticides in *The Silent Spring*. Some of his comments may be heard, paraphrased, or even verbatim today.
22. Robert Bonk, *Pharmacoeconomics in Perspective*, Pharmaceutical Products Press, 1999. The author describes it as a "Primer". Indeed it is! Succinct and very usable. A true "Cookbook" in the field.
23. J. Lyle Bootman, Raymond J. Townsend and William F. McGhan, *Principles of Pharmacoeconomics*, Second Edition, Harvey Whitney Books, 1996.

24. William Kelly, *Prescribed Medications and Public Health*, Pharmaceutical Product Press, 2006. Primarily about adverse drug reactions and how to prevent and deal with them. The role of Big Pharma is briefly but cogently presented.
25. Thomas Jacobsen and Albert Wertheimer, *Modern Pharmaceutical Industry: A Primer*, Jones and Bartlett, 2010. An excellent and very readable description of the workings and decision-making of a drug company. Short, but insightful look at what constitutes the "real" price of a drug.
26. Gregory Higby and Elaine Stroud, *The Inside Story of Medicine*, The American Institute of the History of Pharmacy, 1997, Proceedings of a Symposium sponsored by Glaxo Wellcome, part of an exhibit of the Smithsonian.
27. J. Tyrone Gibson, *Medication Law and Behavior*, Wiley, Inter-Science, 1976. Thoughtful, somewhat theoretical and in many ways brilliant exposition of the nature of law, medicine, and human behavior.
28. Alan Escovitz and Dev Pathak, Eds., *Health Outcomes and Pharmaceutical Care*, Pharmaceutical Products Press, 1997. Health outcomes are essentially "bang for the buck" as relative to drug cost. The 5 D's of outcomes as presented are: Death, Disease, Disability, Discomfort, and Dissatisfaction.
29. Dev Pathak and Alan Escovitz, Eds., *Managed Competition and Pharmaceutical Care*, Pharmaceutical Products Press, 1996. Excellent series by contributors, assessing the role of managed care in affecting drug prices.
30. Henry Steele, "Patent Restrictions and Price Competition in the Ethical Drug Industry", *Journal of Industrial Economics*, 1964, pp. 198–223. Widely quoted following the 1962 Drug Amendments.
31. Winston Churchill, *My Early Life*, Simon and Schuster, 1930. No relevance to this book, but everyone should read Churchill occasionally.
32. Sheila Shulman, Elaine Healy and Louis Lasagna, *PBMs: Re-shaping the Pharmaceutical Distribution System*, Pharmaceutical Products Press, 1998.
33. Delbert Konnor, Ed., *Pharmacy Law Desk Reference*, Haworth Press, 2007. Some twenty-six contributors with 25 chapters. Focus on Pharmacy practice but with some coverage of FDA, patents, and trademarks.
34. Lisa Basara and Michael Montagne, *Searching for Magic Bullets*, Pharmaceutical Products Press, 1994. The definitive work and a good bit extra.
35. Thomas Hager, *Ten Drugs*, Abrams Press, 2019. Thoughtful and engaging story of drug discovery through serendipity and a few fortunate accidents.
36. Anonymous, *Pharmaceutical Manufacturers Association*, remarks to the American Pharmaceutical Association, 1972.
37. *Competitive Problems in the Drug Industry*, Hearings before the Subcommittee on Monopoly, U.S. Senate Select Committee on Small Business.
38. T. Levitt, *The Marketing Imagination*, Free Press, 1986.
39. J. Fred Weston, *Issues in Pharmaceutical Economics*, Lexington Books, 1979.
40. John McWhorter, *Words on the Move*, Henry Holt Publisher, 2016. Written by a "lexicographer". A challenging read but often "down to earth and humorous". Explains some of the communication problems between Congress and Big Pharma.

41. Bernard Barber, *Drugs and Society*, 1967, Russell Sage Foundation, with permission.
42. Louis Lasagna, *Life, Death and the Doctor*, Alfred Knoph Publishers, 1968.
43. Daniel Klein, *Every Time I Find the Meaning of Life, They Change It*, One World Publishing, 2015. A lighthearted review of some of the great philosophers.
44. Timothy Harper, *The Complete Idiot's Guide to the U.S. Constitution*, Penguin Group. This is just excellent, 2007. Readable, thorough, and quotable. As noted before, it should be a required reading for anyone wishing to serve in Congress.
45. William Shakespeare, *Hamlet*, Act 3, Scene 1, Apologies to the Bard of Avon.
46. George Urdang, *The Workings and Philosophies of the Pharmaceutical Industry*, National Pharmaceutical Council, 1959.
47. Gerald Carson, *One for Man, Two for a Horse*, Doubleday, 1961. Wonderful, lavishly illustrated, view of the "patent medicine era". Lots of fun!
48. Paul Talalay, Ed., *Drugs and Society*, Johns Hopkins Press, 1964.
49. Peter Temin, *Taking Your Medicine, Drug Regulation in the United States*, Harvard University Press, 1980. Brilliant! As of 1980, a thorough examination of history and rationale of drug regulation as it affects public policy.
50. George Squibb in Ref. 8, a somewhat different view from a well-known name.
51. *Pharmaphoram* – Website, *Deep Dive*, a digital magazine with "objective, issue-driven analyses, high-level interviews and unique research for pharmaceutical companies".
52. Lucas Richart, *Strange Trips*, McGill-Queens Press, 2019.
53. Wayne O. Evans and Nathan S. Kline, Eds., *Psychotropic Drugs in the Year 2000, Use by Normal Humans*, Charles C. Thomas Publisher, 1971. Fascinating predictions by a distinguished list of contributors twenty-five years before the year 2000. New intoxicants, aphrodisiacs, life pattern alternates, and use of psychotropics in geriatrics and in criminals.
54. W. Marvin Davis, *Consumers Guide to Dietary Supplements and Alternative Medicines*, Pharmaceutical Products Press, 2006. The definitive book for consumers. Philosophy, science and humor.
55. W. Steven Pray, *A History of Non-prescription Products Regulation*, CRC Press, 2003. (Author of Chapter 15 of this Book.)
56. Thomas R. Fulda and Albert I. Wertheimer, Eds., *Handbook of Pharmaceutical Public Policy*, Pharmaceutical Products Press, 2007.
57. Gaylord Nelson, "How Fair is the Price of Brand Name Pharmaceuticals?" *Medical World News*, Vol. 8, September, 1967.
58. Estes Kefauver, "The Determination of Price", pp. 30–34 (in 59).
59. Estes Kefauver, *In A Few Hands*, Pantheon Books, 1965.
60. Raymond A. Bauer and Mark G. Fields, "Ironic Contrast: U.S. and U.S.S.R. Drug Industries", *Business Review*, September–October 1962: 94.22. Widely quoted comparison of the drug industries in two different political systems.
61. Alfred W. Hubbard, "The Expanding Role of Government in Medicine", *Modern Medicine Topics*, November, 1967.

62. A. Mason Harlow, "Pharmaceutical Marketing and the Public Interest – In Perspective," Proceedings of the 1966 World Congress, American Marketing Association, Chicago, 1966.
63. Lawrence Lessing, "Laws Alone Can't Make Drugs Safe," *Fortune*, March, 1963, p. 123.
64. Anonymous, "Medical Advertising, State of the Craft and Regulations, *FDA Papers*, February 1967, pp. 14–16.
65. George Squibb, "Drug Prices" – The Achilles Heel of the Pharmaceutical Industry, pp. 151–160 (Ref. 8).
66. Joseph D. McEvilla, "Price Determination in the Pharmaceutical Industry", *Drug and Cosmetic Industry*, Vol. 82, 1958, p. 34.
67. Milton Moscowitz, "The Drugstore: Outlet or Bottleneck?" *Drug and Cosmetic Industry*, Vol. 88, 1961, p. 725.
68. Joseph A. Ingolia, "Is Ethical Drug Marketing in Step with Medical Practice?" *Pharmaceutical Marketing and Media*, Vol. 2, 1967.
69. John T. Conner, "The Functions of the Pharmaceutical Industry in our Society", (in Ref. 48).
70. John K. Crellin, *A Social History of Medicines in the Twentieth Century*, Pharmaceutical Products Press, 2004. Scholarly and engaging with an incisive look at industry practices.
71. Madhu Agrawal, *Global Competitiveness in the Pharmaceutical Industry*, Pharmaceutical Products Press, 1999.
72. Susan A. Simmons, Bruce C. Payne and Mickey C. Smith, "Marketing Medicaid Drugs: An Analysis of Cost Factors", *Journal of Health Care Marketing*, Vol. 6, No. 3.
73. Susan A. Simmons, S. Cabell Shull and Mickey C. Smith, "Production Costs in the Pharmaceutical Industry", *Atlantic Economic Review*, November-December, 1975.
74. S. A. Simmons, S.C. Shull and M. C. Smith, "Rates of Returns on Research and Development in the Pharmaceutical Industry: U.S. vs. U.K.", *Management International Review*, Vol. 4, 1981, p. 62.
75. Lou E. Pelton, David Strutton and Mickey C. Smith "Future Pharmacists and Public Initiative to Control Retail Drug Prices: A Political Economy Framework", *Health Marketing Quarterly*, Vol. 10, p. 241.
76. James A. Visconti and Mickey C. Smith, "Economic Consequences of Adverse Drug Reactions", *Hospitals J.A.H.A.*, Vol. 43, May 1, 1967, p. 85.
77. Herman L. Lazarus, Mickey C. Smith and Dewey D. Garner, "A Study of Cost Control as a Function of the P&T Committee", *Hospital Formulary Management*, Vol. 6, No. 8, 1971, p. 10.
78. Mick Kolassa and Mickey C. Smith, "The Effects of Acquisition Costs and Budget Based Compensation on the Attitudes of Pharmacy Directors toward the Adoption of a Cost-Effective Drug", *Pharmaceconomics*, Vol. 13, 1998, p. 223. Some evidence that hospital pharmacy directors whose salary is based on their budget will resist adding a new drug to their formulary.

79. Mickey C. Smith, "Outcomes Research: The Way We Were", *Journal of Research in Pharmaceutical Economics*, Vol. 7, No. 4, p. 5, 1996.
80. John E. Ware, Jr., "Outcomes Research: Implications for Improving Health Care Delivery", *Journal of Research in Pharmaceutical Economics*, Vol. 7, No. 4, 1996, p. 13.
81. Mickey C. Smith, "The Neglected "P" in the Four "P's" of Pharmaceutical Marketing", *Product Management Today*, December, 1982.
82. Mickey C. Smith, "The Cost of Drugs", *Journal of the American Medical Association*, Vol. 235, No. 3, 1976, p. 294.
83. Lon L. Larson, Mickey C. Smith, Thomas R. Sharpe, Ronn Hy and Dewey D. Garner, "Government Regulation and the Believability of Prescription Drug Advertising, An Application of Attribution Theory", *Drug Intelligence and Clinical Pharmacy*, Vol. 11, No. 6, June, 1977, p. 339.
84. Mickey C. Smith, John Juergens and William Jack, "Medication and the Quality of Life", *American Pharmacy*, Vol. NS 31, No. 4, April 1991, p. 278.
85. Richard Levy and Mickey Smith, "Rx Marketing's Real Value", *Pharmaceutical Executive*, Vol. 14, No. 10, October 1994, p. 66.
86. E. Dichter, *Handbook of Consumer Motivations*, McGraw-Hill, 1964.
87. M. C. Smith, T. R. Sharpe and B. F. Banahan, "Patient Response to Symptoms", *Journal of Clinical and Hospital Pharmacy*, Vol. 6, 1981, p. 267.
88. Agatha Christie, *What Mrs. McGillicudy Saw*, Pocket Books, 1957, p. 167.
89. Walter J. Primeaux and Mickey C. Smith, "Pricing Patterns and the Kinky Demand Curve", *Journal of Law and Economics*, Vol. 19, April 1976, p. 142.
90. Irwin M. Rosenstock, "Historical Origins of the Health Belief Model", *Health Education Monographs*, Vol. 2, winter 1974, p. 334.
91. D. E. Knapp, R. E. Oeltjen and D. A. Knapp", "An Anatomy of an Illness", *Medical Marketing and Media*, Vol. 9, July 1974, p. 20.
92. Robert B. Settle and Pamela L. Alreck, *Why They Buy*, John Wiley & Sons, 1986. Fascinating psychological and sociological analysis. Relation to drugs possible by extension.
93. J. B. Griffin, *Medicines: Regulation, Research and Risk*, Greystone Books, 1992. Based on experiences in the United Kingdom.
94. J. L. Bootman, *Pharmacoeconomics*, CMR, N.D. Intended as a "cookbook" for applicants for status as a Certified Medical Representative. CMR designation was intended for "detail" persons, modeled after CLU – Certified Life Underwriter.
95. Hugh D. Walker, *Market Power and Price Levels in the Ethical Drug Industry*, Indiana University Press, 1971.
96. B. S. Wallston and K. A. Wallston, "Locus of Control and Health: A Review of the Literature", *Health Education Monographs*, Vol. 6, 1979, pp. 107–117.
97. Alison Masson and Robert L. Steiner, *Generic Substitution and Prescription Drug Prices*, Federal Trade Commission, 1985. Written with 1980 data, but a comprehensive look at "substitution" at the time.
98. Joseph L. Fink, Jesse C. Vivian and Ilisa B.G. Berstein, *Pharmacy Law Digest*, 2006. The "Bible" of pharmacy law on local, state and national levels.

99. Robert B. Helms, Ed., *Drug Development and Marketing*, American Enterprise Institute for Public Policy Research, 1975. Proceedings of a two-day conference sponsored by the Center. Thirty high-powered contributors and some equally high- powered economics. Lively discussions, often at odds with one another. (One discussant describes the presentation by another contributor as "extremely weak, combining flimsy evidence with a theoretical procedure of dubious validity.) Only two participants from Big Pharma.
100. E. Freidson, *Profession of Medicine*, Dodd, Mead, 1970.
101. Robert P. Brady, Richard M. Cooper and Richard S. Silverman, Eds., *Fundamentals of Law and Regulations*, Food and Drug Law Institute, 1997. Massive, but very readable. Only about 20 percent concerns drugs, the rest being foods, veterinary medicines and cosmetics.
102. Eliot Freidson, *Professional Dominance*, Atherton Press, 1970.
103. David Schwartzman, *Innovation in the Pharmaceutical Industry*, Johns Hopkins University Press, 1976. Good review of the pharmacoeconomic literature of the time. A bit heavy on formulas.
104. Milton Silverman and Phillip R. Lee, *Pills, Profits, and Politics*, University of California Press, 1974. Well researched, with distinguished group of contributors.
105. Jeannette Y. Wick, *Pharmacy Practice in an Aging Society*, Pharmaceutical Products Press, 2006.
106. Charles Levinson, *The Multinational Pharmaceutical Industry*, International Federation of Chemical and General Workers' Unions, ND. Mostly British, with good international comparisons.
107. Stuart Walker, *Pharmaceutical Patents*, Centre for Medicines Research, ND. Good discussion of effective patent life.
108. David Schwartzman, *The Expected Return from Pharmaceutical Research*, American Enterprise Institute, 1975.
109. Anonymous, *The Pharmaceutical Industry, Profits Patents and Promotion*, 1980. A pamphlet detailing PMA's response to criticism as of 1980.
110. Robert L. McCarthy, *Introduction to Health Care Delivery*, Aspen Publishers, 1998. Intended as a Pharmacy textbook. Broad, covers the issues from Pharmacy perspective with twenty contributors.
111. Jack E. Fincham, *Patient Compliance with Medication*, Pharmaceutical Products Press, 2007. A comprehensive look at why people use prescription drugs improperly, or not at all. Solutions are provided.
112. John Lidstone, *Marketing Planning for the Pharmaceutical Industry*, Gowen Press, 1989. A rather cursory "how to" book for product managers. U.K. oriented.
113. Arthur Hailey, *Strong Medicine*, Doubleday, 1994, a novel. The story of a strong woman whose career involves her in the fascinating business of pharmaceuticals.
114. Linda Marsa, "A Five Point Plan to Lower Rx Prices", *AARP Bulletin*, May, 2019.
115. Barry Werth, *The Billion Dollar Molecule*, Simon and Schuster, 1984.
116. Barry Werth, *The Antidote*, Simon and Schuster, 2004.

117. Mickey C. Smith, *Principles of Pharmaceutical Marketing*, Third Edition, Lea and Febiger, 1983.
118. E. J. McCarthy, *Basic Marketing, A Managerial Approach*, Richard D. Irwin Publishers, 1981.
119. Mickey C. Smith, Ed, *Studies in Pharmaceutical Economics*, Pharmaceutical Products Press, 1999. A state of the art summary of the subject up to the time of publication. Thirty-three chapters by fifty-eight contributors.
120. Bernard G. Keller and Mickey C. Smith, *Pharmaceutical Marketing: An Anthology and Bibliography*, Williams and Wilkins, 1969.
121. Sam Peltzman, *Political Participation and Government Regulation*, University of Chicago Press, 1998. Very heavy economics. Nothing about drugs.
122. *Majority Staff Report*, "Skyrocketing Prescription Drug Prices", Special Committee on Aging, U.S. Senate, 1980.
123. *Competitive Problems in the Drug Industry*, Proceedings, Monopoly Subcommittee of the Select Committee on Small Business, Parts 1–33, U.S. Senate, 1967–1979.
124. *Administered Prices*, Proceedings, Subcommittee on Antitrust and Monopoly, Committee on the Judiciary, U.S. Senate, 1960–1961.
125. *Advertising of Proprietary Medicines*, Proceedings, Subcommittee on Monopoly of the Select Committee on Small Business, U.S. Senate, 1971–1977.
126. Federal Food, Drug, and Cosmetic Act, as amended, October 1976.
127. *Agency Hearings*, Proceedings, Committee on Interstate and Foreign Commerce, U. S. House of Representatives, 1967.
128. *Inter-Agency Drug Coordination*, Report, Committee on Government Operations, Subcommittee on Reorganization and International Organizations, U.S. Senate, 1964.
129. *Drug Industry Antitrust Act*, Proceedings, Antitrust Subcommittee, of the Committee on the Judiciary, U.S. House of Representatives, 1962.
130. *Drug Safety*, Proceedings, Intergovernmental Relations Subcommittee of the Committee on Government Operations, U. S. House of Representatives, 1964.
131. *Examination of the Pharmaceutical Industry*, Proceedings Subcommittee on Health of the Committee on Labor and Public Welfare, U. S. Senate, 1974.
132. *Physician Ownership in Pharmacies and Drug Companies*, Proceedings, Subcommitttee on Antitrust and Monopoly, Committee on the Judiciary, 1964.
133. *Substitute Prescription Drug Act*, Sub-Committtee on Consumer Protection and Finance of the Committee on Interstate and Foreign Commerce, U. S. House of Representatives, 1978.
134. *The Medical Restraint of Trade Act*, Proceedings Subcommittee on Antitrust and Monopoly of the Committee on the Judiciary, U.S. Senate, 1967.
135. *The Relationship Between Drug Abuse and Advertising*, Proceedings Consumer Subcommittee of the Committee on Commerce, U.S. Senate, 1970.
136. *The Regulation of New Drugs by the Food and Drug Administration: The New Drug Review Process*, Proceedings, Subcommittee on Intergovernmental Relations and Human Resources, U.S. House of Representatives, 1982.

137. *Drug Regulation Reform Act of 1978*, Proceedings, Subcommittee on Health and the Environment of the Committee on Interstate Commerce, U. S. House of Representatives, 1976.
138. *Oversight: The Food and Drug Administration's Process for Approving New Drugs*, Proceedings, Subcommittee on Science, Research and Technology of the Committee on Science and Technology, U. S. House of Representatives, 1979.
139. *Small Business Problems in the Drug Industry*, Proceedings, Subcommittee on Activities of Regulatory Agencies of the Select Committee on Small Business, U. S. House of Representatives, 1967.
140. *Safety and Efficacy of Over the Counter Drug Use by the Elderly*, Proceedings, Subcommittee on Health and Long-Term Care of the Select Committee on Aging, U.S. House of Representatives, 1983.
141. *The Safety and Effectiveness of New Drugs*, Proceedings Subcommittee on Intergovernmental Relations of the Committee on Government Operations, U. S. House of Representatives, 1971.
142. *Drug Use and Misuse: A Growing Concern for Older Americans*, Proceedings Subcommittee on Health and Long Term Care, of the Select Committee on Aging, U.S. House of Representatives, 1983.
143. *The Patent Term Restoration Act of 1981*, Committee on the Judiciary, Proceedings U.S. Senate, 1981.
144. *Prescription Drug Advertising and Price Advertising*, Proceedings Subcommittee on Consumer Protection and Finances of the Committee on Interstate and Foreign Commerce, U.S. House of Representatives, 1976.
145. *Drug Efficacy, Parts 1 and 2*, Proceedings Intergovernmental Relations Subcommittee of the Committee on Governmental Operations, U. S. House of Representatives, 1969.
146. *Prescription Drug Advertising*, Proceedings Subcommittee on Intergovernmental Relations of the Committee on Government Operations of the U. S. House of Representatives, 1970.
147. *Regulatory Policies of the Food and Drug Administration*, Proceedings Subcommittee on Intergovernmental Relations of the Committee on Government Operations of the U.S. House of Representatives, 1970.
148. *The Safety and Effectiveness of New Drugs*, Proceedings Subcommittee on Intergovernmental Relations of the Committee on Government Operations of the U.S. House of Representatives, 1971.
149. *Food and Drug Administration Act*, Proceedings Subcommittee on Public Health and Environment of the Committee on Interstate and Foreign Commerce, U.S. House of Representatives, 1972.
150. *Review of Transactional Provisions in Drug Amendments of 1962*, Proceedings Subcommittee on Public Health and Environment of the Committee on Interstate and Foreign Commerce of the U.S. House of Representatives, 1971.
151. *Pricing of Drugs, 1977*, Proceedings Subcommittee on Antitrust and Monopolies of the Committee on Human Resources, and the Subcommittee on Health and Scientific Research, U.S. Senate, 1977.

152. *Pharmaceutical Innovation-Promises and Problems*, Proceedings Subcommittee on National Resources and the Environment and Subcommittee on Investigations and Oversight of the Committee on Science and Technology, U.S. House of Representatives, 1981.
153. *Polydrug Abuse-The Response of the Medical Profession and the Pharmaceutical Industry*, Proceedings Select Committee on Narcotics Abuse and Control, Ninety-Fifth Congress, 1979.
154. Sam Peltzman, *Regulation of Pharmaceutical Innovation*, America Enterprise Institute for Public Policy Research, 1974. An eminent economist concludes that delays resulting from the 1962 Amendments caused medical and economic losses.
155. Richard Harris, *The Real Voice*, Macmillan, 1964. Popular account of the Kefauver Hearings.
156. H. Somers and A. R. Somers, *Doctors, Patients and Health Insurance*, The Brookings Institution, 1961.
157. Mickey C. Smith, *The Rexall Story: A History of Genius and Neglect*, Pharmaceutical Products Press, 2004.
158. Mickey C. Smith, David P. Lipson and G. Joseph Norwood, "Drug Clerks: How Much Influence on OTC Purchases?" *Medical Marketing and Media*, September, 1987.
159. Avedis Donabedian, *Aspects of Medical Care Administration: Specifying Requirements for Health Care*, Harvard University Press, 1973. This is as good as it gets! Thoughtful, wide-ranging. Though little attention is given to all specific topics in the Book, everything in this wonderful text applies.
160. D. M. Berman, *In Congress Assembled*, McMillan, 1964.
161. D. P. Moynihan, "What is 'Community Action'?" *The Public Interest*, fall, 1966.
162. Courtney Davis and John Abraham, *Unhealthy Pharmaceutical Regulation*, Palgrave/Macmillan, 2013. Essentially limited to the U.K.
163. Francis Narin, James C. Corrigan, and Michael G. Gallagher, *The Quest for Knowledge: Contribution of U.S. Pharmaceutical Industry Scientists*, CHI Research/Computer Horizons, 1986, Pamphlet, paid for by R.M.A. A comparison of literature contributions by Big Pharma scientists and NIH funded authors.
164. Gary L. Nelson, *Pharmaceutical Company Histories*, UK Publishing, 1983.
165. Medical Advertising Hall of Fame, *Medicine Avenue*. Published by the Hall of Fame with no one claiming authorship. Beautifully illustrated. An inside look at medical advertising into the 90's.
166. Mickey C. Smith, "Lay Periodical Coverage of the Minor Tranquilizers", *Pharmacy in History*, Vol. 25, No. 3, 1983. A survey of lay periodical coverage of what was a new class of drugs (in 1954) until the middle 80's.
167. *Use and Misuse of Benzodiazepines*, Proceedings Subcommittee on Health and Scientific Research of the Committee on Labor and Human Resources, U.S. Senate, 1979.
168. *Drug Literature*, Proceedings Subcommittee on Reorganization and International Organizations, Committee on Governmental Operations, U.S. Senate, 1963.

169. President Clinton's Health Care Reform Proposal: *Health Security Act, 1993*.
170. Paul S. Rhodes, "The Doctors Dilemma – Drug Therapy and the Facts of Life", *Archives of Internal Medicine*, Vol. 107, June 1961, pp. 810–812.
171. New York Academy of Medicine Committee on Public Health, "Pharmaceutical Advertising", *Bulletin of the New York Academy of Medicine*, January 1962.
172. *Skyrocketing Prescription Drug Prices*, Proceedings Special Committee on Aging, U.S. Senate Proceedings, 1989.
173. Katherine Eban, *Bottle of Lies*, Harper Collins, 2019. A detailed look inside the world of generics. The focus is on the Indian Company, Kanbaxy, but the workings of the FDA receive a thorough treatment.
174. Mickey C. Smith and David A. Knapp, *Pharmacy, Drugs and Medical Care*, Three Editions, Williams and Wilkins, 1981. An introductory textbook for pharmacy students.
175. Congressional Research Service, Library of Congress, *Competitive Problems in the Drug Industry, Psychotropic Drugs, Summary and Analyses*, Report to Select Committee on Small Business of the U.S. Senate, 1979.
176. Donald Drake and Marian Uhlman, *Making Medicine, Making Money*, Andrews and McMeel, 1993. The authors are from the *Philadelphia Inquirer*.
177. *Use of Advisory Committees by the Food and Drug Administration*, Proceedings Subcommittee on Intergovernmental Relations and Human Resources of the Committee on Government Operation of the U.S. House of Representatives, 1975.
178. *Medicare Catastrophic Coverage Act of 1988*, Commerce Clearing House, 1988.
179. *FDA's Regulation of Zomax*, Proceedings of the Subcommittee on Intergovernmental Relations and Human Resources of the Committee on Government Operations, of the U.S. House of Representation, 1983.
180. L.L. Maine and R. P. Penna in C. Knowlton and R. Penna, Eds, *Pharmaceutical Care*, Chapman and Hall, 1996.
181. L.M. Strand et al., "Drug Related Problems: Their Structure and Function", *DICP Annals of Pharmacotherapy*, Vol. 24, 1990, pp. 1093–1097, with permission.
182. D. P. Moynihan, "What is 'Community Action?" *The Public Interest*, Vol. 5, 1996.
183. W. F. Murphey and C. H. Pritchett, "Statutory Interpretation", in *Courts, Judges and Politics*, Random House, 1961.
184. Stuart Anderson, Ed., *Making Medicines*, Pharmaceutical Press, 2005. A British perspective with a good account of the Thalidomide tragedy.
185. Jim Cox, *Sold on Radio*, McFarland and Company, 2008. A survey of radio advertising in radio's "Golden Age". Good review of OTC ads.
186. Mickey C. Smith, "Portrayal of the Elderly in Prescription Drug Advertising", *The Gerontologist*, Vol. 16, 1976. A pilot study in 1970 of ads in *Medical Economics and Geriatrics*.
187. Mickey C. Smith, "The Cost of Drugs", *Journal of the American Medical Association*, Vol. 235, January 1976, pp. 294–295.
188. Mickey C. Smith, "Appeals Used in Advertisements for Psychotropic Drugs: An Exploratory Study", *American Journal of Public Health*, Vol. 67, No. 2, 1977, pp. 171–173.

189. Mickey C. Smith, "Where Are the Blacks in Prescription Drug Advertising?" *Medical Marketing and Media*, Vol. 12, May 1977, pp. 47–49.
190. Michael Ryan and Mickey C. Smith, "Dissonance and the Physician", *Pharmaceutical Marketing and Media*, Vol. 3, November, 1968.
191. E. M. Kolassa et al., "The Effects of Acquisition Cost and Budget-Based Compensation on the Attitudes of Pharmacy Directors toward the Adoption of a Cost-Effective New Drug", *Pharmacoeconomics*, Vol. 13, February 1998, pp. 223–230.
192. Mickey C. Smith and E. M. "Mick" Kolassa, "Nobody Wants Your Products. They are Negative Goods", *Product Management Today*, Vol. 12, December, 2001.
193. Sheryl L. Szeinbach et al., "Content Analysis of Pharmacoeconomic Appeals in Pharmaceutical Drug Product Advertisements", *Journal of Research in Pharmaceutical Economics*, Vol. 3, No. 3, 1991, pp. 75–90.
194. Masako Nagasawa Murphy, Mickey C. Smith and John P. Juergens, "The Synergic Impact of Promotion Intensity and Therapeutic Novelty on Market Performance of Prescription Drug Products", *The Journal of Drug Issues*, Vol. 22, No. 2, 1992, pp. 305–316.
195. Lon L. Larson and Mickey C. Smith, "An Analysis of 'Fair Balance' in Prescription Drug Advertising", *Medical Marketing and Media*, Vol. 13, June 1978, pp. 2–6.
196. Mickey C. Smith, "Drug Product Advertising and Prescribing: A Review of the Evidence", *American Journal of Hospital Pharmacy*, Vol. 34, November 1977, pp. 1208–1224.
197. John R. Neill, "A Social History of Psychotropic Drug Advertisements", *Social Science in Medicine*, Vol. 28, No. 4, 1989, pp. 333–338. Only ads in psychiatric journals are cited. Emphasis is on neuroleptics (major tranquilizers). Based on an unspecified number of ads from 1955 to 1980. The author's views are "impressionistic".
198. Lon N. Larson et al., "Governmental Regulations and the Believability of Prescription Drug Advertising", *Drug Intelligence and Clinical Pharmacy*, Vol. 11, June 1977, pp. 338–343.
199. Mickey C. Smith, "Drug Advertising to Pharmacists: Danger and Opportunity", *Medical Marketing and Media*, March 1979.
200. Foo Nin Ho and Mickey C. Smith, "Portrayal of the Elderly in Over-the-Counter Drug Television Advertisements", *Journal of Pharmaceutical Marketing and Management*, Vol. 6, No. 4, 1992, pp. 21–31.
201. David J. McCaffrey, Benjamin F. Banahan and Mickey C. Smith, "Pharmacy Support Staff and OTC Recommendation", *Pharmacy Times*, Vol. 58, September 1992, p. 48.
202. Mickey C. Smith, "The Prescription: Unwanted Good and Social Object", *Pharmacy Business*, Winter 1993.
203. "Medicine in the Public Interest", *Therapeutic Substitution Symposium*, 1985.
204. Richard Hughes and Roberto Brewin, *The Tranquilizing of America*, Harcourt, Brace, Jovanovich, 1979.

205. W. Van Elmeren and B. Horisberger, Eds., *Socioeconomic Evaluation and Drug Therapy*, Springer-Verlag, 1988. Proceedings of a conference sponsored by Ciba-Geigy.
206. Albert I. Wertheimer and Mickey C. Smith, *A Casebook in Social and Behavioral Pharmacy*, Harvey Whitney Books, 1987.
207. Arnold D. Kaluzny and James E. Veney, *Health Service Organizations*, McCuthan Publishing, 1980. A "technique" book for analyzing organizations.
208. W. Jack Duncan, Peter M. Gunter and Linda E. Swayne, *Strategic Management of Health Care Organizations*, PWS-Kent Publishing, 1992.
209. John T. Hill, *Don't Blame the Medicine*, Merrybook Publishing, 1993.
210. National Pharmaceutical Council, *Pharmaceutical Benefits under State Medical Assistance Programs*, various dates. A yearly guide to Medicaid drug programs.
211. Max A. Ferm, *How to Save Money with Generic Drugs*, William Morrow Company, 1984. A consumer's guide to generics.
212. John T. Fay, *Distributor's Digest*, Wholesale Drugs Magazine, 1992. A humorous look at drug wholesaling.
213. C. Huttin and N. Bosanquet, *The Prescription Drug Market*, North Holland Publishers, 1992. Proceedings of a European Conference.
214. Styli Engel, *Pharmaceutical Marketer's Handbook*, Engel Publishing, 1995. A virtual dictionary. Useful reference for both newcomers and veterans. Wonderfully detailed.
215. Wilson F. Neuhauser, *Health Services in the United States*, Second Edition, Ballinger Publishing, 1985.
216. D. L. Patrick and P. Erickson, "Assessing Health-Related Quality of Life for Clinical Decision Marking", in S. R. Walker and R. M. Rosser, Eds., *Quality of Life-Assessment and Application*, MTP, 1987.
217. G. Teeling-Smith, *Measurement of Health*, Office of Health Economics, 1985.
218. Stan Finkelstein and Peter Temin, *Reasonable Rx: Solving the Drug Price Crisis*, FT Press, 2008. Provides a solution to "the drug price crisis". Fantasy but with good background work.
219. M.C. Smith, "The Prescription: Everything You Wanted to Know but Didn't Think to Ask", *American Pharmacist*, Vol. 18, 1978, pp. 30–33.
220. American Pharmaceutical Association, *Professionalism American Pharmacist*, Vol. 24, 1984.
221. CBS Television Network, "The CBS Consumer Model: A study of Attitudes, Concerns and Information Needs for Prescription Drugs and Related Illnesses", Corporation for Public Broadcasting, 1984.
222. D. C. Brodie, *The Challenge to Pharmacy in Times of Change*, American Pharmaceutical Association and American Society of Hospital Pharmacists, 1965.
223. *The Rx Legend*, Food and Drug Administration, 1966.
224. N. B. Talbot, "Concerning the Need for Behavioral and Social Science in Medicine", in J. H. Knowles, Ed., *Views of Medical Education and Medical Case*, Harvard University Press, 1968.
225. R. M. Nixon, "Message to the Congress of the United States", February, 1971.

226. Rene' Dubos, *The Mirage of Health*, Anchor Books, 1959. Deep, thoughtful, wonderful book. The word "Mirage" in the title tells it all.
227. I. M. Rosenstock, "Why People Use Health Services", in D. Mainland, Ed., *Health Services Research*, Milbank Memorial Fund, 1967.
228. R. Slack and A. W. Nineham, *Medical and Veterinary Chemicals*, Pergamon Press, 1968.
229. J. C. Krantz, "Home Remedies as Sources of Modern Medicine", in H. E. Whipple, Ed., *Home Medication and the Public Welfare*, Annals of the New York Academy of Science, Vol. 120, 1965.
230. L. Lasagna, "The Pharmaceutical Revolution", *Science*, Vol. 166, 1969, pp. 1227–1233. Keen insights by one of the most articulate observers of the drug industry.
231. M. M. Wintrobe, "The Therapeutic Millennium and It's Price", in Talalay (48).
232. H. W. Haggard, *Devils, Drugs, and Doctors*, Harper & Row, 1929.
233. Marcia Angell, *The Truth About the Drug Companies-How They Deceive Us and What to Do About It*, Random House, 2004.
234. Jerry Avorn, *Powerful Medicine: The Benefits, Risks, and Costs of Prescription Drugs*, Knoph, 2004.
235. Mickey C. Smith, *Pharmacy and Medicine on the Air*, Scarecrow Press, 1988.
236. *Medicare Catastrophic Coverage Act of 1988*, Commerce Clearing House, Clinton's Bill, 1988.
237. Nathaniel M. Rickles, Albert I. Wertheimer and Mickey C. Smith, *Social and Behavioral Aspects of Pharmaceutical Care*, Second Edition, Jones & Bartlett, 2010.
238. M. C. Gerald, "Judging OTC's Science Narrows Choices", *American Pharmacy*, NS19, 1979.
239. Anonymous, "OTC's Under Review", *American Pharmacy*, NS20, 1980.
240. H. I. Silverman, "What Lies Ahead for Rx to OTC Switches", *Drug and Cosmetic Industry*, Vol. 141, 1981.
241. A. Blenkinsopp and C. Bradley, "Patients, Society and the Increase in Self-Medication", *British Medical Journal*, Vol. 312, 1996.
242. D. M. Vickery, "A Medical Perspective", *Drug Information Journal*, Vol. 19, 1985.
243. Report of a Working Party, "Abuse of Medicines, Part One, Self-Medication", *Drug Intelligence and Chemical Pharmacy*, Vol. 10, 1976.
244. D. Cargill, "Self-Treatment as an Alternative to Rationing of Medical Care", *The Lancet*, Vol. 289, 1967, pp. 1377–1378.
245. P. V. Rosenau and C. Thoer, "The Liberalization of Access to Medication in the United States and Europe", in E. David, Ed., *Contested Ground: Public Purpose and Private Interest in the Regulation of Prescription Drugs*, 1967.
246. G. Rivett, *From Cradle to Grave: Fifty Years of the NHS*, King's Fund, 1998.
247. Richard R. Abood and David Brushwood, *Pharmacy Practice and the Law*, Aspen, 2001.
248. B. Berabe, "Rx to OTC: Bringing in the Switch Hitters", *Canadian Pharmaceutical Journal*, Vol. 124, 1991.

249. Anonymous, "Americans at Risk from Self-Medication", *American Journal of Health Systems Pharmacy*, Vol. 54, 1997.
250. Anonymous, "Cosmetic OTC Sales Rise by 10%", *The Pharmaceutical Journal*, Vol. 268, 2002.
251. I. Illich, *Limits to Medicine-Medical Nemesis: The Expropriation of Health*, McClelland and Stewart, 1976.
252. R. Moynihan, *Too Much Medicine? The Business of Health*, ABC Books, 1998.
253. C. Medawar, "Data Sheets: A Consumer's Perspective", *The Lancet*, Vol. 331, 1988, pp. 777–778.
254. Paul Starr, *The Social Transformation of American Medicine*, Basic Books, 1982.
255. Ernest Greenwood, "Attributes of a Profession", *Social Work*, Vol. 2, 1957, pp. 45–55.
256. Terence E. Johnson, *Professions and Power*, Macmillan, 1972.
257. Karl Mannheim, *Essays on the Sociology of Knowledge*, Routledge and Kegan Paul, 1952.
258. Kenneth Arrow, "Uncertainty and the Welfare Economics of Medical Care", *American Economic Review*, Vol. 53, 1963.
259. Daniel H. Funkelstein, *Medical Students, Medical Schools and Society during Five Eras*, Ballinger, 1978.
260. I. M. Rosenstock, "Why People Use Health Services", *Milbank Memorial Fund Quarterly*, 1966.
261. Talcott Parsons, "Definitions of Health and Illness in the Light of American values and Social Structure", in E. G. Jaco, Ed., *Patients, Physicians, and Illness*, Free Press of Glencoe, 1959.
262. H. E. Sigerist, *On the Sociology of Medicine*, M. D. Publications, 1960.
263. A. L. Strauss, *Chronic Illness and the Quality of Life*, C. V. Mosby Co., 1960, with permission.
264. L. M. Verbrugge and F. J. Ascione, "Exploring the Iceberg", *Medical Care*, 1987.
265. David Mechanic, *Medical Sociology*, Free Press, 1978.
266. J. P. McEvoy, A.C. Howe and G.E. Hogarty, "Differences in the Nature of Relapse and Subsequent Inpatient Course Between Medication Compliant and Non-Compliant Schizophrenic Patients", *Journal of Nervous and Mental Disease*, Vol. 172, 1984.
267. N. Col, J. E. Fanale and P. Kronholm, "The Role of Medication Non-Compliance and Adverse Drug Reactions in Hospitalizations of the Elderly", *Archives of Internal Medicine*, Vol. 150, 1990.
268. J. J. Green, "Frequent Re-hospitalization on Non-Compliance with Treatment", *Hospital and Community Psychiatry*, Vol. 39, 1988.
269. Mickey C. Smith and Albert I. Wertheimer, *Social and Behavioral Aspects of Pharmaceutical Care*, Pharmaceutical Products Press, 1996.
270. Mickey C. Smith, *A Social History of the Minor Tranquilizers*, Pharmaceutical Products Press, 1985.
271. B. A. Myers, *A Guide to Medical Care Administration*, American Public Health Association, 1965.
272. H. L. Lennard et al., *Mystification and Drug Misuse*, Jossey-Bass, 1971.

273. National Analysts, Inc., *A Study of Health Practices and Opinions*, National Technical Information Service, 1970.
274. Harry Heller Research, *Health Care Practices and Perceptions*, Harry Heller Research, 1984.
275. T. J. Scheff, *Being Mentally Ill*, Aldine Publishing, 1966.
276. B. Ehrenreich, "Gender and Objectivity in Medicine", *International Journal of Health Services*, Vol. 4, 1974, pp. 617–623.
277. R. Cooperstock, "Sex Differences in the Use of Mood-Modifying Drugs: An Explanatory Model", *Journal of Health and Social Behavior*, Vol. 12, 1971, pp. 238–244.
278. Elissa H. Mosher, "Portrayal of Women in Drug Advertising: A Medical Betrayal", *Journal of Drug Issues*, Vol. 6, 1976, pp. 72–78.
279. R. L. Ackoff, "Towards a Behavioral Theory of Communication", *Management Science*, Vol. 4, 1958, pp. 218–234.
280. Wroe Alderson, "Advertising Strategy and Theories of Motivation", in Robert Ferber and Hugh G. Wales, Ed., *Motivation and Morbet Behavior*, Richard D. Irwin, 1958.
281. Staff Report to the U. S. Senate Committee on Finance, "Medicare and Medicaid: Problems, Issues and Alternatives", 1970.
282. Edmund S. Phelps, Ed., *Private Wants and Public Needs*, University of Pennsylvania Press, Norton, 1962.
283. W. J. Cohen, "Hospital Insurance for the Aged", *Mimeographed*, 1965.
284. Robert N. Wilson, *The Sociology of Health: An Introduction*, Random House, 1970.
285. Thomas R. Oliver, Philip R. Lee and Helene C. Lipton, "A Political History of Medicare and Prescription Drug Coverage", *The Milbank Quarterly*, Vol. 82, 2004, pp. 283–354.
286. Julie Rovner, "Congress' Catastrophic Attempt to Fix Medicare", in *Intensive Care: How Congress Shapes Health Policy*, T. E. Mann and N. Ornstein, Eds., American Enterprise Institute, 1995.
287. Matthew Boyle, "Drug Wars", *Fortune*, 2005.
288. Steven Lukes, "Power and Authority", in Robert Nesbit and Tom Bottomore, Eds., *A History of Sociological Analysis*, Basic Books, 1974.
289. Hannah Arendt, *Between Past and Future*, Viking, 1961.
290. Patricia Likendall, "Medical Specialization: Trends and Contributing Factors", in R. H. Coombs and C. E. Vincent, Eds., *Psychosocial Aspects of Medical Training*, C. Thomas, 1971.
291. Marshall H. Becker, Ed., *The Health Belief Model and Personal Health Behavior*, Health Education Monographs, Vol. 2, 1974.
292. *Skyrocketing Prescription Drug Prices*, Proceedings Special Committee on Aging of the U. S. Senate, 1989.
293. Mickey C. Smith, "Drug Advertising as a source of Therapeutic Information", *American Journal of Hospital Pharmacy*, Vol. 25, June 1968, pp. 46–52.
294. B. L. Svarstad, "The Sociology of Drugs", in H. I. Wertheimer and M. C. Smith, Eds., *Pharmacy Practice*, University Park Press, 1981.

295. G. Grob, "The Social History of Medicine and Disease in America: Problems and Possibilities", in P. Bracin, Ed., *The Medicine Show*, Science History Publications, 1977.
296. A. Barger, "History", in E. Usdin, Ed., *Psychotherapeutic Drugs, Part 1 – Principles*, Marcel Dekker, 1976.
297. G. Klerman, "Drugs and Social Values", *International Journal of Addictions*, Vol. 5, 1970.
298. Paul Stolley, "Cultural Lag in Health Care", *Inquiry*, Vol. 8, 1971.
299. D. Manheimer et al., "Popular Attitudes and Beliefs about Tranquilizers", *American Journal of Psychiatry*, Vol. 130, 1973.
300. J. Najman, D. Klein and C. Munro, "Patient Characteristics Negatively Stereotyped by Doctors", *Social Science and Medicine*, Vol. 14A, 1982.
301. J. Morgan, "The Politics of Medication", in L. Lasagna, Ed., *Controversies in Therapeutics*, W. B. Sanders, 1980.
302. R. Miller, "Prescribing Habits of Physicians", *Drug Intelligence and Clinical Pharmacy*, Vol. 8, 1974, p. 261–264.
303. A. Schmidt, "Comment", *American Journal of Psychiatry*, Vol. 13, 1978.
304. *False and Misleading Advertising of Prescription Tranquilizing Drugs*, Proceedings Subcommittee on Legal and Marketing Affairs of the U. S. House of Representatives Committee on Government Operations, 1958.
305. K. Hammond and C. Joyce, *Psychoactive Drugs and Social Judgment*, John Wiley and Sons, 1977.
306. Durand F. Jacobs, "The Psychoactive Drug Thing: Coping or Cop Out?" *Journal of Drug Issues*, Vol. 27, 1971.
307. J.W. Marks, *The Benzodiazepines*, University Press, 1981.
308. J. Rogers, "Drug Abuse-Just What the Doctor Ordered", *Psychology Today*, Vol. 12, 1971.
309. L. Koran, "Psychiatric Manpower Ratios", *Archives of General Psychiatry*, Vol. 36, 1975.
310. P. Hesbacher et al., "Setting, Patient and Doctor Effects on Drug Response in Neurotic Patients", *Psychopharmacology*, Vol. 18, 1970.
311. Edward W. McCranie, Alan J. Horowitz and Richard M. Marine, "Alleged Sex-Role Stereotyping in the Assessment of Women's Physical Complaints. A Study of General Practitioners", *Social Science and Medicine*, Vol. 12, 1978, pp. 111–116.
312. Constance A. Nathanson, "Social Roles and Health Status among Women: The Significance of Employment", *Social Science and Medicine*, Vol. 14A, 1980, pp. 463–471.
313. David Mechanic, "Sex, Illness, Illness Behavior, and the Use of Health Services", *Social Science and Medicine*, Vol. 12B, 1978, pp. 207–214.
314. Ronald C. Kessler, Roger L. Brown and Clifford L. Bowman, "Sex Differences in Psychiatric Helpseeking", *Journal of Health and Social Behavior*, Vol. 22, 1981, pp. 49–64.
315. Ruth Cooperstock and Henry L. Lennard, "Some Social Meanings of Tranquilizer Use", *Sociology of Health and Illness*, Vol. 1, 1979, pp. 331–347.

316. A. Donagan, "How Much Neurosis Should We Bear?", in H. Engelhardt and S. Spencer, Eds., *Mental Health, Philosophical Perspectives*, D. Reidel, 1978.
317. H. T. Engelhardt, in (346).
318. Michael E. Porter, *Competitive Strategy*, The Free Press, 1980.
319. M. L. Fones, "Self-Regulation of Pharmaceutical Advertising?", *Medical Marketing and Media*, Vol. 7, 1972, pp. 8–10.
320. *NWDA Executive Newsletter*, Vol. 18, 1963.
321. Pharmaceutical Manufacturers Association, "Issues and Answers", Comment to Senator Kennedy, 1973.
322. Wroe Alderson, *Dynamic Marketing Behavior*, Richard D. Irwin, 1965.
323. D. D. Adams and W. E. Nelson, "The Drug Amendments of 1962", *New York University Law Review*, Vol. 38, 1963.
324. C. C. Edwards, "Closing the Gap: OTC Drugs", *FDA Consumer*, 1972.
325. Anonymous, "Drug Pricing and the Rx Police State", *Consumer Reports*, 1970.
326. Anonymous, "Drug Trends", *FDC Reports*, 1970.
327. R. H. Hensel, "Consumerism: A Decision by Next Wednesday", *Medical Marketing and Media*, Vol. 6, 1971.
328. A. M. Harlow, *Pharmaceutical Marketing in Perspective*, Mosby, 1973.
329. D. B. Manischevitz and J. A. Stuart, "Marketing under Attack", *Journal of Marketing*, Vol. 26, 1962, pp. 1–6.
330. Mickey C. Smith, "Drugs and the Right to Happiness", *Drug Intelligence and Clinical Pharmacy*, Vol. 14, 1980.
331. C. B. Chapman and J. M. Talmadge, "The Evaluation of the Right-to-Health Concept in the United States", in M. B. Vischer, Ed., *Humanistic Perspectives in Medical Ethics*, Prometheus Books, 1972.
332. D. Callahan, "Biomedical Programs and the Limits of Human Health", in R. M. Veatch and R. Branson, *Ethics and Health Policy*, Ballinger, 1976.
333. G. G. Reader, "Community and Government Responsibility in the Delivery of Medical Care", in E. D. Kilbourne and W. G. Smile, Eds., *Human Ecology and Public Health*, Macmillan, 1969.
334. M. B. Balter, In. (99).
335. R. M. Veatch, *Ethics and Health Policy*, Ballinger, 1976.
336. K. Lewin, *A Dynamic Theory of Personality: Selected Papers*, Translated by D. K. Adams and K. E. Zener, McGraw-Hill, 1935.
337. M. Richard, *The Real Voice*, Macmillan, 1964.
338. Michael G. Wokasch, *Pharmaplasia*, Wokasch Consulting, 2010.
339. W. D. Reekie and M. H. Weber, *Profits, Politics and Drugs*, Macmillan Health, 1979.
340. Victor Fuchs, *Who Shall Live?* Basic Books, 1974.
341. D. S. Pathak, A. Escovitz and S. Kucuklavslan, Eds., *Promotion of Pharmaceuticals: Issues, Trends, Options*. Proceedings of a Conference at Ohio State University, 1995.
342. J. F. Weston, *Pricing in the Pharmaceutical Industry*, University of California Press, 1971.

343. D. Schwartzman, *The Expected Return from Pharmaceutical Research*, American Enterprise Institute, 1975.
344. J. Schnee, "Innovation and Discovery in the Drug Industry", in E. Mansfield et al., Eds., *Research and Innovation in the Modern Corporation*, Macmillan, 1971.
345. R. M. Cooper, "The Food and Drug Administration's Authority to Regulate Miscellaneous Statements by Pharmaceutical Manufacturers", in (371). A detailed legal analysis of "free speech" versus commercial speech.
346. D. G. Adams, "Pharmaceutical Advertising: Education versus Promotion", in (371).
347. Samuel Merwin, *Rise and Fight Againe*, Albert and Charles Boni, Inc., 1935.
348. Paul DeHaen, *Development Schedule of New Drug Products*, Romaine Pearson, 1949. A "step-by-step" description of the development of a new drug as seen 50 years ago.
349. Task Force on Prescription drugs, *Approaches to Drug Insurance Design*, U. S. Department of HEW, 1969.
350. Louis Lasagna and Joseph Cooper, Ed., *Decision-Making on the Effectiveness and Safety of Drugs*, The Interdisciplinary Communication Associates, 1971.
351. Anonymous, *Hospital Pharmacy*, Vol. 7, 1971.
352. L. S. Linn, "Physician Characteristics and Attitudes toward the Legitimate Use of Psychotherapeutic Drugs", *Journal of Health and Social Behavior*, Vol. 12, 1971, pp. 132–140.
353. H. F. Dowling, "The Prescribed Environment", *Saturday Review*, April 3, 1971.
354. Robert Seidenberg, "Drug Advertising and Perception of Mental Illness", *Mental Hygiene*, Vol. 55, 1971.
355. J. S. Szasz, *The Myth of Mental Illness*, Harper, 1964.
356. Wayne G. Menke, "Professional Values in Medical Practice", *New England Journal of Medicine*, Vol. 280, 1969, pp. 930–936.
357. Max Weber, *Essays in Sociology*, Oxford Press, 1958.
358. E. L. Koos, *The Health of Regionville*, Columbia University Press, 1954.
359. Robert P. Hudson, "Polypharmacy in Twentieth Century America", *Clinical Pharmacology and Therapeutics*, Vol. 9, 1968, pp. 2–10.
360. J. A. Visconti and M. C. Smith, "Appeals Used in Prescription Drug Advertising", *Hospital Pharmacy*, Vol. 3, 1968, pp. 5–13.
361. Anonymous, *FDC Reports*, Vol. 33, 1971.
362. D. C. Brodie, *Drug Utilization and Drug Utilization Review and Control*, U. S. Department of HEW, 1970.
363. S. Potter, *One Upmanship*, Holt, Rinehart and Winston, 1951.
364. Donald R. Kirsch and Ogi Ogas, *The Drug Hunters*, Arcade Publishing, 2017. This is simply a terrific book. It is literate, fascinating and fun. Even better than *Ten Drugs* (35).
365. Daniel L. Azarnoff, Donald B. Hunninghake and Jack Wortman, "Prescription Writing by Generic Name and Drug Cost", *Journal of Chronic Disease*, Vol. 19, 1966, pp. 1253–1256.
366. Marcia Angell, *The Truth About the Drug Companies*, Random House, 2005.

367. Daniel Carpenter, *Reputation and Power*, Princeton University Press, 2010.
368. Philip J. Hilts, *Protecting America's Health*, Alfred H. Knopf, 2003.
369. Peter Martin, *The Dictionary Wars*, Princeton University Press, 2019.
370. D. McCaffrey, M. C. Smith and B. Banahan, "Economic Losses Associated with Unclaimed Prescriptions", *Product Management Today*, April 1994, pp. 20–24.
371. Rita Ricardo Campbell, *Drug Lag*, Hoover Institution Press, 1976.
372. John F. Cady, *Drugs on the Market*, Lexington Books, 1975.
373. F. Marion Fletcher, *Market Restraints in the Retail Drug Industry*, University of Pennsylvania Press, 1967.
374. Norman Cousins, *Anatomy of an Illness*, Norton, 1979, with permission.
375. Clement Bezold, Ed., *Pharmaceuticals in the Year 2000*, Institute for Alternative Futures, 1983.
376. John F. Early, "Unplugging the Third Rail", *Policy Analysis*, Cato Institute, June 2019.
377. Norman Sartorius, "The Meaning of Health and Its Promotion", *Croatian Medical Journal*, Vol. 47, August 2006, p. 662.
378. N. B. Talbot, "Concerning the Need for Behavioral and Social Science in Medicine", in J. H. Knowles, Ed., *Views of Medicine Education and Social Science in Medical Care*, Harvard University Press, 1966.
379. George E. Pickett, "The Basics of Health Policy: Rights and Privileges", *American Journal of Public Health*, Vol. 65, 1961, pp. 236–240.
380. D. Callahan, "Biomedical Progress and the Limits of Human Health", (in Veatch -335).
381. G. C. Reader, "Community and Governmental Responsibility in the Delivery of Medical Care to the Individual", in E. D. Kilbourne and W. G. Smillie, Eds., *Human Ecology and Public Health*, Macmillan, 1969.
382. Anonymous, "Committee for a National Health Service", *American Journal of Public Health*, Vol. 67, 1977.
383. M. E. Roemer and S. J. Axelrod, "A National Health Service and Social Security", *American Journal of Public Health*, Vol. 67, 1978.
384. B. L. Svarstad, "Sociology of Drugs", in A. I. Wertheimer and M. C. Smith, Eds., *Pharmacy Practice*, Williams and Wilkins, 1981, with permission.
385. Mickey C. Smith, "The Prescription: Every Thing You Wanted to Know but Didn't Think to Ask", *American Pharmacist*, Vol. NS18, 1978, pp. 30–33.
386. W. F. Murphey and C. H. Pritchett, "Statutory Interpretation", *Courts, Judges and Politics*, Random House, 1961.
387. Michael R. Pollard, "Managed Care and a Changing Pharmaceutical Industry", *Health Affairs*, Vol. 9, 1990, pp. 55–65.
388. Ted Klein and Fred Danzig, *Publicity: How to Make the Media Work for You*, Scribners, 1985.
389. Emily Chang, Mickey Smith and Ben Banahan, "Opinions of Mississippi Pharmacists on the OTC Status of Ibuprofen", *Journal of Pharmaceutical Marketing and Management*, Vol. 3, 1988, pp. 117–123.
390. Roger J. Traynor, "The Ways and Meanings of Defective Products and Strict Liability", *Tennessee Law Review*, Vol. 32, 1965, p. 363.

391. Marilyn Ferguson, *The Aquarian Conspiracy: Personal and Social Transformation in the 1980's*, J. P. Archer, 1980, with permission.
392. J. J. Hanlon, *Principles of Public Health Administration*, Mosby Company, 1969.
393. Harry F. Dowling, *Medicines for Man*, Alfred A. Knopf, 1970.
394. John T. Fay, Jr., *Managing Healthcare Distribution, 1876–2001*, E. L. F. Publications, 2001. A beautiful history by a wholesaling icon.
395. Dennis B. Worthen, *A Roadmap to a Profession's Future*, Gordon and Breach Science, 1999, with permission. Contains full text of the Millis Commission Report.
396. Howard S. Frazier and Frederick Mosteller, *Medicine Worth Paying for: Assessing Medical Innovations*, Harvard University Press, 1995. Individual economic analyses of medical advances.
397. Milton Moskowitz, "The Drugstore: Outlet or Bottleneck", *Drug and Cosmetic Industry*, Vol. 88, 1961.
398. James R. Philip, "Rational Prescribing and Drug Usage", *American Journal of Hospital Pharmacy*, Vol. 27, 1970, pp. 659–665.
399. D. McCaffrey et al. "The Financial Implications of Initial Non-Compliance: An Investigation of Unclaimed Prescriptions in Community Pharmacies", *Journal of Research in Pharmaceutical Economics*, Vol. 6, 1995, pp. 38–64.
400. Anonymous, *F. D. C. Reports*, Vol. 33, 1971.
401. A. Sheldon, F. Baker and C. McGlaughlin, Eds., *Systems and Medical Care*, MIT Press, 1970.
402. R. Ferber and H. G. Wales, *The Effectiveness of Pharmaceutical Promotion*, University of Illinois Press, 1958.
403. J. S. Coleman, E. Katz and H. Menzel, *Medical Innovation, A Diffusion Study*, Bobbs-Merrell, 1966.
404. Lawrence S. Linn and Milton S. Davis, "Physicians Orientation toward the Legitimacy of Drug Use and Their Preferred Source of Drug Information", *Social Science and Medicine*, Vol. 6, 1972, pp. 199–203.
405. Gregory R. Mundy et al., "Current Medical Practice and the Food and Drug Administration", *Journal of the American Medical Association*, Vol. 229, 1974, pp. 1744–1748.
406. Peter A. Parish, "Sociology of Prescribing", *British Medical Journal*, Vol. 30, 1974, pp. 214–217.
407. Russell R. Miller, "Prescribing Habits of Physicians, Part VII", *Drug Intelligence and Clinical Pharmacy*, Vol. 9, 1974, pp. 81–91.
408. N. S. Kline, "Antidepressant Medications", *Journal of the American Medical Association*, Vol. 227, 1974.
409. M. B. Balter in Helms (99).
410. Anonymous, "A Study of Advertising Effects in Modern Medicine", *Modern Medicine Publications*, 1970.
411. D. S. Conger, *Social Interventions*, Modern Press, 1974.
412. J. R. Crout, (Testimony), Competitive Problem Hearings, Part 30, (1976) in Ref. 123.

413. Franz L. Ingelfinger, "Annual Discourse – Swinging Copy and Sober Discourse", *New England Journal of Medicine*, Vol. 281, 1969, pp. 526–532.
414. Paul D. Stolley, "Assuring the Safety and Efficacy of Therapies", *International Journal of Health Services*, Vol. 4, 1974, pp. 131–145.
415. R. W. Fassold and C. W. Gowdy, "A Survey of Physicians' Reactions to Drug Promotion", *Canadian Medical Association Journal*, Vol. 98, 1968, p. 701.
416. Arthur Ruskin, "A Survey of Information Needs and Problems Associated with Communications Directed at Practicing Physicians, Part 1", *National Technical Information Services*, 1974.
417. Thelma H. McCormack, "The Druggists' Dilemma: Problems of a Marginal Occupation", *American Journal of Sociology*, Vol. 61, 1956, pp. 308–315.
418. Dennis B. Worthen, *A Road Map to a Profession's Future*, Gordon and Breach, 1999.
419. Charles D. May, "Selling Drugs by Educating Physicians", *Journal of Medical Education*, Vol. 36, 1961, pp. 1–23.
420. Mickey C. Smith and L. Griffin, "Rationality of Appeals Used in the Promotion of Psychotropic Drugs: A Comparison of Male and Female Models", *Social Science and Medicine*, Vol. 11, 1977, pp. 409–414.
421. Mickey C. Smith, P. Strecker and J. Hair, "Sex Appeals in Prescription Drug Advertising", *Medical Marketing and Media*, Vol. 12, 1977, pp. 68–70.
422. Mickey C. Smith, "Portrayal of the Elderly in Prescription Drug Advertising", *Gerontologist*, Vol. 16, 1976, pp. 329–334.
423. Mickey C. Smith, "Where Are the Blacks in Prescription Drug Advertising?" *Medical Marketing and Media*, Vol. 12, 1977.
424. P. A. Parish, "What Influences Have Led to Increased Prescribing of Psychotropic Drugs?" *Journal of the Royal College of General Practitioners*, Vol. 23, 1973, p. 49.
425. Jacob Jacoby and Constance Small, "The FDA Approach to Defining Misleading Advertising", *Journal of Marketing*, Vol. 39, 1975, pp. 65–68.
426. Leslie Hendeles, "Need for 'Counter-Detailing' Antibiotics", *American Journal of Hospital Pharmacy*, Vol. 33, 1976, pp. 918–924.
427. George J. Stigler, "The Economics of Information", *Journal of Political Economics*, Vol. 69, 1961, pp. 213–225.
428. P. Nelson, "Information and Consumer Behavior", *Information Journal*, Vol. 78, 1970, p. 135.
429. M. R. Ryan and Mickey C. Smith, "Are Physicians Dissonant?" *Pharmaceutical Marketing and Media*, Vol. 4, 1969, p. 42.
430. J. F. Sadusk (Letter), *Annals of Internal Medicine*, Vol. 75, September 1971.
431. F. J. Ingelfinger, "Advertising: Informational but Not Educational", *New England Journal of Medicine*, Vol. 296, 1972, pp. 1318–1319.
432. G. Teeling-Smith, "Psychotropic Drugs and Society", *Journal of the Royal College of General Practitioners*, Vol. 23, 1973, p. 58.
433. D. L. Wade, "Adverse Reactions to Psychotropic Drugs", *Journal of the Royal College of General Practitioners*, Vol. 23, 1973.

434. J. Stetler, "Commentary", *F.D.C. Reports*, Vol. 38, 1976.
435. Anonymous, "Findings and Conclusions of the NCCC Project on Drug Advertising", *Journal of Drug Issues*, Vol. 4, 1974.
436. Mickey C. Smith, "A Colloquy on Pharmaceutical Advertising", *Pharmaceutical Marketing and Media*, Vol. 11, 1967.
437. Mickey C. Smith, "Who Are the Pharmacists?" *Medical Marketing and Media*, March, 1986.
438. Metta Lou Henderson and Dennis B. Worthen, *American Women Pharmacists, Contributions to the Profession*, CRC Press, 2002.
439. V. Petkova and Z. Dimitrova, "Asthma Drug Medication and Non-Compliance", *Bollettino Chimico Farmaceutico*, Vol. 141, 2002, pp. 355–356.
440. Morton Mintz, *The Therapeutic Nightmare*, Houghton Mifflin Company, 1965.
441. George Bender and Robert Thom, *Parke-Davis Pictorial Annals of Medicine and Pharmacy*, The Warner Lambert Company, 1999.
442. Louis Lasagna, *Life, Death and the Doctor*, Alfred Knopf, 1968.
443. Steven Pray, *A History of Non-Prescription Drug Regulation*, Pharmaceutical Products Press, 2003.
444. Phillip Hilts, *Protecting America's Health*, University of North Carolina Press, 2003.
445. R. S. Epstein and M. G. McGlynn, "Disease Management: What Is It?" *Disease Management and Health Outcomes*, Vol. 1, 1997.
446. Office of the Inspector General, "Experiences of Health Maintenance Organizations with Pharmacy Benefit Management Companies", OIG Report OEI-01-95-00110, 1997.
447. G. Aston, "Discord on Managed Care Standardss", *American Medical News*, Vol. 40, 1997, pp. 1–34.
448. M. A. Rodwin, "Consumer Protection and Managed Care", *Health Affairs*, Vol. 15, 1996.
449. J. N. and R. O. Snyder, "A Review of Sexual Behavior in the United States", *American Journal of Psychiatry*, Vol. 40, 1992.
450. Ernest Dichter, *Handbook of Consumer Motivations*, McGraw-Hill, 1996, with permission.
451. A. C. Twaddle and A. M. Hessler, *A Sociology of Health*, C.V. Mosby Co., 1977 with permission.
452. Patricia J. Bush, "Pathways to Medicine Use", *Journal of Health and Social Behavior*, Vol. 19, 1978, pp. 179–189.
453. American Pharmaceutical Association, *Communicating the Value of Comprehensive Pharmaceutical Services to the Consumer*, A.Ph.A., 1973.
454. L. M. Verbrugge and F. J. Ascione, "Exploring the Iceberg", *Medical Care*, Vol. 24, 1987 pp. 539–569.
455. Y. N. Harari, *Homo Deus*, Harper Perennial, 2017.
456. M. H. Becker and L. A. Maiman, "Socio-Behavioral Determinants of Compliance with Health and Medical Care Recommendations", *Medical Care*, Vol. 13, 1975, pp. 1–24.
457. "Pharmaceutical Focus on Adherence", *PM 360*, August 2019.

458. Ivan Illich, *Limits to Medicine – Medical Nemesis*, McClelland and Stewart, 1976.
459. Y. N. Harari, *Sapiens*, Harper Perennial, 2018.
460. Michael H. Cooper, *Prices and Profits in the Pharmaceutical Industry*, Pergamon Press, 1966.
461. Mickey C. Smith, *The Problems of Economic and Marketing Research in the Pharmaceutical Industry*, Ph.D. Dissertation, University of Mississippi, 1964.
462. Laura Keras et al., "Limited Distribution Networks Stifle Competition in Generic and Biosimilar Industries", *American Journal of Managed Care*, Vol. 24, April 4, 2018, pp. 122–127.
463. *Majority Staff Report*, "Skyrocketing Prescription Drug Prices: Turning a Bad Deal into a Good Deal", Special Committee on Aging, U.S. Senate, January 1990.
464. J. C. Krantz, "Home Remedies as Sources of Modern Medicine", in H. E. Whipple, Ed., *Home Medication and the Public Welfare*, New York Academy of Sciences, 1965, p. 829–832.
465. William Doyle and A. R. Savina, "Development and Marketing of Pharmaceutical Specialties", *Drug and Cosmetic Industries*, 1946.
466. Richard Moulton, "The General Foods Check List for Development of New Products", 1948.
467. Carl Djerrasi, *The Politics of Contraception*, W. W. Norton, 1979.
468. J. M. Firestone, "A Price Index for Drugs", *Drug and Cosmetic Industry*, Vol. 87, 1963, p. 34.
469. G. M. Lebhar, "The Story of Drug Chains", *Chain Store Age*, Vol. 25, 1950, p. 2.
470. D. Gilbert, T. Walley and B. New, "Lifestyle Medicines", *British Medical Journal*, Vol. 321, 2000, p. 1341.
471. J. Laurance, "Health: Should Self-Esteem Be Available at NHS?" *Independent*, 2001, p. 9.
472. S. Overman, "Warning: Viagra May Cause Headaches for Health Insurers", *HR Magazine*, January 9, 1998, p. 1.
473. Anonymous, "Go On, It's Good for You", *The Economist*, August 8, 1998, p. 348.
474. J. Delgado, quoted in 53, p. 82.
475. R. Rychlik, *Strategies in Pharmacoeconomics and Outcomes Research*, Pharmaceutical Products Press, 2002.
476. Meagan Rosenthal, E. Holmes and B. Banahan, *Research in Social and Administrative Pharmacy*, Vol. 3, p. 1.
477. A. A. Scitovsky and D. P. Rice, "Estimates of the Direct and Indirect Costs of Acquired Immunodeficiency Syndrome in the United States, 1985, 1986, 1991", *Public Health Reports*, Vol. 102, pp. 5–17, 1987.
478. D. P. Rice, "Estimating the Cost of Illness", DHEW Publications, No. 947-6, 1966.
479. D. P. Rice, T. A. Hodgstein, "The Economic Cost of Illness: A Replication and Update", *Healthcare Financing Review*, Vol. 7, 1985, pp. 61–80.
480. A. A. Scitovsky, "The Economic Impact of AIDS", *Health Affairs*, Vol. 7, 1988, pp. 32–45.

481. S. J. Jachuk et al., "The Effect of Hypotensive Drugs on Quality of Life", *Journal of the Royal College of General Practitioners*, Vol. 32, 1982, pp. 103–105.
482. R. Diamond, "Drugs and the Quality of Life: The Patient's Point of View", *Journal of Clinical Psychiatry*, Vol. 46, 1985, pp. 29–35.
483. R. A. Pearlman and R. F. Uhlmann, "Quality of Life in Chronic Diseases", *Journal of Gerontology*, Vol. 43, 1958, pp. 25–30.
484. W. E. Morton and L.A. Hahn, "Epidemiology of Genital Health Disease", *Journal of the American Medical Association*, Vol. 195, 1966, p. 129.
485. E. A. Suchman, *Sociology in the Field of Public Health*, Russell Sage Foundation, 1963, p. 53.
486. Anonymous, *The Control of Communicable Diseases in Man*, American Public Health Association, 1960.
487. A. A. Scitovsky, "High Cost of Dying" *The Economist*, Vol. 93, 2005, pp. 825–841.
488. M. Bergner et al., "The Sickness Impact Profile: Validation of a Health Status Measure", *Medical Care*, Vol. 14, No. 1, 1986, pp. 57–67.
489. C. Bomhardier et al., "Auranofin Therapy and Quality of Life in Patients with Rheumatoid Arthritis: Results of a Multicenter Trial", *American Journal of Medicine*, Vol. 81, 1986, pp. 565–578.
490. M. S. Thompson et al., "The Cost-Effectiveness of Auranofin: Results of a Randomized Clinical Trial", *Journal of Rheumatology*, Vol. 145, 1988, pp. 35–42.
491. M. S. Thompson, "Willingness to Pay and Accept Risks to Cure Chronic Disease", *American Journal of Public Health*, Vol. 76, 1986, pp. 392–396.
492. C.R.B. Joyce, "Quality of Life: The State of the Art in Clinical Assessment", in Stuart Walker and Rachel Rosser, Eds., *Quality of Life: Assessment and Application*, MTP Press, 1987.
493. M. E. Pichichero, "Short Course Antibiotic Therapy for Respiratory Infections", *Pediatric Infectious Disease Journal*, Vol. 19, 2000, pp. 929–937.
494. J. A. Rizzo and W. A. Simons, "Variations in Compliance Among Hypertensive Patients by Drug Class: Implications for Health Care Costs", *Clinical Therapeutics*, Vol. 19, 1997, pp. 1446–1457.
495. R. M. Schulz et al., "Drug Use Behavior Under the Constraints of a Medicaid Prescription Cap", *Clinical Therapeutics*, Vol. 17, 1995, pp. 330–340.
496. S. D. Sullivan, "Noncompliance with Medication Regimens and Subsequent Hospitalizations: A Literature Analysis and Cost of Hospitalization Estimate", *Journal of Research in Pharmaceutical Economics*, Vol. 2, 1990, pp. 467–479.
497. Ed Schoonveld, *The Price of Global Health*, Routledge, 2015.
498. G. M. Kolassa, *Elements of Pharmaceutical Pricing*, Pharmaceutical Products Press, 1997.
499. David Cleeton, Valy Goepfrich and Burton Weisbrod, "What Does the Consumer Price Index for Drugs Really Mean?" *Health Care Financing Review*, Vol. 13, No. 3, 1992, pp. 45–52.
500. P. Branca, *The Medicine Show*, Science History Publications, 1983.
501. Anonymous, "The Skies Grow Friendlier", *Time*, August 17, 1981.

502. N. Winkelman, "The Use of Neuroleptic Drugs in the Treatment of Nonpsychotic Psychiatric Patients", in F. Ayd, Ed., *Rational Pharmacology and the Right to Treatment*, Ayd Medical Communications, 1975, p. 161.
503. Frank Berger, "Anxiety and the Discovery of the Tranquilizers", in F. Ayd and B. Blackwell, *Discoveries in Biological Psychiatry*, J. B. Lippincott, 1970.
504. Leo Sternbach, "The Benzodiazepine Story", *Journal of Medicinal Chemistry*, Vol. 22, 1979, p. 2.
505. K. Hammond and C. Joyce, *Psychoactive Drugs and Social Judgement*, John Wiley & Sons, 1973.
506. D. Jacobs, "The Psychoactive Drug Thing: Coping or Cop Out?" *Journal of Drug Issues*, Vol. 1, 1971, p. 264.
507. Alexander Schmidt, "Comment", *American Journal of Psychiatry*, Vol. 135, 1978, p. 1057.
508. G. Aden, "Forward", in W. Clark and J. del Giudice, Eds., *Principles of Psychopharmacology*, Second Edition, Academic Press, 1978, p. 2.
509. Anonymous, "Over-coping with Valium", *FDA Consumer*, Vol. 13, 1980, pp. 21–23.
510. T. D. Rucker, "Production and Prescribing of Minor Tranquilizers: A Macro View: Paper presented to the American Ortho-Psychiatric Association, April 19, 1980.
511. J. Morgan, "The Politics of Medication", in L. Lasagna, *Controversies in Therapeutics*, W. B. Saunders, 1980, pp. 16–22.
512. J. R. Neill, "A Social History of Psychotropic Drug Advertisements", *Social Science and Medicines*, Vol. 28, No. 4, 1989, pp. 333–338.
513. H. Parry, "Patterns of Psychotropic Drug Use Among American Adults", *Journal of Drug Issues*, Vol. 1, 1971, p. 264.
514. D. Manheimer, G. Mellinger and M. Balter, "Psychotherapeutic Drugs", *California Medicine*, Vol. 109, 1964, p. 109.
515. G. Mellinger et al., "Patterns of Psychotherapeutic Drug Use Among Adults in San Francisco", *Archives of General Psychiatry*, Vol. 25, 1971, p. 25.
516. B. Blackwell, "Minor Tranquilizers: Use, Misuse or Overuse", *Psychosomatics*, Vol. 16, 1975, p. 26.
517. D. Greenblatt, R. Shader and J. Koch-Wesser, "Psychotropic Drug Use in the Boston Area", *Archives of General Psychiatry*, Vol. 32, 1975, p. 518.
518. M. Balter and J. Levine, "Character and Extent of Psychotherapeutic Drug Usage in the United States", *Psychiatry I*, Vol. 23, 1971, p. 80.
519. H. Parry et al., "National Patterns of Psychotherapeutic Drug use", *Archives of General Psychiatry*, Vol. 28, 1973, p. 769.
520. L. Smith, "Citation Analysis", *Library Trends*, Vol. 30, 1981, p. 81.
521. B. Blackwell, "Psychotropic Drugs in Use Today", *Journal of the American Medical Association*, Vol. 225, 1973, p. 224.
522. D. Greenblatt and R. Shader, "Meprobamate: A Study of Irrational Drug Use", *American Journal of Psychiatry*, Vol. 127, 1971, p. 127.
523. M. C. Smith and J. Juergens, "Two Tranquil: The Epidemiology of an Idea", *Clinical Research Practices and Drug Regulatory Affairs*, Vol. 3, 1987, pp. 147–153.

524. G. Bylinsky, "Future Drugs that Will Be Lifesavers for the Industry Too", *Fortune*, Vol. 3, 1987, pp. 147–153.
525. R. M. Sade, "Medical Care as a Right: A Refutation", *New England Journal of Medicine*, Vol. 285, 1971, pp. 1287–1292.
526. E. J. McCarthy, *Basic Marketing: A Managerial Approach*, Richard D. Irwin, 1964.
527. Sandoz Newsletter to Pharmacists, N.D.
528. M. C. Smith, "Practicing Mail-Order Pharmacy is a Violation of Pharmacy's Code of Ethics", *Mississippi Pharmacist*, Vol. 18, 1991, p. 17.
529. M. C. Smith, "A Colloquy on Pharmaceutical Advertising", *Medical Marketing and Media*, Vol. 11, 1967, p. 48.
530. W. J. Goode, "Encroachment, Charlatanism and the Emerging Profession", *American Sociological Review*, Vol. 25, 1960, p. 902.
531. T. H. McCormick, "The Druggists' Dilemma: Problems of a Marginal Profession", *American Journal of Sociology*, Vol. 61, 1956, p. 308.
532. A. A. Done, "Differences Between Advertised and Medical Uses of Drugs", *Journal of Advertising Research*, Vol. 1, 1960, pp. 18–21.
533. Mickey C. Smith, "Practicing Mail-Order Pharmacy is a Violation of Pharmacy's Code of Ethics", *Mississippi Pharmacist*, May 1991, p. 17.
534. Winifred Gallagher, *How the Post Office Created America*, Penguin Press, 2015.
535. Monica Williams-Murphy, *It's Ok to Die*, Murphy & Murphy Publishers, 2011.
536. J. M. Fletcher, "The Price of Public Respect", in Ref. 8.
537. Bryan R. Luce and Anne Elixhauser, "Socioeconomic Evaluation and the Health Care Industry", *Journal of Research in Pharmaceutical Economics*, Vol. 2, No. 4, 1990.
538. D. Neuhauser, *Survey of Research Results and Current States of CBA/CEA in Technology Assessment: Cimetidine as a Model*, Leonard Davis Institute of Health Economics, University of Pennsylvania, 1981.
539. K. Johnson, "AMA Guidelines: We'll Stay the Course", *Medical Marketing and Media*, 1991, pp. 82–88.
540. D. Kessler, "Drug Promotions and Scientific Exchange", *New England Journal of Medicine*, Vol. 325, 1991, pp. 201–203.
541. P. H. Rubin, "Economics of Prescription Drug Advertising", *Journal of Research in Pharmaceutical Economics*, Vol. 3, No. 4, 1991, p. 29.
542. Syed Usman, C. Marshall and M. Smith, "Differences Between Actual and Advertised Uses of Drugs – A Replicated Study", *Journal of Advertising Research*, Vol.19, 1979, p. 65.
543. Mike Magee, *Code Blue*, Atlantic Monthly Press, 2019.
544. Ben Goldacre, *Bad Pharma: How Drug Companies Mislead Doctors and Harm Patients*, Faber and Faber, 2013.
545. The Wilkerson Group, "The Challenge of Neuroscience: Clinical Perspectives and Commercial Prospects", *Pharmaceutical Executive*, October, 1990, with permission.
546. A. H. Maslow, *Motivation and Personality*, Harper Brothers, 1954.

547. Elizabeth Moench, "What Does DM Mean to Patients", *Pharmaceutical Executive*, May 1995, p. 52.
548. C. Huttin and N. Bosanquet, *The Prescription Drug Market*, North Holland, 1992.
549. Chip Walter, *Immortality, Inc.*, National Geographic, 2020.
550. G. Bylinsky, "Future Drugs That will be Lifesavers for the Industry Too", *Fortune*, Vol. 94, pp. 152–162.
551. H. E. French and Richard Miller, Jr., *The Productivity of Health Care and Pharmaceuticals*, AEI Press, 1999. An international study concluding that, "Increased pharmaceutical consumption helps improve mortality outcomes, especially for those at middle age and beyond".
552. Earl L. Koos, *The Health of Regionville*, Hafner Publishing, 1967.
553. Gerald Posner, *Pharma*, Avid Reader Press, 2020.

Chapter 13 References

554. W. Steven Pray, *Nonprescription Product Therapeutics*. Second Edition. Baltimore, MD: Lippincott Williams & Wilkins, 2006.
555. W. Steven Pray, *A History of Nonprescription Product Regulation*. New York: Pharmaceutical Products Press, 2003.
556. Anonymous, "Understanding Over-the-Counter Medicines", Food and Drug Administration. https://www.fda.gov/drugs/buying-using-medicine-safely/understanding-over-counter-medicines. Accessed September 30, 2019.
557. Anonymous, "White Paper: Value of OTC Medicines to the U.S. Healthcare System", Consumer Healthcare Products Association. http://overthecounter-value.org/white-paper/. Accessed September 30, 2019.
558. "CPG Sec. 120.500 Health Fraud-Factors in Considering Regulatory Action", Food and Drug Administration. https://www.fda.gov/ICECI/ComplianceManuals/CompliancePolicyGuidanceManual/ucm073838.htm. Accessed September 30, 2019.
559. James H. Young, *The Medical Messiahs*. Princeton, NJ: Princeton University Press; 1967.
560. "War on Cut Drug Prices", *New York Times*, May 4, 1900.
561. Samuel H. Adams, "The Great American Fraud", *Collier's*, October 7, 1905, p. 14.
562. "Do not Want to Make Alcohol Conspicuous", *New York Times*, September 21, 1906.
563. Joshua J. Pray and W. Steven Pray. "Nonpharmacy OTC Sales: Patients Lose", *Medscape*. https://www.medscape.com/viewarticle/456001_3. Accessed September 30, 2019.
564. Anonymous, "About CHPA", Consumer Healthcare Products Association. https://www.chpa.org/About.aspx. Accessed September 30, 2019.
565. Anonymous, "NDMA Board Votes Name Change", NDMA Special Report, January 29, 1999.

566. S. Levy, "It's Now Official: NDMA is CHPA", *Drug Topics*, Vol. 143, No. 7, 1999, p. 43.
567. "NDMA gets a consumer-friendly name", *US Pharm*, Vol.24, No. 3, 1999, p. 55.
568. Anonymous, "Consumer Healthcare Products Association", *Weekly Pharmacy Reports*, February 1, 1999, p. 1.
569. Anonymous, "Annual Report", Consumer Healthcare Products Association. https://www.chpa.org/CHPAAnnualReport.aspx. Accessed October 1, 2019.
570. "Drug Act Widened in Tugwell Draft", *New York Times*, May 16, 1933.
571. "Tugwell Assailed on Advertising Act", *New York Times*, October 11, 1933.
572. "Witnesses Assail Food and Drug Bill", *New York Times*, December 9, 1933.
573. "Copeland Offers Revised Drug Bill", *New York Times*, January 5, 1934.
574. "Drug Trade to Back Black Bill", *New York Times*, January 7, 1934.
575. "Fight for Drug Act to Be Continued", *New York Times*, December 5, 1934.
576. "Drug Act Revisions Will Be Supported", *New York Times*, December 6, 1934.
577. "Industry to Seek Drug Act Changes", *New York Times*, January 13, 1935.
578. "Drug Act Hearing Expected in March", *New York Times*, February 24, 1935.
579. "Drug Advertisers See Threat in Bill", *New York Times*, April 7, 1935.
580. "Suggests Changes in Drug Measure", *New York Times*, January 10, 1937.
581. Anonymous, "Food & Drug Bill Passed at Last", *Business Week*, June 18, 1938.
582. "Proprietary Group Assails Drug Bill", *New York Times*, May 15, 1951.
583. "Drug Makers Hit Control Measure", *New York Times*, August 22, 1962.
584. K. Gannon, "Cope: The Year in OTCs—Progress and Challenges", *Drug Topics*, Vol. 136, No. 12, 1992, p. 60.
585. K. Gannon, "NDMA's Cope Upholds Consumer's 'Rights' on OTCs", *Drug Topics*, Vol. 138, No. 11, 1994, p. 80.
586. Anonymous, "NDMA Group Provides Extensive Input as the Last OTC Review Panel Ends!" *NDMA Executive Newsletter*, December 4, 1998, p. 3.
587. Anonymous, "CHPA Urges Different Approach for OTC Review", *CHPA Executive Newsletter*, March 4, 2000, p. 2.
588. Anonymous, "OTC Industry Asks Changes at FDA", *NDMA News Release*, August 3, 1990.
589. M. F. Conlan, "Three Familiar with Pharmacy Issues Named to FDA's OTC Panel", *Drug Topics*, Vol. 136, No. 23, 1992, p. 94.
590. M. F. Conlan, "Mist-ified: Should Some OTCs Receive a New Classification?" *Drug Topics*, Vol. 139, No. 14, 1995, p. 16.
591. Anonymous, "Warn of Self-Medication with O.T.C. Drugs", *Pharmacists Financial News*, June 1992.
592. Anonymous, "OTC Overdose", *NARD Journal*, Vol. 114, No. 6, 1992, p. 11.
593. Anonymous, "FDA Got 131,000 Complaints About Rxs and OTCs", *Drug Topics*, Vol. 141, No. 3, 1997, p. 8.
594. "Drug Outlet Issue up to Trial Judge", *New York Times*, December 12, 1952.
595. M. Q. Bectel, "The Rx-OTC Switch: Good for Pharmacy", *American Pharmacy*, Vol. NS24, No. 4, 1984, p. 20.
596. J. Covert, "Making the Most of the Rx-OTC Switch", *American Pharmacy*, Vol. NS24, No. 2, 1984, p. 34.

597. J. P. White, "Third Class of Drugs Opens up First-Class Feud", *Drug Topics*, Vol. 128, No. 17, 1984, p. 38.
598. Anonymous, "RPh's United on Need for 'Pharmacist Legend' Class of Rx Drugs that Go OTC", *American Druggist*, Vol. 201, No. 11, 1984, p. 17.
599. Anonymous, "OTC Drug Labels: 'Must Reading'", *FDA Consumer*, Vol. 19, No. 10, 1985, p. 33.
600. K. Gannon, "Rx-to-OTC Switches Raise New Call for Third Class", *Drug Topics*, Vol 133, No. 19, 1989, p. 48.
601. R. Harkness, "Going Third Class", *Drug Topics*, Vol. 134, No. 5, 1990, p. 8.
602. Anonymous, "Third Class of Drugs", *Nonprescription Drug Manufacturers Association Position Paper*, June 26, 1990 (revised).
603. M. Segal, "Rx to OTC-The Switch is on", *FDA Consumer*, Vol. 25, No. 3, 1991, p. 9.
604. M. Segal, "Rx-OTC...The Switch is on", NDMA Reprint.
605. S. Martin, "Is a Third Class of Drugs in Pharmacy's Future?" *American Pharmacy*, Vol. NS32, No. 4, 1991, p. 36.
606. F. Gebhart, "California Pushing Hard for Third Class of Drugs", *Drug Topics*, Vol. 135, No. 7, 1991, p. 28.
607. A. E. Vasa, "For 'Pharmacists Only'", *Drug Topics*, Vol. 135, No. 11, 1991, p. 13.
608. J. T. Walden, "We are Unique", *Drug Topics*, Vol. 135, No. 18, 1991, p. 10.
609. R. Lauring, "Stop the Madness", *Drug Topics*, Vol. 136, No. 2, 1992, p. 10.
610. Anonymous, "NDMA Counters "New" Third Class Push", *NDMA Executive Newsletter*, September 6, 1991, p. 1.
611. Anonymous, "Third Class Briefing Kit", *Nonprescription Drug Manufacturers Association*, September 4, 1991.
612. Anonymous, "Third Class of Drugs is "Perennial Sub-Issue" with Little Congressional Support", *Weekly Pharmacy Reports*, September 16, 1991, p. 2.
613. Anonymous, "The Benefits of a Pharmacist Legend Category", *NARD Journal*, Vol. 113, No. 10, 1991, p. 18.
614. Anonymous, "NDMA Attacks NARD's Transitional Drug Category", *NARD Journal*, Vol. 114, No. 3, 1992, p. 24.
615. F. Gebhart, "FDA Nixes Third Class of Drugs Once Again", *Drug Topics*, Vol. 136, No. 15, 1992, p. 69.
616. R. P. Marshall, "A Transition Category of Drugs: Win-Win-Win-Win?" *American Pharmacy*, Vol. NS33, No. 10, 1992, p. 64.
617. Anonymous, "Third Class of Drugs Cited in NDMA Briefing Book as a 'Special Problem'", *Weekly Pharmacy Reports*, March 15, 1993, p. 3.
618. Anonymous, "GAO Frowns on Third Drug Class", *American Druggist*, Vol. 212, No. 10, 1995, p. 18.
619. Anonymous, "GAO Rejects Third Class of Drugs", *NDMA Executive Newsletter*, September 8, 1995, p. 2.
620. S. Talkington, "Drug Firms Pleased with FDA's Increased Emphasis on OTCs", *Drug Topics*, Vol. 140, No. 11, 1996, p. 118.
621. C. Blank, "Is this the Right Time for a Third Class of Drugs?" *Drug Topics*, Vol. 141, No. 11, 1997, p. 106.

622. M. J. Mehlman, "Quackery", *American Journal of Law & Medicine*, Vol. 31, 2005, pp. 349–363.
623. V. S. Cowart, "Health Fraud's Toll: Lost Hopes, Misspent Billions", *JAMA*, Vol. 259, 1988, pp. 3229–3330.
624. J. E. Dodes and M. J. Schissel, "Quacks Among us", *New York State Dental Journal*, Vol. 61, 1995, pp. 16–17.
625. J. S. Goodwin and M. R. Tangum, "Battling Quackery", *Archives of Internal Medicine*, Vol. 158, 1998, pp. 2187–2191.
626. M. L. Brigden, "Unorthodox Therapy and Your Cancer Patient", *Postgraduate Medical Journal*, Vol. 81, 1987, pp. 271–272;275–277;280.
627. S. Barrett, "Fighting Quackery-A Quick-Reference Guide", *Postgraduate Medical Journal*, Vol. 81, 1987, pp. 13;16;21.
628. V. Herbert, "Unproven (Questionable) Dietary and Nutritional Methods in Cancer Prevention and Treatment", *Cancer*, Vol. 58(Supplement), 1986, pp. 1930–1941.
629. B. P. Squires, "Why Quackery Thrives", *CMAJ*, Vol. 138, 1988, pp. 999–1000.
630. M. Bigby, "Snake Oil for the 21st Century", *Archives of Dermatology*, Vol. 134, 1998, pp. 1512–1514.
631. D. M. Brunette, "Alternative Therapies: Abuses of Scientific Method and Challenges to Dental Research", *Journal of Prosthetic Dentistry*, Vol. 80, 1998, pp. 605–614.
632. T. T. Perls, "Anti-Aging Quackery: Human Growth Hormone and Tricks of the Trade—More Dangerous Than Ever", *The Journals of Gerontology Series A Biological Sciences and Medical Sciences*, Vol. 59, 2004, pp. 682–691.
633. R. B. Stevenson, "Quackery, Fraud, and Denturists", *Journal of the American College of Dentists*, Vol. 70, 2003, pp. 34–37.
634. D. W. Chambers, "Quackery and Fraud: Understanding the Ethical Issues and Responding", *Journal of the American College of Dentists*, Vol. 70, 2003, pp. 9–17.
635. Anonymous, "The Ethics of Quackery and Fraud in Dentistry: A Position Paper", *Journal of the American College of Dentists*, Vol. 70, 2003, pp. 6–8.
636. K. E. Follmar, "Taking a Stand Against Fraud and Quackery in Dentistry", *Journal of the American College of Dentists*, Vol. 70, 2003, pp. 4–5.
637. W. T. Jarvis, "Quackery: A National Scandal", *Clinical Chemistry*, Vol. 38, 1992, pp. 1574–1586.
638. S. H. Short, "Health Quackery: Our Role as Professionals", *Journal of the American Dietetic Association*, Vol. 94, 1994, pp. 607–611.
639. E. Ascher, "Nostrums, Quackery, and Ethics in Vascular Surgery: How to Remain True to the Path of Hippocrates and Still Feed Our Families", *Journal of Vascular Surgery*, Vol. 40, 2004, pp. 389–394.
640. Anonymous, *Quackery-the Billion Dollar Miracle Business (Pamphlet)*. Rockville, MD: Food and Drug Administration, 1990.
641. K. L. Milstead, "Enforcement of Antiquackery Laws", *Journal of the American Pharmacists Association*, Vol. NS3, 1963, pp. 458–460.
642. M. J. Schissel and J. E. Dodes, "Dentistry and Alternative Therapy", *New York State Dental Journal*, Vol. 63, 1997, pp. 32–37.

643. D. E. Hanson, "Different Viewpoints on Alternative Medicine (Letter)", *American Family Physician*, Vol. 55, 1997, pp. 2080–2082.
644. W. I. Wardwell, "Alternative Medicine in the United States", *Social Science & Medicine*, Vol. 38, 1994, pp. 1061–1068.
645. M. Baum, "Quack Cancer Cures or Scientific Remedies", *Journal of the Royal Society of Medicine*, Vol. 89, 1996, pp. 543–547.
646. R. L. Koretz, "Is Alternative Medicine Alternative Science?" *Journal of Laboratory and Clinical Medicine*, Vol. 139, 2002, pp. 329–333.
647. E. Ernst, M. H. Pittler and C. Stevinson, "Complementary/Alternative Medicine in Dermatology: Evidence-Assessed Efficacy of Two Diseases and Two Treatments", *American Journal of Clinical Dermatology*, Vol. 3, 2002, pp. 341–348.
648. F. A. Sonnenberg, "Health Information on the Internet", *Archives of internal medicine*, Vol. 157, 1997, pp. 151–152.
649. B. Keoun, "Cancer Patients Find Quackery on the Web", *Journal of the National Cancer Institute*, Vol. 88, 1996, pp. 1263–1265.
650. K. Schmidt and E. Ernst, "Assessing Websites on Complementary and Alternative Medicine for Cancer", *Annals of Oncology*, Vol. 15, 2004, pp. 733–742.
651. A. J. Iannarone, "Scientific Basis for Health Claims for Dietary Supplements", *Food and Drug Law Journal*, Vol. 47, 1992, pp. 665–676.
652. J. H. Young, "The Development of the Office of Alternative Medicine in the National Institutes of Health", *Bulletin of the History of Medicine*, Vol. 72, 1998, pp. 279–298.
653. Anonymous, "The NIH Almanac-Organization", National Center for Complementary and Alternative Medicine. https://www.nih.gov/about-nih/what-we-do/nih-almanac/national-center-complementary-integrative- health-nccih. Accessed September 30, 2019.
654. Anonymous, "About the National Center for Complementary and Alternative Medicine", The National Center for Complementary and Alternative Medicine. https://nccih.nih.gov. Accessed September 30, 2019.
655. T. N. Gorski, "Current Issues in Protecting the Public from Health Fraud: 'Dietary Supplements' as a Public Health Problem", Testimony before the U.S. Senate Special Committee on Aging, 2001, Quackwatch. http://quackwatch.org/01QuackeryRelatedTopics/Hearing/gorski.html. Accessed September 30, 2019.
656. K. C. Atwood, IV. "The Ongoing Problem with the National Center for Complementary and Alternative Medicine", Committee for the Scientific Investigation of Claims of the Paranormal. https://skepticalinquirer.org/2003/09/the_ongoing_problem_with_the_nccam/. Accessed September 30, 2019.
657. W. I. Sampson. "Why the National Center for Complementary and Alternative Medicine Should Be Defunded", *Quackwatch*. http://www.quackwatch.org/01QuackeryRelatedTopics/nccam.html. Accessed September 30, 2019.

658. B. J. Tesch. "Herbs Commonly Used by Women: An Evidence-Based Review", *American Journal of Obstetrics and Gynecology*, Vol. 188(Suppl) , 2003, pp. S44–S45.
659. Anonymous, "Study Shows St. John's Wort Ineffective for Major Depression", *FDA Consumer*, Vol. 36, No. 3, 2002, p. 8.
660. Anonymous, "Kava and Severe Liver Injury", *FDA Consumer*, Vol. 36, No. 3, 2002, p. 4.
661. "How to Spot Health Fraud", Food and Drug Administration. https://www.fda.gov/Drugs/EmergencyPreparedness/BioterrorismandDrugPreparedness/ucm137284.html. Accessed September 30, 2019.
662. Anonymous, "Health Fraud", *MedlinePlus*. https://medlineplus.gov/healthfraud.html. Accessed October 1, 2019.
663. "Miracle Health Claims", Federal Trade Commission. https://www.consumer.ftc.gov/articles/0167-miracle-health-claims. Accessed September 30, 2019.
664. R. A. Buerki and L. D. Vottero, *Ethical Responsibility in Pharmacy Practice*. Madison, WI: American Institute of the History of Pharmacy, 2002.
665. Anonymous, "Code of Ethics for Pharmacists", American Pharmacists Association. https://www.pharmacist.com/code-ethics. Accessed September 30, 2019.
666. Anonymous, "Improving Medication Use. Advancing Patient Care", American Pharmacists Association. http://www.aphanet.org/AM/Template.cfm?Section=About_APhA&CONTENTID=2410&TEMPLATE=/CM/HTMLDisplay.cfm. Accessed January 5, 2006.
667. Anonymous, *Final Program. American Pharmaceutical Association 142nd Annual Meeting & Exposition*. Washington, DC: American Pharmaceutical Association, 1995, p. 53.
668. E. G. Feldman, "Harmless, but Ineffective, Remedies (Editorial)", *Journal of Pharmaceutical Sciences*, Vol. 64, 1975, p. 1584I.
669. D. Foreman, "Lifesaving Bacteria", *Pharm Today*, Vol. 11, No. 5, 2005, p. 6.
670. Anonymous, "Product Showcase", *Pharm Today*, Vol. 11, No. 8, 2005, p. 6.
671. Anonymous, "Hyland's Complete Flu Care 4 Kids", *MyHealthCare21.com*. http://www.myhealthcare21.com/HY152/Complete-Flu-Care.html. Accessed January 6, 2006.
672. E. W. Guthrie, "Lessons Learned from Early Americans", *Pharm Today*, Vol. 11, No. 9, 2005, p. 6.
673. D. Foreman, "The Ancient Beverage That Heals", *Pharm Today*, Vol. 11, No. 9, 2005, p. 12–31.
674. M. Slezak, "Practicing on Pins and Needles", *American Druggist*, Vol. 213, No. 11, 1996, pp. 26;28–30.
675. M. Slezak, "Rite Aid Advertises Its Vitamin Expertise", *American Druggist*, Vol. 214, No. 11, 1997, p. 13.
676. F. Batz, "Integrating Herbal Therapy into Practice", *American Druggist*, Vol. 215, No. 5, 1998, pp. 5858–5865.

677. V. E. Tyler, "Why Many 'Health Foods' are Not Safe and Effective", *Pharm Times*, Vol. 49, No. 3, 1983, pp. 35–37.
678. C. Grauds and J. Cox, "Introduction to Aromatherapy", *Pharm Times*, Vol. 65, No. 9, 1999, p. 80.
679. C. Grauds, "Selenium Reduces Incidence of Prostate Cancer", *Pharm Times*, Vol. 65, No. 7, 1999, p. 83.
680. C. Grauds, "Milk Thistle: A Potential Life-Saver", *Pharm Times*, Vol. 62, No. 3, 1996, p. 95.
681. C. Grauds, "Treating Migraine and Arthritis with Feverfew", *Pharm Times*, Vol. 61, No. 7, 1995, pp. 32–34.
682. M. Sherman, "Natural Medicines: A Rare Opportunity for Pharmacists", *Pharm Times*, Vol. 63, No. 11, 1997, pp. 80–82.
683. E. McCormick, "Modern and Traditional Medicines: Can They Coexist?" *Pharm Times*, Vol. 64, No. 10, 1998, pp. 71–72.
684. RONH10@JUNO.com, "Concern Over Herbals (Letter)", *Pharm Times*, Vol. 63, No. 12, 1997, p. 8.
685. D. J. Pacy, "Unleashed Herbal Explosion (Letter)", *Pharm Times*, Vol. 65, No. 8, 1999, p. 12.
686. Y. C. Terrie, "Antisnoring Products", *Pharm Times*, Vol. 71, No. 8, 2005, pp. 11;15–16.
687. Anonymous, "OTC Product News. Alphactif for Men", *Pharm Times*, Vol. 71, No. 8, 2005, p. 18.
688. A. D. Garrett, "Complementary Medicine and Diabetes: What's Fact, What's Fiction?" *Pharm Times*, Vol. 71, No. 8, 2005, p. 34.
689. Anonymous, "Appearex (Advertisement)", *Pharm Times*, Vol. 71, No. 8, 2005, p. 35.
690. W. S. Pray, "Quackery, a Deadly Threat to Health", *US Pharmacist*, Vol. 16, No. 5, 1991, pp. 35–36;39–40.
691. C. Kwong-Robbins, "Traditional Chinese Medicine – A Natural and Holistic Approach", *US Pharmacist*, Vol. 27, No. 12, 2002, pp. 44;46;48–50.
692. C. Kwong-Robbins, "The Art and Science of Chinese Herbal Medicine", *US Pharmacist*, Vol. 28, No. 3, 2003, pp. 62;65;68;71;75.
693. Anonymous, "Drug Store News", *Drug Store News*. http://www.drugstorenews.com/. Accessed January 6, 2006.
694. J. B. Lavalle, "Treating Women's Health the Natural Way", *Drug Store News*, Vol. 8, 1998, p. CP31.
695. R. Eder, "OTC Giants Join Herbal Game", *Drug Store News*, Vol. 7, 1997, p. 27.
696. Anonymous, "Nature's Essence Blood Tonic Syrup (Advertisement)", *Drug Store News*, Vol. 8, 1998, p. CP14.
697. K. Snyder, "R.Ph.s Can Learn More About CAM", *Drug Topics*, Vol. 140, No. 22, 1996, p. 52.
698. J. Bennett, "The Best Pharmacy Practices: Innovative or Diverse Services", *Drug Topics*, Vol. 141, No. 8, 1997, pp. 96–105.

699. K. Snyder, "Cold-Eeze Lozenges Are Taking the Nation by Storm", *Drug Topics*, Vol. 141, No. 3, 1997, pp. 16;19.
700. W. M. Davis, "The Role of Glucosamine and Chondroitin Sulfate in the Management of Arthritis", *Drug Topics* (supplement), Vol. 142, No. 8, 1998, pp. 1S–15S.
701. E. Portyansky, "Alternative Medicine-How Bountiful is the Harvest?" *Drug Topics*, Vol. 142, No. 7, 1998, pp. 44–45;47;49–50.
702. G. M. Tarlach, "Turning Herbs 'N2' Profits", *Drug Topics*, Vol. 142, No. 2, 1998, p. 66.
703. S. Levy, "M.D.s Issue Call for Testing Alternative Medications", *Drug Topics*, Vol. 142, No. 19, 1998, p. 21.
704. M. Angell and J. P. Kassirer, "Alternative Medicine-The Risks of Untested and Unregulated Remedies (Editorial)", *NEJM*, Vol. 339, 1998, pp. 839–841.
705. H. Fleming, Jr., "A Natural Progression", *Drug Topics*, Vol. 142, No. 18, 1998, p. 74.
706. S. Levy, "Reading, Writing…and Complementary Care", *Drug Topics*, Vol. 143, No. 21, 1999, pp. 42;44.
707. S. Levy, "Don't Miss This Boat", *Drug Topics*, Vol. 143, No. 5, 1999, pp. 41–42;44;49.
708. S. Levy, "R.Ph. Finds Consumers Becoming Complementary Care Friendly", *Drug Topics*, Vol. 143, No. 20, 1999, p. 61.
709. H. Fleming, Jr., "Two in One", *Drug Topics*, Vol. 143, No. 2, 1999, p. 15.
710. J. S. Williamson and C. M. Wyandt, "New Perspectives on Alternative Medicine", *Drug Topics*, Vol. 145, No. 1, 2001, pp. 57–66.
711. A. M. Kratz, "Flawed Article (Letter)", *Drug Topics*, Vol. 145, No. 5, 2001, p. 18.
712. Anonymous, "Allen Kratz", Premiere Speakers Bureau. http://premierespeakers.com/1066/index.cfm. Accessed January 9, 2006.
713. C. Kwong-Robbins, "Setting Record Straight on Herbs (Letter)", *Drug Topics*, Vol. 145, No. 13, 2001, pp. 12,15.
714. Anonymous, "New Product Bulletin, Alpha CF (Advertisement)", *NARD Journal*, Vol. 111, No. 9, 1989, p. 12.

Chapter 15 References

715. E. M. "Mick" Kolassa and B. F. Banahan. *Growing Competition in the Pharmaceutical Industry; A Response to the PRIME Institute Report*. Technical Report PPN 95-001, University of Mississippi Research Institute of Pharmaceutical Sciences, 1995.
716. *Pharma Pricing USA: A Comprehensive Review of Pharmaceutical Pricing in the Mid-1990s,* London: IMS Pharma Strategy Group, 1995.

717. *Health Economics in the USA: Expectations, Applications, & Future Directions.* Plymouth Meeting, PA: IMS America Health Economics Solutions Group, 1996.
718. R. Corey, *Industrial Marketing: Cases and Concepts*, Third Edition, Prentice-Hall, Inc., 1983.
719. T. T. Nagle and R. K. Holden. *The Strategy and Tactics of Pricing: A Guide to Profitable Decision Making*, Second Edition, Prentice-Hall Inc., 1994.
720. J. C. Goodman and E. G. Dolan. *Economics of Public Policy*, West Publishing Company, 1985.
721. C. M. Kozma, C. E. Reeder and E. W. Lingle, "Expanding Medicaid Drug Formulary Coverage: Effects on Utilization of Related Services", *Medical Care*, Vol. 28, 1990, pp. 963–976.
722. R. Choich, "Product and Service Compensation", in T. R. Brown, Ed., *The Handbook of Institutional Pharmacy Practice*, Third Edition, American Society of Hospital Pharmacists, 1992.
723. F. R. Curtiss, "Current Concepts in Hospital Reimbursement", *American Journal of Hospital Pharmacy*, Vol. 40, 1983, pp. 586–591.
724. S. M. Smythe, "Prescription Pricing: A GAO Evaluation", *Journal of Research in Pharmaceutical Economics*, Vol. 3, No. 1, 1991, pp. 55–64.
725. D. Pryor, "Commentary: A Prescription for High Drug Prices", *Health Affairs*, Vol. 9, 1990, pp. 101–109.
726. C. E. Danials and A. I. Wortheimer, "Analysis of Hospital Formulary Effects on Cost Control", *Topics in Hospital Formulary Management*, Vol. 2 (August), 1982, pp. 32–47.
727. T. D. Rucker and G. Schiff, "Drug Formularies: Myths-in-Formation", *Medical Care*, Vol. 28, 1990, pp. 928–39.
728. S. D. Horn et al., "Intended and Unintended Consequences of HMO Cost-Containment Strategies", *American Journal of Managed Care*, Vol. 22, 1966, pp. 253–254.
729. W. D. Reekie, *Pricing New Pharmaceutical Products*, Croom Helm, 1977.
730. S. Greenfield et al., "Variations in Resource Utilization among Medical Specialties and Systems of Care", *Journal of the American Medical Association*, Vol. 257, 1992, pp. 1624–1630.
731. R. N. Zelnio and J. P. Gagnon, "The Effects of Price Information on Prescription Drug Product Selection", *Drug Intelligence and Clinical Pharmacy*, Vol. 13, 1979, pp. 156–159.
732. E. M. Kolassa, "The New Environment for Pharmaceutical Pricing", *Product Management Today* (January), 1993, pp. 221–22.
733. G. Squibb, "Drug Prices: The Achilles Hill of the Pharmaceutical Industry", in M. C. Smith and B. G. Keller, Eds., *Pharmaceutical Marketing: An Anthology and Bibliography*, Williams and Wilkins, 1969.
734. J. D. Kleinke, "Just What the HMO Ordered: The Paradox of Drug Costs", *Health Affairs*, Vol. 19, No. 2, 2000, pp. 79–91.

Cross Index

Author's Name	Reference Number
Abood	247
Ackoff	279
Adams, D. D.	323
Adams, D. G.	346
Aden	508
Administered Prices	124
Advertising Proprietary	125
Agency Hearings	127
Agrawal	71
Alderson	280,322
American	220,453
Anderson	184
Angell	233,366
Anonymous	36,64,109,239,249,250,325,326,351,361, 382,400,410,435,473,486,501,509
Arendt	289
Arrow	258
Aston	447
Avorn	234
Azarnoff	365
Balter	334,409,514,518
Barber	41
Basara	34
Bauer	60
Becker	291,456
Bender	441

(*Continued*)

Author's Name	Reference Number
Berabe	248
Berger	503
Bergner	488
Berman	160
Bezold	375
Blackwell	516,521
Blenkinsopp	241
Bomardier	489
Bootman	23,94
Bonk	22
Bottomore	288
Boyle	287
Brady	101
Branca	500
Brodie	222
Brodsky	356
Burger	296
Bush	452
Bylinsky	550
CBS	221
COL	267
Cady	372
Callahan	332,380
Campbell	371
Cargill	244
Carson	47
Chang	389
Chapman	331

(*Continued*)

Author's Name	Reference Number
Christie	88
Churchill	31
Cleeton	499
Clinton, Bill (President)	169
Cohen	283
Coleman	403
Competitive	37,123
Congressional	175
Conger	411
Conley	17
Conner	69
Cooper, M. H.	460
Cooper, R. M.	345
Cooperstock	277,315
Cox	185
Cousins	374
Crellin	70
Crout	412
Davis, C.	162
Davis, M.	54
DeHaen	348
Delgado	474
Diamond	482
Dichter	86,450
Djerassi	467
Donagan	316
Done	532
Dowling	353,393

(*Continued*)

Author's Name	Reference Number
Doyle	465
Donabedian	159
Drake	176
Drug Efficacy	145
Drug Industry Antitrust	129
Drug Literature	168
Drug Regulation Reform	137
Drug Safety	130
Drug Use – Older Americans	142
Dubos	226
Duncan	208
Early	376
Eban	173
Engelhardt	317
Ehrenreich	276
Epstein	445
Eskovitz	28
Evans	53
Examination	131
FDA's Regulation	179
Fassold	415
Fay	212,394
Ferber	402
Ferguson	391
Fincham	111
Fink	98
Finkelstein	218
Firestone	468

(Continued)

Author's Name	Reference Number
Fletcher, J.	536
Fletcher, M.	373
Folsom	551
Food and Drug Administration	149
Frazier	396
Freidson	100,102
Fuchs	340
Fulda	56
Funkelstein	259
Gallagher	534
Gerald	238
Gibson	27
Goldacre	544
Goode	530
Greenblatt	517,522
Griffin	93
Grob	295
Hager	35
Hailey	113
Hammond	305
Harlow	62
Hanlon	392
Harari	455,459
Harper	44
Harris	155
Harry	274
Hendeles	426
Henderson	438

(*Continued*)

Author's Name	Reference Number
Hesbacher	310
Hill	209
Hilts	368
Ho	200
Hubbard	61
Hughes	204
Huttin	548
Illich	251
Ingelfinger	413,431
Ingolia	68
Inter-Agency	128
Jachuk	481
Jacobs	306
Jacobsen	25
Johnson, K.	539
Johnson, T.	256
Joyce	305,492,505
Kaluzny	207
Kefauver	58,59
Keller	120
Kelly	24
Kendall	290
Keras	462
Kessler, D.	540
Kessler, R.	314
Kirsch	364
Klerman	297
Klein, D.	43,300

(Continued)

Author's Name	Reference Number
Klein, T.	388
Kline	53,408
Knapp, D. A.	91,174
Knapp, D. E.	91
Kolassa, E. M.	10,11,78,191,192,498
Konnor	33
Koos	552
Koran	309
Larson	83,195
Lasagna	42,230,350
Laurance	471
Lazarus	77
Lebhar	469
Lennard	315
Lessing	63
Levinson	106
Levitt	38
Levy	85
Lewin	336
Lidstone	112
Linn	352,404
Luce	537
Magee	543
Majority	122
Manischevitz	329
Mannheim	257
Manheimer	299,514
Marks	307

(*Continued*)

Author's Name	Reference Number
Marsa	114
Martin	369
Maslow	546
Masson	97
May	419
McCaffrey	201,370,399
McCarthy, E. J.	118
McCarthy, R.	110
McCormick	531
McEvilla	66
McEvoy	266
McWhorter	40
Mechanic	265,313
Medawar	253
Medical Advertising	64,165
Medical Restrain	134
Medicare	236,178
Medicine	203
Merwin	347
Miller	302
Mintz	21
Moench	547
Morgan	301
Mosher	278
Morton	484
Moskowitz	397
Moulton	466
Moynihan	161,252

(Continued)

Author's Name	Reference Number
Mundy	405
Murphy, M.	194
Myers	271
Najman	300
Narin	163
Nathanson	312
National	210
National Analysts	273
Neill	197
Nelson, Gary	164
Nelson, Gaylord	57
Nelson, P.	428
Neuhauser, D.	538
Neuhauser, W. F.	215
New York	171
NWDA	320
Oliver	285
Overman	472
Oversight	138
Parish	406,424
Parry	513,519
Parsons	261
Patent	143
Pathak	29,341
Pearlman	483
Pelton	75
Petkova	439
Peltzman	121,154

(*Continued*)

Author's Name	Reference Number
Pickett	379
Pharmaceutical	321
Pharmaceutical Innovation	152
Pharmaphoram	51
Phelps	282
Philip	398
Physician Ownership	132
Pichichero	493
Polydrug Abuse	153
Porter	318
Posner	553
Potter	363
Pray	55
Prescription Drug Advertising	144, 146
Pricing	151
Primeaux	89
Reader	381
Reekie	339
Regulation – New Drugs	136
Regulatory Policies	147
Relationship	135
Report	243
Review	150
Rhodes	170
Rice	478, 479
Richart	52
Rickles	237
Rivett	246

(Continued)

Author's Name	Reference Number
Rizzo	494
Rodwin	448
Roemer	383
Rogers	308
Rollins	13
Rosenau	245
Rosenstock	90,227
Rosenthal	476
Rovner	286
Rubin	541
Rucker	510
Ryan	190,429
Sade	525
Sadusk	430
Safety and Effectiveness	141
Safety and Efficacy	140
Sandoz	527
Sartorius	377
Scheff	275
Schnee	344
Schoonveld	497
Schulz	495
Schwartzman	103,108
Scitovsky	477,480,487
Seidenberg	354
Seidman	449
Settle	92
Sewak	18

(*Continued*)

Author's Name	Reference Number
Shakespeare	45
Sheldon	401
Shulman	32
Sigerist	262
Skyrocketing	172
Silverman, H.	240
Silverman, M.	104
Simmons	72–74
Slack	228
Small Business	139
Smith, A.	19
Smith, L.	520
Smith, M. C.	1–9,79,81,82,84,87,117,119,157,158,166,174,186–189, 192,196,199,202,219,235,270,293,330,385,420–423, 436,437,461,523,528,529,533
Somers	156
Sonnedecker	20
Spilker	16
Squib	50,65
Staff	281
Starr	254
Steele	30
Sternbach	504
Stetler	434
Strand	181
Stigler	427
Stolley	298,414
Substitute	133
Suchman	485

(*Continued*)

Author's Name	Reference Number
Sullivan	496
Svarstad	294
Szeinbach	193
Talalay	48
Talbot	224,378
Teeling-Smith	217,432
Temin	49
Thompson	490,491
Traynor	390
Twaddle	451
Use and Misuse	167
Use of Advisory	177
Usman	542
Van Elmeren	205
Veatch	335
Vickery	242
Visconti	76,360
Vogel	15
Wade	433
Walker, H.	95
Walker, S.	107
Walter	549
Ware	80
Werth	115,116
Wertheimer	12,206
Weston	39,342
Wick	105
Wilkerson Group	545

(Continued)

Author's Name	Reference Number
William-Murphy	535
Wilson, R. N.	284
Wilson, W. F.	215
Winkelman	502
Wokasch	338
Worthen	395

Appendix B – Some Useful Quotes

A Quotation on Quotations

In Boswell's, *The Life of Samuel Johnson*, he relates the following: "(An acquaintance) censures quotation as mere pedantry". Johnson's reply: "No sir, it is a good thing: there is a community of mind in it. Classical quotation is the parole of literary men all over the world".

In his humorous and philosophical book, *Every Time I find the Meaning of Life, They Change It*, (43), the author describes his collection of short quotes from various philosophers as "Pithies". Here, usually relating to the subject at hand, are some of my "Pithies".

- As long as Big Pharma puts money over health, they are unworthy of being the sole developers of new drugs. I think that we can find other models, based on public funding for the public good (Hager, *Ten Drugs*).
- The best way to get a long-lasting blockbuster (drug) is to make sure it doesn't cure anything (Hager, *Ten Drugs*).
- The fact that no one knows anything about the future makes all business forecasters much more sure (Mattson and Dick in *Pharmaceutical Marketing in the 21st Century*).
- He that will not apply new remedies must expect new evils, for time is the greatest innovator (Francis Bacon 1625).
- It is the abiding belief of the author that good marketing makes good medicine …when the system works. Bad marketing never succeeds for long and neither does bad medicine (Mickey Smith, *Pharmaceutical Marketing, Principles, Environment, and Practice*).

- A profession and a society which are so concerned with physical and functional well-being as to sacrifice civil liberty and moral integrity must inevitably press for a scientific environment similar to that provided laying hens on chicken farms ... hens who produce eggs industrially and have no diseases or other cares (Eliot Freidson).
- Drug prices are way too high (Jesse Dukes, a personal communication from my very excellent handyman).
- He (sic) who orders does not pay, and he who pays does not order (Estes Kefauver).
- I firmly believe that if the whole materia medica, as now used, could be sunk to the bottom of the sea it would be all the better for mankind, and all the worse for the fishes (Oliver Wendell Holmes).
- The moral of the drug bill is that even on an exceedingly complex issue the legislative branch can perform in the manner intended by (the Founding Fathers)...the Congress can prove itself to assume leadership in the legislative process (Estes Kefauver).
- Whatever waste and cynicism may be charged to the profit system, it has no equal in creativity, in productivity and above all, in responsiveness, to the mandates of the market (Paul Talalay).
- The desire to take medicine is perhaps the greatest feature which distinguishes man from animals (William Osler).
- Tied in with the government investigation is the belief by a substantial segment of the general public that drug prices are too high...In all likelihood, this is a passing phenomenon built up by misunderstanding and suspicion and by the resentment of people who grudgingly spend money on medical care regardless of need (Herbert Wilkinson, Abbott Labs, 1959).
- This is the formula for love: the conferral of survival benefits upon the other in a creatively enlarging manner (Paul Montague).
- If a law is not absolutely necessary, then it is absolutely necessary that there not be a law (Lord Acton).
- The people have spoken, the bastards...(?).
- A politician has two important goals: first, to get elected and, second to get re-elected (?).
- Let us go forward together. Winston Churchill used it many times. Could, should, serve as a motto for Congress. Maybe emblazoned on the Capitol. (Don't hold your breath!)
- The nearest approach to immortality on Earth is a Government bureau (James Byrnes).

- "We are not the end product of evolution; we are only the product so far...we have a long way to go. The reptiles evolved themselves out of existence too. The successful ones did...they are called mammals now" (John Campbell, science fiction writer).
- The future is repriced every day (Barry Werth in *The Antidote*).
- It is hard to believe that a man is telling you the truth if you know that you would lie if you were in his place (H.L. Mencken).
- Sickness is catching: O were favor so, (William Shakespeare, *A Midsummer Night's Dream*).
- Half the money I spend on advertising is wasted; the trouble is I don't know which half (John Wanamaker).
- People who cannot find time for recreation are obliged sooner or later to find time for illness (John Wanamaker).
- My doctors treated my alcoholism as a Valium deficiency (?)
- Most of the time, we think we are sick. It's all in the mind (Thomas Wolfe).
- After all, a doctor is just to put your mind at rest (Petronius).
- If is part of the cure to wish to be cured (Seneca).
- The miserable have no other medicine but only hope (Shakespeare).
- We are, all of us, in the gutter, but some are looking at stars (Oscar Wilde).
- Medicinal discovery. It moves in mighty leaps. It leapt straight past the common cold and gave it us for keeps (Pam Ayres).
- A desperate disease requires a dangerous remedy (Guy Fawkes).
- If a patient turns out to be really ill, after all, it is always possible to look grave at the same time and say "You realize, I suppose, that twenty-five years ago you'd be dead" (Stephen Potter).
- A miracle drug is any drug that will do what the label says it will do (Eric Hodgins).
- Medicine is a collection of uncertain prescriptions, the results of which, taken collectively, are more fatal than useful to mankind (Napoleon Bonaparte).
- Scientists do not discover in order to know, they know in order to discover (Edward Wilson).
- Science has promised us truth – an understanding of such relationships as our minds can grasp; it has never promised us either peace or happiness (Gustav Le Bon).
- The saddest aspect of life right now is that science gathers knowledge faster than society gathers wisdom (Isaac Azimov, "Cultural Lag" in this Book).

- Here's the rule for bargains: "Do unto other men, for they would do for you. That's the true business precept, (Charles Dickens)".
- A hundred doses of happiness are not enough: send to the drug store for another bottle and, when that is finished, for another. There can be no doubt that, if tranquilizers could be bought as easily as aspirin, they would be consumed, not by the billions, as they are at present but by the scores and hundreds of billions. And a good, cheap, stimulant would be almost as popular (Aldous Huxley).
- Courage is being scared to death – but you still saddle up (John Wayne).
- The power to prescribe is the power to destroy (Paul Swann).
- There are three kinds of lies: lies, damn lies, and statistics, (Benjamin Disraeli).
- A statistician is someone with a talent for numbers but without the personality to be an accountant (Dr. John Bentley).
- The natural role of the twentieth century man is anxiety (Norman Mailer).
- A very good thing is veal pie when you know the lady who made it and are quite certain it ain't kittens (Charles Dickens, *Pickwick Papers*).
- Striving to better oft we mar what's well, (William Shakespeare). Mississippi version: If it ain't broke, don't fix it.
- The scientific environment allows a minority viewpoint not only to exist, but to flourish (Phillip Hilts).
- Men are linked by pain and suffering. Men are also limited by common joy of conquering disease and disability. (Findings, Senate Sub-committee on Reorganization and International Organizations.)
- Developing a drug is as important as inventing it (Nicholas Kittrie).
- Where the probable may prove to be impossible, the impossible may suddenly be achieved (Austin Smith).
- The nature of man is not what he is born as, but what he was born for (Aristotle).
- Please don't send out any small bore detail men (William Haddad).
- You wouldn't say that if my writers were here (Jack Benny).
- Complete freedom from disease and struggles is almost incompatible with the process of living (Rene Dubos).
- The faith in the magic power of drugs is not new. In the past, as today, it contributed to give medicine the authority of priesthood and to recreate the glamor of ancient mysteries (Rene Dubos).
- All my means are sane; my motives and objects mad (Herman Melville, *Moby Dick*).

- There are no specific diseases. There are specific disease conditions (Florence Nightingale).
- Where understanding fails, there immediately comes a word to take its place (Goethe).
- We hold these truths to be self-evident, that all men evolved differently, that they are born with certain mutable characteristics, and that among these are life and the pursuit of pleasure (Yuval Harari).
- That boy ain't got a lick o'sense (my father).
- To ward off disease men, as a general rule, find it easier to depend on healers than to attempt the more difficult task of living wisely (Rene Dubos).
- To bring into the world an unwanted human being is as antisocial an act as murder (Gore Vidal).
- In general, the art of government consists in taking as much money as possible from one class of citizens and to give it to the other (Voltaire).
- Nothing that is worth knowing can be taught (Oscar Wilde).
- I can resist everything except temptation (Oscar Wilde).
- Instead of monopolizing the seat of judgment, journalism should be apologizing in the dock (Oscar Wilde).
- In this world there are only two tragedies, one is not getting what one wants and the other is getting it (Oscar Wilde).
- Before you go anywhere you have to fix the God-damn car (John Gardner).
- Man is born to live and not to prepare to live (Boris Pasternak).
- Chance favors the trained mind (Louis Pasteur).
- The good Lord gave me money (John D. Rockefeller).
- The men with muckrakes are often indispensable to the well-being of society; but only if they know when to stop raking the muck (Theodore Roosevelt).
- Every man desires to live long, but no man would be old (Jonathan Swift).
- There will always be the one right word. Use it despite its foul or merely ludicrous associations (Dylan Thomas).
- How many a man has dated a new era in his life from the reading of a book (Henry David Thoreau).
- Here am I laid, my life and misery done, ask not my name, I curse you everyone (Timon, Epitaph).
- I never give them hell. I just tell the truth and they think it is hell (Harry S. Truman).

- To do nothing is sometimes a good remedy (Hippocrates).
- Extreme remedies are very appropriate for extreme diseases (Hippocrates).
- Words are, of course, the most powerful drug used by mankind (Rudyard Kipling).
- A woman is only a woman, but a good cigar is a smoke (Rudyard Kipling).
- A great literature is chiefly the product of inquiring minds in revolt against the memorable certainties of the nation (H. L. Mencken).
- Humanity has but three great enemies: fever, famine and war...by far the most terrible is fever (William Osler).
- Society is produced by our wants and government by our wickedness (Thomas Paine).
- Medicine is not merely a science but an art. The character of the physicians may act more powerfully upon the patient than the drugs employed (Paracelsus).
- Medicine is increasingly focused on upgrading the healthy rather than healing the sick (Yuval Harari).
- A growing percentage of the population is taking psychiatric medicines on a regular basis not only to cure debilitating mental illnesses, but also to face more mundane depressions and the occasional blues (Yuval Harari).
- It is not easy to live knowing that you are going to die, but it is even harder to believe in immortality and be proven wrong (Yuval Harari).
- You cannot count on death to save you from becoming irrelevant (Yuval Harari).
- The truth shall make you free, but first it will make you miserable (Douglas Preston).
- Anyone can predict the future, but getting it right...(?) (Mickey Smith).
- The real voyage of discovery consists not in seeking new landscapes but in having new eyes (Marcel Proust).
- The gut is an organ not well suited to reasoning (Oliver Wendell Holmes).
- All medicines are poisons...the right dose differentiates a poison from a remedy (Paracelsus).
- Well done is better than well said (Ben Franklin).
- Though it is worthwhile to attain the end merely for one man, it is finer and more godlike to attain it for a nation (Aristotle).

- If I had my way, I'd make health catching instead of disease (Robert Ingersoll).
- I am in a moment of pretty wellness (Horace Walpole).
- There is no health; Physicians say that we, at best, enjoy a Nutrilite (John Donne).
- A general practitioner can no more become a specialist than an old shoe can become a dancing slipper. Both have developed habits which are immutable (Frank Kittredge Paddock).
- The problem is to induce people to pay twenty-five cents for the liver-encouraging, silent-perambulating, family pills, which cost three cents to make (Josh Billings).
- Apothecary, The physician's accomplice, undertaker's benefactor, and grave worm's provider (Ambrose Bierce).
- We can buy human life. Each country within certain limits decides its own death rate (Paul Hawley).
- The apothecary is neither to diminish nor decrease the physician's prescriptions. He is to meddle only in his own vocation and to remember that his office is only to be the physician's cook (William Bulleia).
- Two minutes with Venus, two years with Mercury (Earl Moore).
- If you think you have caught a cold, call in a good doctor. Call in three doctors and play bridge (Robert Benchley).
- (The Apothecary's) reward, therefore, ought to be suitable to his skill and his trust, and it arises generally from the price at which he sells his drugs (Adam Smith).
- Though the apothecary sells (his drugs) for three or four hundred, or at a thousand per cent profit, this may frequently be no more than the reasonable wages of his labor charged, in the only way he can charge them upon the price of his drugs (Adam Smith).
- Mankind cannot always stand aghast (Rene' Dubos).
- The strongest argument for "private enterprise" is not the function of profit. The strongest argument is the function of loss (Peter Drucker).
- The best we get from government in the welfare state is competent mediocrity (Peter Drucker).
- When a minority becomes a majority, and seizes authority, it hates a minority (L. H. Robbins).

Appendix C – The Saga of Vitamin B$_{13}$ – A Pharmaceutical Triumph

By M. Patrick O'Meara

(**Author's Note:** This is satire as it should be writ. I included it in one of my first Books (8) and it is as brilliant now as it was then, in 1960. Read it and enjoy!)

You are all, I am sure, familiar with each chapter of the remarkable story of vitamin B$_{13}$ as it unfolded. But this exciting tale of discovery and development, exemplifying of the pharmaceutical industry's endless quest for betterment, deserves a recapitulation at this time.

It was back in late 1960, nearly 2 years ago. Hans Schuller-Christian, the brilliant professor of medicine at one of the most important Eastern medical schools, had been lured a short time before into the research ranks of Pfizz, Upchuck, and Groan by an offer of 3,000 shares of PU&G stock, an annual salary of $75,000, plus an attractive continuing stock option arrangement.

Pfizz, Upchuck, and Groan itself had just experienced a managerial revolution, with the presidency and all policy-making power passing into the hands of the Advertising and sales branch of the corporation, in the person of Harry "Hard-Sell" Cradshaw. "Hard-Sell" had earned his reputation as director of sales and Advertising for the Pulley Brothers soap empire. His Promotion of "Love", the liquid detergent, as the "Cream of Passion" to be used only by those "daring souls seeking the delicious intoxication of romance" was a masterpiece of Advertising technique. In 1 year it made

"Love" the largest selling detergent and doubled the value of Pulley Brothers' common stock. PU&G captured Cradshaw following this *tour de force* with an offer of the presidency and a free hand in reorganization.

Displaying his hard-headed managerial ability upon his arrival at PU&G, "Hard-Sell" ordered George Beardsley, his Vice-President in charge of research, to obtain for him "the smartest young research brain in American medicine". After intensive inquiry and consultations, Beardsley brought Schuller-Christian to the Chief. Cradshaw hired him immediately as Director of Research at the previously cited bountiful recompense. The 38-year-old Schuller-Christian whose $15,000 yearly salary was near his peak earning capacity in academic circles, was dazzled by the offer, and accepted; agreeing to Cradshaw's only stipulation that he be a loyal member of the PU&G team.

Cradshaw decided that an entirely new direction was needed in research and product development. With serendipity remarkable for one so new to the Drug game, he fell upon the answer himself. He noted that the B vitamins, long big earners for the Drug Houses, were in a quiescent state. The discovery of vitamin B_{12} had now dimmed. As a specific for "that tired feeling", it had gradually lost out to the psychic energizers.

"Hard-Sell" sent a memo to Schuller-Christian with the succinct notion – "Research up a vitamin B_{13}! Make it Big, Really BIG!"

S.-C. was still adjusting himself to the philosophy and pace of pharmaceutical research, so different from that of the ivory towers of academic medicine, and the memo from the Chief came as a jolt. After briefly reviewing the vitamin field, he presented his objections to Cradshaw. "You just can't conjure up a new vitamin out of thin air", he tried to explain.

"Nonsense", snorted Cradshaw, over-riding the protest. "Twelve and one make thirteen, don't they? Tell our synthetic chemists to combine B_{12} and B_1, and we will have the hottest wonder drug of this decade". "But we don't have any idea what this combination would do, much less whether it would have any therapeutic value", continued Schuller-Christian.

"You give us the drug and we will decide what it's good for", the hard-headed Chief persisted. "I can think of at least a dozen maladies that it would be the best damn drug for yet – housewife's fatigue, salesman's nerves, the 3 o'clock letdown, flaccidity of middle-aged men – why our list of indications will cover 3 pages by the time we're through. You just produce the B_{13}, and keep this top secret. We'll call it 'Operation Panacea'".

Schuller-Christian was dejected following this encounter with "Hard-Sell". Only the discouragement of his wife, who had quickly become adapted to living in the Grand Fashion, kept him at PU&G. He even decided that the old boy might be right. Maybe the combination of cyanocobalamin and thiamine would be interesting.

The synthetic chemists at PU&G were a talented lot, and under Schuller-Christian's direction, they systematically subjected the B_1 and B_{12} to a wide variety of biosynthetic maneuvers. They finally achieved a linkage between the phosphate of the cyanocobalamin and the thiazole N of the thiamine, while maintaining the integrity of the rest of the component molecules.

The resultant cyanocothiamine (or vitamin B_{13}, as it was quickly called, in deference to the Chief) proved to be an astonishing substance biologically. Extensive and exhaustive testing in a wide variety of laboratory animals from the suckling hamster to the corn-fed capon proved it to be absolutely inert. Even in massive doses of more than 1 gm daily, it had no effect on growth, metabolism, hormone output, behavior, or any other discernible parameter. In addition, it showed no B_1 or B_{12} activity.

After the heroic testing program, which strained the facilities of PU&G's huge animal farm, Schuller-Christian reported the negative results to the Chief, hoping that this would end the costly project.

But Cradshaw's interest turned to enthusiasm as S.-C., reported one negative result after another. "Wonderful!" he exclaimed. "The perfect drug – absolutely no side effects! This will make you famous and PU&G rich, Hans! We'll sink 10 million in a clinical testing and Promotion program that will set American medicine on its ears!"

Supplies of JP1313, as the cyanocothiamine was secretively called, were distributed, with accompanying brochures hinting that this was the long desired elixir of life. The negative animal studies were cited in support of the idea that this was a super vitamin, specific for and active in only the highest animal – man. Only the most remarkable results could be expected from such a remarkable agent. And its absolute safety was repeatedly emphasized.

In addition to the "Big Name Labs", as the PU&G People referred to the prestige investigators, hundreds of "Small Fish" also received supplies of JP1313. "Small Fish" was the trade appellation for the many eager self-styled "clinical investigators" made up of young residents in training, happy to break into the literature via the Drug-testing route, as well as established practitioners, equally enthused to be able to see 40 patients a day and still "do research". The "Small Fish" received the JP1313, grants to cover all expenses, and of course, the brochures. The researchers then proceeded to try JP1313 in every conceivable medical situation. Gynecologists used it for the menopause; psychiatrists tested it in neurotic and psychotic states; urologists tried it for impotence; general practitioners as well as every species and subspecies of specialist got into the act.

Not all the Drug testers were uncritical. The quick screening by the PU&G area research directors did not keep out a few People who were determined to perform objective and carefully controlled studies. However, the work of the later misfits was ignored, never to see the light of publication, as the mass of Reports was returned.

Most of the studies were of a testimonial nature. The researchers were given the cards on which they recorded the daily dose, periodic laboratory tests, and the response of the patient. Mrs. Jones had suffered from "gas" for years. After 2 days of this new special medicine, doled out so carefully, and with such a background of precaution and interest, she was miraculously degassed! Likewise old Mr. Smith; after one dose he felt more sprightly than he had felt in 20 years. "Danced a jig today" was the notation written for the first follow-up visit.

This pattern was repeated thousands of times. "Hard-Sell" had been conservative; the list of indications would exceed ten pages. As the research progressed, PU&G invited the more enthusiastic of its volunteer workers to all-expense-paid company conferences, where they were amply wined and dined and given the opportunity to share their wonderful results with each other. Their fervor heightened, they returned to the precincts to grind out more affirmative ballots for JP1313.

After several months, began the reaping of the harvest of thousands of cards. The well-staffed and efficient editorial department of Pfizz, Upchuck, and Groan did all the work. The researchers just sent in the cards. Some of the more conscientious tallied up their own totals, but largely this was left to the company statisticians. The votes were counted and PU&G writers composed the papers. The latter modestly refused to take authorship credit for their labors but gave the glory for this latest medical advance to the volunteer researchers.

The PU&G editorial department had a knack for getting its papers into publication quickly. The many dozen provincial medical journals throughout the country often had trouble filling their pages. The well-written and well-illustrated "original research" papers submitted by PU&G were appreciated.

Nor was the fact that the journals were heavily subsidized by Advertising income from PU&G and other Drug Houses ever forgotten. So within a month, the first Reports began to appear in such periodicals as the *West Rockland Journal of Medicine,* the *Mohawk Valley Medical Gazette,* and of course the giveaways.

While these momentous events were taking place, the important question of naming the new wonder Drug was being debated in PU&G's Nomenclature Section. Normally the name of a new Drug was selected from about half a dozen submitted by the company Univac computer. But Cradshaw insisted on bypassing the computer on this, his pet Drug, and announced that the name of JP1313 or vitamin B_{13} would be simply VIM.

"If one syllable can sell soap, it should sell drugs", the Chief argued.

The old hands in the Nomenclature Section, tactfully persuaded "Hard-Sell", to alter it to BioVIM, to give the name a more professional ring. A quick consumer-response survey by the motivational research section confirmed the choice. BioVIM had only the most favorable connotations, the dissection of consumer entrails by the MR augurs revealed. So B_{13}, the lucky vitamin, became BioVIM!

Before the first medical article appeared in print, PU&G began its Promotion of BioVIM to doctors. Here again "Hard-Sell" Cradshaw lived up to his reputation for imaginative salesmanship.

The Promotion experts at PU&G were about to begin a campaign based on the usual techniques. There would be gaudily colored and extravagantly phrased (BioVIM adds Vim to Life!) mailings originating in Addis Ababa, Montevideo, Tahiti, Pocatello, Idaho, and a submarine under the Arctic icecap. These would be timed to arrive in the doctor's offices on consecutive days. When resistance had been softened by 2 weeks of this long-range saturation bombardment, the PU&G shock troops, the detail men, would storm the ramparts, bribing their way past the receptionists manning the outer defenses, and bursting into the sancta sanctorum, armed with preprints, charts, graphs, and of course samples (with vitamins for the kiddies).

It was an expensive and ambitious campaign that had been planned, but "Hard-Sell" vetoed it.

Humdrum! No imagination!" he roared. "All old tricks. Not a new damn idea in the whole plan! But I've got some new ideas even if you old tired hucksters haven't. What's the one thing that'll catch a doctor's attention these days? Not post cards from Timbuktu, you can be sure. It's S-T-O-C-K-S, Stocks! That's what!"

"We're going to give every doctor in the country one share of PU&G common for 'good-will.'" Cradshaw continued, "together with the hint that the stuff will skyrocket when BioVIM hits the drugstores. And with every visit by one of our detail men they will get a certificate permitting them to get another share at half price. They will be clamoring for visits from the detail men. We'll have to double the force to meet the demand. Every doc in the U.S. will be a co-owner of PU&G and will be pushing BioVIM for all he's worth".

The sales and Promotion staff stood open-mouthed and silent in awed respect to the genius of the Chief.

His plan was followed in every detail. The only concession to standard promotional technique was the planting of articles in the lay press. Nearly every magazine and newspaper in the country from the *Wall Street Journal* to *McCall's* soon featured lurid stories about this sensational new Drug. The *Reader's Digest* had a lead article entitled "The Divine Drug" which described in exciting detail how cases of nearly every type of illness affecting heart, liver, lung or what have you responded miraculously to BioVIM. "Such a wonder drug is truly a gift from God, the Divine Healer," the article concluded. These releases preceded the appearance of the articles in the professional journals, as is the usual practice. The result of this was to build up a tremendous consumer demand that even the most scrupulous physician would find hard to resist.

I need not recount the fantastic success scored by BioVIM; you are all familiar with it. Selling at 90 cents per 100 mg. tablet ("A regular supply costs less than feeding the children"), BioVIM within 2 months earned all the millions spent in "research and development". Within 1 year, it had earned 200 million for PU&G and had become the all-time high earner for the Drug industry. Pfiss, Upchuck, and Groan stock did indeed skyrocket; Cradshaw and Schuller-Christian received fat bonuses; and medical science chalked up another dazzling triumph.

Source: M. Patrick O'Meara, "The Saga of Vitamin B_{13} – A Pharmaceutical Triump", *Harvard Medical Alumni Bulletin*, pp. 16–18, July 1960, with permission from Harvard Medical Alumni Association and Harvard Medical School.

Authors

Dr. Mickey C. Smith is author or editor of more than a score of Books as well as 400+ papers in more than 100 different journals. His work has been translated into Chinese, Japanese, Russian, Spanish, and Korean. Among his national and international awards are: Distinguished Educator from the American Association of Colleges of Pharmacy (first time given), Fellowship in the Institute of Pharmacy International, Australian Institute of Pharmacy Management, and an Honorary Doctorate from his alma mater, the St. Louis College of Pharmacy. Smith has served as a consultant to the FDA, FTC, WHO, and served as a member of Big Pharma. Smith is Barnard Professor Emeritus of Pharmacy Administration and of Management and Marketing at the University of Mississippi.

Dr. E.M. (Mick) Kolassa is a retired professor of Pharmaceutical Marketing and Economics at the University of Mississippi. His experience in the pharmaceutical industry includes key positions in Pricing and Economic Policy with the Upjohn Company and Sandoz. He also founded Medical Marketing Economics, a firm that focuses on value-based pricing of medical products and services. Kolassa is author/editor of the two definitive Books on Drug Prices: *Elements of Pharmaceutical Prices* (translated into Japanese) and *The Strategic Pricing of Pharmaceuticals*. He also served as editor of the *Journal of Pharmaceutical Marketing and Management*.

Currently, Dr. Kolassa occupies his time as a blues musician and is CEO of Endless Blues Records.

Walter Steven Pray, B.S. (Pharm), M.A., M.P.H., PhD, taught a wide variety of courses and labs at Southwestern Oklahoma State University's College of Pharmacy for over 42 years. He published over 400 articles in pharmacy, medical, and dental journals. His first textbook, *Nonprescription*

Product Therapeutics, was widely used in pharmacy colleges. His second Book, a *History of Nonprescription Product Regulation*, was a detailed history of nonprescription product Legislation. His Books were translated into Portuguese and Korean.

Dr. Pray is qualified as an expert witness on nonprescription products in federal and state litigations. His doctoral research won the Lyman Award as the most outstanding article published in the *American Journal of Pharmacy Education* in 1985. He was awarded the Bernhardt Professorship in 2002 for sustained excellence in scholarship, teaching, and service. He received the Henry Cade Award from the National Association of Boards of Pharmacy. He has been a consultant for the Centers for Disease Control and the Environmental Protection Agency.

Index

Note: **Bold** page numbers refer to tables and *italic* page numbers refer to figures.

AAC *see* Actual Acquisition Cost (AAC)
AAM *see* Association for Accessible Medicines (AAM)
AARP *see* American Association of Retired Persons (AARP)
AARP Bulletin 255
Abbreviated New Drug Application (ANDA) 146, 147, 156, 315
AbbVie 241
Acton, Lord 133
Actual Acquisition Cost (AAC) 366
acute illness, sick role in 204–207
Adams, S. H. 297, 298
adversaries, advocates and 179
advertisers, DTC 387
advertising
    agencies 57, 248
    direct-to-consumer (DTC) 31, 48–50
    listing in direct to consumer 41
    medical, failings in **163**
advocates and adversaries 179
After Shock (Chopra) 388
agencies
    advertising 57, 248
    Federal Agencies 153, 293, 297
    Federal regulatory Agency 276
    State Agencies 153
aging, future drugs for 285–286
aging society, drugs in 284–285
AIDS 209
Alderson, W. 29, 43, 134, 154
Alzheimer's disease 365, 389

American Association of Retired Persons (AARP) 102, 176, 179, 218, 219, 372
    and Greedy Big Pharma 255–256
American Druggist (AD) 335
American Medical Association (AMA) 173, 235
American Medical Association House of Delegates 6
American Pharmaceutical Association (APhA) 305
American Public Health Association 6
Anatomy of an Illness (Couzins) 20
ANDA *see* Abbreviated New Drug Application (ANDA)
Angell, M. 219
anti-discriminatory pricing 175
apologia 391–392
Apple, W. Dr. 91
arthritis, rheumatoid 207–208
Association for Accessible Medicines (AAM) 244
asthma 349
attitudes and evaluation of drugs 193–195, **194**
Average Wholesale Price (AWP) 43, 366, 367–369, **369**
Avorn, J. Dr. 121, 134
AWP *see* Average Wholesale Price (AWP)
Azulfidine 161

Beardsley, G. 456
Bentham, J. 133
Bernstein, E. Dr. 121

463

Bezold 154
Biden, J. 140
"Big Bio" 245–246
Big Pharma 16–17
   alternative view 228–231
   Congress and Greedy 256–258
   conference on Drugs and Society in 1963 226–228
   Greedy Big Pharma 253
      AARP and 255–256
      Congress and 256–258
      parts of Greedy 253–255
   ideas for 232–238
   response of Big Pharma to people 232
Billings, J. 188
Bill of Rights 14
bills and sponsors 140–142, **142–145**
biological entity, woman as 4, 4–5
Blair, F. A. 302
Blair, J. M. 165
BLS see Bureau of Labor Statistics (BLS)
"blunderbuss" approach 267
Bok, E. 298
Bosch, H. 391
Boswell, J. 447
Bureau of Labor Statistics (BLS) 255
Bush, P. J. 198

Callahan, D. 7, 8
CAM see Complementary and Alternative Medicine (CAM)
Campbell, R. R. 19
cardiovascular diseases 349
Carney, W. 115, 116
Catastrophic Coverage Bill 148
Catastrophic Drug Act 56
   Repeal of Catastrophic Drug Act (1989) 149–150
CBA see cost-benefit analysis (CBA)
CEA see cost-effectiveness analysis (CEA)
Centers for Medicare and Medicaid Services (CMS) 167
Certified Medical Representative (CMR) 46
CFR see Code of Federal Regulations (CFR)
CGMP see Current Good Manufacturing Practices (CGMP)
Chapman, C. B. 6

Cheney, F. J. 297
Chinese Opium Wars 151
chlorothiazide 265
Chopra, S. Dr. 388
CHPA see Consumer Healthcare Products Association (CHPA)
chronic illness, sick role in 204–207
claim adjudication 181
claims processing standards 181
Clark, R. 111
Clayton Act 165
Cleeton, D. 254
clinical medicine 265
Clinton, B. 150, 151, 324
CMR see Certified Medical Representative (CMR)
CMS see Centers for Medicare and Medicaid Services (CMS)
Code of Federal Regulations (CFR) 153, 170
COI see cost-of-illness (COI)
colitis, ulcerative 208
community pharmacy networks 181
Complementary and Alternative Medicine (CAM) 339
compliance, sick role and 214–217
compounding pharmacists 247–248
Comprehensive Drug Abuse Prevention Control Act of 1970 93
Congress and Greedy Big Pharma 256–258
Connor, J. T. 226
Consumer Healthcare Products Association (CHPA) 298, 314
Consumer Price Index (CPI) 254
Consumer Product Safety Commission (CPSC) 165
Cope, J. D. 323, 324
Copeland Bill 302, 303
Copeland, R. 301
Corey, R. 356
cosmic rays 285
cost-benefit analysis (CBA) 343
cost-effectiveness analysis (CEA) 343
cost-of-illness (COI) 344–346
cost savings, through marketing directly to patients 236–237
cost-utility analysis (CUA) 344
council, on drug policy 389

Couzins, N. 20
CPI *see* Consumer Price Index (CPI)
CPSC *see* Consumer Product Safety Commission (CPSC)
Crout, R. Dr. 110, 111
CUA *see* cost-utility analysis (CUA)
Current Good Manufacturing Practices (CGMP) 164
cyanocothiamine 457

DEA *see* Drug Enforcement Administration (DEA)
Decision-making, price 369–375
  Reekie's three basic pricing strategies 371, *372*
DIA *see* Drug Information Association (DIA)
diabetes 349
Dickens, C. 391
Dietary Supplement Health and Education Act (DSHEA) 313, 330–331
Dingell, J., business problems in drug industry 89–91
direct-to-consumer (DTC)
  advertising 31
  promotions of prescription Drugs 274–275
direct-to-customer (DTC) drug 241
Dirksen, E. 63, 70, 71, 73, 88
Dis-Ease *see individual entries*
Distaval 1
disutility 21
Dixon, P. R. 63–64, 85
Djerassi, C. 270
Donabedian, A. 9, 14, 20
Douglass, G. L. 297
Dowling, H. 61
drug(s)
  in aging society 284–285
  attitudes and evaluation of 193–195
  development, curiosities and surprises 279–280
  discovery 277–279
  functions of **10, 13**
    human motives and **12**
  invention 277–279
  lifestyle 286–288
  names 168–170

origins of 263–264, **264**
over the counters (OTCs) 36–37
prescription *see* prescription drugs
product development 267–269
drug abuse
  Moss, F. 93
Drug Amendments (1962) 148–149, 154
drug efficacy problems
  Fountain, L. H. 91–93
Drug Efficacy Study Implementation (DESI) 157, 306
Drug Enforcement Administration (DEA) 166–167
drug industry
  business problems in 89–91
  federal laws affecting **134**
  legislation to **139**
  self-regulation 175
Drug Information Association (DIA) 223
Drug Lag 19, 107, 108, 113, 118, 149, 154, 167, 171, 280–281, 384
Drug Literature 98
drug misadventure 1, 2
drug policy 11–16
  council on 389
  implementation of 12
  investigations 15
  legislation 14
  regulations 15
drug price 38
  controversy 381
  issues 148
  marketing exerts downward pressure on 234–235
  regulation 242
Drug Reform Act of 1978 154
drug-related problems 18–19
  categories of **18**
drug-related tragedies 1–2
drugs of abuse, narcotics and 151
drug's true effects, evaluation of 193–195
drug-taking behaviors 193
drug utilization review (DUR) programs 362
DSHEA *see* Dietary Supplement Health and Education Act (DSHEA)
DTC advertisers 387
Dubos, R. 20, 23, 220, 261

Dunlop, J. T. Dr. 128–130
Durham–Humphrey Amendment 138, 146, 276, 304–305, 316
Durrett, J. J. 301
Dynamic Tension 13, 24, 31, 57, 156, 175, 183, 386, 389, 391

Economic Bill of Rights 6
economic epidemiology 351–354
  aims and purposes of 353
economics of non-compliance 349–351
Edwards, C. C. 94
EEC see European Economic Community (EEC)
Elixhauser, A. 342
emphysema 208–209
End Taxpayer Subsidies for Drug Ads Act 387
environmental developments, marketing in last century **276,** 276–277
enzyme inhibition 265
European Economic Community (EEC) 257
Evans, W. O. 219, 285, 287, 391
Every Time I find the Meaning of Life, They Change It 447

FAA see Federal Aviation Administration (FAA)
Fair Packaging and Labeling Act 159
Fair Trade 271
Faust, R. 116
FCC see Federal Communications Commission (FCC)
FDA see Food and Drug Administration (FDA)
Federal Agencies 153, 293, 297
Federal Aviation Administration (FAA) 387
Federal Communications Commission (FCC) 47, 166
Federal Food, Drug and Cosmetic Act 162
Federal Government Policy 16
federal laws, affecting drug industry **134**
Federal regulatory Agency 276
Federal Trade Commission (FTC) 47, 85, 165, 294
Fierce Pharma 386, 388
Finch, R. H. 128
Fincham, J. E. 349
Finkelstein, S. 247, 258

Firestone, J. 271
"focus group" technique 250
Food and Drug Administration (FDA) 26, 106–109, 154
  accelerates its anti-quackery activity 329–330
  FDA Report (1993) 329
  labeling and promotion 159–164
  manufacturing 164
  Modernization Act 89
  Modernization Act of 1997 50
  and quackery post-DSHEA 331–332
  regulatory authority 164–165
  regulatory process for new drug **157**
  remedies 164–165
  safety and effectiveness 156–158
Food and Drug Administration's review of OTC products
  benefits of FDA OTC Review 310
  criticism of FDA OTC review 312
  genesis of FDA OTC review 306–307
  nonprescription products not reviewed 312–313
  organizing the review 307
  OTC Label 310–312
  OTC manufacturers and the review 313–314
Food Drug and Cosmetic Act 50, 159
  Food, Drug, and Cosmetic Act (1938) 301–303
formularies 178
  management 182
Fountain, L. H. 84–85, 94–96, 101–102, 117–119
  drug efficacy problems 91–93
"Four P's" 25–26; *see also* marketing mix/the "Four P's"
  government and 55–56
Frazier, K. 17
FTC see Federal Trade Commission (FTC)
Fulda, T. R. 134
Furness, B. 89

General Accounting Office (GAO) of the U.S. Government 324
Generic Drug(s) 35, 50, 147, 167, 243, 355, 366, 368–369

industry 22, 140, 141, 146, 161, 243
  products 34
Generic Drug Fee Amendment Act 244
generic pharma 243–244
Generic Pharmaceutical Association 244
generic products 34–35
generics, appearance and labeling of
  244–245
Gibson, J. T. 160
Glenn, J. 119
Goddard, J. Dr. 84, 161
Goldberg, Dr. 101
gonorrhea 208
Gore, Al
  on pharmaceutical R&D 113–117
Gosselin, R. A. 249
Gottlieb, S. 388
government and Four P's 55–56
Goyan, J. 320
The Great American Fraud (Adams) 297
Greedy Big Pharma 253
  AARP and 255–256
  Congress and 256–258
  parts of Greedy 253–255
Greedy Big Tech 259–261

Haddad, W. F. 140, 141
Hailey, A. 218
Halberstam, M. Dr. 112–113
Hamilton, W. 165
Handbook of Nonprescription Drugs
  (HND) 333
HAQ *see* Health Assessment Questionnaire
  (HAQ)
Harari, Y. 219, 287, 388
Harkness, R. 321
Harrison Narcotic Act (1914) 151, 300–301
Harris, R. 165
Hatch, O. 109, 140, 330
Hawley, J. 259
Hayes, A. H. Dr. 114
HBM *see* Health Belief Model (HBM)
HCFA *see* Health Care Financing
  Administration (HCFA)
health, definition 2–3
Health and Human Services (HHS) 258
Health Assessment Questionnaire (HAQ) 347

health behavior, sick role 201, 202
Health Belief Model (HBM) *189,* 189–190
  case study 190–192
health care and rights 6–9
"Health Care Delivery System" 11
Health Care Financing Administration
  (HCFA) 167
Health Care goods and services 361
Health Care insurance plans 361
Health Care laws 135
Health Care market 237
health care marketing system 30
health care policy 12
health care system 136, **136–137,** 237–238
health maintenance organizations
  (HMO's) 257
hearings, drug related **142–145**
Heinz, C. 120–121
Henderson, D. 387
Henry VI 134
HHS *see* Health and Human Services (HHS)
Hill, C. 56
Hillary Care 150–151
Hilts, P. J. 2
*A History of Non-Prescription Drug
  Regulation* (Pray) 22
HMO's *see* health maintenance
  organizations (HMO's)
Hoge, J. F. 302, 305
Holden, R. K. 357
Homo Deus (Harari) 219, 388
Hooper, C. 387
hospital-dispensed drug, price for *368*
Hruska, R. 61, 70, 72–74, 88
Huhn, L. A. 351
Humphrey, H. 98–99
Hutt, P. B. 101
Huxley, A. 270
hydrochlorothiazide (HCTZ) 191

IACP *see* International Academy of
  Compounding Pharmacists (IACP)
Illich, I. 218
illness behavior, sick role 202–204
Immortality (Walter) 286
infectious disease 349
Ingelfinger, F. J. 54

inhibition, enzyme 265
International Academy of Compounding Pharmacists (IACP) 247
Investigational New Drug (IND) Application 157, 158

Jacobsen, T. 33
Join Commission for the Accreditation of Healthcare Organizations (JCAHO) 182
Joyce, C. R. B. 348, 349

Kefauver, E. 17, 59, 61–65, 80–82, 140, 148, 229, 260, 276, 306
  on brand names 67–68
  on competition 66
  minority views 70–77
  on patents 65–66
  on prices 68–70
  on profits 68
  on promotion 66–67
  resignation and whistle blower 77–80
Kefauver–Harris Amendment (1962) 156, 306
Kelsey, F. Dr. 117
Kemp, E. F. 301
Kennedy, E. 44, 59, 85–89, 102–106, 109–111, 140
Kilgore, S. 102–103
Kirsch, D. R. 267
Kleinke, J. D. 377
Kline, N. S. 285, 287, 288
Kolassa, E. M. Dr. 20–22, 38, 342, 461
Koop, C. E. 238

Ladies' Home Journal (Bok) 298
laws
  and policy 135–139
  regulated nonprescription products 299–306
  state 151
  Waxman–Hatch Law 146–148
lawyers 178–179
lay referral system 197, 204
Lee, P. Dr. 125, 130
legislation
  to drug industry **139**
  drug policy 14
  and regulation 135
Lehman, H. 285
Lennard, H. L. 11
Ley, H. Dr. 92
The Life of Samuel Johnson (Boswell) 447
lifestyle drugs 286–288
Limits to Medicine – Medical Nemesis (Illich) 218
Liu, A. 388
Lovesey, P. 261
Lower Drug Costs Now Act 383–384
L-tryptophan 329
Luce, B. R. 342

MAC *see* maximum allowable cost (MAC)
Magee, M. Dr. 261
mail-order pharmacy 180
mail-order services 181–182
managed care myopia 359–360
managed care organizations (MCO) 360, 361
Manischewitz, D. B. 222, 224
marketing
  as actualizing process 26–27
  communications by pharmaceutical companies 235–236
  concept 26
  development 268
  directly to patients, cost savings 236–237
  in last century 269
  practitioners, efforts of 26
  research 249–251
marketing exerts downward pressure, on price of medicines 234–235
marketing mix/the "Four P'S" 27–29
market opportunities, on unmet needs **288–290**
Maslow, A. 186
maximum allowable cost (MAC) 42, 366
McCaffrey, D. J. 350
McCain, J. 119
McCarthy, E. J. 31
McEvilla, J. 38, 42, 90, 271, 272
McMahon, Dr. 115–116
MCO *see* managed care organizations (MCO)
Medicaid 175

prescription drug programs 257
   programs 257
medical advertising, failings in **163**
medical folklore, search for new drugs
   in 264
medical models, assumptions underlying
   different **5–6**
Medicare 175
   program 167
Medicare Catastrophic Coverage Act 149–150
Medicare Catastrophic Protection Act of
   1987 125
medication regimens
   compliance with 209–214
   factors affecting compliance *213*
   non-compliance with 209
medication use, influences on 217–218
medicines
   clinical medicine 265
   marketing exerts downward pressure on
      price of 234–235
   "packaged medicines" 301
   patent medicines 295
      characteristics of 295–296
      fight against 298–299
      manufacturers 296–298
   self-regulation 173–174
Metzenbaum, H. 111–112
Michaelson, J. Dr. 96
Miller, A. 49
Mims, C. 259
Mintz, M. 82
Mirage of Health (Dubos) 20, 23
Modern Pharmaceutical Industry (Jacobson
   and Wertheimer) 33
monographs, PMA 239
Morton, W. E. 351
Moss, F.
   drug abuse 93
Mossinghoff, G. 123–124, 223
Moulton, B. Dr. 77–80, 108
Moynihan, R. 14
myopia, managed care 359–360

Nader, R. 88
Nagle, T. T. 357
narcotics and drugs of abuse 151

NARD *see* National Association of Retail
   Druggists (NARD)
National Association of Boards of Pharmacy
   (NABP) 180
National Association of Retail Druggists
   (NARD) 90, 323
National Center for Complementary and
   Alternative Medicine (NCCAM)
   328–329
National Consumers League 322–323
National Council for Prescription Drug
   Programs, Inc. (NCPDP) 181
National Disease and Therapeutic Index
   (NDTI) 249
National Drug Testing and Evaluation
   Center Act 85
National Education Service 9
natural products, exploration of 266
NCCAM *see* National Center for
   Complementary and Alternative
   Medicine (NCCAM)
NCPDP *see* National Council for Prescription
   Drug Programs, Inc. (NCPDP)
NDA *see* New Drug Application (NDA)
NDMA *see* Nonprescription Drug
   Manufacturers Association (NDMA)
NDTI *see* National Disease and Therapeutic
   Index (NDTI)
Nelson, G. 51, 59, 81–84, 109, 228, 260
networks, community pharmacy 181
New Drug Application (NDA) 157, 158, 307
New England Journal of Medicine
   (NEJM) 54, 337
New Testament 205
Nineham, A. W. 267
non-compliance, economics of 349–351
Nonprescription Drug Manufacturers
   Association (NDMA) 297, 313,
   321–324
non-prescription drugs *see* nonprescription
   products
nonprescription products 295–299
   and devices lacking proof of safety and
      efficacy 325–329
   laws regulating 299–306
Noonan, P. 260
Novitch, M. 119–120

Nutrition Labeling and Education Act of 1990 328

Obamacare 150–151
Ogas, O. 267
Old Testament 205
O'Meara, M. P. 455–460
Omnibus Budget Reconciliation Act of 1990 366
Orphan Drug Act 89, 149
over the counter (OTC) 34, 294
   drugs 36–37
   manufacturers, opposition from 318–325
   marketplace 185
   medications 293
over the counter products, FDA's review of
   benefits of FDA OTC Review 310
   criticism of FDA OTC review 312
   genesis of FDA OTC review 306–307
   nonprescription products not reviewed 312–313
   organizing the review 307
   OTC Label 310–312
   OTC manufacturers and the review 313–314

PA *see* Proprietary Association (PA)
"packaged medicines" 301
Parsons, T. 201, 205
patent medicines 295
   characteristics of 295–296
   fight against 298–299
   manufacturers 296–298
Patent Restoration Act 167
patents and trademarks 167
patient behavior 206
patient needs, communicating with prescribers linking products to 235–236
patient package insert (PPI) 94, 160
Patman, W. 89–90
PBAs *see* pharmaceutical benefits administrators (PBAs)
PBMs *see* pharmaceutical benefits managers (PBMs)
PCAB *see* Pharmacy Compounding Accreditation Board (PCAB)
PCCA *see* Professional Compounding Centers of America (PCCA)
PDP *see* Prescription Drug Plan (PDP)
Pearlman, R. A. 346
Peltzman, S. 52, 149
people as patients 185–186
   demographics 186
   needs and wants 186–188
Pepper, C. 119–121
Pfizer product 246
pharmaceutical benefits administrators (PBAs) 180
pharmaceutical benefits management (PBM) firms 180
pharmaceutical benefits managers (PBMs) 176, 384
   basic services **177**
   controversies in PBM industry 182–183
   enhanced services **177**
   future of 183
   intermediate services **177**
   and outcomes management 180
pharmaceutical companies, marketing communications by 235–236
pharmaceutical distribution, developments in 272, **272**
Pharmaceutical Economics and Public Policy 261
pharmaceutical firms 376
pharmaceutical industry 25, 26
   pricing practices in 38–39
   wholesaler segment of 36
The Pharmaceutical Industry Prices, Profits, Patents and Promotion 239
The Pharmaceutical Journal 1
Pharmaceutical Manufacturers Association (PMA) 17, 223, 227
   monographs 239
pharmaceutical marketers 237
pharmaceutical marketing system 29–30, 222
   fundamental role of 233
   place 30, 35–37
      mail-order prescriptions 37
      wholesaler 37–38
   price 30, 38
      hospital pricing 43

listing in direct to consumer
advertising 41
retail pricing 42–43
summary of factors influencing
39–40
product 30, *32,* 32–33
generic products 34–35
from medicine to your mouth 33–34
molecular modification 34
promotion 30–31, 43–45
direct-to-consumer advertising (DTC)
48–50
forms of promotion 47–48
meetings and exhibits 48
"Off-Label" Information 50
personal selling–detailing 45–46
print media 46–47
samples 48
social costs and benefits of 51–53
public perceptions of 232
stimulates demand 237–238
pharmaceutical marketplace, environmental
developments in 276, **276**
pharmaceutical pricing 357, 366–367, *368*
Actual Acquisition Cost (AAC) 366
Average Wholesale Price (AWP) 366,
367–369, **369**
developments in 271, **271**
direct price 366
future of 377–381
growing importance of 361–363
important terms in 366
maximum allowable cost (MAC) 366
OBRA 90 366
Prisoner's Dilemma 379–381
rebate 366
pharmaceutical pricing philosophy 364
pricing on purpose 365
willingness to pay 364–365
pharmaceutical products development *269*
pharmaceutical promotion development
274, **275**
Pharmaceutical Research and Manufacturers
Association (PhRMA) 17
Pharmaceutical Research and Manufacturers
of America (PhRMA) 31
pharmaceuticals, value of 375–377

pharmaceutics 34
pharmacist
compounding 247–248
counseling 318
role 214
Pharmacists Planning Service (PPSI)
322–324
pharmacoeconomics 341–342
developments in 234
emergence of socioeconomic research
342–345
socioeconomic evaluations
definition 342–343
types 343–345
pharmacogenetics 389
pharmacy
mail-order 180
network management 181
self-regulation 174
pharmacy codes of ethics, change to
embrace quackery 332–333
Pharmacy Compounding Accreditation
Board (PCAB) 247
pharmacy networks, community 181
pharmacy services, specialty 182
pharmacy textbooks endorse quackery
333–334
Pharmacy Times 335
phenylpropanolamine (PPA) 322
Phillips, V. 62
physico-chemical-pharmaceutical
development 267
Pickett, G. Dr. 8
place
government and "Four P's" 56
marketing in last century **272,** 272–274
pharmaceutical marketing system 30,
35–37
mail-order prescriptions 37
wholesaler 37–38
PMA *see* Pharmaceutical Manufacturers
Association (PMA)
policy
drug policy 11–16
council on 389
implementation of 12
investigations 15

Index ■ 471

policy (*cont.*)
    legislation 14
    regulations 15
  federal 128
  health care 12
  laws and 135–139
Pollard, M. R. 16
POTUS 387
PPI *see* patient package insert (PPI)
PPSI *see* Pharmacists Planning Service (PPSI)
Pray, W. S. Dr. 22, 461, 462
prescribers linking products, to patient needs 235–236
Prescription Drug Plan (PDP) 380
prescription drugs
  Manufacturer 257
  Task Force on 124–125
    drug benefits for aged 126
    Dunlop Report 128–130
    economic issues 127
    federal policy 128
    government regulatory duties 127–128
    professional education/proficiency 127
    quality of care: drug use process 126
    research, findings, and recommendations 125–126
prescription limitations 178
prescription-to-OTC switch 314
  factors considered in approving an Rx-to-OTC Switch 316–317
  methods 314–316
  switches types 317
press and media, self-regulation 174–175
Prevacid 359
Preyer, W. Y. 98, 302
price
  government and "Four P's" 56
  for hospital-dispensed drug *368*
  marketing in last century *271*, 271–272
  pharmaceutical marketing system 30, 38
    hospital pricing 43
    listing in direct to consumer advertising 41
    retail pricing 42–43
    summary of factors influencing **39–40**
  for retail-dispensed outpatient drug *368*

price decision-making 369
  company abilities 374–375
  company needs 374
  competition 371, *371*
  decision-making process 373
  disease characteristics 373–374
  factors in pricing decision 369–371, **370**
  patient characteristics 372–373
  public policy considerations 375, *375*
  Reekie's three basic pricing strategies 371, *372*
Price index 271
pricing 356–357
  anti-discriminatory 175
  fear of 358–359
  managed care myopia 359–360
  market segments 358
  need to price on purpose 361
  new product dilemma 357
  pharmaceutical 357, 366–367, *368*
    Actual Acquisition Cost (AAC) 366
    Average Wholesale Price (AWP) 366, 367–369, **369**
    developments in 271, **271**
    direct price 366
    future of 377–381
    growing importance of 361–363
    important terms in 366
    maximum allowable cost (MAC) 366
    OBRA 90 366
    Prisoner's Dilemma 379–381
    rebate 366
  policies 41
  terminology 365
"Pricing of Drugs, 1977" 102
product
  development 233–234
  marketing in last century *269*, 269–270
  pharmaceutical marketing system 30, *32*, 32–33
    generic products 34–35
    from medicine to your mouth 33–34
    molecular modification 34
Professional Compounding Centers of America (PCCA) 247, 248
promotion
  government and "Four P's" 57

marketing in last century 274–275, **275**
marketing mix/the "Four P's" 29
pharmaceutical marketing system 30–31, 43–45
   direct-to-consumer advertising (DTC) 48–50
   forms of promotion 47–48
   meetings and exhibits 48
   "Off-Label" Information 50
   personal selling–detailing 45–46
   print media 46–47
   samples 48
   social costs and benefits of 51–53
Proprietary Association (PA) 296–298
Pryor, D. 59, 122–124, 256, 258
public perceptions, of pharmaceutical marketing 232
public scrutiny 25
Pure Food and Drugs Act (1906) 297, 299–300
"push/pull" effect 200

QOL *see* quality of life (QOL)
quackery 325–326
   conspiracy to legitimize 326–328
   FDA accelerates its anti-quackery activity 329–330
   FDA and quackery post-DSHEA 331–332
   new names confer false respectability 339
   pharmacy codes of ethics change to embrace 332–333
   pharmacy journals endorse 334–339
   pharmacy textbooks endorse 333–334
quality of life (QOL)
   assessment 346–349
   measurements 349
Quality of Well-Being (QWB) 347
quantitative analysis 34

radiation 285
Rathbun, F. 323, 324
rays, cosmic 285
rebate, pharmaceutical pricing 366
Reekie's three basic pricing strategies 371, *372*
regulations 170
   enacted by State Legislation and Boards of Pharmacy **169**
   on pharmaceutical promotion 160
   regulatory reform 171
REMS *see* Risk Evaluation and Mitigation Strategies (REMS)
Resale Price Control 271
response to government 223–224
   counterattack 224–225
   guilty 225–226
   not guilty 224
retail-dispensed outpatient drug, price for *368*
reward *versus* risk 258
Rheinstein, P. Dr. 118
rheumatoid arthritis 207–208
Rice, D. 345
rights, health care and 6–9
right to health care 7
Risk Evaluation and Mitigation Strategies (REMS) 246
risk *versus* reward 258
Robinson–Patman Act 89
Rogers, P. C. 96
Roosevelt, F.
   Economic Bill of Rights 6
Roosevelt, T. 299, 301
Rovner, J. 150
Rubin, P. 237
Rucker, T. D. Dr. 125
ruminations 386
Rx-to-OTC switch
   examples of 317
   factors considered in approving an 316–317
   movement 314

Sadusk, J. F. 52
Sapiens (Harari) 388
Sartorius, N. 2, 3
Scheuer, J. 107, 108, 113
Schifrin, L. 60
Schmidt, A. 101
Schoonveld, Ed 354
Schwartzman, D. 51, 52
Scitovski, A. 345
Securities and Exchange Commission (SEC) Regulations 183
self-actualization 187

self-care actions 203
Self-Medication's Role in U.S. Health Care 324
self-regulation 173
  congress 174
  drug industry 175
  medicine 173–174
  pharmacy 174
  press and media 174–175
Sewell, W. 99
sickness career 195–197, *196*
sick role 201
  in acute and chronic illness 204–207
  behavior 202
  and compliance 214–217
  health behavior 201, 202
  illness behavior 202–204
Sigerist, H. 351
Silverman, M. Dr. 125
Slack, R. 267
Smith, A. 59, 62–65, 72, 85
Smith, M. C. Dr. 461
SmithKline Beecham, (SKB) 346, 348
social entity, woman as *4*, 4–5
society, drugs and role in 9–11, **10**
soothing syrups 300
specialty drugs 246
specialty pharmacy services 182
sponsors, bills and 140–142, **142–145**
Squibb, B-M. 246
Squibb, G. 228, 229, 231, 377
Starr, P. 284, 386
State Agencies 153
state laws 151
State Legislation and Boards of Pharmacy, regulations enacted by **169**
state regulations 168
statesmanship 240–241
Stern, G. 89
Stetler, J. J. 85–87, 223
Stigler, G. J. 51
Strand, L. M. 18
Strong Medicine 218
Stuart, J. A. 222, 224
Switch Regulation 314
syphilis 208
syrups, soothing 300

Talmadge, J. M. 6
TAP's proton pump inhibitor 359
Task Force (TF) on Prescription Drugs 124–125
Tax Equity and Fiscal Responsibility Act (TEFRA) 362
Taylor, K. 318
TEFRA *see* Tax Equity and Fiscal Responsibility Act (TEFRA)
Temin, P. 19, 247, 258
thalidomide 1
  tragedy 2, 19, 276
third parties/managed care controls 175–176
Thurmond, S. 104, 106, 140
Till, I. 165
trademarks, patents and 167
trends 386–388
  immortality 388
  slow/stop the aging process 388–389

Uhlmann, R. F. 346
ulcerative colitis 208
United States Vitamin (USV) company 306
Unmet needs, market opportunities in **288–290**
U.S. Adopted Names Council (USAN) 168
U.S. Health Care industry 16
USP *see* U.S. Pharmacopeia (USP)
U.S. Pharmacopeia (USP) 168–169

Van Deerlin, L. 100–101
"vicarious search" 29
Von Bismarck, O. 133

Walden, J. T. 322
Walker, S. 116
Wall Street Journal 387–389
Walter, C. 286
Wanamaker, J. 44
Warner, J. 123
Waxman–Hatch Law 35, 146–148, 355
Waxman–Hatch Patent Extension Act 276
Wegner, F. 105
Weidenbruch, J. 322
Weinberger, C. 141

Welch, H. Dr. 77
Werth, B. 280
Wertheimer, A. I. Dr. 33, 134, 391
Weston, J. F. 38
Wiley, A. 71, 76
Wiley, H. W. Dr. 298
Willingness to Pay (WTP) 348
Wolfe, S. Dr. 88, 141, 142

woman, as biological and social entity 4, 4–5
"Wonder Drugs" 61
World Health Organization (WHO) 2, 259
Wright, C. 261
Wyden, R. 323

Zomax 121